D1227130

JAMES BALDWIN
THE FBI FILE

Also by William J. Maxwell

New Negro, Old Left:
African American Writing and Communism between the Wars (1999)

Claude McKay, *Complete Poems* (editor, 2004)

F. B. Eyes:
How J. Edgar Hoover's Ghostreaders Framed African American Literature (2015)

JAMES BALDWIN
THE FBI FILE

EDITED AND WITH
AN INTRODUCTION AND NOTES BY
WILLIAM J. MAXWELL

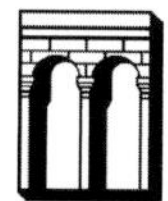

Arcade Publishing · New York

SOMERSET CO. LIBRARY
BRIDGEWATER, N.J 08807

Copyright © 2017 by William J. Maxwell

All rights reserved. No part of this book may be reproduced in any manner without the express written consent of the publisher, except in the case of brief excerpts in critical reviews or articles. All inquiries should be addressed to Arcade Publishing, 307 West 36th Street, 11th Floor, New York, NY 10018.

First Edition

Arcade Publishing books may be purchased in bulk at special discounts for sales promotion, corporate gifts, fund-raising, or educational purposes. Special editions can also be created to specifications. For details, contact the Special Sales Department, Arcade Publishing, 307 West 36th Street, 11th Floor, New York, NY 10018 or arcade@skyhorsepublishing.com.

Arcade Publishing® is a registered trademark of Skyhorse Publishing, Inc.®, a Delaware corporation.

Visit our website at www.arcadepub.com.

10 9 8 7 6 5 4 3 2 1

Library of Congress Cataloging-in-Publication Data

Names: Maxwell, William J. (College teacher), author.
Title: James Baldwin : the FBI file / William J. Maxwell.
Description: New York : Arcade Publishing, 2017.
Identifiers: LCCN 2016058378 | ISBN 9781628727371 (paperback)
Subjects: LCSH: Baldwin, James, 1924-1987. | African American Authors—Biography. | American literature—African American Authors—History and criticism. | United States. Federal Bureau of Investigation—History—20th century. | BISAC: HISTORY / United States / 20th Century. | BIOGRAPHY & AUTOBIOGRAPHY / Literary. | SOCIAL SCIENCE / Ethnic Studies / African American Studies.
Classification: LCC PS3552.A45 Z822 2017 | DDC 818/.5409 [B]—dc23 LC record available at https://lccn.loc.gov/2016058378

Cover design by Erin Seaward-Hiatt
Cover photo by Dave Pickoff: Associated Press

ISBN: 978-1-62872-737-1
Ebook ISBN: 978-1-62872-738-8

Printed in China

CONTENTS

JAMES BALDWIN
THE FBI FILE

Introduction

BALDWIN AND HIS FILE AFTER BLACK LIVES MATTER

Born-Again Baldwin

James Baldwin, buried on December 8, 1987, often looks like today's most vital and most cherished new African American author. This impression doesn't rest on the faith in bodily resurrection that Baldwin abandoned along with his teenage ministry in Harlem. Nor does it slight Teju Cole, Natasha Trethewey, Kevin Young, and the rest of the emerging literary competition—though it's true that one leading light in that competition, Ta-Nehisi Coates, has suffered as well as profited from Toni Morrison's pronouncement that he fills "the intellectual void" opened by Baldwin's passing. Instead, the impression that Baldwin has returned to preeminence, unbowed and unwrinkled, reflects his special ubiquity in the imagination of Black Lives Matter. As Eddie Glaude Jr. observes, "Jimmy is *everywhere*" in the advocacy and self-scrutiny of the young activists who bravely transformed the killings of Trayvon Martin, Michael Brown, Natasha McKenna, and far too many others into a sweeping national movement against police brutality and campus racism. For these activists, disruptive and creative and warning of new fires next time, Jimmy himself has filled the void traced to his death. Something like the Shakespeare of Stephen Dedalus, the Baldwin of Black Lives Matter is his own true father—one who rehearsed for the role, it's worth remembering, by raising several of his eight younger siblings and by peppering his live speech and written dialogue with the hip endearment of "baby." With ironic paternalism, Baldwin habitually applied this sweet nothing to that set of permanent children proud of their whiteness.

"So I give you your problem back," he schooled a not especially fresh-faced interviewer in 1963, "You're the nigger, baby, it isn't me."

It's no state secret, of course, that Black Lives Matter, or BLM for short, is a movement fueled by electronic social media, by the graphic smartphone video followed by the mobile demonstration advertised on Facebook and choreographed in real time via Twitter. "The thing about [Martin Luther] King or Ella Baker" and the rest of the civil rights pantheon, explains DeRay Mckesson, the most prominent face of the movement's techno-optimism, "is that they could not just wake up and sit at breakfast and talk to a million people. The tools that we have to organize and resist are fundamentally different than what's existed before in black struggle." Regardless of the new advantages of instant mass communication, however, BLM has also begun to reorder the slow time of the African American literary canon like the Civil Rights Movement before it. Whatever BLM's cumulative political significance will be—the jury remains out amid white backlash, the election of backlasher-in-chief Donald Trump, the tragic assassination of police officers in Dallas and Baton Rouge, and the slow fade of direct action as a defining BLM tactic—it has already adopted more than one literary muse and has already stamped black literary history.

Considered as a generational sensibility indebted but not confined to the #BlackLivesMatter platform launched in 2013, BLM has embraced a lyrically withering essayist, the previously mentioned Coates, and has appointed an academic poet laureate, the National Book Award finalist Claudia Rankine. It has recuperated a militant memoirist, Assata Shakur, whose 1987 autobiography, written in Cuban exile, now rivals *The Autobiography of Malcolm X* (1965) as a passport to 1960s-style Black Nationalism. The medley of poetry, radical confession, selective legal history, and anti-racist name-taking in *Assata*—an unexpected pre-echo of Rankine's multigeneric collection *Citizen* (2014)—has also yielded BLM's best-loved poem, a rewrite into rough ballad meter of the climax of *The Communist Manifesto* memorized and mass-chanted by thousands of protestors in dozens of American cities. "It is our duty to fight for our freedom," Shakur's twice-historical lines direct,

It is our duty to win.
We must love each other and support each other.
We have nothing to lose but our chains.

Yet while Shakur is the author of BLM's "If We Must Die," its street-tested anthem of unity-in-resistance, Baldwin reigns as the movement's literary conscience, touchstone, and pinup, its go-to ideal of the writer in arms whose social witness only enhances his artfulness. It's Baldwin's good name and impassioned queer fatherhood that aspiring movement intellectuals invoke in Twitter handles such as #SonofBaldwin, #Flames_Baldwin, and #BaemesBaldwin. It's Baldwin's distilled racial wisdom, often mined from his heated Black Power-era interviews, that fortifies these intellectuals' posts and tweets. (See, for instance, the viral social-media resharing of Baldwin's correction of an *Esquire* magazine reporter in 1968: "I object to the term 'looters' because I wonder who is looting whom, baby.") It's Baldwin's longer, formal prose that's recommended by BLM protesters for its uncanny relevance, its vintage elegance combined with the tight fit with present emergencies that, according to rapper-activist Ryan Dalton, "says a lot about Baldwin's writing, but also about how little progress we've made." It's the glossy black-and-white Library of America edition of Baldwin's *Collected Essays* that rivals "Assata Taught Me" hoodies and DeRay Mckesson's blue down vest as an iconic movement accessory. It's the second thoughts on Richard Wright and retaliatory violence in Baldwin's essay "Many Thousands Gone" that Rankine samples in detail in the "World Cup" section of *Citizen*. And it's *The Fire Next Time* (1963), Baldwin's unforgettable but often misremembered meditation on the Islam of Elijah Muhammad and the Christianity of and against Martin Luther King, that underwrites the whole of Coates's *Between the World and Me* (2015), on whose dust jacket Toni Morrison declares the author the most gifted Son of Baldwin of all. Coates is happy to admit his bestseller's steep debt to the older writer; the influence became inevitable, he tells us, after he reread *The Fire Next Time* and asked himself "why don't people write short, powerful books like this [anymore], a singular, hundred-page essay?" One reason why more people don't, it's fair to say, is that Baldwin is now, practically speaking, back among us to write such books on his own.

Why is Baldwin's work so alive in the tide of Black Lives Matter, flourishing more thoroughly now than during his own day of struggle, when King privately lamented his poetic license and Eldridge Cleaver of the Black Panthers publicly shamed the imaginary castration, extending "to the center of his burning skull," he supposedly suffered as a black gay man? One reason involves an irony of history identified by the Paris-based

African American writer Thomas Chatterton Williams. To Williams's mind, the very "same characteristics of the Baldwin brand that so 'estranged' him from the concerns of his generation and of black America writ large—his intersectionality before that was a thing—are what make him such an exemplar of the queer-inflected mood of the Black Lives Matter era now." In other words, for Williams, Baldwin's variously queer misalignment with the social history of his present assures his model alignment with ours.

Williams's observation may well exaggerate the extent of Baldwin's alienation from his original cohort and country. Despite his many French and Turkish addresses and all the dim-witted, homophobic cracks about "Martin Luther Queen," just how estranged from the evolving concerns of mid-century black America was this card-carrying senior member of SNCC, a nonviolent marcher from Selma to Montgomery who moved on to counsel Black Panther Huey Newton in a California prison? (Baldwin was far less estranged, it's certain, than Ralph Ellison, the author of *Invisible Man* (1952), a fellow apprentice-turned-sworn enemy of Richard Wright's social realism, and maybe the most deliberately American black author of any generation.) Williams is on the money, however, in suggesting that Baldwin's renewed appeal is linked to the queer theory and queerer memory of Black Lives Matter. The movement's queer leadership—Mckesson, Patrisse Cullors, Alicia Garza, Opal Tometi, and scores of others—refuses to think about race apart from the proto-intersectional Baldwinian question of race-and-sex-and-more. Their rebalancing of the history of black protest, designed to highlight what Garza dubs the neglected heroism of "Black queer and trans folks" along with black women, black prisoners, and other groups traditionally "marginalized within Black liberation movements," enthrones Baldwin near the heart of the black progressive tradition.

BLM's queer revisionism, a boost to Baldwin's sales figures, is not the usual campaign to comfort an anxious radical present with the names and slogans of an admiring past. In the movement's grasp of time after Michael Brown, a proudly improper civil rights epoch has escaped the prim tomb of Martin Luther King Day and has returned intact as neither tragedy, nor farce, nor civics lesson but as an urgent ethical test. "If you EVER wondered who you would be or what you would do if you lived during the Civil Rights Movement, stop," commands Shaun King, the controversial BLM journalist. "You are living in that time, RIGHT NOW." Tef Poe, the St. Louis rapper and Ferguson protest regular, has quotably insisted that

BLM "ain't your grandparents' Civil Rights Movement." Even in this slogan in favor of young blood, however, the generation of Diane Nash and Bayard Rustin qualifies as a blood relation whose legacy demands fresh but comparable styles of political devotion.

For all its urgency, BLM's elevation of Baldwin would remain strategic, short on emotional magnetism, if his commentary on subjects pressing to the movement didn't seem eloquently fitting. Yet his collected writing makes the curating of a BLM Baldwin as respectful as it is self-flattering. In broad strokes, the pro-BLM voice to be built from this writing seconds the movement in content and schools it in form. The Baldwin so assembled offers committed readers a compelling blend of confirmation and challenge, a mirror of shared social analysis offset by a not-just-stylistic question: namely, to paraphrase Ta-Nehisi Coates, Why don't people write *sentences* like this anymore?

Read in tune with Black Lives Matter, Baldwin's best-known essays and novels cast the physical precariousness of black American life, its disproportionate exposure to injury and murder, as white racism's steady baseline. The "Negro's past," Baldwin maintains in *The Fire Next Time*, is a thing of hard-earned, precious beauty—and "of rope, fire, torture, castration, infanticide, rape," of the constant, humiliating fear, "deep as the marrow of the bone," of "death." Like BLM, this Baldwin paints the red record of white terrorism as an obsession with breaking the black form, its erotic power above all. "A Black man has a prick, [therefore] they hack it off," Baldwin cynically reasoned in dialogue with Audre Lorde. Sanctioning the secular materialism of a Coates, for whom the "particular, specific" black body is the final horizon of emancipation, Baldwin projects an electrically embodied post-Christian era, one in which the teary kiss and "protecting arm" of the lover outstrip any sacred blessing at the close of his autobiographical first novel, *Go Tell It on the Mountain* (1953).

Also like Black Lives Matter, this Baldwin sees the integrity of the black body menaced by a conspiracy between two outwardly opposed faces of white supremacy. The first of these faces is white innocence, redefined in the Norman Mailer–haunted essay "The Black Boy Looks at the White Boy" as a willful offense and "the thing that most white people imagine that they can salvage from the storm of life." The second face is the keeper and enforcer of this fantasy of deliverance, the white police. It's a white cop who teaches Rufus Scott, the martyred jazz drummer at the hub of *Another Country*

(1962), just "how to hate." And Scott, the keeper of Harlem's beat, collectively played by "hands, feet, tambourines, drums, pianos, laughter, curses, razor blades," is a black everyman here as elsewhere. "Rare, indeed," Baldwin testified in the essay "Fifth Avenue, Uptown," "is the Harlem citizen, from the most circumspect church member to the most shiftless adolescent, who does not have a long tale to tell of police incompetence, injustice, or brutality." As this reference to the cop-victimized church member hints, Baldwin upholds BLM in scorning the wager that freedom will follow respectability. The gay landmark *Giovanni's Room* (1956) is only the least closeted statement of his faith that the flight from shame to safety—racial, sexual, and existential—is an immoral ugly Americanism. Seen through Baldwin's eyes, the challenge of his time, and of BLM's, is to accept that liberation can be won only "if you will *not* be ashamed, if you will only *not* play it safe." This weighing of daring and principled self-transformation over settled demands for reform—denounced as pre-political self-indulgence by some in Baldwin's day, and some in ours—is sympathetic music to BLM, a movement drawn to energized friendship circles above obedient membership lists.

All of these parallels have joined to make Baldwin the most-tweeted literary authority of Black Lives Matter. The blend of political prophecy and theatrical self-exposure in nearly all of his essays, regardless of their topic, indeed anticipates the very twenty-first-century job description of the freedom fighter/social media star. Yet Baldwin is also appreciated by movement voices for the fundamental *un*-tweetability of his prose at its most identifiable, for the long and gracefully overstuffed sentences, immersed in the syntax of two royal Jameses, King and Henry, that confirm his share of historical remoteness. Tweet *this*, the lavish Baldwin sentence seems to say, as in this stem-winder from "Everybody's Protest Novel," the sentimentally Oedipal 1949 essay that made Baldwin's name on two sides of the Atlantic: "Sentimentality, the ostentatious parading of excessive and spurious emotion, is the mark of dishonesty, the inability to feel; the wet eyes of the sentimentalist betray his aversion to experience, his fear of life, his arid heart; and it is always, therefore, the signal of a secret and violent inhumanity, the mask of cruelty." In the relatively few, firmly vernacular words of a tweet by a Brooklyn BLM supporter, Baldwin is due homage because such "sentences be a page long and still grammatically correct. That boy ice cold."

On his own Twitter account, Coates has similarly celebrated Baldwin's control of the more-than-140-character formula; and in *Between the World and Me*, he channels both the low page total and the lingering, spun-out phrasing of *The Fire Next Time*, one of the fullest short books in American literature. It's no accident that Rankine chooses to integrate Baldwin into *Citizen* through a long, grammatically correct, and paradoxically languid quotation (here cut for length) describing a temptation to violence: "And there is no [black American] who has not felt, briefly or for long periods, with anguish sharp or dull, in varying degrees and to varying effect, simple, naked, and unanswerable hatred; who has not wanted to smash any white face he may encounter in a day, to violate [it], out of motives of the cruelest vengeance . . . ," etc. Baldwin's mushrooming commas and semicolons are a far cry from *Citizen*'s interspersed images and rapid jump cuts. But the inclusion of the former devices in Rankine's work demonstrates the historical pedigree of her interest in the dilemma of black vengeance—a pedigree signaled in part by Baldwin's distance from her economical formal repertoire. Baldwin's selected opinions have made him a virtual contemporary of Black Lives Matter. His lush and unpragmatic style, by contrast, is a tool through which the felt pastness of a selective black past can be measured for present use.

Filed-Again Baldwin

The FBI file excerpted and reproduced in this book contains no evidence that J. Edgar Hoover ever remarked on Baldwin's generous sentence lengths. But this same file, absorbing paperwork generated from 1958 (perhaps even 1944) to 1974 and topping out at 1,884 pages, stands as the longest yet extracted on an African American author active during Hoover's five decades as a Bureau executive. Part of the reason for the FBI's great expense of ink and labor on Baldwin can be detected in a handwritten note that Hoover scrawled on an internal Bureau memo in 1964. "Isn't Baldwin a well known pervert?" the semi-permanent FBI director demanded, his participation in the worst-hidden gay marriage in official Washington visible just beyond the margins. Despite the career-threatening context, M. A. Jones, an officer of the FBI's Crime Records Division, elected to answer Hoover's question by carefully distinguishing between fictional and personal testimonies. "It is not a matter of official record that [Baldwin] is a pervert," Jones specified in a meticulous communication to Hoover, even though "the theme of homosexuality has figured prominently in two of his three published novels.

Baldwin has stated that it is also 'implicit' in his first novel, *Go Tell It on the Mountain*. In the past, he has not disputed the description of "autobiographical" being attached to the first book. . . . While it is not possible to state that he is pervert," Jones concluded, Baldwin "has expressed a sympathetic viewpoint about homosexuality on several occasions, and a very definite hostility toward the revulsion of the American public regarding it."

Hoover, typically hostile to any queer man less powerfully insulated than himself, did not glide gently into agreement with Jones's subtle distinctions between sexual acts, sympathies, and representations. The FBI director continued to entertain voices inside and outside the FBI interested in banning Baldwin's explicitly erotic third novel, *Another Country*—this despite the Bureau's refusal to act against the book under the Interstate Transportation of Obscene Matter Statute and the report of the Justice Department's General Crimes Section that "*Another Country* by James Baldwin has been reviewed . . . and it has been concluded that the book contains literary merit and may be of value to students of psychology and social behavior." With rival units in Justice discovering the novel's redeeming social importance, it was left to Hooverite sticklers to contemplate *Another Country*'s resemblance to earlier benchmarks of modernist indecency. "[I]n many aspects it is similar to the 'Tropic' books by [Henry] MILLER," wrote Washington, DC's special agent in charge.

Well-informed literary comparisons and blurb-worthy praise are not the norm in Baldwin's FBI file. The Justice Department's General Crimes Section looks to be a better source of legalistic jacket copy applauding "literary merit" and "value to students of psychology and social behavior." Yet the incongruous thoughtfulness of M. A. Jones's reply to Hoover's insulting question, its outstripping of the need to label, discipline, and punish, illustrates the grudging respect that some Bureau agents felt for the writers they furtively "ghostread" and harassed. Hoover himself possessed an inflated fear and regard for the authors who doubled as "thought-control relay stations," as he classified them. Authorial relay stations of prominence, Baldwin included, were spared in-person interviews by Bureau agents impressed by their "access to the subversive press," a megaphone whose range the FBI tended to exaggerate. Despite Hoover's ugly, destructive, and sometimes criminal hostility to the Black Freedom Movement beginning no later than the riot-torn "Red Summer" of 1919, the encounters of his FBI with African American writing could not always resist the pleasures of the enemy text. Likely the single thing that Hoover's Bureau shares with Black Lives Matter, in fact, is the once-uncommon judgment that Baldwin was the sixties' most significant black author.

Eldridge Cleaver's reproach be damned, the ingredients of Baldwin's FBI file match BLM revivalism in centering their subject at the intersection of black art and Black Power politics. Beginning in 1963, forms in the file place Baldwin on Hoover's notorious Security Index of imminently arrestable threats to the state, citing the collective risk of his "outspoken stand on the civil rights issue, his current prominence as an author and the inflammatory nature of his writings which show him to be a dangerous individual who could be expected to commit acts inimical to the national defense and public safety of the United States in time of emergency." Convinced that the state of emergency has come, a 1968 Bureau document installs Baldwin near the top of a list of "Independent Black Nationalist Extremists," a ranking that followed several mentions of the author in tapped telephone calls from Nation of Islam headquarters in Chicago. Malcolm X, his private conversations recorded in hundreds of FBI documents, is overheard endorsing the eloquence of "Brother Baldwin," highly "influential among the intellectuals." The hip vocabulary of the brother's private speech is an object of Bureau attraction, one source, possibly, of the over-eager slang that white FBI agents deployed when ghostwriting would-be black poems, letters, and manifestoes for the anti-Black Nationalist COINTELPRO program: "It is noted that in greeting . . . BALDWIN stated 'Hello, baby, how are you' and in closing the conversation stated that 'It's good to hear from you, baby.'" Agent memos welcome Baldwin's titles into the FBI's research library in Washington, from *Another Country* and *The Fire Next Time* to the lynching drama *Blues for Mister Charlie* (1964) and the acidic memoir *No Name in the Street* (1972). Confidential accounts of dozens of speaking engagements validate Baldwin's suspicion that there was often "a CIA or FBI agent in the group" when he publicly unloaded his mind. Bureau informants followed his talks from Mississippi farm fields to a Manhattan dinner of the Emergency Civil Liberties Committee, where Baldwin shared the dais with a certain guitar-playing "Bobby Dillon." In distinction to Baldwin's lucid address, an FBI mole recounted, the musician's "was rather one of free association." Not even the Bureau, a clearinghouse of conspiracy theories and implausible alibis, predicted that Dylan would beat Baldwin to the Nobel Prize for literature.

Along the trail of speaking engagements, Baldwin conducts an unhidden running battle with Bureau surveillance, climaxing in the promise that he will publish an anti-FBI screed with the power to expose Hoover's racism at last. A book-in-possible-progress named *The Blood Counters,* supposedly titled after "the negroes' nickname for the FBI" and said to "depict the work of the FBI in the South during . . . recent civil rights incidents," was touted by Baldwin in *Playbill* and the *New York Herald Tribune* and taken seriously enough to become the talk of Bureau critic-spies in 1963 and 1964. Baldwin's sometime lawyer Clarence Jones was captured on an FBI wire during this period boasting that his client's assault on the Hooverites will "be like an atom bomb." Despite Jones's overheard assurance, Baldwin's manuscript never reached waiting arms at the Dial Press—a firm where one of the Bureau's "contacts in the publishing field" purportedly stood ready to "secure the proofs" and forward them to Bureau headquarters. According to James Campbell, the Scottish biographer who first pried loose the bulk of Baldwin's FBI file, the abandonment of *The Blood Counters* is one sign of the Bureau's responsibility for the author's shrunken productivity after 1963, the year not just of John F. Kennedy's traumatic slaying but of Baldwin's outraged discovery of FBI spying on civil rights protestors in Selma, Alabama. "It's hard to write between assassinations," Baldwin mordantly explained when asked about the slow-forming novel after *Another Country.* And it's even harder, adds Campbell, "when everyone . . . is listening to the writer's private conversation with himself"—everyone, that is, but the anxious, distracted, and phone-tapped writer in question.

The open secret of FBI surveillance drove Baldwin closer to creative silence and too close to clinical paranoia, speculates Campbell. But it's no more speculative to claim that Baldwin drove the FBI mad in turn, his real and virtual communications to the Black Freedom Movement compulsively screened, catalogued, and reviewed by the Bureau at the cost of thousands of dollars and agent-hours. From its inception, Baldwin's Hoover-bashing *Blood Counters* may have been a phantom text never planned for print, a high-risk conceptual artwork from the golden age of such artwork. Its target audience may have been the excitable interpretive community of Hoover's ghostreaders, and its mission accomplished the second a slice of America's national police force neglected other duties to shadow an imaginary manuscript. The same spectral book that Campbell understands as proof of forced abandonment, Baldwin could have taken as evidence of the power of words not seen. John A. Williams, the black mega-novelist, set the stakes of a consciously anti-FBI literature this way in *The Man Who Cried I Am* (1967), the great African American countersurveillance novel of the 1960s: "the secret to converting *their* change to *your* change," he wrote, "was *letting them know that you knew*" you were watched. The form in which the black artist should let them know, Williams indicates, was that artist's tactical business, and a feint (*The Blood Counters*, say) might do as well as a hammer (*The Man Who Cried I Am* itself).

The activists of Black Lives Matter, some of whom have tweeted and lamented Baldwin's FBI file, have reason to see themselves reflected in his cat-and-mouse game with US government espionage. In July 2015, documents unearthed by journalists armed with the Freedom of Information Act disclosed that the Department of Homeland Security (DHS) began monitoring BLM protesters mere days after the killing of Michael Brown in a St. Louis suburb. DHS, coincidentally led by Jeh Johnson, a grandson of the Harlem Renaissance patron Charles S. Johnson, had vacuumed up data from Facebook, Twitter, and Vine to track the movements of key black organizers and to reproduce a map of "conflict zones" where they were expected to practice their craft. The department "fully supports the right of individuals to exercise their First Amendment rights," affirmed a spokesman after the revelations, but DHS remained responsible for "providing situational awareness and establishing a common operating picture for the federal government." A month later, BLM learned more of what the quest for situational awareness and a common operating picture entailed. Published exposés confirmed that "crisis management" reports on well-networked "threat actors" had been purchased from the cybersecurity firm ZeroFox and shared with the FBI, the NYPD, and the Baltimore Police. Leaked copies of these reports placed Johnetta Elzie, the Ferguson-raised co-founder of We the Protesters, on a list of sixty-two such actors for whom "immediate response is recommended." Elzie was unsurprised by the evidence she was hounded for her "massive" Twitter following, as a star-struck ZeroFox termed it. "I never needed paper confirmation" of the surveillance, she noted, "but I guess it made it real for other people who didn't think it was possible." In March 2016, BLM organizers struck back with paper confirmation of their own, a friend-of-the-court letter in favor of Apple's war with the FBI over the hacking of a terrorist's iPhone. "One need only look to the days of J. Edgar Hoover and the wiretapping of Rev.

Martin Luther King, Jr.," wrote Opal Tometi, Shaun King, and a coalition of civil rights groups, "to recognize that the FBI has not always respected the right to privacy for [those] it did not agree with." "In the context of white supremacy and police violence," tweeted signee Malkia Cyril, "Black people need encryption." With the ghosts of Hoover-era counterintelligence programs hovering over their shoulders, BLM representatives then attended a pro-Apple protest in front of the FBI's J. Edgar Hoover Building on Pennsylvania Avenue. Finished and dedicated in 1975, the Brutalist concrete of this headquarters structure was specially reinforced to hold the weight of millions of pages of surveillance files, Baldwin's included.

The drama of historical repetition staged before the Hoover Building brings us to a final question: How should we understand the recurrence of the surveillance that now targets Black Lives Matter as it once targeted Baldwin, BLM's favorite pipeline to the black literary past? Or, more to the point, how can this repetition be survived and defeated? Simone Browne's 2015 book *Dark Matters*, a pioneering study of the racial history of twenty-first-century surveillance technologies, offers deep-rooted guidance. She begins with a cousin of the Baldwin file—the FBI's relatively thin dossier on Frantz Fanon, the black radical psychiatrist—and by telegraphing her desire to outrun the ruling emotion of "Afro-pessimism," an academic label for the growing sense among black activists and intellectuals that the bonds of slavery remain depressingly unbroken in our era of Trumpism, mass black incarceration, and the "New Jim Crow": "I enter *Dark Matters*," Browne declares, "with this sense of optimism in mind: that in Fanon's works and in the writings of black feminist scholars, another mode of reading surveillance can be had." Browne's alternative mode of reading reveals the surveillance of blackness visible most everywhere but in the academic field of surveillance studies, a place where race too often figures as an unnamable matter. In an act of creative translation, she follows the surveillance scholar Steve Mann in altering a French prefix from *sur*, or "on," to *sous*, or "below," and invents the counter-concept of "dark sous-veillance." Under this concept's umbrella, she highlights performances of black freedom in the face of white surveillance that could by rights include Baldwin's *Blood Counters* as well as BLM's commitment to capturing police abuse via cellphone. Yet Browne's optimistic revisionism ultimately finds its historical ballast in the same territory as Afro-pessimism. The history of "transatlantic slavery must be engaged," she maintains, "if we are to create a surveillance studies that grapples" with the past and present of "unfinished emancipation." In Browne's work as a whole, state surveillance and dark sous-veillance each build on knowledge of black resistance born under slavery and illuminated by it even now. Baldwin sometimes typified the 1960s, the high watermark of civil rights agitation, as "the last slave rebellion." But Browne's book argues that the long war against slave-watching power rages fifty years on. Viewed through her lens, Baldwin's and BLM's skirmishes with the FBI each look like the latest—not the last—revolt of the slaves.

For their part, Baldwin's file and the rest of the FBI's many dossiers on twentieth-century African American authors imply something different about the nature of racial surveillance. These strange documents of both literary criticism and secret police work reveal that Hoover's Bureau, the dominant institution in US domestic intelligence from 1919 to 1972, never acted from the premise that black writers were akin to slaves. The founding premise beneath the Bureau's extensive surveillance of twentieth-century African American authors was an opposite one, in fact, a vision of liberation rather than of captivity. In the teens and 1920s, Hoover and his G-Men witnessed the initial chapters of the New Negro or Harlem Renaissance and the epochal social movement of black migration northward and resolved that a previously imprisoned population had become highly literate, increasingly free in movement and expression, and modern, all too modern.

Robert Adger Bowen, a white writer of black dialect fiction and the FBI executive primarily responsible for the Bureau's first published work of literary criticism, confessed the following in a special report to J. Edgar Hoover dated 1919: the "marked ability" of Claude McKay and other first-wave Harlem Renaissance authors, he had discovered, broke sharply from the "bombast and nonsense" he associated with the "plantation negro preacher." The New Negro writer "means business," Bowen concluded, "and it would be well to take him at his word." James Weldon Johnson, the author of *The Autobiography of an Ex-Colored Man* (1912), a crucial herald of Harlem's rebirth, reviewed a related FBI report on African American writing in the black-owned *New York Age* and underscored that the honing of a "clear, intelligent, and forcible" New Negro voice "is what shocks the writer of the report more than anything else." The Bureau agent responsible for reviewing New Negro literature was "a man who has evidently, like many others, been asleep on the Negro," Johnson deduces, and what "astonishes him most is the fact that these articles are written by Negroes who know how to use the English language."The FBI snooping that pained and inspired James Baldwin forty years later stemmed from much the same astonishment over black literary sophistication and influence, the enduring product of the national security state's apprehension that modern black literacy had trumped modern black slavery. This too, then, is part of James Baldwin's legacy to Black Lives Matter: history's notice that surveillance is not cemented exclusively to the position of the slave but is also uneasily applied to those most free and those best equipped to say so.

What's in—and Not in—This Edition of the Baldwin File

The once-secret documents presented in this book are taken from the long FBI file on James Baldwin first obtained by James Campbell after a successful 1998 court challenge. As a declassified US government record, this file now sits in the public domain. All of its 1,884 pages can be found at my online F.B. Eyes Digital Archive (http://digital.wustl.edu/fbeyes/), though scores of passages and pages have been redacted by the FBI for reasons of privacy, law enforcement, or national security. Redacted portions of the file, whether blacked out in part or removed whole pages at a time and replaced by explanatory legal memos, are minimized in my selections here for reasons of interest and convenience. Readers should remember that the full file is studded with evidence that aspects of the Bureau's hostile tango with Baldwin are still censored.

The file pages included in this book are reproduced just as they are in copies of the Baldwin file provided directly by the FBI. This does not mean that these pages are always crystal clear. There is confusing overwriting generated as documents traveled within the Bureau and to other federal agencies, with stamps, signatures, marginal comments, and various page numbers overlaid on typewritten reports. There is blurriness thanks to the mixed quality of Bureau Xeroxing in response to initial FOIA requests. Readers can rest assured, however, that in holding this book they hold something close to the shape and story of the original FBI paperwork. Tedious repetitions in the file have not made the cut, but the documents included were chosen to reflect the file's complete range, from plainly mistaken information on Baldwin's marital status to piercing insight into his social and artistic commitments. Taken as a whole, these documents compose a sometimes accurate, often infuriating, and always enlightening police-authored biography of James Baldwin in his prime. Now the most revered African American writer of his time, he is here profiled as a first-class threat to J. Edgar Hoover's FBI and its ideal of the American order, racial, sexual, and cultural.

Sources of Quotations in the Introduction

"[T]he intellectual void," Toni Morrison on the dust jacket of Ta-Nehisi Coates, *Between the World and Me* (New York: Spiegel & Grau, 2015). **"Jimmy is *everywhere*,"** Eddie Glaude Jr., "James Baldwin and Black Lives" (online video, *C-Span.org*, 8 May 2015). **"So I give you your problem back,"** James Baldwin, "Who Is the Nigger?" (online video, *YouTube*, 23 April 2010). **"The thing about [Martin Luther] King or Ella Baker. . .,"** DeRay Mckesson, quoted in Bijan Stephen, "Get Up, Stand Up: Social Media Helps Black Lives Matter Fight the Power" (*Wired*, Nov. 2015, web). **"It is our duty to fight for our freedom. . .,"** Assata Shakur, *Assata: An Autobiography* (Chicago: Lawrence Hill Books, 2001), 52. **"I object to the term 'looters' . . . ,"** James Baldwin, quoted in "James Baldwin Tells Us All How to Cool It This Summer" (*Esquire*, July 1968, web). **"[S]ays a lot about Baldwin's writing . . . ,"** Ryan Dalton/capetownbrown (Tweet, 4 Aug. 2015). **"[W]hy don't people write short, powerful books. . .,"** Ta-Nehisi Coates, interviewed by Mary Ann Gwinn (*Seattle Times*, 23 October 2015, web). **"[T]o the center of his burning skull,"** Eldridge Cleaver, *Soul on Ice* (New York: Dell, 1968), 101. **"[S]ame characteristics of the Baldwin brand that so 'estranged' him . . . ,"** Thomas Chatterton Williams, Breaking into James Baldwin's House" (*The New Yorker*, 28 October 2015, web). **"Black queer and trans folks . . . ,"** Alicia Garza, "A Herstory of the #BlackLivesMatter Movement" (*The Feminist Wire*, 7 October 2014, web). **"If you EVER wondered . . . ,"** Shaun King (*Facebook* post, 10 November 2015). **"[A]in't your grandparents' Civil Rights Movement,"** Tef Poe, quoted in Keeanga-Yamahtta Taylor, *From #BlackLivesMatter to Black Liberation* (Chicago: Haymarket Books, 2016), 161. **"Negro's past . . . ,"** James Baldwin, *The Fire Next Time*, in *Collected Essays* (New York: Library of America, 2015), 342. **"A Black man has a prick . . . ,"** James Baldwin, interview with Audre Lorde, "Revolutionary Hope" (*Essence*, December 1984), 133. **"[P]rotecting arm,"** James Baldwin, *Go Tell It on the Mountain*, in *Early Novels and Stories* (New York: Library of America,

1998), 213. **"[T]he thing that most white people . . . ,"** James Baldwin, "The Black Boy Looks at the White Boy," in *Collected Essays*, 270. **"[H]ow to hate"** and **"hands, feet, tambourines . . . .,"** James Baldwin, *Another Country*, in *Early Novels and Stories*, 370. **"Rare, indeed . . . ,"** James Baldwin, "Fifth Avenue, Uptown," in *Collected Essays*, 176. **"[I]f you will *not* be ashamed . . . ,"** James Baldwin, *Giovanni's Room*, in *Early Novels and Stories*, 267. **"Sentimentality, the ostentatious parading . . . ,"** James Baldwin, "Everybody's Protest Novel," in *Collected Essays*, 12. **"[S]entences be a page long . . . ,"** Hello Brooklyn (Tweet, 23 May 2013). **"And there is no [black American] who has not felt . . . ,"** James Baldwin, "Many Thousands Gone," quoted in Claudia Rankine, *Citizen: An American Lyric* (Minneapolis: Graywolf Press, 2014), 124. **"Isn't Baldwin a well known pervert?"** J. Edgar Hoover, marginal comment in the James Baldwin FBI file, July 1964. **"It is not a matter of official record that [Baldwin] is a pervert . . . ,"** M. A. Jones in the James Baldwin FBI file, July 1964. **"*Another Country* by James Baldwin has been reviewed . . . ,"** in the James Baldwin FBI file, Sept. 1963. **"[I]n many aspects it is similar to the 'Tropic' books . . . ,"** in the James Baldwin FBI file, September 1962. **"[T]hought-control relay stations,"** J. Edgar Hoover, quoted in Natalie Robins, *Alien Ink: The FBI's War on Freedom of Expression* (New York: William Morrow, 1992), 50. **"[A]ccess to the subversive press,"** in the W. E. B. Du Bois FBI file, October 1960. **"[O]utspoken stand on the civil rights issue . . . ,"** in the James Baldwin FBI file, December 1963. **"Independent Black Nationalist Extremists,"** in the James Baldwin FBI file, January 1968. **"Brother Baldwin . . . ,"** Malcolm X, quoted in the James Baldwin FBI file, July 1961. **"It is noted that in greeting . . . ,"** in the James Baldwin FBI file, January 1964. **"[A] CIA or FBI agent in the group,"** James Baldwin, quoted in the James Baldwin FBI file, August 1968. **"Bobby Dillon"** and **"was rather one of free association,"** in the James Baldwin FBI file, January 1964. **"[T]he negroes' nickname for the FBI . . . ,"** James Baldwin, quoted in the James Baldwin FBI file, July 1964. **"[B]e like an atom bomb,"** Clarence Jones, quoted in the James Baldwin FBI file, June 1963. **"[C]ontacts in the publishing field . . . ,"** in the James Baldwin FBI file, August 1964. **"It's hard to write between assassinations,"** James Baldwin, quoted in James Campbell, *Syncopations: Beats, New Yorkers, and Writers in the Dark* (Berkeley: University of California Press, 2008), 100. **"[W]hen everyone . . . is listening to the writer's private conversation**

. . . ," James Campbell, *Syncopations*, 100. **"[T]he secret to converting *their* change to *your* change . . . ,"** John A. Williams, *The Man Who Cried I Am* (New York: Overlook, 2004), 386. **"[C]onflict zones,"** quoted in George Joseph, "Feds Regularly Monitored Black Lives Matter since Ferguson" (*The Intercept*, 24 July 2015, web). **"[F]ully supports the right of individuals . . . ,"** Department of Homeland Security, quoted in George Joseph. **"[C]risis management . . . ,"** Brandon Ellington Patterson, "Black Lives Matter Organizers Labeled as 'Threat Actors' by Cybersecurity Firm" (*Mother Jones*, 3 August 2015, web). **"[I]mmediate response is recommended . . . ,"** quoted in Brandon Ellington Patterson. **"I never needed paper confirmation . . . ,"** Johnetta Elzie, quoted in Brandon Ellington Patterson. **"One need only look to the days of J. Edgar Hoover . . . ,"** Opal Tometi and company, quoted in Jenna McLaughlin, "The FBI vs. Apple Debate Just Got Less White" (*The Intercept*, 8 March 2016, web). **"In the context of white supremacy . . . ,"** Malkia Cyril, quoted in Jenna McLaughlin. **"I enter *Dark Matters* . . . ,"** Simone Brown, *Dark Matters: On the Surveillance of Blackness* (Durham: Duke University Press, 2015), 6. **"[T]ransatlantic slavery must be engaged . . . ,"** Simone Brown, 13. **"[T]he last slave rebellion,"** James Baldwin, quoted in *Conversations with James Baldwin*, edited by Fred L. Standley and Louis H. Pratt (Jackson: University Press of Mississippi, 1989), 194. **"[M]arked ability"** and **"bombast and nonsense . . . ,"** Robert Adger Bowen, "Radicalism and Sedition among the Negroes as Reflected in Their Publications," Robert Adger Bowen Papers, Clemson University, Box 10, Folder 86. **"[C]lear, intelligent, and forcible. . ."** and **"a man who has evidently . . . ,"** James Weldon Johnson, "Report of the Department of Justice on Sedition among Negroes" (*New York Age*, 12 December 1919).

Permissions

Portions of the introduction and of my commentaries on individual FBI documents are adapted with permission from my article "Born-Again, Seen-Again James Baldwin," published in the journal *American Literary History* in the winter of 2016 (copyright © 2016 by Oxford University Press); and from my book *F.B. Eyes: How J. Edgar Hoover's Ghostreaders Framed African American Literature* published in 2015 (copyright © 2015 by Princeton University Press).

Acknowledgments

My gratitude to the brave eloquence of James Baldwin; to the artists and activists of Black Lives Matter who reinvented him for our time; to the many scholars of the FBI and James Baldwin who paved the way, David Leeming, Dwight McBride, and the file mavens James Campbell and Douglas Field high among them; to my rock-solid and discerning editor, Cal Barksdale, who suggested such a book in the first place; to the rest of the team at Arcade/Skyhorse who made realizing the object a rare pleasure; and, as always, *alla famiglia*. This is for the incomparable Jules, Bix, and Elvis; Steph, Anna, Lizzie, and Carolyn; Oreon and Evelyn; and Sarah, Liz, and Louis.

JAMES BALDWIN'S FBI FILE, SAMPLED AND EXPLAINED

1.

GRAPHIC EVIDENCE

1963, 1964, AND 1966

James Baldwin is the twentieth-century African American author most honored in the twenty-first. All the same, his FBI dossier begins like a common criminal case file with an envelope of graphic evidence. The first significant item in the envelope is an identifying photo of Baldwin at age thirty-nine, fresh from the success of *The Fire Next Time*, his now-classic reflection on the religion of the Civil Rights Movement and its Black Muslim skeptics, initially published in January 1963. Surprisingly, the FBI or another police force did not take the photo, distorted by Bureau reproduction, though later documents in the file prove that Bureau agents quietly photographed Baldwin as he protested in Selma that October. Instead, the photo was borrowed from a positive article in *The Militant*, the newspaper of the Socialist Workers Party, run as Baldwin lectured across the American South in support of the Congress of Racial Equality (CORE) and its philosophy of nonviolent but dynamic confrontation with racism. A flattering publicity portrait repurposed as a mugshot prefaces Baldwin's FBI file—not the only time the Bureau turned the tools and fruits of his literary success into investigative weapons against him.

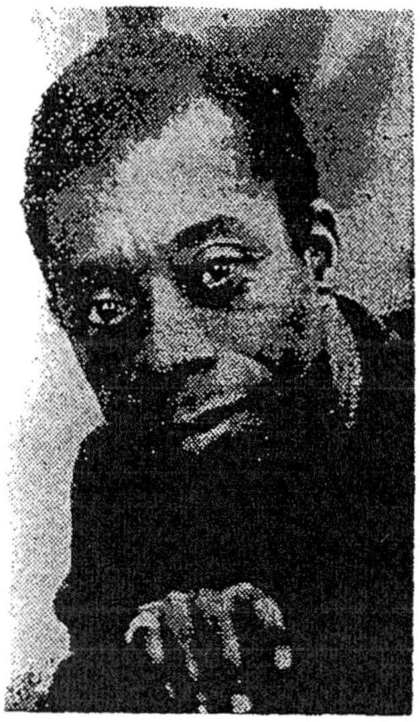

James Baldwin

The second item in the envelope is a copy of an impassioned 1964 fund-raising letter Baldwin wrote for the Mississippi Freedom Project led by the Student Nonviolent Coordinating Committee (SNCC), a group he joined well after his student days. This highly choreographed, often mythologized voter registration project drew over a thousand out-of-state volunteers, 90 percent of them white, into contact with experienced SNCC organizers and thousands of local African American citizens risking their lives for voting rights in the summer of 1964. It also drew the FBI into the business of investigating violence against civil rights workers: after years of Bureau inaction, Attorney General Robert F. Kennedy persuaded J. Edgar Hoover to probe the brutal "Mississippi Burning" murders of Freedom Project participants James Chaney, Andrew Goodman, and Michael Schwerner. Baldwin's letter, written while the bodies of the trio were still missing, paints the Project as an existential advance and a virtuous children's crusade, "an act of faith and courage" by young men and women "that is so extraordinary that I find myself struggling for words to describe my feelings toward them." Why did the FBI find Baldwin's appeal important enough to collect through a "Confidential Mail Box" set up to receive radical publications? In part because the Bureau, unlike Baldwin's radical critics, consistently saw him as a militant protest leader as well as an influential author and commentator. Baldwin would in fact support SNCC's turn to a combative Black Nationalism in 1966. SNCC chairman Stokely Carmichael's call for Black Power, Baldwin argued, harmonized with at least one respected "canon of Western thought: the self-determination of peoples." As the decade wore on, Baldwin's continued sympathy for SNCC increasingly alarmed FBI headquarters, and became one justification for his official relisting as an "Independent Black Nationalist Extremist" in 1968.

PLEASE DO NOT REMOVE
THIS SLIP FROM EXHIBIT
NY 100-146553-TAI

ALL INFORMATION CONTAINED
HEREIN IS UNCLASSIFIED
DATE 5-22-89 BY

AN URGENT MESSAGE FROM: Ruby Dee

Dear Friend:

As you are reading this letter, the young men and women shown above are in Mississippi performing an act of faith and courage that is so extraordinary that I find myself struggling for words to describe my feelings toward them.

They are some of the more than 1000 volunteers who have come from all over our country to spend this summer in the most terror-stricken area of the south -- Mississippi where 900,000 Negroes live in feudal conditions unimaginable to the outsider.

The gravest of dangers await these courageous workers. Some details of what they face are given in the enclosed article reprinted from Newsweek. The first of the summer volunteers have already been arrested; project offices have been attacked and even bombed. God knows what may happen between now, as I write this letter, and when you receive it.

All of us are waiting anxiously and still praying for the safety of the three young people who have disappeared.

And yet, they are coming; teachers, nurses, technicians, college students, legal advisors -- both Negro and white.

They are coming: on a unique mission, an unofficial peace corps for the south, bringing their skills and courage to communities which have been almost completely shut off from the American mainland.

(over please)

These courageous young people will staff a wide range of programs whose goal is nothing less than to help bring the Mississippi Negro into the 20th century. Their undertakings will include: 1) the establishment of Freedom Schools teaching everything from the techniques of non-violent protest to technical skills and remedial reading; 2) expanded voter registration drives; 3) supporting Negro candidates for public office; 4) the creation of community centers across the state.

The director of the Mississippi Summer Project is Robert Moses, a leader of the Student Nonviolent Coordinating Committee. SNCC will be the driving force in carrying out the entire project. Bob Moses is a brilliant, 29-year old Negro who was educated at Hamilton and Harvard, then gave up an excellent teaching appointment to work in the civil rights movement.

Not many of us can leave jobs and families to spend a whole summer in Mississippi. But all of us can help see to it that these courageous young people have enough food to eat - sorely needed books and teaching materials - medicines for illness and injury- legal aid to keep them (or get them) out of jail.

These young people belong to us -- they are our sons and daughters. But just being proud of them won't help. Mayor Thompson of Jackson Miss., says "They won't have a chance." I ask you to help give them a chance by sending a generous contribution for the Mississippi Summer Project and to send it NOW. Please send as much as you can -- every dollar you can spare will be put to direct and immediate use.

Sincerely yours,

James Baldwin

James Baldwin

P.S. Time is so short - the need so immediate! Please send your contribution now to me at SNCC - 100 Fifth Ave., New York 11, N. Y. Make all checks payable to SNCC.

PLEASE DO NOT REMOVE
THIS SLIP FROM EXHIBIT
NY 100-146553-102

REPRINTED FROM
Newsweek February 24, 1964

MISSISSIPPI:

Allen's Army

The second summer of the Negro revolt was still months off. But ever since the first, Allen Thompson, the graying, satin-smooth mayor of unreconstructed Jackson, Miss., has been acting as though Armageddon were just around the corner.

Girding for a new wave of civil-rights demonstrations this summer, Thompson is massing an impressive—and expensive—deterrent force of men and military hardware. To defend the capital city of 144,422, he is building up his young, tough, riot-trained police force from 390 to 450, plus two horses and six dogs. The force is "twice as big as any city our size," Thompson boasted last week—and it will be backed by a reserve pool of deputies, state troopers, civilian city employes, and even neighborhood citizen patrols.

With a hefty $2.2 million budget to spend, the department recently bought 200 new shotguns, stockpiled tear gas, and issued gas masks to every man. Its motor fleet includes three canvas-canopied troop lorries, two half-ton searchlight trucks, and three giant trailer trucks to haul demonstration POW's off to two big detention compounds. "I think we can take care of 25,000," the mayor said.

Weepers: But the pride of Allen's Army is Thompson's Tank—the already popular nickname for a 13,000-pound armored battlewagon built to the mayor's specifications at roughly $1 a pound. The twelve-man tank, abristle with shotguns, tear-gas guns, and a submachine gun, flopped on its first mission—putting down a demonstration at all-Negro Jackson State College two weeks ago. As it rolled up, a tear-gas shell went off inside, and all twelve men stumbled out crying. Nevertheless, Thompson says reverently: "It's a wonderful thing."

Would a collision come? Thompson thought so—and so did the young war-hawks of the Student Nonviolent Coordinating Committee, already mapping a massive summer campaign in Mississippi. SNCC was dispatching questionnaires last week to prospective recruits for its own nonviolent army of 500 to 1,000—mostly college students—to staff

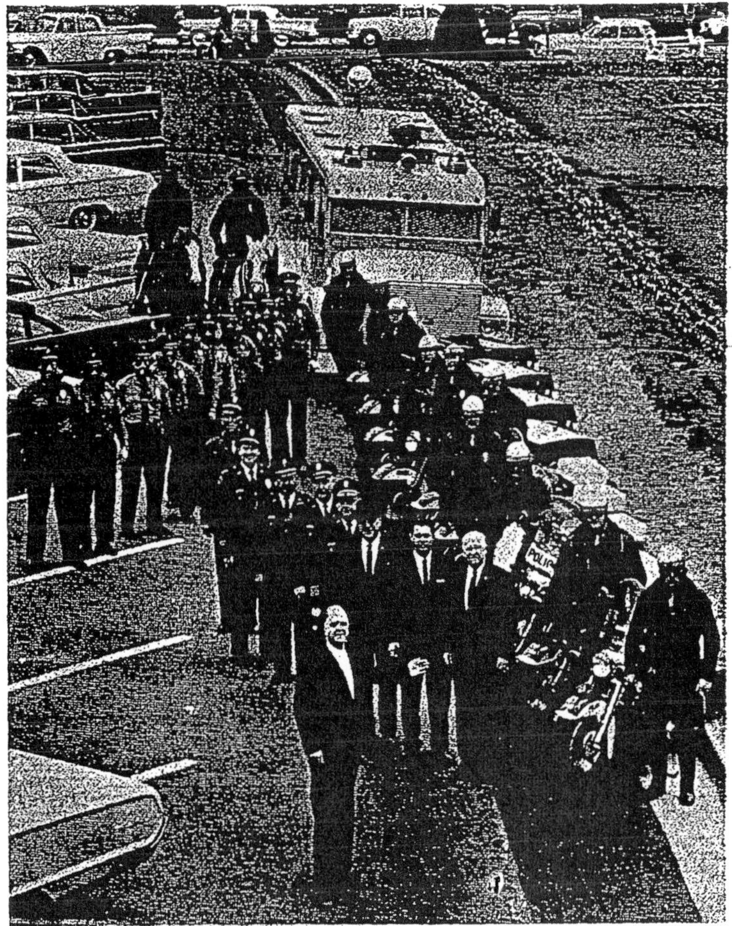

Thompson, troops—and armor

"freedom schools," community centers, and voter-registration drives. "The summer of 1964," SNCC chairman John Lewis said, "could really be *the* year for Mississippi. Before the Negro people get the right to vote, there will have to be a massive confrontation, and it probably will come this summer . . . We are going to Mississippi full force."

And when they come, Thompson feels he has the means to contain them. "There will be no unlawful marching and peaceful picketing," he vowed. "We are not going to let them come into the downtown area."

The mayor insists his army is only a second-strike force designed to preserve law and order. "We have to wait," he told NEWSWEEK's Karl Fleming, "until they start trouble." But Thompson is certain trouble will come. "This is it," he said. "They are not bluffing and we are not bluffing. We're going to be ready for them . . . They won't have a chance."

ALL INFORMATION CONTAINED
HEREIN IS UNCLASSIFIED
DATE 5-22-89 BY

PLEASE DO NOT REMOVE
THIS SLIP FROM ~~EXHIBIT~~
NY 100-146553-1A2

FIRST CLASS
Permit No. 31978
New York, N. Y.

BUSINESS REPLY MAIL
No Postage Stamp Necessary if Mailed in the United States

POSTAGE WILL BE PAID BY—

James Baldwin
Suite 803
100 Fifth Avenue
New York, N. Y. 10011

ALL INFORMATION CONTAINED
HEREIN IS UNCLASSIFIED
DATE 5-22-89 BY [illegible]

PR

Mr. Baldwin:

Enclosed please find my contribution of $____________
for the Mississippi Summer Project.

NAME________________________

ADDRESS________________________

CITY/STATE________________ Zipcode__________

Please make checks payable to SNCC

"...They won't have a chance." *Mayor Thompson of Jackson, Miss.*

Please—Give them that chance—NOW!

GRAPHIC EVIDENCE

The final item in the envelope heading up Baldwin's file is another portrait photograph, this one hijacked from a 1966 version of his US passport. This second photo, just three years older than the first, reveals the FBI's determination to keep an up-to-date headshot of Baldwin at the ready, the better to identify and detain him as a security risk in times of national emergency, as other documents in the file confirm. The source of the headshot testifies to the Bureau's close coverage of Baldwin's travels as a frequent transatlantic flyer (not just the concern of the CIA, officially charged with collecting national intelligence outside the US). Baldwin's confident look at the camera and firm signature across the photo predict his efforts, unveiled elsewhere in the file, to spy on and write about the Bureau in return—to do unto the FBI, in other words, what its file had done to him. As the cultural historian Maurice Wallace sees it, Baldwin's prominent eyes staring back from his Bureau dossier reflect "an eyeballing disposition of his own."

JAMES ARTHUR BALDWIN
PP/APP DTD. 8/2/6

2.

BALDWIN'S "FRECH ACCENT" ON AFRICAN INDEPENDENCE

JUNE 1961

Indexes in the file refer to stray FBI paperwork on Baldwin dating from 1958 and 1960, perhaps even from 1944, the year the apprentice author first met Richard Wright and launched the manuscript that became his debut novel, *Go Tell It on the Mountain* (1953). But the earliest complete document in the file comes from 1961 and concerns a public gathering of the Liberation Committee for Africa (LCA). This small, New York–based Pan-Africanist group is best remembered for publishing the *Liberator*, a leading political and cultural journal founded in response to the death of Patrice Lumumba, the Congolese independence leader assassinated with help from the CIA. Baldwin became a regular *Liberator* contributor and lent his voice to a June 1961 LCA meeting at a Broadway hotel whose audience included an undercover FBI spy. The three-page informer's report that followed the meeting begins with a dreary account of a "heavy traffic tie-up on approaching the Lincoln Tunnel." It nears its end with a bang, however, describing "the last speaker and the most forceful of the evening," the "author of 'Go Tell It on the Mountain'" who "realyy capivtated the audience with his frech [French] accent." Despite the comic misinterpretation of the sources of Baldwin's elaborate English, not to mention the malapropisms and spelling mistakes, the informer's account succeeds in capturing the excited response to Baldwin's embrace of the African revolution. At the same time, it corroborates Baldwin's belief that CIA or FBI agents lurked whenever he addressed a crowd. The extent of the CIA's surveillance of Baldwin remains murky, but his FBI file serves as a ready record of many of his speeches on political topics in the 1960s and early 1970s. Where the FBI was concerned, chronicling these often ephemeral talks—more than a few consciously delivered in the presence of government spies—was as vital as collecting Baldwin's publications.

OPTIONAL FORM NO. 5010-104-01

UNITED STATES GOVERNMENT

Memorandum

CONFIDENTIAL

TO : SAC, [100-45587)] DATE: 6/13/61

FROM : SA

SUBJECT: LIBERATION COMMITTEE FOR AFRICA; IS - C

Action - None recommended.

On 6/7/61, who has furnished reliable information in the past, personally provided a written statement to SA This statement is maintained in

8 - New York (RM)
1 - 105- (AFRICAN ACTIVITIES IN US)
(SOUTH AFRICAN UNITED FRONT)
(LIBERATION COMMITTEE FOR AFRICA)
1 -
1 -
1 -
1 - (JOHN KILLENS)
1 - (JAMES BALDWIN)
1 -
1 -

18 - Philadelphia
1 - 100-45587
17 - Other Philadelphia Files

CTA:fkd
(26)

Classified by
Declassify on: OADR

File Reviewers
Review CFs and Refs.

DECLASSIFIED BY
ON

SEARCHED INDEXED
SERIALIZED FILED
JUN 1 6 1961
FBI — NEW YORK

CONFIDENTIAL

"NATIONISLAM, COLONIALISM, and the UNITED STATES ONE MINUTE TO 12:

"Auspices of The Liberation Committee for africa
Place Martinique Hotel
22nd, Street and Broadway, New York City

"Friday, June 2, 1961
"8:30 P.M.

b7C-4
b7D-2

"Due to the heavy traffic tieup on approaching the Lincoln Tunnel the buss did not arrive in New York until eight-thirty o'clock. The auditorium was crowded when we arrived but the program had not started. Daniel Watts who was the chairman of the affair greeted the group and we were admitted without the stated fee of $1.00. The program started at nine oclock the chairman, Daniel Watts, stated the purpose of the meeting designed for positive action for freedom of the African people and to aid in the struggle to end conialism abraid and discrimination at home (X)

"The first speaker was Mr. John Killens author of 'Then We Heard the Thunder,' 'Young Blood' and 'Odds Against Tomorrow,' Mr. Killens stated that the period in which we areliving is one of great up surge of the common people. That the colored peope of the world are on the move to attain their freedom, liberty and justice. He was not (X)

CONFIDENTIAL

CONFIDENTIAL

"a very force___ speaker as most of his speech was from prepared manuscript. The next speaker was James Higgins, editor of the York Gazette and Daily. Mr. Higgins addressed the audience in his usual witty style which drew many hearty laughs from the audience. He told of the embarrassment of the officials in regards to Cuban fiasco and ended with a serious note from the writings of the American revolution. (C)

"Mr. James Baldwin was the last speaker, William ~~Worthy, the third speaker~~, told of a conference from which he had just returned in Washington, D.C., where some the countries leading interlectuals had assembled for a conference on the building of the nations character. The eme of his address was the seeming lack of understanding of what is taking place in the world and the utterly impossibility to continue along the same path that we are now treading. And that he had quite bluntly told them that the majority peoples of the world who are colored are no longer going to be content with a second class position in the world. At this point the chairman called for a collection to help to defray the expenses of the Committee and to pay some of its debts. This amounted to only $182.00 whibh was small considering the size of the audience which was at least two-thirds white middle class Jews. The next speaker was Vusumi Make of The South Africa United Front. His was critical of the role of the United States in regards to the sub-human role of the Union of South Africa and of the obsession of the American Government on the question of Communism. He stated that how the representatives of America claim to be against Colonialism and oppression yet in the United Nations they vote to support these Nations Colonial policies. Mr. Make presented a constructive plea for support of the oppressed majority the South African Natives. The last speaker and the most forceful of the evening was that of James Baldwin author of 'Go Tell It On The Mountain.' Mr. Baldwin whom it had been explained had spent the last nine years in Paris, Frances, realyy capivtated the audience with his frech accent and the courageousness of his message. He stated that it was a priod of revolution that confronts the world and that America has taken a position throughout the world against revolutions. And that only in revolution will the problems of this country be solved. The audience was quite enthusiastic in its acceptance of this speech as it seemed to go along with the ideas of most of those present. (C)

CONFIDENTIAL

CONFIDENTIAL

"We were welcomed by Gunther and several members of the Socialist Workers Party at the meeting. (X)

"Though the chairman had expressed prively that he did not wish his movement to be dominated by the communist and other radicals this seems to be the case. There seemed to be no representative of any of the Muslim groups present and this is strange as they are foremost in the fight for African liberation. The Buss for Philadelphia left New York at one-thirty oclock P.M. arriving in Philadelphia at 4:15 A.M." (X)

3.

MALCOLM X AND ELIJAH MUHAMMAD PRAISE BROTHER BALDWIN

JULY 1961

Another cache of 1961 documents consists of digests of phone-tapped conversations between Elijah Muhammad, the leader of the Nation of Islam (NOI) between 1934 and 1975, and a number of his followers including Malcolm X, Muhammad's most brilliant pupil, later his most disillusioned rival. In *The Fire Next Time*, Baldwin recounts a dinner invitation to Muhammad's South Side Chicago mansion, which he accepted in part to protest the "really cowardly obtuseness of white liberals" mystified by NOI's doctrine of black self-defense. Over a simple meal and two incongruous glasses of milk (Baldwin generally preferred Scotch), Muhammad praised the writer for his televised attacks on white hypocrisy and racist violence. "[I]t seemed to him," notes Baldwin, "that I was not yet brainwashed and was trying to become myself." In the digest of NOI phone traffic assembled by Chicago FBI agents, the course of Muhammad's outreach to Baldwin is clarified. It was Malcolm X, the classified record shows, who was asked to communicate the elder leader's "best love" to Baldwin—"there was no 'Tom' in him," thought Muhammad—and who passed the author's New York telephone number on to his spiritual father. These early pages of Baldwin's file dramatize one of the perverse ironies of questionably legal Bureau eavesdropping: it could capture and preserve history in the making with rare intimacy. Hoover's Bureau largely missed this implication of its phone-tapping, of course, much as it ignored Baldwin's final rejection of NOI's political theology in *The Fire Next Time*. Schooled by the not-too-distant memory of the Holocaust, Baldwin concluded there that "[t]he glorification of one race and the consequent debasement of another always has been and always will be a recipe for murder."

UNITED STATES GOVERNMENT

MEMORANDUM

TO : SAC, BOSTON (97-145) DATE: 7-28-61

FROM : SAC, CHICAGO (100-35635)

SUBJECT: NATION OF ISLAM
IS - NOI

ALL INFORMATION CONTAINED
HEREIN IS UNCLASSIFIED
DATE 5-22-89 BY [illegible]

The information set forth hereinafter was made available on the dates indicated by [redacted] who has furnished reliable information in the past. b2-1

6/26/61

[redacted] as the call was long distance from Newark, New Jersey) was in contact with ELIJAH MUHAMMAD. b7C-2

[redacted] stated he was calling to tell MUHAMMAD about the wonderful turnout (probably the 6/25/61 "feast" sponsored by Temple No. 4, Washington, D.C.). [redacted] stated it was full to the brim. MUHAMMAD stated he had been watching some of it on TV and added his "bronchitis" got worse Saturday night and I wasn't able to do any talking and my breath was too short and my voice was so that I could hardly talk without coughing. So I told my wife I can't make it because I wouldn't be fit to be sitting among people coughing and spitting up mucus all the time, and it would be a disgrace and I just can't make it. MUHAMMAD went on to say that he felt better around noon and had tried to get something out, but it was too late.

2-Boston (RM)
1-100- [redacted]
4-Indianapolis (25-9290) (Info) (RM)
1-100- [redacted]
1-100- [redacted]
1-100- (Gary "Crusader") b7C-3
2-Miami (105-544) (Info) (RM)
1-100- [redacted]
1-Newark (100- [redacted] (Info) (RM) 100-146553
3-New Orleans (100-15908) (Info) (RM)
1-100- [redacted]
1-100- [redacted]

(copies continued on i page)

SEARCHED INDEXED
SERIALIZED FILED
JUL 3 1 1961
FBI — NEW YORK

100-0-135703

CG 100-35635

3-New York (105-7809) (Info) (RM)
1-100-8999 (MALCOLM X LITTLE)
1-100- (JAMES BALDWIN)
3-Philadelphia (25-26091) (Info) (RM)
1-100-
1-100-
2-Phoenix (105-93) (Info) (RM)
1-100- (ELIJAH MUHAMMAD)
1-San Francisco (25-29163) (Info) (RM)
1-Washington Field (100-22829) (Info) (RM)
9-Chicago
1-100-6989 (ELIJAH MUHAMMAD)
1-100-32519
1-100-37886
1-100-27167
1-100-26797
1-100-37129
1-100-28457
1-100-31176 ("Crusader")
JRS:BMC
(31)

Jam 0
Jimmy 0

b7C-3

[redacted] told MUHAMMAD he would like to come out and see MUHAMMAD next week. MUHAMMAD told [redacted] he should call towards the end of this week to see if he would still be here as he had been thinking of going to Arizona until he gets rid of the bronchitis. MUHAMMAD stated that medicine just gave him temporary relief and added that he needs a long rest. MUHAMMAD went on to thank [redacted] and all the followers who were in Washington yesterday and who carried out such an orderly and wonderful mass meeting. MUHAMMAD added he was proud of his followers. MUHAMMAD also wanted to make known to [redacted] his regrets that the officer here did not escort him to the airport the last time he was here, adding it was stupid of the officials and MUHAMMAD would not let it happen again. MUHAMMAD stated he had bawled them out for this neglect, adding they should have escorted him to the airport to show their thanks for the good work he did here for a whole week in his efforts to convert the "dead."

b7C-2

6/26/61

A Brother Minister, believed to be MALCOLM X LITTLE, Minister of Temple No. 7, New York City, was in contact with [redacted] (believed to be [redacted] and the Holy Apostle. MUHAMMAD thanked MALCOLM and the other believers and followers for all the noble work they did there (probably Washington, D.C.) after adding it was wonderful. MUHAMMAD stated that "the whole world should bear witness; there is no God but Allah and that MUHAMMAD is his servant; that progress is being made in the wilderness; that his name is being known in the wilderness where the dragon of the evil world lives..." MUHAMMAD stated he would have put aside a million dollars in cold cash if he could have been there, but he wasn't able and Allah knows best. MUHAMMAD stated he took worse on Saturday night and it would have been impossible for him to get up on Sunday to make a speech.

MUHAMMAD then spoke about Brother BALDWIN, adding he had heard him speak this morning and stated that he was wonderful. MALCOLM stated he was just talking with Brother BALDWIN. MUHAMMAD told MALCOLM to give him his best love and he thought he was wonderful; that MALCOLM should tell him if he had known his telephone number he would have called him as soon as he was through looking at him. MALCOLM gave MUHAMMAD telephone number WA 9-5921 for Mr. JAMES BALDWIN in New York City. MALCOLM stated BALDWIN was very influential among the intellectuals there.

MALCOLM told MUHAMMAD they were blessed with a very large flock there and he believes there were a thousand "originals" down there who came down in cars.

A discussion ensued about MUHAMMAD's health and MALCOLM told MUHAMMAD he hoped he would do what he did before, adding that if it involves any cost it would be easy for them to arrange a plan which would be nothing to anyone. MUHAMMAD stated they did not even have to think about it as everything is taken care of and they already have enough. MUHAMMAD stated they are doing that every time they go to the temple. MUHAMMAD added that if it would get hot here it would be good, but added that this is the worst place. MUHAMMAD stated they had to turn on the heat yesterday and added that it was 97 in Phoenix yesterday. MUHAMMAD stated he did not think he could get out there this week, but possibly next week.

MALCOLM stated that the month ends Friday and he asked if MUHAMMAD would like him to do "that thing" all around there. MUHAMMAD told him to go ahead. MALCOLM stated he thought it would probably be better on Monday. MUHAMMAD replied it would, adding he should notify them to close them on "you" and on Tuesday he could close in on the other Party.

MUHAMMAD mentioned that [redacted] (probably [redacted] of Newark) called and wanted to see him. MUHAMMAD told MALCOLM that if he talked to [redacted] he should tell him he should come in with MALCOLM and he would be expecting him on Tuesday. b7c-2

MALCOLM and MUHAMMAD then spoke of something for the second Sunday in August, the 13th. MUHAMMAD stated that if he felt good he might take a "light one" on the West Coast as the waters have been stormy for a long time. MUHAMMAD stated he might take one in San Francisco next month.

b7c-2

6/26/61

[redacted] was in contact with [redacted] (ELIJAH MUHAMMAD). ELIJAH stated he had just listened to [redacted] speech on the tape and thought it was wonderful. MUHAMMAD stated he was proud of [redacted] and thought Allah [redacted] MUHAMMAD told [redacted] he thought he had really lashed their number one enemy. [redacted] and ELIJAH discussed how wonderful BALDWIN (JAMES BALDWIN of New York) was, stating there was no "Tom" in him. MUHAMMAD expressed a hope to be able to help [redacted] out sometime this summer adding that it may be one week next month if he felt all right. MUHAMMAD stated he would go to the other place (New York) in August.

6/27/61

[redacted] (probably [redacted] calling long distance from Boston) was in contact with ELIJAH MUHAMMAD.

[redacted] told MUHAMMAD that they had a wonderful time on Sunday (in Washington), but had missed MUHAMMAD. [redacted] expressed a desire to come to Chicago to see MUHAMMAD in the near future. MUHAMMAD instructed [redacted] to come in next Tuesday, adding Brother MALCOLM and Brother JAMES of Newark would be there. [redacted] stated that he and his followers wanted MUHAMMAD to take a rest until he is well.

6/27/61

[redacted] (probably [redacted] of the NOI) was in contact with [redacted] in Monroe, Louisiana. [redacted] asked if he should make out a check to [redacted] stated it would be all right to make it out to him or to [redacted] It was indicated this would be a cashier's check so [redacted] stated he did not see why it could not be made out to a court official there. [redacted] instructed [redacted] to send the check to Post Office Box [redacted] stated he would send the check special delivery so he could get them "out" as soon as possible. [redacted] asked if TROY (TROY CADE, Minister of the NOI group in Monroe, Louisiana) had received the envelope as yet. [redacted] stated he had not given it to TROY as they had thought it best not to give it to him as they did not know what he contains. [redacted] added TROY knows about it, however.

b7C-2

6/27/61

[redacted] (probably [redacted] of Miami, Florida) was in contact with ELIJAH MUHAMMAD. [redacted] indicated he was in court at the time of this contact and wanted to check with MUHAMMAD before he made any statement. MUHAMMAD instructed [redacted] to say that Islam is for peace, that their people have never been aggressive, but wanted to live in peace and dignity. MUHAMMAD told [redacted] to beg the court's forgiveness and say they did not know that anything they did was against the law. MUHAMMAD instructed [redacted] to not to try to get smart. [redacted] stated he would like to come and see MUHAMMAD. MUHAMMAD instructed [redacted] to write first, adding that he may be going back to Phoenix.

6/28/61

[redacted] was in contact with MALCOLM (LITTLE) at New York and stated ELIJAH MUHAMMAD wanted JOHN (probably JOHN 4X SIMMONS) and MALCOLM to make a tape and send it down for national distribution; that in this tape they should give MUHAMMAD's regrets for not being in Washington and bless all those who were there.

6/28/61

An unidentified brother was in contact with [redacted] (probably [redacted] The brother stated that Minister TROY (TROY CADE of Monroe, Louisiana) had called and stated he was released this afternoon; that TROY was not harmed or mistreated, but is weak from the poor conditions and from poor food; that they had TROY in a special hole and that probably all he got was bread and water. The unidentified brother stated that the minister wants to know what he should do now. ELIJAH MUHAMMAD came to the phone and told the unidentified brother to tell the minister to go ahead just the way they planned.

b7C-2

6/30/61

[redacted] was in long distance contact with [redacted] at the residence of ELIJAH MUHAMMAD. [redacted] stated he had told her he would call her. [redacted] replied that he had said he would call at 9 o'clock. [redacted] stated he would call her back.

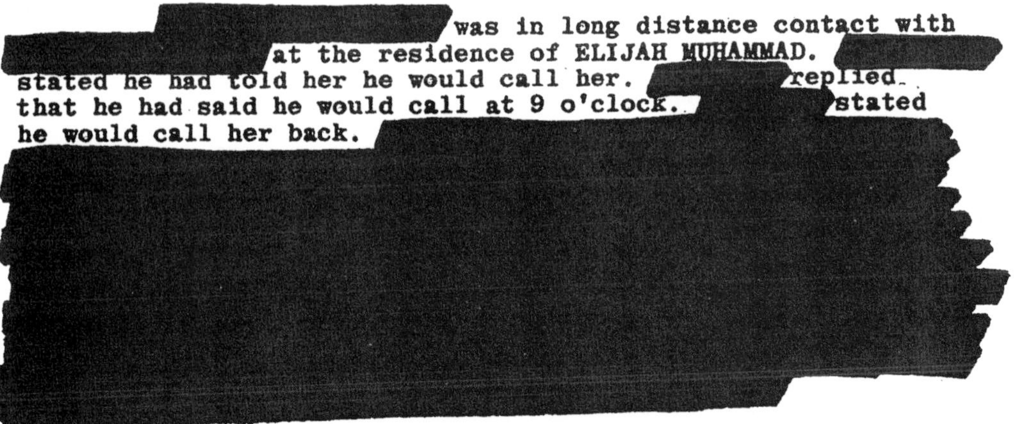

6/30/61

[redacted] to Mr. MUHAMMAD (ELIJAH) and [redacted] told MUHAMMAD that one of his employees whom he had trusted had stolen six checks worth $1000; that the boy enlisted in the Army on the 27th and that his name is [redacted] and he has a warrant out for him. [redacted] continued that he, MUHAMMAD, and [redacted] are becoming very popular, as the "Calumet Index" devoted about 4000 words to them in which they were all given the devil. [redacted] stated he has [redacted] with him now and he wants his money for the printers. [redacted] stated he had been unable to get in touch with the brothers down there; that he even loaned the one $350 of his own money and has not heard from them and they have only sent him a check for $300 thus far.

b7C-2

[redacted] then spoke to [redacted] and told him that Brother [redacted] and Brother [redacted] borrowed 350 for the Gary "Crusader" and went ahead and sold ads so they have an eight page paper; that all they sent was a check for 300 and that does not pay anything for last week's or this week's paper. [redacted] stated he was sticking his neck out and the printer was going along only because of him. [redacted] stated he has [redacted] at [redacted] and [redacted] at [redacted], but has not been able to reach them. [redacted] stated he would talk with them and if they owe this money he will tell them to pay up. It was indicated the office number is Turner 5-4357. It was further indicated they print 5,000 copies there.

4.

ANOTHER COUNTRY AS OBSCENE SPECIMEN

SEPTEMBER AND OCTOBER 1962

James Baldwin's third novel, *Another Country*, published in June 1962, represented what he called a "universal blues" rooted in the bohemian particulars of postwar Harlem and Greenwich Village. The novel's exploration of the risk of love and the greater risk of love's repression located this saving emotion in a variety of unconventional places: in bisexual and adulterous sex, in romances between blacks and whites, between jaded existentialist Americans and unstereotypically innocent Europeans. As a result, *Another Country* earned a place on the bestseller list, wildly mixed reviews, and numerous charges of obscenity. Correspondence in Baldwin's file from the fall of 1962 reflects the verdict of the Washington, DC, police department that *Another Country* might be illegally indecent. A copy of the novel was sent from the department's Morals Division to the FBI's Washington field office, whose "SAC," or special agent in charge, then sent the book up the ladder to FBI director J. Edgar Hoover. Hoover's personal as well as criminological interest in obscenity was familiar to Bureau executives, but the FBI's private copy of *Another Country* initially languished as a sterile "specimen" in the FBI crime laboratory. Washington's SAC—the first FBI agent to be pressed into service as a ghostreader of Baldwin's work—knew enough of the history of avant-garde literature to note the many similarities between Baldwin's novel and "the 'Tropic' books by [Henry] MILLER," subjects of obscenity lawsuits in at least twenty-one US states. He knew enough of the official morality of his employer, meanwhile, to instruct that Baldwin's suspect text "need not be returned" to his office.

OPTIONAL FORM NO. 10
5010-101

UNITED STATES GOVERNMENT

Memorandum

TO : DIRECTOR, FBI

DATE: 9/19/62

ATTENTION: FBI LABORATORY

FROM : SAC, WFO (145-0)

SUBJECT: JAMES BALDWIN; THE DIAL PRESS
NEW YORK, NEW YORK
ITOM

403878

Enclosed is a book entitled "Another Country" written by JAMES BALDWIN. This book was published in 1962 by the Dial Press, New York, New York. This novel was received from [redacted] Morals Division, M Metropolitan Police Department. In many aspects it is similar to the "Tropic" books by MILLER. It need not be returned.

b7C-7

3 - Bureau (Enc.1)
1 - WFO

ENCLOSURE

VJG:mpc
(4)

COPY & SPECIMENS RETAINED IN LAB. FOR LAB ACTION & REPORT

INDEXED FILES

REC-6

EX-113

145-2625-1

4 SEP 21 1962

EX

7-1b

REPORT
of the

FEDERAL BUREAU OF INVESTIGATION
WASHINGTON, D. C.

To: FBI, Washington Field Office

Date: October 3, 1962
FBI File No. 145-2625
Lab. No. D-403878 AV

Re: JAMES BALDWIN; THE DIAL PRESS
NEW YORK, NEW YORK
ITOM

Specimens received 9/21/62

Q1 One hard-bound book entitled "Another Country" written by James Baldwin

Result of examination:

The book described above as specimen Q1 was not identified with material of a similar nature which has been forwarded previously to the Laboratory.

Specimen Q1 is being added to the Bureau's files.

Q1 added to O.F. 10/2/62 cwb

CWB:ch (4)

Tolson
Belmont
Mohr
Callahan
Conrad
DeLoach
Evans
Malone
Rosen
Sullivan
Tavel
Trotter
Tele. Room
Holmes
Gandy

MAIL ROOM ☐ TELETYPE UNIT ☐

5.

"WHAT DO OUR FILES SHOW ON JAMES BALDWIN?"

MAY 1963

Baldwin's FBI file, like many others on public figures, doubles as a clipping file, a collection of cut-and-pasted newspaper and magazine articles that ironically resembles the kind of scrapbook once kept by adoring fans. The earliest article saved for the Baldwin file was an opinion piece by Warren Rogers, the chief Washington correspondent of the *New York Journal American*, touching on the writer's meeting with Attorney General Robert F. Kennedy and other civil rights intellectuals in May 1963. Baldwin had acted nothing like the flattered guest at Joseph Kennedy's New York apartment, taking the brother of the president to task for ignoring the historical differences between Irish and African Americans, not least the fact that only the latter group was "still required to supplicate and beg you for justice." Rogers panned the meeting as Kennedy's "disastrous sortie into the lofty levels of Negro intellectualism," a trying place where the likes of Baldwin, "the bitter and brilliantly articulate spokesman," had to be reckoned with—not just as equals, but as potential superiors. Kennedy, for his part, was humiliated by Baldwin's sharpness at the meeting and may have ordered a sweep of FBI records on the author. At the bottom of Rogers's article is a handwritten note by Clyde Tolson, Hoover's second-in-command at the Bureau and all-but-legal husband. "What do our files show on James Baldwin?" Tolson asked, with the answer arriving in the form of several summary reports inspiring a decade of stiffened FBI surveillance. In

"Re/Member This House," an unfinished memoir written in the 1980s, Baldwin lashed back at the Kennedy-FBI nexus with a colorful image of an intimidating, cigar-chomping Bobby Kennedy carrying "an FBI file cabinet in his brain."

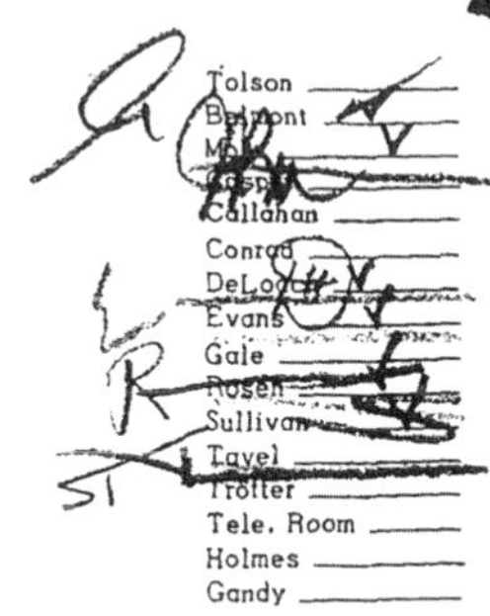

THE RACIAL ISSUE

RFK in Fight Of His Life-- And Knows It

By WARREN ROGERS
N. Y. Journal-American Chief Washington Correspondent With Hearst Headline Service

WASHINGTON: Attorney General Robert F. Kennedy is in the fight of his life, and he knows it. The racial issue will make or break him, and it may well decide his brother's place in history.

Bob Kennedy took over the Justice Department with some misgivings. He had listened to all the arguments against it—that he was too young, too untested as a lawyer, too close to the President to occupy Cabinet status, too inexperienced to handle all the myriad details of an excruciatingly difficult office.

In the end, after much soul-searching, he decided he could do it. And he surprised a number of his critics by doing a lot of it well. Except for the case of Jimmy Hoffa, where he has apparently bogged down in a pursuit as dogged and as fruitless as Hamlet's search for justice, the young man who managed his brother into the White House has managed his affairs exceedingly well.

Articulate Spokesman for U. S.

Bob Kennedy has been more than an Attorney General. He has been the ramrod behind much of America's foreign policy endeavors, notably the mess after the Bay of Pigs fiasco and the first decisive effort to settle the South Viet Nam problem. He emerged, in a trip around the world, as an articulate spokesman for American leadership of the newly developing nations.

But Bob Kennedy will be less than an Attorney General—at least in the judgment of history—if he does not solve the racial problem. It is, without any doubt, the gravest problem facing the country today.

There are clear signs that he is working at it, almost to the exclusion of anything else. He has been quietly holding meetings with various businessmen throughout the country in an effort to explain to them his feeling that—no matter how strong are the

Bobby Kennedy In Fight of His Life

Continued from First Page

prejudices of the people of their community—the American philosophy embodied in the Fourteenth Amendment must be maintained.

He had one disastrous sortie into the lofty levels of Negro intellectualism a few days ago. That was his meeting with James Baldwin, the bitter and brilliantly articulate spokesman for the Negro who says, "integration now." Baldwin and others with whom Kennedy talked in New York did not budge an inch, and it now is clear the meeting might better not have been held.

He had another disastrous junket into hard-core segregationist territory. That was his session at Montgomery, Ala., with Alabama's Gov. George Wallace. Afterward, Kennedy came away shaking his head and saying it was like talking to a foreign government, which is just about the way he must have felt after his bout with Baldwin.

It can be predicted that, in the future, Bob Kennedy will not make such mistakes again. He has learned that little can be gained and much can be lost by trying to deal directly with people like Wallace and Baldwin who are at the absolute opposite ends of the integration-segregation spectrum.

The key to the problem lies in between, with those whom the extremists on both sides call "Uncle Toms," "handkerchief heads," "radicals," "moderates," and much, much worse. The key also lies in the economic field. The greatest pressure for a solution in Birmingham was brought by U. S. Steel on its Birmingham subsidiary, Tennessee Coal and Iron.

Businessmen, whether big or little, whether local or absentee owned, are not going to stand idly by and watch a racial dispute destroy their businesses. It has happened in Little Rock, New Orleans, Birmingham, and wherever else the canker gnaws. It is here—among business, professional, clerical and other leaders who are not entirely bigoted, one way or the other—that solutions are going to be worked out. And they had better be.

ALL INFORMATION CONTAINED
HEREIN IS UNCLASSIFIED
DATE 5/16/89 BY [illegible]

62-108763-3

NEW YORK JOURNAL AMERICAN
New York, New York
5/28/63

What do our files show on James Baldwin?

ENCLOSURE

OPTIONAL FORM NO. 10

UNITED STATES GOVERNMENT

Memorandum

Tolson
Belmont
Mohr
Casper
Callahan
Conrad
DeLoach
Evans
Gale
Rosen
Sullivan
Tavel
Trotter
Tele. Room
Holmes
Gandy

TO : Mr. A. Rosen

DATE: May 29, 1963

FROM : Mr. [redacted]

SUBJECT: JAMES ARTHUR BALDWIN
INFORMATION CONCERNING

ALL INFORMATION CONTAINED
HEREIN IS UNCLASSIFIED
DATE 5-16-89 BY

SYNOPSIS:

On the attached clipping from the New York "Journal American" of 5-28-63, Mr. Tolson inquired as to information in our files concerning James Baldwin who recently met with the Attorney General.

Bureau files reveal that Baldwin, a Negro author, was born 8-2-24 in New York City and has lived and traveled in Europe. He has become rather well-known due to his writings dealing with the relationship of whites and Negroes. In 1960 he sponsored an advertisement of the Fair Play for Cuba Committee and was identified as one of its prominent members. This group is a pro-Castro propaganda organization in the United States. In 1961 he sponsored a news release from the Carl Braden Clemency Appeal Committee distributed by the Southern Conference Educational Fund, the successor to the Southern Conference for Human Welfare cited as a communist front by the House Committee on Un-American Activities (HCUA). Braden was a communist convicted of contempt of the HCUA. In 1962 Baldwin signed a clemency petition for Junius Scales, a communist convicted under the Smith Act. In April, 1961, he sponsored a rally to abolish the HCUA.

Baldwin has supported organizations supporting integration and in 1961 reportedly stated a period of revolution confronted the world and only in revolution could the problems of the United States be solved. He has advocated the abolishment of capital punishment and criticized the Director stating

Enclosure

GHS:bep
(8)
1 - Mr. Belmont
1 - Mr. Mohr
1 - Mr. Rosen
1 - Mr. DeLoach
1 - Mr. Evans
1 - Mr. [redacted]
1 - Name Check Section

REC-73 162-108763-3

11 JUN 13 1963

62 JUN 25 1963

that Mr. Hoover "is not a lawgiver, nor is there any reason to suppose him to be a particularly profound student of human nature. He is a law-enforcement officer. It is appalling that in this capacity he not only opposes the trend of history among civilized nations but uses his enormous power and prestige to corroborate the blindest and basest instincts of the retaliatory mob." He has also indicated he feels the Attorney General and the President have been ineffective in dealing with discrimination and in this connection has urged the removal of the Director.

ACTION:

For information. Information concerning Baldwin and the other individuals who participated in the recent conference with the Attorney General is being incorporated into informative memoranda for dissemination to the Attorney General.

DETAILS:

James Arthur Baldwin was born on August 2, 1924, in New York City to David Baldwin, a part-time clergyman, and Berdis Emma Baldwin, nee Jones. The eldest of nine children, James Baldwin was reared entirely in New York and in 1942 graduated from DeWitt Clinton High School where he served as a student judge and magazine editor. Baldwin has received many fellowships and awards which enabled him to live and write in Europe for approximately eight years during the 1950's. He has traveled to many other parts of the world including Palestine, Africa and many of the Asiatic countries.

JAMES ARTHUR BALDWIN

The April 6, 1960, edition of "The New York Times" contained an advertisement by the Fair Play for Cuba Committee and Baldwin was one of the sponsors of the committee. The April 16, 1960, edition of "The Crusader" identified Baldwin as one of the prominent members of the committee. This Committee is a pro-Castro propaganda organization in the United States.

Baldwin spoke before a mass rally of the Washington, D. C., Chapter of the Congress of Racial Equality for the "Original Freedom Riders" on 6-11-61 and stated in substance that the white race had better realize the emerging strength of the Negro and that he would not care to be in the shoes of the white man when the African nations become stronger.

The 10-2-61 issue of the "National Guardian" carried an advertisement of The Monroe Defense Committee listing Baldwin as one of the sponsors thereof. This committee was formed to tell the story of the racial violence which occurred in Monroe, North Carolina, on 8-27-61.

Baldwin was one of the authors of a letter to the editor in the 6-17-61 edition of the "New York Herald Tribune" which advocated the abolishment of capital punishment and in this connection he criticized the Director stating that Mr. Hoover "is not a lawgiver, nor is there any reason to suppose him to be a particularly profound student of human nature. He is a law-enforcement officer. It is appalling that in this capacity he not only opposes the trend of history among civilized nations but uses his enormous power and prestige to corroborate the blindest and basest instincts of the retaliatory mob."

The Liberation Committee for Africa held a celebration on 6-2-61 at which Baldwin was listed as one of the principal speakers. During his address he stated a period of revolution confronted the world and that America has taken a position throughout the world against revolutions, and then asserted that only in revolution could the problems of the United States be solved.

Baldwin's name appeared as a sponsor on a news release in August, 1961, from the Carl Braden clemency appeal committee which was being distributed by the Southern Conference Educational Fund. This organization is the successor to the Southern Conference for Human Welfare cited by the House Committee on Un-American Activities (HCUA) as a communist front. Braden was sentenced to prison for contempt of the HCUA.

The 1-10-63 issue of the "National Guardian" revealed that Baldwin was among the signers of a statement urging the Anti-Defamation League to withdraw its award, "democratic legacy," to President Kennedy unless the Department of Justice drops its "harassment" of William Worthy, Jr. Worthy is a Negro journalist who has been in trouble with United States officials as he traveled without a passport both through Red China and to Cuba.

The 4-17-61 issue of the "National Guardian" announced a rally to abolish the HCUA and Baldwin was listed as a sponsor of the rally. In April, 1962, Baldwin was among the 550 signers of a clemency petition for convicted communist Junius Scales who was convicted for violating the Smith Act.

The 5-17-63 issue of "Time" magazine devotes its cover to Baldwin and the magazine describes some of his recent efforts in behalf of integration. He is described as a "nervous, slight, almost fragile figure, filled with frets and fears. He is effeminate in manner, drinks considerably, smokes cigarettes in chains and he often looses his audience with overblown arguments." The May, 1963, issue of "Mademoiselle" contains an interview-type article with James Baldwin in which he gibes to both whites and Negroes concerning the Negro situation in the United States. During this article he indicated that he was illegitimate. On the subject of homosexuality, Baldwin states "American males are the only people I've ever encountered in the world who are willing to go on the needle before they'll go to bed with each other. Because they're afraid of this, they don't know how to go to bed with women either. I've known people who literally died out of this panic. I don't know what homosexual means any more, and Americans don't either... If you fall in love with a boy, you fall in love with a boy. The fact that Americans consider it a disease says more about them than it says about homosexuality."

In connection with a discussion of why he feels both Robert Kennedy, the Attorney General, the Justice Department and President Kennedy are ineffective in dealing with discriminatio with the Negroes in the South, Baldwin makes the statement that he is weary of being told that desegregation is legal. He then states "...because first of all you have to get Eastland out of

Congress and get rid of the power that he wields there. You've got to get rid of J. Edgar Hoover and the power that he wields. If one could get rid of just those two men, or modify their power, there would be a great deal more hope..."

A United Press International release dated April 29, 1963, revealed that David Susskind was fired on that day by the Metropolitan Broadcasting Company and his television program "Open End" was being removed from the air. According to the news release a dispute between Susskind and the television broadcasting company started when Susskind announced plans to present author James Baldwin and singer Harry Belafonte on a program called "The American Negro Speaks His Mind." Officials of the television company objected to the program by Susskind on the basis that the combination of Baldwin and Belafonte "would not offer a broad enough basis of enlightened opinion."

6.

BALDWIN AS HOMOSEXUAL—AND PUBLIC ENEMY

MAY 1963

The summary records the FBI compiled on Baldwin after his tense meeting with Bobby Kennedy were explicitly angled to supply information "of a derogatory nature." As this memo from a New York supervisor indicates, the Bureau's search for dirt concentrated on two matters: the evidence "that Baldwin is a homosexual" and that he had "made derogatory remarks in reference to the Bureau." Both uncloseted homosexuality and open criticism of the FBI were capital offenses in Hoover's extra-legal criminal code, and Baldwin was especially suspect for combining them in one super-articulate package. As we'll see, however, the FBI's effort to punish Baldwin for these sins was baffled by his willingness to defend them in writing.

OPTIONAL FORM NO. 10
5010-104-01

UNITED STATES GOVERNMENT

Memorandum

ALL INFORMATION CONTAINED HEREIN IS UNCLASSIFIED EXCEPT WHERE SHOWN OTHERWISE

TO : SAC, NY (100-16553) DATE: 5/29/63

FROM : [redacted] SUPERVISOR, #12

b7C-1

SUBJECT: JAMES ARTHUR BALDWIN
INFORMATION CONCERNING

Mr. [redacted] Crime Records, Bureau, on 5/21/63 requested a check of the NYO indices and also established sources for any information, particularly of a derogatory nature, concerning captioned. Information had been developed by the Bureau that BALDWIN is a homosexual, and on a recent occasion made derogatory remarks in reference to the Bureau.

b2 b7D-1

The indices of the NYO disclose two pertinent files identical to the captioned: 100-16553 and [redacted]

(S)(U)

Records of the NYCPD disclose that JAMES BALDWIN was arrested on 9/3/54 for Disorderly Conduct, was arraigned before Judge BALSAM and received a suspended sentence. The Disorderly Conduct charge was for refusal to move on order of a policeman. At that time JAMES BALDWIN was described as Negro, age 30, novelist, residence 63 West 97th Street.

The records of Selective Service disclose that JAMES ARTHUR BALDWIN originally registered on 12/26/42, giving his residence as 2171 Fifth Avenue, NYC, employment Belle Meade Quartermaster Depot, Belle Meade, New Jersey. His mother was listed as Mrs. BERDIS BALDWIN, same address. He again registered on 9/17/48, at which time his residence was given as 46 West 131st Street, apartment 5-E, NYC. The person listed as always knowing his whereabouts was CONSTANCE WILLIAMS, 99 West 10th Street. His date of birth was shown as 8/2/24. He was classified 1-A on 11/8/48 and 5-A on 8/14/50. His address for 12/13/48 was shown as 269 Rue Jacques, Paris, France, and on 5/1/52, 800 Oxford Road, Ann Arbor, Michigan.

b7C-6

Through [redacted]

DECLASSIFIED BY [illegible]
ON 2-13-90
89-3016 1 - 100-16553 NJ-ZR.

CONFIDENTIAL 100-146553-18

MMO'R:enc
(1)

Classified by [illegible]
Declassify on: OADR 5-22-89

CONFIDENTIAL

NY 100-16553

Time Inc., newspaper clips and the results of their research for an article that was done in "Time" on JAMES BALDWIN were obtained and Photostats were forwarded to the Bureau. NYO maintained no copies.

This information was telephonically furnished to Supervisor [redacted], who stated no confirmatory letter was necessary.

b7c-1

CONFIDENTIAL

CONFIDENTIAL

CONFIDENTIAL

7.

THE WHITE HOUSE LISTENS IN

JUNE 1963

Before the FBI began its notorious wiretapping of Martin Luther King in November 1963, it installed bugs—what it liked to call "technicals"—on the phones of two of his closest advisers: Stanley Levison, King's longtime sounding board and literary editor, and Clarence Jones, a Harlem-based movement lawyer and King traveling buddy who also sometimes served as Baldwin's attorney. The Jones wiretap often delivered the latest confidential news on Baldwin straight to Bureau headquarters. In this highly secret document from June 1963, excluded for years "from automatic downgrading and declassification," Hoover in turn sent the latest on Baldwin straight to the White House. Jones and Levison had discussed plans for the upcoming March on Washington with black labor leader A. Philip Randolph, Hoover reported, and had worried over the slant of a forthcoming profile of King in the white-bread *Saturday Evening Post*. More to the point, Jones and Levison had also talked about linking a planned Baldwin statement on the Bureau's failings in the civil rights field to one contemplated by King. Feeding Levison's worry that Baldwin was prone to "a kind of poetic exaggeration," Jones boasted that "I have seen some statements on the FBI but I have never seen one like this. He (Baldwin) is going to nail them to the wall." This account of Baldwin's intentions was never forgotten or forgiven by the Bureau, whose obvious anger forced it to assure the White House that there was no truth to the rumor "that Agents of our New York City Office" had stalked Baldwin and "attempted to enter [his] apartment." The Bureau's promise that "we have not conducted any investigation of

Baldwin" was insincere, however, given the contents of this and other documents in his FBI file. The regular appearance of Baldwin's name and voice on the Bureau's wiretaps of King's inner circle was a hidden reason why the FBI treated him as a civil rights VIP.

CONFIDENTIAL

1-Mr. Belmont
1-Mr. Rosen
1-Mr. Malley
1-Mr. McGowan
1-Mr. Lavin
1-Mr. Mohr
1-Mr. DeLoach
1-Mr. Evans

62-108763

June 6, 1963

BY COURIER SERVICE

REC'D-READING ROOM
FBI
JUN 6 5 27 PM '63

Honorable P. Kenneth O'Donnell
Special Assistant to the President
The White House
Washington, D. C.

My dear Mr. O'Donnell:

Attached for your information is a memorandum prepared by our New York Office dated June 4, 1963, setting forth information concerning a discussion held by Reverend Martin Luther King, Jr., Clarence Jones and Stanley Levison on June 1 and 2, 1963. Levison and Jones are more fully identified in the memorandum.

In addition to the information contained in the memorandum, a confidential source, who has furnished reliable information in the past, advised on June 4, 1963, that on June 4, 1963, Stanley Levison was in contact with Clarence Jones. Levison inquired of Jones when "Phil," presumably A. Philip Randolph, was coming back. Jones indicated that "Phil" was at the Hamilton Hotel in Chicago and would return on Thursday. Jones indicated that "Phil's" reaction was positive but desired to know to what extent the employment issue would be played up and that "Phil" thought it would be "anticlimatic to have a march in October."

Jones indicated to Levison that "Phil" wants to talk to "Martin," presumably Martin Luther King, Jr., and added that he, Jones, has been unable to reach "Martin." Jones felt that "Martin" should call "Phil."

ORIGINAL FILED IN

BY COURIER SVC.
47 JUN - 6
COMM-FBI

CONFIDENTIAL
DECLASSIFIED BY
ON 5/16/89

GROUP 1
EXCLUDED FROM AUTOMATIC
DOWNGRADING AND
DECLASSIFICATION

Tolson
Belmont
Mohr
Casper
Callahan
Conrad
DeLoach
Evans
Gale
Rosen
Sullivan
Tavel

RBL:cag (10)

53 JUN 27 1963

MAIL ROOM ☐ TELETYPE UNIT ☐

Honorable P. Kenneth O'Donnell

Jones also indicated to Levison that he had spent all day Sunday and Sunday evening with James Baldwin and that he had gone into some detail with Baldwin concerning political action this summer. Jones commented to Levison that if King issues a statement then he, Baldwin, would like to know about it because he would also issue a statement supporting it, and he believes such action might be helpful.

Jones indicated to Levison that the statement would be made around the 12th. Jones stated that Baldwin agrees with the statement very much which is the important thing. Baldwin reportedly gave Jones a blank check to do whatever he wanted to in his name.

Jones informed Levison of a statement that Baldwin is preparing and mentioned to Levison, "I have seen some statements on the FBI but I have never seen one like this. He (Baldwin) is going to nail them to the wall." Levison inquired if this was because of the questioning of the people who were at the meeting, which presumably refers to a conference the Attorney General held in New York on May 24, 1963. Jones told Levison that Baldwin's statement was not because of the alleged interviews of persons at the meeting but was because of the harassment of himself and Baldwin reportedly told Jones that "This is going to be like an atomic bomb when it is dropped." Levison agreed with this, commenting that "It really will because he (Baldwin) is a name in the news." Levison then asked Jones, "Have they been harassing him? What idiots, how idiotic."

It should be noted that an allegation had previously been made that Agents of our New York Office had attempted to enter Mr. Baldwin's apartment on May 27, 1963, and the further allegation had been made that persons attending the conference on May 24, 1963, had been interviewed by Agents following the conference. Both allegations are completely without foundation. In addition, we have not conducted any investigation of Baldwin and he has not been harassed in any way by Agents of this Bureau.

Honorable P. Kenneth O'Donnell

Levison then commented to Jones that there is only one thing that bothers him about Baldwin's statements. Levison stated, "I think he is overstating the situation in the North. There is more of a kind of poetic exaggeration." Jones replied, "There is some poetic exaggeration, that is true." Levison then commented, "It troubles me because what it can lead to is the expectation of something and when something less occurs, it leads to an attitude of well, now they have miscalculated. I just do not have the same feeling about the intensity of attitudes here." Jones replied, "He (Baldwin) and I differ on this, but he feels strongly about it."

Our source indicated that Levison and Jones next discussed a forthcoming article to appear in "The Saturday Evening Post" concerning Reverend Martin Luther King, Jr. Levison indicated that King was apprehensive about the article because the interviewer appeared to be somewhat hostile. Levison informed Jones that he had spoken to the public relations man from "The Saturday Evening Post" and Levison is of the opinion that the forthcoming article may only be generally favorable to Reverend Martin Luther King, Jr.

As additional information is obtained concerning the plans of Reverend Martin Luther King, Jr., Jones and Levison, this information will be promptly brought to your attention.

The Attorney General is being furnished a copy of the attached New York memorandum and the information set forth above.

Sincerely yours,
J. Edgar Hoover

Enclosure

NOTE: This memorandum is being classified "Confidential" because it contains information from a source, the unauthorized disclosure of which would seriously impair the investigation of the Communist Party, USA, and such impairment could have an adverse effect upon the national defense interests of the country.

CONFIDENTIAL

8.

THE BUREAU PREPARES ITS COUNTERATTACK

JUNE 1963

How did the FBI respond to Baldwin's threat to "nail [it] to the wall?" This memo from M. A. Jones, an officer of the Crime Research Section—the FBI's public relations department in all but name—counts the ways. FBI ghostwriters prepared "a suggested statement by the Director," subject to Hoover's final approval, "which can be made in the event Baldwin should make false charges against the Bureau." Other FBI agents monitored and transcribed Baldwin's television appearances, arranging for the national crime laboratory, usually associated with more serious hair- and blood-sample analysis, to record public TV programs before the invention of the DVR. Still other agents seeded anti-Baldwin stories in sympathetic newspapers, as in this clipped *Daily Oklahoman* column attacking the "outlandish slander" the "prominent Negro author . . . had previously directed against the Federal Bureau of Investigation." (Historians have shown that the Bureau planted multiple stories—signed and unsigned—smearing Martin Luther King in the same period.) Evidence here and elsewhere in the file shows that Baldwin was a writer who inspired diverse types of FBI writing and ghostwriting. His overheard intention to attack the Bureau in print prolonged a literary back-and-forth between the FBI and African American authors first triggered when the young Hoover's Radical Division publicly slammed the young Harlem Renaissance in 1919.

OPTIONAL FORM NO. 10

UNITED STATES GOVE[RNMENT]

Memorandum

Tolson
Belmont
Mohr
Casper
Callahan
Conrad
DeLoach
Evans
Gale
Rosen
Sullivan
Tavel
Trotter
Tele. Room
Holmes
Gandy

TO : Mr. DeLoach

DATE: 6-7-63

FROM : M. A. Jones

SUBJECT: JAMES BALDWIN

b7C-1

BACKGROUND:

We have received information to the effect that Baldwin, an author who has been critical of the Bureau and has been connected with communist front and integration activities, is allegedly preparing a statement concerning the FBI which supposedly "is going to nail them to the wall" and "is going to be like an atom bomb when it is dropped." A suggested statement by the Director which can be made in the event Baldwin should mak[e] false charges against the Bureau has previously been prepared and will be issued if the circumstances warrant. (WILL, OF COURSE, BE SUBMITTED FOR APPROVAL.)

CURRENT DEVELOPMENT:

A review of today's television listing reflects that a program concerning the "Integration Crisis" will be heard this evening at 9:30 p.m. on local Channel 26. Baldwin will be interviewed by Kenneth Clark of the City College of New York. Also schedul[ed] a statement by Malcolm X, leader of the Black Muslims. Channel 26 is the local educa-tional television station, WETA.

Arrangements have been made for the Laboratory to record this program a[t] 9:30 this evening. A representative of the Crime Research Section will also be pres[e]nt a[t] that time to monitor the program.

CONCERNING KENNETH CLARK

Baldwin and other individuals had a meeting with the Attorney General in New York City on May 24, 1963, at which time racial matters were discussed. One of those attending this meeting was a Dr. Kenneth Clark, who is a psychologist at the City College of New York. Clark has never been investigated by the Bureau. Clark has been very active in the integration movement as well as in the affairs of the National Association for the Advancement of Colored People. In 1959, he was a member of the New York Cit[y] Board of Education's Commission on Integration in the Schools. In 19[58], Minnijean Br[own] was reportedly staying at the home of Dr. and Mrs. Clark. Minnijean Brown, in 1958 the 16-year-old girl who was expelled from Central High School in Little Rock, Arkan[sas]

RECOMMENDATION:

For information.

1 - Mr. Tolson
1 - Mr. DeLoach
1 - Mr. Conrad
CJH:jaf
(7)

ALL INFORMATION CONTAINED
HEREIN IS UNCLASSIFIED
DATE 5/16/89 BY [illegible]
292325

REC-58

62-108763

12 JUN 11 1963

5 JUN 1963

1009

OPTIONAL FORM NO. 10
MAY 1962 EDITION
GSA GEN. REG. NO. 27

5010-106

UNITED STATES GOVERNMENT

Memorandum

TO : Mr. DeLoach

DATE: 6/7/63

FROM : M. A. Jones

SUBJECT: JAMES BALDWIN
TELEVISION INTERVIEW
JUNE 7, 1963

Tolson
Belmont
Mohr
Casper
Callahan
Conrad
DeLoach
Evans
Gale
Rosen
Sullivan
Tavel
Trotter
Tele. Room
Holmes
Gandy

b7C-1

A filmed interview of author James Baldwin and Malcolm X, Black Muslim, by Dr. Kenneth Clark was shown on Channel 26, WETA, on June 7, 1963, at 9:30 p.m. A 30-minute film of the Baldwin interview was shown first and followed by a 30-minute filmed interview of Malcolm X. It was announced prior to the films that the Baldwin interview was conducted "shortly after" Baldwin and other Negro leaders met with Attorney General Robert Kennedy in New York on May 24, 1963.

There was no reference to the FBI during these interviews. Baldwin made reference to the interview with the Attorney General stating that he was shocked at the lack of "real understanding" by the Attorney General of the Negro problem. Malcolm X made his reference to the Attorney General stating that he had talked to the wrong group, referring to Baldwin and the other Negro leaders, concerning the Negro problem.

REC-73 62-108763-2

RECOMMENDATION:

2 JUN 13 1963

None. For information.

1 - Mr. DeLoach
1 - Mr. Conrad

RWG:alk
(5)

ALL INFORMATION CONTAINED
HEREIN IS UNCLASSIFIED
DATE 5/16/89 BY [illegible]

63 JUN 21 1963

FD-350 (4-3-62)

(Mount Clipping in Space Below)

Mr. Tolson
Mr. Belmont
Mr. Mohr
Mr. Casper
Mr. Callahan
Mr. Conrad
Mr. Evans
Mr. Rosen
Mr. Sullivan
Mr. Tavel
Mr. Trotter
Tele. Room
Miss Holmes
Miss Gandy

b7C-1

Fulton Lewis Jr.

FBI Impartial In Rights Cases

IT is the anguished cry of James Baldwin that Attorney General Robert Kennedy could not "communicate" during their recent closed-door session held as a meeting of the minds on Americans racial problems.

There would have been even less communication, however, if Kennedy had heard the outlandish slander that Baldwin, prominent Negro author, had previously directed against the Federal Bureau of Investigation.

Had Baldwin repeated his statements at their conference, the attorney general would undoubtedly have set the record straight. As much as any man, Bob Kennedy is cognizant of the job the FBI has performed in the civil rights field.

The bureau, being strictly an investigative agency, doesn't side with segregationists or integrationists, despite what Baldwin and others charge. Southern racists assail the FBI as a Gestapo agency.

FBI investigations in this field are conducted thoroughly, promptly and impartially without apology to anyone. They are handled by special agents who have completed special training which specifically qualifies them to conduct civil rights investigations.

It is the FBI that has laid the groundwork for thousands of previously disenfranchised Negroes to register and vote. Bureau agents late last year conducted investigations involving more than 100 counties in which racial discrimination was reported to exist.

(Indicate page, name of newspaper, city and state.)

14 THE DAILY OKLAHOMAN
OKLAHOMA CITY, OKL.

ALL INFORMATION CONTAINED HEREIN IS UNCLASSIFIED DATE 5/16/89 BY

Date: JUNE 7 1963
Edition: MORNING
Author: FULTON LEWIS J
Editor:
Title: CIVIL RIGHTS, FEDERAL BUREAU OF INVESTIGATION
Character: or Classification:
Submitting Office: OKLA CITY

NOT RECORDED
149 JUN 17 1963

9.

BUCKLEY VERSUS BALDWIN

JUNE 1963

Before Baldwin defeated William F. Buckley Jr., the intellectual "Father of American Conservatism," by 544 to 164 votes in a legendary (now YouTubed) debate at the Cambridge University Union in 1965, the FBI staged a contest between the two thinkers in Baldwin's FBI file. In addition to collecting less brainy pieces on Baldwin published in the national and international press, the FBI clipped and saved several of Buckley's columns elegantly railing against Baldwin's supposed goal of unconditional white surrender. In this example from June 1963, circulated among the Bureau's upper echelon, Buckley links Baldwin's "crushing hortatory eloquence" to his "raw nervous temperament" and his impossible dream of the final "evanescence of color." To Buckley's divided mind, *The Fire Next Time* is at bottom a "poignant essay threatening the whites." While Buckley was far more articulate than most FBI commentators about both his racial paranoia and his appreciation of Baldwin's literary gifts, his split judgment on Baldwin was not that far from the Bureau's collective opinion. Like Buckley, the creator of the *National Review*, the flagship journal of the modern American right, Hoover's foundational conservative institution saw Baldwin as fundamentally wrongheaded but too fluently expressive to ignore.

19 (Rev. 10-15-62)

On the Right:

Baldwin's Call To Color Blindness

By WILLIAM F. BUCKLEY JR.

"MARTIN LUTHER KING is a great man," James Baldwin said a week ago, "but he has come to the end of his rope." Baldwin is the Negro novelist and essayist and the principal catalyst of the policy of unconditional surrender (he wants the white population: 1. to give their power to the Negroes, 2. to renounce their civilization, and 3. to despise their God). He means that Dr. King has nowhere left to take his people by any of the conventional forms of protest. "Look about you," Baldwin says in effect, "and what do you see? A Supreme Court that outlawed segregated schools nine years ago, and a South that is still 91 per cent segregated; a Chicago—far, far away from the South—where 90 per cent of Negro children go to schools that are preponderantly Negro."

BUCKLEY

That is not the kind of progress that satisfies a man of the raw nervous temperament of James Baldwin; and so, with that crushing hortatory eloquence that no other writer living today can successfully imitate, he calls for the total liberation of the Negro, for the end of Christian civilization, and, beginning immediately, for personal action by the President. Two weeks ago he proposed to Robert Kennedy that JFK personally escort the two Negro students scheduled to enroll at the University of Alabama on June 10 over the protest of Gov. Wallace. Robert Kennedy is said to have laughed. This is no laughing matter, harrumphed the New York Times.

Indeed it isn't. It is a tragic matter, tragedy here defined as an irresistible force moving on collision course towards an immovable body. What Baldwin has asked for is nothing less than the evanescence of color. He wants the day to come—soon; if not by June 10, not long after; certainly within his lifetime—when color-consciousness will disappear, when you and I, entering a room, will not have noticed even at the time we leave, who there, if anyone, was black, who was white.

Moreover, in pursuing his goal of an end to racial self-consciousness, his instrument is, of all things, racial self-consciousness. He wants a mobilized Negro community who will view all life as Baldwin does, with direct relation to the goal of absolute integration.

Baldwin's Negro, every time he drinks a cup of coffee, must brood over the behavior of the white waitress who handed it to him—did she act unnaturally? Resentfully? Condescendingly? And every time he listens to Ella Fitzgerald sing, he must writhe in resentment over the racial tribulations that gave birth to the blues. In order to abolish a society of Blacks and Whites, it is necessary, Baldwin seems to be saying, for the Blacks to be 110 per cent Black.

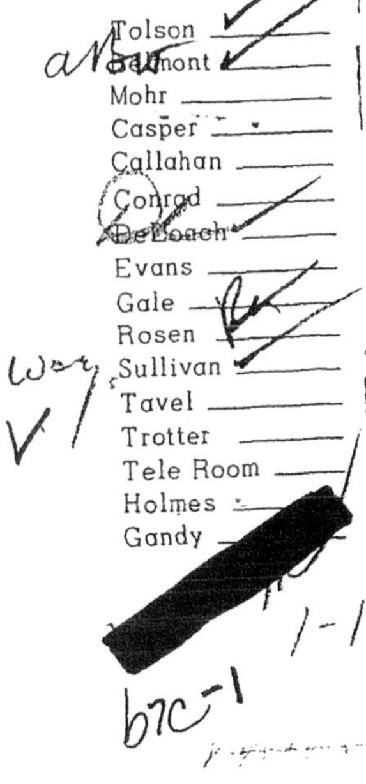

b7C-1

ALL INFORMATION CONTAINED HEREIN IS UNCLASSIFIED DATE 5/16/89 BY

The Washington Post and Times Herald
The Washington Daily News
The Evening Star
New York Herald Tribune
New York Journal-American 10
New York Mirror
New York Daily News
New York Post
The New York Times
The Worker
The New Leader
The Wall Street Journal
The National Observer
Date

JUN 8 1963

NOT RECORDED
149 JUN 14 1963

58 JUN 17 1963

* * *

ASSUMING WE WERE willing to put the entire legal resources of this country at the disposal of James Baldwin, what would he do with them, to eliminate race prejudice? In his poignant essay threatening the whites with The Fire Next Time unless we now reform, he cites two typical humiliations, one from his early childhood, when an Irish policeman in downtown Manhattan yelled at him to go back to Harlem "where the Niggers belong," another that happened to him only last year, at age 38, when a bartender at the Chicago Airport refused to serve him a drink, affecting not to be able to tell whether he was over eighteen. How can such meanness be cured by legislation?

What shall we do, in the new order, to that policeman and that bartender? Shoot them? It is more to the point to shoot human nature, whence the troubles really come, but there seems to be no practicable way to do that.

If I am born different — whether a Negro like Baldwin, a hunchback like Quasimodo, a beauty like Elizabeth Taylor, or a conservative like myself — I shall be treated "differently." Sometimes that difference should be cherished (it is a fact that here and there a young Negro lawbreaker is dealt with more tolerantly because he has not had the same advantages as the white boy from the middle class neighborhood). So long as the eyes remark the difference between black and white, existential differences, of greater or lesser consequence, but of meaning just the same, will exist.

The job at hand is not to try to obliterate differences which only autohypnotic color blindness could achieve, but to stimulate man's capacity for love and his toleration, understanding, and respect for other, different people.

What is important about Baldwin is that he is a great artist, not that he is an evangelist of racial reconciliation. In the latter capacity he will, pursuing his present course, do great harm; in the former capacity, he has greatly raised the prestige of the Negro in the world of letters; that is a true step forward for his people.

10.

ANOTHER COUNTRY'S "VALUE TO STUDENTS OF PSYCHOLOGY AND SOCIAL BEHAVIOR"

JUNE, AUGUST, AND SEPTEMBER 1963

The FBI's interest in *Another Country* wasn't confined to its year of publication—1962—or its fate in the hands of the Morals Division of the Washington police. In June and July 1963, newspaper clippings on the novel's censorship battles beyond DC piled up in Baldwin's file. The Bureau paid special attention to the book's reception in New Orleans, where Jim Garrison, the open-minded district attorney (later a prominent Kennedy assassination conspiracy theorist), clashed with Edward Pinner, an assistant city attorney convinced that Baldwin had written fiction "so sickening that if the obscenity were removed, you'd have nothing but the covers left." In August, Hoover acted as a kind of national police librarian and lent the Bureau's shelved copy of *Another Country* to the Criminal Division, another branch of the Justice Department, after the latter fielded complaints about the book from a number of citizens. The division's review of the novel, a month in the making, reinforced the FBI's earlier decision not to conduct an investigation into Baldwin's "possible violation of the Interstate Transportation of Obscene Matter Statute." When all was read, said, and done, *Another Country* "contains literary merit and may be of value to students of psychology and social behavior," the review declared. Echoing the much-quoted criterion of "redeeming social importance" enforced by the US

Supreme Court in 1957, the Justice Department judged the novel both too revealing and too well written to be obscene. Not every federal ghostreader of Baldwin's work, it turns out, was immune to its power. This ghostreader's words, at least, could have been used for a blurb on *Another Country*'s paperback edition.

FD-350 (4-3-62)

Mr. Tolson
Mr. Belmont
Mr. Mohr
Mr. Casper
Mr. Callahan
Mr. Conrad
Mr. DeLoach
Mr. Evans
Mr. Gale
Mr. Rosen
Mr. Sullivan
Mr. Tavel
Mr. Trotter
Tele. Room
Miss Holmes
Miss Gandy

(Mount Clipping in Space Below)

BOOK CHARGES REFUSED BY DA

Raps 'Censorship' of Baldwin Novel

Decrying "censorship," Dist. Atty. Jim Garrison refused Tuesday to take charges against sellers of a book by controversial Negro novelist James Baldwin.

Garrison attacked the police file on a dozen or more such books and the arrest of book store employes.

Frank P. Rossetter, 55, manager of the Doubleday Book Store, 633 Canal, and an employe, George E. Deville, 17, were arrested by police vice squad officers for selling the novel, "Another Country," by author James Baldwin.

COPIES SEIZED

Police confiscated all copies of the book.

The book store is part of a nationwide chain. The company's attorney in New Orleans, Wood Brown, said that to his knowledge no other arrests have been made because of selling "Another Country" and that the book has not been declared obscene elsewhere.

The police file on books and publications ruled obscene by the police or the city attorney's office is about two inches thick and consists mainly of magazines and paperback novels. The Baldwin book and the "Tropic of Cancer" by Henry Miller are the only two written by nationally known authors and published by large publishing houses.

IDEA IS ASSAILED

Garrison said, "The idea of a police officer walking into a legitimate bookstore, removing a book from the shelf that is written by a reputable author and has been critically acclaimed and then arresting the store manager is outrageous.

"It disregards the fundamental concepts of freedom of expression and freedom of the press.

"All that is needed now is to have a ceremony in which the books are burned.

"In my opinion the employes of Doubleday did not commit an offense. I think there is no place in this city for censorship . . . it is true some persons may consider the book obscene. However, many others may not and it should be left up to the individual to decide."

"Those persons who consider it obscene don't have to read it."

File 8 88

b7C-1

(Indicate page, name of newspaper, city and state.)

Page 3 Sec. 3

THE TIMES PICAYUNE
NEW ORLEANS, LA.

Date: 6/19/63
Edition:
Author:
Editor:
Title: District Attorney Orleans Parish, La.
Character:
or
Classification: 80-
Submitting Office: New Orleans

NOT RECORDED
191 JUL 3 1963

FD-350 (4-3-62)

Mr. Tolson
Mr. Belmont
Mr. Mohr
Mr. [illegible]
Mr. [illegible]
Mr. [illegible]
Mr. [illegible]
Mr. Evans
Mr. Gale
Mr. Rosen
Mr. Sullivan
Mr. Tavel
Mr. [illegible]
Tele. Room
Miss Holmes
Miss Gandy

(Mount Clipping in Space Below)

CHARGES IN CITY COURT READIED

Book Store Manager Target, Says Pinner

Edward Pinner, assistant city attorney, said Thursday night that charges against the manager of Doubleday Book Store here will be filed Friday in Municipal Court.

Similar charges were originally brought to District Attorney Jim Garrison, who refused to accept the charges and the police department arrest "censorship."

The charges are being brought in connection with the store manager's displaying and selling the controversial novel "Another Country" by Negro author James Baldwin, who is frequently bitter in condemnation of racial segregation.

The book, with a plot set in the lower socio-economic strata of New York City, hit the best seller list shortly after publication last year and has been under fire ever since from groups who brand it as osbcene.

Pinner said that the manager, after having been informed that sale of the book would be in violation with city ordinances pertaining to the sale of obscene and pornographic literature, kept the book on the shelves.

He said that the race issue in the novel had no bearing on the city attorney's charges. Several inter-racial relationships are chronided in the Baldwin book.

Pinner said that after reading the book, he was convinced that "it is the most filthy and poronographic book I have ever read, and I am shocked that persons could condone the sale of such literature, which is so sickening that if the obscenity were removed, you'd have nothing but the covers left."

(Indicate page, name of newspaper, city and state.)

Page 7 Sec. 1

THE TIMES PICAYUNE
NEW ORLEANS, LA.

Date: 6/21/63
Edition:
Author:
Editor:
Title: District Attorney Orleans Parish, La.

Character:
or
Classification: 80-
Submitting Office: New Orleans

V45
NOT RECORDED
184 JUL 3 1963

56 JUL [illegible]

1625

PUBLISHERS FIGHT BALDWIN BOOK BAN

3 Take Legal Action Against New Orleans' Move

By HENRY RAYMONT

Three publishers here have retained attorneys to defend James Baldwin's novel, "Another Country," against a threatened ban in New Orleans on the ground of obscenity.

Criminal charges against shops selling the novel have been threatened by Edward Pinner, New Orleans assistant city attorney, who has called it "the most filthy and pornographic book I have ever read."

Richard Baron, head of The Dial Press, publisher of the hard-cover edition of the novel, said yesterday he had retained Horace Manges, attorney for the American Book Publishers Council, to head the legal battle.

The novel, widely praised by critics, is about unfulfilled and rebellious artists in New York and dwells on the fate of Negro intellectuals in America.

The Dell Publishing Company which put out the paperback edition, and Doubleday & Co. have hired Richard Galen and James F. Dwyer to work on the case.

Mr. Manges said he expected to hear next week if Mr. Pinner would press charges against Frank P. Rossiter, manager of the Doubleday Bookshop in New Orleans, and George E. Deville, assistant manager.

The two were arrested June 18 for having sold the book after the City Attorney's office had demanded its withdrawal. They were held an hour and released on parole.

The arrest has been criticized by other New Orleans authorities and newspapers and broadcasting stations there.

District Attorney James Garrison of New Orleans has said he does not believe the Doubleday employes committed an offense.

"I think there is no place in this city for censorship," he has said. "True, some persons may consider the book obscene. However, others may not and it should be left to the individual to decide."

If the criminal charges against the two are dropped, Mr. Manges said, he will seek a declaratory judgment by the New Orleans court to clear the book.

He said that the publishers and New Orleans bookstores had temporarily agreed to halt sales of the book until a court ruling had been obtained.

Mr. Baron said he had received reports of pressure on New Orleans bookstores and public libraries by the Citizens Council, a white-supremacist organization, to have them withdraw the novel.

Such pressure began, he said, shortly after Mr. Baldwin addressed a meeting of the Congress of Racial Equality at Tulane University in New Orleans.

It was the first time that an obscenity charge had been brought against the work of the 40-year-old writer, Mr. Baron asserted.

The charges against the Doubleday employes, filed with the New Orleans Municipal Court, are based on a city ordinance forbidding the sale of obscene literature.

ALL INFORMATION CONTAINED HEREIN IS UNCLASSIFIED DATE 5-22-89 BY [illegible]

CLIPPING FROM THE

NY Times

EDITION Final

DATE 6/30/63

PAGE 47

FORWARDED BY NY DIVISION

NOT FORWARDED BY NY DIVISION

100-146553-21

SEARCHED INDEXED SERIALIZED FILED JUL 2 1963 FBI — NEW YORK

Mr. Herbert J. Miller, Jr.
Assistant Attorney General

August 15, 1963

Director, FBI

James Baldwin

"ANOTHER COUNTRY"
THE DIAL PRESS
INTERSTATE TRANSPORTATION OF OBSCENE MATTER

Enclosed herewith in response to the telephonic request of Mr. Carl W. Belcher of your Division on August 9, 1963, is a copy of the book, "Another Country," by James Baldwin. This book was furnished to our Washington Field Office in September, 1962, by the Morals Division of the Metropolitan Police Department, Washington, D. C. No investigation has been conducted by this Bureau concerning the interstate transportation of same in possible violation of the Interstate Transportation of Obscene Matter Statute.

It is requested that this book be returned upon completion of your review.

Enclosure

145-2625-2

1 - Mr. [redacted]
JAC:mlt
(5)

REC-115

19 AUG 15 1963

b7C-1

NOTE:

Mr. Belcher telephonically inquired of SA [redacted] on 8-9-63 as to whether we had available a copy of instant book, stating they had received several citizens' inquiries concerning same and desired to review it. This book submitted to Bureau by WFO letter dated 9-19-62. Bureau file 145-2625.

AUG 15 9 59 AM '63

MAILED 2
AUG 15 1963
COMM-FBI

Tolson
Belmont
Mohr
Casper
Callahan
Conrad
DeLoach
Evans
Gale
Rosen
Sullivan
Tavel
Trotter
Tele. Room
Holmes
Gandy

MAIL ROOM ☐ TELETYPE UNIT ☐

REC'D

55 AUG 19 1963

F 147

File in 145-2625

JAC

UNITED STATES GOVERNMENT

DEPARTMENT OF JUSTICE

Memorandum

TO : Director, Federal Bureau of Investigation

DATE: September 13 1963

HJM:HWA:rmr

FROM : Herbert J. Miller, Jr.
Assistant Attorney General
Criminal Division

SUBJECT: "Another Country", The Dial Press, Interstate Transportation of Obscene Matter

This refers to your memorandum dated August 15, 1963, concerning the above subject.

"Another Country" Book by James Baldwin has been reviewed in the General Crimes Section of this Division and it has been concluded that the book contains literary merit and may be of value to students of psychology and social behavior. There is no basis for investigation.

In accordance with your request the book is returned herewith.

Attachment

COPY & SPECIMENS RETAINED IN LAB FOR ... ACTION & REPORT

ENCLOSURE

b7c-1

145-2625-3

REC-85

25 SEP 1963

EX-112

F-40

INDEX LAB FILES

64 SEP 30 1963

11.

"BETTER QUALIFIED TO LEAD A HOMO-SEXUAL MOVEMENT THAN A CIVIL RIGHTS MOVEMENT"

SEPTEMBER 1963

It's unclear whether this "Airtel" message—the product of a now-abandoned FBI rapid communication system—stemmed from the Bureau's bugging of Clarence Jones or (more probably) its tap of Stanley Levison's telephone. In either case, the message reveals tensions between Baldwin's and Levison's responses to the infamous Birmingham church bombing that killed four young black Sunday school students on September 15, 1963—tensions that reflected growing strains between Martin Luther King and more militant civil rights protestors exasperated by his steadfast nonviolence and careful outreach to white progressives, Levison included. Peaceful, go-slow liberals, Baldwin declared at a press conference, were among those "responsible for Birmingham."The firmer stand advocated by Baldwin "and his group with respect to the Birmingham situation" was "extremely ridiculous," Levison snapped. More surprisingly, Levison disparaged Baldwin and his allies as "not 'too deep intellectually,'" seemingly confusing political pragmatism with analytical strength. Asked about the opinion of Bayard Rustin, the veteran gay organizer of the March on Washington, Levison replied that Rustin joined Baldwin in "being better qualified to lead a homo-sexual movement than a civil rights movement." The FBI welcomed news of Levison's resort to homophobia, not unique in a civil rights leadership that sometimes insulted Baldwin as "Martin Luther Queen." Hoover's Bureau, led by a gay-baiting non-heterosexual, largely shared Levison's prejudice and also appreciated evidence of any rift within the Civil Rights Movement—evidence that could be exploited in counterintelligence campaigns if necessary.

9/23/63

AIRTEL REGISTERED

TO: DIRECTOR, FBI (157-6-34)

FROM: SAC, NEW YORK (157-892)

SUBJECT: RACIAL SITUATION
NEW YORK DIVISION
RACIAL MATTERS

ALL INFORMATION CONTAINED
HEREIN IS UNCLASSIFIED
DATE 5/23/89

b2-1

[redacted] advised on 9/22/63, that on that date STANLEY LEVISON conferred with [redacted] They discussed the stand taken by JAMES BALDWIN and his group with respect to the Birmingham situation. They agreed that the entire business of their condemnation of the Presidential commission to study the Birmingham situation, and also their idea of boycotting Christmas shopping, were extremely ridiculous. STANLEY LEVISON expressed the opinion that this group of BALDWIN's was not "too deep intellectually." b7C2

[redacted] asked what BAYARD RUSTIN's position was with BALDWIN and LEVISON replied that in his opinion, the two were better qualified to lead a homo-sexual movement than a civil rights movement.

3 - BUREAU (157-6-34)(RM)
1 - NY 100[redacted](414) b7C-3
1 - NY 100- (JAMES BALDWIN)(412)
1 - NY 100-46724 (BAYARD RUSTIN)(424)
1 - NY 100-111180 (STANLEY LEVISON)(414)
1 - NY 157-892 (412)

FTL:mfd (#414)
(9)

100-146553-33

SEARCHED INDEXED
SERIALIZED FILED
SEP 23 1963
FBI — NEW YORK

12.

BALDWIN BAITS J. EDGAR HOOVER—AND BUREAUCRATIC HELL BREAKS LOOSE

SEPTEMBER 1963

In late September 1963, the Bureau finally received confirmation of the criticism from Baldwin it had anticipated for months. During both a press conference and a television appearance, the writer charged out loud that the FBI was a hazard to the Civil Rights Movement and that Hoover effectively placed the awesome power of the Justice Department on the side of the segregationists. This "letterhead memo" detailing Baldwin's accusations, likely based on the Clarence Jones phone tap rather than on a human confidential source, was originally held as highly secret, its exposure considered a threat to the "national defense." Its contents disclose that Baldwin and Jones were livid about the decision of the United States Information Agency (USIA) to delete Baldwin's negative comments on the FBI from the transcript of a government-sponsored television program. "[A]ny legitimate critical opinion of the FBI is apparently 'off limits or taboo,'" Jones protested. Baldwin's critical opinion of the Bureau came through more clearly at an uncensored New York press conference. The letterhead memo quoted Baldwin's confession there that he "blame[d] J. Edgar Hoover in part" for the Birmingham church bombing, and that African Americans in general had "no cause to have faith in the FBI." More than fifty years on, it is difficult to recapture just how rare—and just how courageous—such public criticisms of the Bureau were. Baldwin's words preceded King's risky 1964 complaint that the FBI was "completely ineffectual in resolving the continued mayhem and brutality inflicted upon the Negro in the Deep South." They outstripped the long tradition of cat-and-mouse exchanges between black writers and the Bureau launched during the Harlem Renaissance. And they rocketed Baldwin, in the mind of Hoover's FBI, to the status of genuine national security threat.

FD-36 (Rev. 12-13-56)

FBI

Date: 9/24/63

~~CONFIDENTIAL~~

Transmit the following in PLAIN TEXT

(Type in plain text or code)

AIRTEL

Via

(Priority or Method of Mailing)

TO: DIRECTOR, FBI
(ATT: CIVIL RIGHTS SECT. GENERAL INVESTIGATIVE DIV.)

FROM: SAC, NEW YORK (100-146553)

SUBJECT: JAMES BALDWIN
RACIAL MATTERS
SM - C

CLASSIFIED AND
EXTENDED BY
REASON FOR EXTENSION
FCIM, II, 1-2.4.2
DATE OF REVIEW FOR
DECLASSIFICATION

Enclosed herewith are ten (10) copies of a letterhead memo reflecting the conversation between CLARENCE JONES and JAMES BALDWIN, as received by [redacted] on 9/19/63.

The source utilized to characterize CLARENCE JONES is [redacted] in 1954. Also used to characterize CLARENCE JONES is [redacted]

The letterhead memo is classified "Secret" due to the extreme sensitive nature of [redacted] The unauthorized disclosure of this information could reveal the identity of the source and thereby impair investigation of subversive matters, which could be injurious to the national defense.

Characterization of CLARENCE JONES is listed at the end of the memo in order to insure continuity of the memo.

ENCLOSURE

DECLASSIFIED BY
ON 10/12/88

5 - Bureau (ENCLS.10)(RM)
(1-100-407018)(CLARENCE JONES)
(1-100-106670)(MARTIN LUTHER KING)
1 - Birmingham (157-867)(ENCLS.1)(INFO)(RM)
1 - Atlanta (100-5586)(ENCLS.1)(INFO)(MARTIN LUTHER KING)(RM)
1 - New York (100-73250)(CLARENCE JONES)
1 - New York (100-136585)(MARTIN LUTHER KING)
1 - New York (100-146553)

Agency C-2, ONI, OSI, CRD, I.S. U.S.I.A

Date Forw.

How Forw.

REC-104

SEP 25 1963

CC - WICK

JPD:mld
(12)

XEROX
OCT 3 1963

~~CONFIDENTIAL~~

ALL INFORMATION CONTAINED
HEREIN IS UNCLASSIFIED

Approved: ____ Sent ____ M Per ____
Special Agent in Charge

SUBV. CONTROL

OCT 14 1963

UNITED STATES DEPARTMENT OF JUSTICE

FEDERAL BUREAU OF INVESTIGATION

In Reply, Please Refer to File No.

New York, New York
September 24, 1963

New York 100-146553

DECLASSIFIED BY 3042 PWT/8K
ON 10/12/88
81-0802 Garrow/King
DP8BTJ/ag
5-16-89
292325

APPROPRIATE AGENCIES AND FIELD OFFICES ADVISED BY ROUTING SLIP(S) OF Declassification DATE 12/9/77 RSS

Re: James Baldwin
Racial Matters; –
Security Matter – C

On September 19, 1963, a confidential source who has furnished reliable information in the past, advised that on that date Clarence Jones (Counsel to Martin Luther King) and James Baldwin (Negro author) held a discussion regarding Baldwin's appearance on the USIA television program in Washington on August 28, 1963. Jones stated that he had requested from USIA a transcript of the entire show and had received this transcript and noted that Baldwin's remarks regarding the Federal Bureau of Investigation (FBI) and Mr.Hoover were not contained therein and therefore Jones assumed that these remarks had been edited out. Baldwin stated that he had witnesses to the statements that he had made on this program. In recalling his statement regarding the FBI, Baldwin stated that the substance of his remarks on this program were "part of the problem in the civil rights movement is J. Edgar Hoover". Jones then stated that he would "like to blow the whistle on this". Jones stated that any legitimate critical opinion of the FBI is apparently "off limits or taboo". Jones further stated that he had composed a letter to the rest of the participants on the USIA show informing them of the deletion made. Jones then stated that he intends to inform the USIA that he knows of the deletion and intends also to bring this information to the attention of the public and the Attorney General. Jones continued that he was going to do this immediately and stated that he would also like to draft a statement and stated "we cannot let this deletion go".

DECLASSIFIED BY 6080
ON 11/1/77

CONFIDENTIAL

~~SECRET~~
~~Group 1~~
~~Excluded from automatic downgrading and declassification~~

CLASSIFIED AND EXTENDED BY
REASON FOR EXTENSION
FCIM
DATE OF REVIEW FOR DECLASSIFICATION

This document contains neither recommendations nor conclusions of the FBI. It is the property of the FBI and is loaned to your agency; it and its contents are not to be distributed outside your agency.

SECRET

James Baldwin

Additionally, Baldwin and Jones discussed Baldwin's public statement of September 18, 1963, issued at a press conference in New York City. According to the "New York Herald Tribune", September 19, 1963, Baldwin is quoted as bitterly criticizing the Kennedy Administration and the FBI for their "lack of action" following the Birmingham bombing, September 15, 1963. The "New York Times" of September 19, 1963, additionally quotes Baldwin as saying "I blame J. Edgar Hoover in part for events in Alabama. Negroes have no cause to have faith in the FBI". This source also stated that Jones told Baldwin that he had received a call from an attorney "who works in an office of the Justice Department". According to this source, this attorney advised Jones that Baldwin's statement had caused "quite a stir", stating further "you're going to be hearing from us".

Jones further advised Baldwin that Baldwin's press statements were a most significant contribution. Jones further stated that he was disturbed over the proposed conference of Negro leaders with the President scheduled for September 19, 1963. Jones felt that this conference could do more harm than good. Baldwin stated that he felt that Kennedy should go to Alabama and Jones replied "the President cannot be let off the hook on this thing". Jones further added that Baldwin's press statement had been a very valuable contribution and that it reflected that general consensus of opinion of the majority of Negroes in Birmingham. Baldwin agreed that the feeling existed not only in Birmingham but elsewhere. Baldwin then spoke of something his sister had said to his mother, "Negroes are thinking seriously of assassinating Martin Luther King". Jones then stated that he believed that the feeling in the South is one of "crisis in the efficacy of non-violent movement".

In a further discussion of the Birmingham bombing Jones questioned the "efficacy of the FBI in cases like this". Jones stated that there had been 45 to 50 bombings since 1947 and not one had been solved. He further stated that "there has been a total absence of FBI infiltrating racist organizations".

SECRET

James Baldwin

As of July 3, 1963, Clarence Jones was the General Counsel forthe Gandhi Society for Human Rights, 15 East 40th Street, New York City.

A second confidential source, who has furnished reliable information in the past, advised that on February 26, 1957, he identified a photograph of Clarence Jones as the person whom he knew during late 1953 or early 1954, to be a member and in a position of leadership in the Labor Youth League (LYL). (C) U

The LYL has been designated pursuant to Executive Order 10450.

(C) U
A third confidential source on August 20, 1963, advised that Clarence Jones was at that time Counsel to Reverend Martin Luther King.

13.

"NEGROES ARE THINKING SERIOUSLY OF ASSASSINATING MARTIN LUTHER KING"

SEPTEMBER 1963

These documents drawn from the FBI's wiretap on Clarence Jones expose additional fallout from divided reactions to the Birmingham church bombing. Disappointed by King's involvement in discussions on appointing a Federal commission to investigate the bombing, Jones sought to rally Baldwin's more confrontational civil rights circle, dominated by intellectuals but earlier dismissed by Stanley Levison as "not 'too deep intellectually.'" According to a digest of several phone calls, Baldwin agreed with Jones that it was "nonsense" to "study the situation" once again: the murderous racism that had doomed the four little girls should be punished and uprooted, not reexamined by the Kennedy administration. Baldwin then conveyed his sister's sense of the severity of the "crisis in the efficacy of non violent movement": "Negroes are thinking seriously," she warned, "of assassinating Martin Luther King." Where Jones had worked months earlier to align King's and Baldwin's attacks on President Kennedy's FBI director, he now criticized King "for allowing himself to be outmaneuvered" by Kennedy, and he encouraged Baldwin to coordinate with fellow African American novelist John Oliver Killens (also a target of Bureau surveillance with his own FBI dossier) to "blast King." In this and other paperwork deposited in the Baldwin file, the FBI recorded deep fault lines in the Civil Rights

Movement that predated the emergence of Black Power. More often than his Black Power-era reputation would suggest, Baldwin was discovered on the radical side of those lines.

SAC, NEW YORK (100-73250) 9/26/63

SA [redacted] b7c-1

CLARENCE JONES
SM-C

ALL INFORMATION CONTAINED
HEREIN IS UNCLASSIFIED
DATE 5/23/89 BY

Identity of Source: [redacted] b2-1
(Conceal & paraphrase)

Reliability: Has furnished reliable information in the past.

Location: 100-73250-1A

On 9/20/63, source indicated that CLARENCE JONES was in contact with JOHN KILLENS (ph). JONES expressed his feelings on the President's decision to appoint a commission. JONES felt a critical comment should be made on this action by the President. KILLENS (ph) will again be in contact with JONES later today.

Source advised on 9/20/63, that [redacted] was in contact with CLARENCE JONES. JONES criticized KING (MARTIN LUTHER KING) for allowing himself to be outmaneuvered by KENNEDY. JONES indicated that JOHN KILLENS (ph) and JAMES BALDWIN are going to blast KING today because of KING's actions in D.C. b7c-2

On 9/20/63, source indicated that CLARENCE JONES was in contact with JOHN KILLEN. They were critical of the results of the meeting of the Civil Rights Leaders and the President. KILLEN felt the man (President) hadn't done a thing and had been let off the hook. JONES though that he, LOUIS LOMAX, JAMES BALDWIN, RUBY DEE, and KILLEN should meet prior to the meeting at 5:00 and plan strategy on a statement to be released. The meeting was to take place at 3:30 pm in Room 440, Hotel Astor.

1 - NY 100-136585 (MARTIN LUTHER KING)
1 - NY 100-146553 (JAMES BALDWIN)
1 - NY 100-102397 (JOHN KILLENS)
1 - NY 100-73250

100-146553-39

JDM:gmh
(4)

On 9/20/63, source advised that CLARENCE JONES left a message for JAMES BALDWIN. There would be a meeting of LOUIS LOMAX, RUBY DEE, KILLEN, JONES, and BALDWIN at 3:30 pm in Room 440 of Hotel Astor.

Source on 9/20/63, indicated that [redacted] (ph) was in contact with CLARENCE JONES. JONES was angry with the results of the meeting between the President and the Civil Rights Leaders. JONES felt that the appointment of a commission is "about the most sophisticated insult you can give to the killing of these six people." He has told JAMES BALDWIN and JOHN KILLEN not to let this thing pass without making some strong comments about it. [redacted] (apparently an actor) criticized the speech the President had made at the U.N.

b7c-2

On 9/20/63, source advised that CLARENCE JONES was in contact with BALDWIN. JONES wants something to be done about the presidential committee. Both thought it was nonsense to study the situation. JONES felt that BALDWIN, KILLEN, and RUBY DEE should make a strong statement on this. Source determined from LUCIAN that the telephone number of KILLEN is SL 6-9270.

Positive identification of JOHN KILLENS is not possible at this time. However, a copy of this memo is being placed in file 100-102397 inasmuch as a possibility exists that it may be identical.

FEDERAL BUREAU OF INVESTIGATION
U. S. DEPARTMENT OF JUSTICE
COMMUNICATIONS SECTION
SEP 19 1963

TELETYPE

URGENT 9-19-63 11-40 AM JLW

TO DIRECTOR

FROM SAC NEW YORK 100-146553 4P

JAMES BALDWIN

SECURITY MATTER - C

RACIAL MATTERS

ALL INFORMATION CONTAINED HEREIN IS UNCLASSIFIED DATE 5-16-89 BY

ON NINE NINETEEN SIXTYTHREE, [redacted] ADVISED THAT ON THAT DATE CLARENCE JONES /COUNSEL TO MARTIN LUTHER KING/ AND JAMES BALDWIN /NEGRO AUTHOR/ HELD A DISCUSSION REGARDING BALDWIN-S APPEARANCE ON THE USIA TELEVISION PROGRAM IN WASHINGTON ON EIGHT TWENTYEIGHT SIXTYTHREE. JONES STATED THAT HE HAD REQUESTED FROM ~~USIA~~ US INFORMATION AGENCY A TRANSCRIPT OF THE ENTIRE SHOW AND HAD RECEIVED THIS TRANSCRIPT AND NOTED THAT BALDWIN-S REMARKS REGARDING THE FBI AND MR. HOOVER WERE NOT CONTAINED THEREIN AND THEREFORE JONES ASSUMED THAT THESE REMARKS HAD BEEN EDITED OUT. BALDWIN STATED THAT HE HAD WITNESSES TO THE STATEMENTS THAT HE HAD MADE ON THIS PROGRAM. IN RECALLING HIS STATEMENT REGARDING THE FBI, BALDWIN STATED THAT THE SUBSTANCE OF HIS REMARKS ON THIS PROGRAM WERE "PART OF THE PROBLEM IN THE CIVIL RIGHTS MOVEMENT IS J. EDGAR HOOVER". JONES THEN STATED THAT HE WOULD "LIKE TO BLOW THE WHISTLE ON THIS". JONES STATED

END PAGE ONE

REC-20 62-108763-4

OCT 3 1963

MR. BELMONT FOR THE DIRECTOR

PAGE TWO

THAT ANY LEGITIMATE CRITICAL OPINION OF THE FBI IS APPARENTLY "OFF LIMITS OR TABOO". JONES FURTHER STATED THAT HE HAD COMPOSED A LETTER TO THE REST OF THE PARTICIPANTS ON THE USIA SHOW INFORMING THEM OF THE DELETION MADE. JONES THEN STATED THAT HE INTENDS TO INFORM THE USIA THAT HE KNOWS OF THE DELETION AND INTENDS ALSO TO BRING THIS INFORMATION TO THE ATTENTION OF THE PUBLIC AND THE ATTORNEY GENERAL. JONES CONTINUED THAT HE WAS GOING TO DO THIS IMMEDIATELY AND STATED THAT HE WOULD ALSO LIKE TO DRAFT A STATEMENT AND STATED "WE CANNOT LET THIS DELETION GO".

ADDITIONALLY, BALDWIN AND JONES DISCUSSED BALDWIN-S PUBLIC STATEMENT OF NINE EIGHTEEN SIXTYTHREE, ISSUED AT A PRESS CONFERENCE IN NEW YORK CITY. ACCORDING TO THE "NEW YORK HERALD TRIBUNE" NINE NINETEEN SIXTYTHREE, BALDWIN IS QUOTED AS BITTERLY CRITICIZING THE KENNEDY ADMINISTRATION AND THE FBI FOR THEIR "LACK OF ACTION" FOLLOWING THE BIRMINGHAM BOMBING NINE FIFTEEN SIXTYTHREE. THE "NEW YORK TIMES" OF NINE NINETEEN SIXTYTHREE, ADDITIONALLY QUOTES BALDWIN AS SAYING "I BLAME J. EDGAR HOOVER IN PART FOR EVENTS IN ALABAMA. NEGROES HAVE NO CAUSE TO HAVE FAITH IN THE FBI". THIS SOURCE ALSO STATED THAT JONES TOLD BALDWIN THAT HE HAD RECEIVED A CALL FROM AN ATTORNEY "WHO WORKS IN AN OFFICE OF THE JUSTICE DEPARTMENT".

END PAGE TWO

ACCORDING TO THIS SOURCE, THIS ATTORNEY ADVISED JONES THAT BALDWIN-S STATEMENT HAD CAUSED "QUITE A STIR", STATING FURTHER "YOU-RE GOING TO BE HEARING FROM US".

JONES FURTHER ADVISED BALDWIN THAT BALDWIN-S PRESS STATEMENTS WERE A MOST SIGNIFICANT CONTRIBUTION. JONES FURTHER STATED THAT HE WAS DISTURBED OVER THE PROPOSED CONFERENCE OF NEGROE LEADERS WITH THE PRESIDENT SCHEDULED FOR NINE NINETEEN SIXTYTHREE. JONES FELT THAT THIS CONFERENCE COULD DO MORE HARM THAN GOOD. BALDWIN STATED THAT HE FELT THAT KENNEDY SHOULD GO TO ALABAMA AND JONES REPLIED "THE PRESIDENT CANNOT BE LET OFF THE HOOK ON THIS THING". JONES FURTHER ADDED THAT BALDWIN-S PRESS STATEMENT HAD BEEN A VERY VALUABLE CONTRIBUTION AND THAT IT REFLECTED THE GENERAL CONSENSUS OF OPINION OF THE MAJORITY OF NEGROES IN BIRMINGHAM. BALDWIN AGREED THAT THE FEELING EXISTED NOT ONLY IN BIRMINGHAM BUT ELSEWHERE. BALDWIN THEN SPOKE OF SOMETHING HIS SISTER HAD SAID TO HIS MOTHER, "NEGROES ARE THINKING SERIOUSLY OF ASSASSINATING MARTIN LUTHER KING". JONES THEN STATED THAT HE BELIEVED THAT THE FEELING IN THE SOUTH IS ONE OF "CRISIS IN THE EFFICACY OF NON VIOLENT MOVEMENT".

IN A FURTHER DISCUSSION OF THE BIRMINGHAM BOMBING JONES QUESTIONED THE "EFFICACY OF THE FBI IN CASES LIKE THIS". JONES STATED THAT THERE HAD BEEN FORTY FIVE TO FIFTY BOMBINGS SINCE NINETEEN FORTY SEVEN AND NOT ONE HAD BEEN SOLVED. HE FURTHER STATED THAT "THERE HAS BEEN A TOTAL ABSENCE OF FBI INFILTRATING RACIST ORGANIZATIONS".

14.

THE BUREAU REVIEWS *THE FIRE NEXT TIME*

OCTOBER 1963

The most significant books acquired for the FBI's national library in Washington, DC, were read and formally reviewed by Bureau agents patrolling the literary front for threats to the health of the state—especially the health of the FBI's reputation. In this example of the eccentric genre of FBI literary criticism, F. J. Baumgardner, a section chief in the Domestic Intelligence Division, reviews Baldwin's *The Fire Next Time*, a collection of two open letters on race, religion, and rights first published in *The New Yorker* and the *Progressive*, respectively. Now ranked as classics of American literature and of the essay form, the acknowledged inspiration for Ta-Nehisi Coates's *Between the World and Me* and dozens of other works, Baldwin's paired letters were immediately praised by the *New York Times* as medleys of "sermon, ultimatum, confession, deposition, testament, and chronicle," united by "searing, brilliant prose." The FBI's contemporary review was less adulatory and more self-concerned. Baumgardner correctly noted that both parts of *The Fire Next Time* "strongly advocate integration," though he missed Baldwin's careful recreation of the racial pain behind the Nation of Islam in "Down at the Cross," the book's second, longer half. Baumgardner joined many other reviewers in emphasizing Baldwin's explosively polarized conclusion: "the relatively conscious whites and blacks" would either "end the racial nightmare, and achieve our country," or fulfill the prophecy of America's destruction by fire. The FBI reviewer was less typical in flagging Baldwin's ironic reference to Christ as a "disreputable sunbaked Hebrew" (a quotation subsequently underlined by another, presumably scandalized Bureau official). And he was on his own in his relieved discovery that J. Edgar Hoover and his Bureau "are not mentioned in the book" despite the phone taps predicting a nuclear-powered Baldwin attack.

OPTIONAL FORM NO. 10
MAY 1962 EDITION
GSA GEN. REG. NO. 27
5010-106

UNITED STATES GOVERNMENT

Memorandum

TO : Mr. W. C. Sullivan

FROM : Mr. F. J. Baumgardner

SUBJECT: "THE FIRE NEXT TIME"
BY JAMES BALDWIN

DATE: October 3, 1963
1 - Mr. Sullivan
1 - Mr. Baumgardner
1 - Mr. [redacted]
(Attn: Miss [redacted])
1 - Mr. [redacted]
1 - Mr. [redacted]

Tolson
Belmont
Mohr
Casper
Callahan
Conrad
DeLoach
Evans
Gale
Rosen
Sullivan
Tavel
Trotter
Tele. Room
Holmes
Gandy

b7C-1

Subject book, published in 1963 by The Dial Press, Inc., New York City, consists of two articles by Baldwin which were previously published in magazines. Both articles strongly advocate integration.

I. "My Dungeon Shook"

In this brief article Baldwin compares Harlem living conditions where he was reared to those described by Charles Dickens existing in London over 100 years ago. Today, with integration, Baldwin says the Negroes must force the whites to stop fleeing from reality and begin to change those conditions.

II. "Down at the Cross" (originally published under the title "Letter from a Region in My Mind")

This lengthy article again mentions Baldwin's past life in Harlem. He had been a preacher on occasion (no mention of being ordained) until he became disillusioned with Christianity. He refers to Christ as a "disreputable sunbaked Hebrew." Baldwin continues: "If the concept of God has any validity or any use, it can only be to make us larger, freer, and more loving. If God cannot do this, then it is time we got rid of Him." Baldwin does not say how. Baldwin does not regard the Negro as inferior to the whites and says the only thing the white man has that the Negro needs is power. He contends the blacks and whites need each other if we are to become a nation and if integration is to be achieved. If the relatively conscious whites and blacks do not falter in their duty to work toward integration, he says, it may be possible to end the racial nightmare. If, on the other hand, they do not try everything to achieve that goal, then "the fulfillment of that prophesy, re-created from the Bible in song by a slave, is upon us: God gave Noah the rainbow sign, no more water, the fire next time!"

ALL INFORMATION CONTAINED
HEREIN IS UNCLASSIFIED
DATE 5-16-89 BY

REC- 5 [illegible]

The Director and the Bureau are not mentioned in the book.

3 OCT 18 1963

1 - 100-3-116 (CPUSA, Negro Question
Communist Influence in Racial Matters)

62-108763
JFM:mls
(7)

5 9 OCT 30 1963

Memorandum to Mr. Sullivan
RE: "THE FIRE NEXT TIME"
BY JAMES BALDWIN
62-108763

Bureau files indicate Baldwin, who was born in 1924 in New York City, has been very active and vocal in the integration movement and his writings deal primarily with that situation. He has lent his name to subversive causes and has been critical of the Director. He has not been investigated.

ACTION:

None. File.

15.

PHOTOS OF BALDWIN IN SELMA

OCTOBER 1963

Baldwin put his body as well as his words on the line in October 1963, jumping directly into the civil disobedience at the heart of the nonviolent Civil Rights Movement. After the Birmingham church bombing that September, sit-ins and voter registration efforts intensified in nearby Selma. SNCC leader James Forman (his last name often misspelled by the FBI) called on Baldwin and comedian Dick Gregory to travel to Alabama to add celebrity glitz to a "Freedom Day" on October 7, during which three hundred African American citizens of voting age would attempt to register at the Dallas County Courthouse. The FBI had advance knowledge of Baldwin's involvement: as this October letter to the Justice Department testifies, the Bureau learned of his arrival at the Birmingham airport through both the Clarence Jones wiretap and a less secretive NBC television report. Baldwin speechified on the big day but also lined up side by side with the protestors, where he saw, at first hand, FBI agents refuse to intervene as Sheriff Jim Clark beat and arrested several would-be voters. Years later, Baldwin recalled asking an FBI representative on the scene if the sheriff—a man whose moral life seemed to be "destroyed by a plague called color"—had "any right to throw us off *Federal* property. *No*, is the answer, *but we can't do anything about it*." Baldwin was incensed by this passivity, further ammunition for his war on the FBI's racial bias. Had Baldwin seen the indistinct black-and-white photographs of him and Forman and other protestors taken by a Bureau agent on Freedom Day, he would have been even angrier. Collecting images of those in the "voter registration line in front of the Dallas County Courthouse" appeared to take precedence over investigating their tormentors.

SECRET

UNITED STATES DEPARTMENT OF JUSTICE

FEDERAL BUREAU OF INVESTIGATION

In Reply, Please Refer to File No.

New York, New York
October 7, 1963

Communist Party, United States
of America (CPUSA)
Negro Question
Communist Influence in Racial Matters
Internal Security - C

On October 6, 1963, a confidential source, who has furnished reliable information in the past, furnished information which indicated that on that date, Clarence Jones expressed concern over James Baldwin (Negro author) travelling to Birmingham, Alabama. Jones instructed his wife to contact local airports to get time and flight of Baldwin's plane to Birmingham. She was then told to contact James Foreman to have him meet Baldwin, scheduled to arrive at 7:25 p.m. the same date aboard United Airlines flight from Newark, New Jersey.

Jones, later the same date, was advised that Baldwin arrived in Birmingham, but was not met by Foreman and is staying at the Gaston Hotel at Birmingham.

Jones was further advised that Baldwin had made a telephone call to the Attorney General. Whether Baldwin actually talked to the Attorney General, or the reason for this contact is unknown by the source at this time.

SECRET
Group I
Excluded from automatic
downgrading and
declassification

DECLASSIFIED BY [illegible]
ON 5/23/89
292325

Searched
Serialized
Indexed
Filed

100-146553-41

This document contains neither recommendations nor conclusions of the Federal Bureau of Investigation (FBI). It is the property of the FBI and is loaned to your agency; it and its contents are not to be distributed outside your agency.

SECRET

CPUSA
Negro Question
Communist Influence in Racial Matters

Baldwin contacted Jones the same date to advise that he was in Birmingham and was deeply concerned as to Foreman's whereabouts since Foreman did not meet him at the airport and that he has heard that Foreman was "running around" with one [redacted] and, according to Baldwin, there is a warrant outstanding for her arrest.

New York National Broadcasting Company (NBC) television newscast at 11 p.m. October 6, 1963, announced that James Baldwin had arrived in Birmingham, Alabama to assist in voting registration.

b7C-4

As of September 15, 1963, Clarence Jones was the General Counsel for the Ghandi Society for Human Rights, 15 East 40th Street, New York City.

A second confidential source, who has furnished reliable information in the past, advised that on February 26, 1957, he identified a photograph of Clarence Jones as a person whom he knew during late 1953 or early 1954, to be a member of and in a position of leadership in the Labor Youth League (LYL).

The LYL has been designated pursuant to Executive Order 10450.

James Foreman is Executive Secretary of the Student Non-Violent Coordinating Committee.

SECRET

UNITED STATES GOVERNMENT

Memorandum

TO : DIRECTOR, FBI (157-6-61) DATE: 10/14/63

FROM : SAC, MOBILE (157-367)(P)

SUBJECT: RACIAL SITUATION,
STATE OF ALABAMA,
SELMA, ALABAMA
RM

ReMolet dated 10/10/63.

Transmitted herewith are three sets of photographs depicting voter registration line in front of the Dallas County Courthouse on October 7, 1963. Photographs taken by SA [redacted] b7C-1

Photograph #1 - Entrance of Dallas County Courthouse before voter registration line formed.

Photographs 2-30 - Sections of voter registration line.

Photographs 31-32 - JAMES FOREMAN, SNCC leader, JAMES BALDWIN, author.

Photographs 33-51 - Sections of voter registration line.

Photographs 52-56 - JAMES FOREMAN, SNCC leader and JAMES BALDWIN, author, attempting to enter Dallas County Courthouse.

2 - Bureau (Encs. 3)(RM)
2 - Mobile
VPD-plw
(4)

ALL INFORMATION CONTAINED HEREIN IS UNCLASSIFIED DATE 2/20/98 BY 6972 FEP/ep 89-3016 JNP

157-6-61-410

REC- 55

ENCLOSURE

ENCLO. BEHIND FILE

1 set photographs sent to CFD

17 OCT 16 1963

OCT 22 1963

1880

#32

#31

#53

#52

#55

#54

#56

16.

A FALLING OUT WITH "SEXUAL PROCLIVITIES"

OCTOBER 1963

In this "urgent" teletype, the Clarence Jones phone tap provides additional up-to-the-minute gossip on tensions within the Civil Rights Movement: in this case, news of an evening argument between Jones and Baldwin that led the former to question his weightiest political commitments. Jones did not follow through on his morning-after threat to abandon the movement along with his representation of Baldwin. Within days, he was speaking and strategizing with Baldwin once again, and he remained a close if sometimes combative adviser to Martin Luther King until King's death in 1968. The teletype nonetheless documents a lasting pattern in Baldwin's intellectual friendships, cemented by "informal nighttime seminars" during which "discussions were frequently heated and there was shouting and sometimes there were tears," as David Leeming explains. The teletype also logs further evidence of the discomfort with Baldwin's "sexual propensities" among King's allies—discomfort based in part on a misdirected fear that sexual scandal would damage the movement. Ironically, it was King's sexual indiscretions that the Bureau abused in the horrifying blackmail letter—the pre-2016 nadir of FBI history—it sent to King's Atlanta home in 1964.

10/10/63

PLAIN TEXT

TELETYPE URGENT

TO: DIRECTOR, FBI (100-3-116)

FROM: SAC, NEW YORK (100-151548)

ALL INFORMATION CONTAINED
HEREIN IS UNCLASSIFIED
DATE 5/23/89 BY

CPUSA NEGRO QUESTION, COMMUNIST INFLUENCE IN RACIAL MATTERS; IS DASH C. OFFICE OF ORIGIN NEW YORK.

ON OCTOBER TEN, SIXTY THREE, [redacted] [redacted] FURNISHED INFORMATION ON THAT DATE WHICH INDICATED THAT CLARENCE JONES TOLD [redacted] THAT HE HAD A FALLING OUT WITH JAMES BALDWIN, NEGRO AUTHOR, LAST NIGHT. AS A RESULT OF THIS, JONES SAID HE IS GETTING OUT OF THE GHANDI SOCIETY AND WAS GETTING OUT OF THE CIVIL RIGHTS MOVEMENT TO DEVOTE HIS TIME TO PRACTICING LAW. JONES SAID HE HAS BEEN CRITICAL OF BALDWIN'S ACTIVITIES, AND MENTIONED THAT BALDWIN'S SEXUAL PROPENSITIES HAVE BECOME KNOWN. JONES ADVISED THAT BALDWIN IS COMING TO THE OFFICE TO ARRANGE FOR THE TRANSFER OF THE FILES. IT WAS INDICATED BALDWIN'S NEW ATTORNEY WOULD BE THEODORE R. KUPFERMAN WITH OFFICES AT

b2-1

b7C-2

1-Supervisor #414
1-NY (100-73250) (CLARENCE JONES) (414)
1-NY (100-) (JAMES BALDWIN)
1-NY (100-151548) (414)
JCS:rmv
(4)

100-146553-48

SEARCHED ... SERIALIZED ...

17.

THE USIA CENSORS BALDWIN

OCTOBER 1963

This letter to J. Edgar Hoover from an official of the United States Information Agency (USIA) dramatizes how other federal agencies tended to respond to FBI pressure on Baldwin and lesser Bureau critics: with anxiety, compliance, and (outward) deference. Paul J. McNichol of the USIA security office assured Hoover that he had nothing to fear from the television program featuring Baldwin that so distressed the Bureau a month earlier. His agency had edited out "[t]he portion of Mr. Baldwin's remarks [that] contained attacks on you and Senator James Eastland." And it had a defensible reason for doing so: "all participants in the round-table discussion" were told "that there would be some editing to make the program fit within normal television time limits." The FBI was not entirely satisfied with the USIA's reaction to this "racial matter," however, and it pressed McNichol for a transcript of the Baldwin remarks it censored. McNichol obliged, and the Bureau discovered that Baldwin hoped to ask Hoover "rude questions such as why the FBI can find a 'junkie' but cannot find a man who bombs the homes of Negro leaders in the deep south." The Bureau was required to dig hard to discover the specifics of Baldwin's insult. But it now had the kind of evidence against him that—at least for the Hooverites—was louder than a bomb.

~~SECRET~~

UNITED STATES INFORMATION AGENCY

WASHINGTON

October 11, 1963

Mr. Tolson
Mr. Belmont
Mr. Mohr
Mr. Casper
Mr. Callahan
Mr. Conrad
Mr. DeLoach
Mr. Evans
Mr. Gale
Mr. Rosen
Mr. Sullivan
Mr. Tavel
Mr. Trotter
Tele. Room
Miss Holmes
Miss Gandy

b7C-1

Dear Mr. Hoover:

This Agency deeply appreciates the information contained in the Bureau's memorandum of September 24, 1963, New York, New York, entitled James Baldwin, Racial Matters; Security Matter - C.

Up to this time the Agency has not received any request from Mr. Baldwin or his attorney concerning the necessary editing done to the videotaped March-on-Washington discussion in which Mr. Baldwin participated.

I thought it would be of interest to you to be informed the content of your memorandum was the subject of a conference of the highest officials in our Agency and if we are required to make some statement on this subject, we will point out that Mr. Alan Carter, Director of the Television Service, clearly informed all participants in the round-table discussion (which was videotaped on August 28) that there would be some editing to make the program fit within normal television time limits. As made, the tape was nearly 33 minutes long and deletions were needed to bring it down to approximately 25 1/2 minutes. In deciding what material would be edited to bring the tape to the proper length, we naturally exercised editorial judgment and we considered that the views of Mr. Baldwin and other participants were adequately expressed without the particular material we deleted.

The portion of Mr. Baldwin's remarks which were removed contained attacks on you and Senator James Eastland and it is Mr. Murrow's established policy in such programs that if an individual is attacked by name in a television program, some

The Honorable
J. Edgar Hoover, Director
Federal Bureau of Investigation
Washington 25, D. C.

REC 14

DECLASSIFIED BY ... ON 1-29-90 Per USIA memo 1.18.90 299013

NOV 5 1963

GROUP 1
Excluded From Automatic Downgrading and Declassification

EXP. PROC.

OCT 14 1963

60 NOV 18 1963

~~SECRET~~

1050

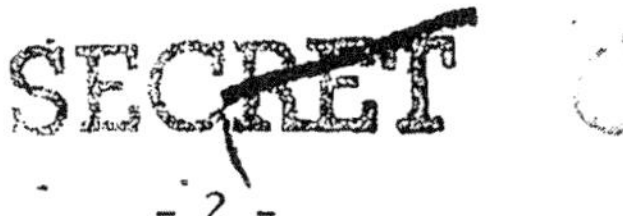

answer to the attack, or some statement of the contrary view, must be included. There were no answers to the attacks on you and Senator Eastland by other members of the group during this particular discussion of the round-table panel, although some members said that if the program had been running a longer time they probably would have made such answering remarks.

I thought you would like to know of the Agency's position in the racial matter which you kindly forwarded to us and of our deep and continuing interest in receiving information of this type.

Warmest personal regards,

Paul J. McNichol

Paul J. McNichol
Director
Office of Security

OPTIONAL FORM NO. 10
MAY 1962 EDITION
GSA GEN. REG. NO. 27

5010-106

SECRET

UNITED STATES GOVERNMENT

Memorandum

ALL INFORMATION CONTAINED HEREIN IS UNCLASSIFIED EXCEPT WHERE SHOWN OTHERWISE

Tolson
Belmont
Mohr
Casper
Callahan
Conrad
DeLoach
Evans
Gale
Rosen
Sullivan
Tavel
Trotter
Tele. Room
Holmes
Gandy

SEE REVERSE SIDE FOR CLASSIFICATION ACTION

TO : Mr. W. C. Sullivan

DATE: 10/28/63

FROM : D. J. Brennan, Jr.

SUBJECT: JAMES BALDWIN
RACIAL MATTERS
SECURITY MATTER - C

Reference is made to letter from Mr. Paul J. McNichol, Director, Office of Security, United States Information Agency (USIA), to the Director dated October 11, 1963. Therein Mr. McNichol expresses appreciation for receipt of information contained in our memorandum of September 24, 1963, captioned as above and setting forth information indicating that Baldwin contemplated protesting certain deletions made by USIA in a videotape of a round-table discussion concerning the March-on-Washington, August 28, 1963.

(U) b7C-1

In reference letter, Mr. McNichol points out that Baldwin's remarks were edited because they amounted to attacks on the Director and Senator James Eastland. He pointed out that it is the established policy of the Director of USIA that if any individual is attacked by name on a television program, some answer to the attack, or some statement of a contrary view, must be included. There being none in this instance, such remarks on the part of Baldwin were edited. (U)

At the request of the Domestic Intelligence Division, Liaison contacted McNichol on October 24, 1963, and requested information as to the nature of Baldwin's remarks regarding the Director. On October 25, McNichol furnished the following verbatim excerpt, which remarks were made by Baldwin during a discussion of the Negro problem and obstacles confronting the Negro:

"It will be a matter of attacking really, J. Edgar Hoover, and asking very rude questions such as why the

1-Mr. Belmont
1-Mr. Sullivan
1-Mr. Sizoo
1-Mr. Baumgardner
1-Mr. [redacted]
1-Liaison
1-Mr. [redacted]

b7C-1

WJM:mer (8)

Classified by [illegible]
Declassify on: OADR

12 NOV 5 1963

60 NOV 14 1963

SECRET

PERS. REC. UNIT

Memorandum to Mr. Sullivan
RE: JAMES BALDWIN
RACIAL MATTERS
SECURITY MATTER - C

FBI can find a 'junkie' but cannot find a man who bombs the homes of Negro leaders in the deep south. They still have not found anyone. These are the questions that one has to be confronted with now. One has got to deal with the fact that if you liberate Negroes in the ghettos of harlem, you have to change New York City."

ACTION:

None. The above is submitted for information and no further action is deemed warranted.

SECRET

18.

ASK J. EDGAR HOOVER—IS BALDWIN "A KNOWN COMMUNIST?"

OCTOBER 1963

Right-thinking, right-leaning Americans had a habit of writing Hoover with their deepest political questions and fears. Among other roles, the FBI director thus served as a national conservative confessor and pen pal who liked giving the impression that he stayed up "past midnight" to make "personal replies to citizens who write to him praising the FBI." In this October 1963 letter from an anticommunist citizen worried over black radicalism and Hoover's rumored retirement, Baldwin (in fact a Trotskyite sympathizer-turned-flexible socialist) is misidentified as a regular writer for the Communist *Daily Worker.* "An evangelist who spoke at our church kept quoting him," the writer explained. "Are you allowed to tell us if a man is a known communist?" The FBI was not allowed to spill the beans held in the Baldwin file, Hoover officially wrote in return. But the FBI director was authorized to insist that he had "no plans to retire." Hoover indeed stayed in the Bureau saddle long enough to receive several other letters from common citizens asking about Baldwin's life, work, and political commitments.

TRUE COPY

[redacted] b7C-5

October 24, 1963

Mr. J. Edgar Hoover, Chief
Federal Bureau of Investigation
Washington, D.C.

ALL INFORMATION CONTAINED
HEREIN IS UNCLASSIFIED
DATE 5-16-89 BY [illegible]

Dear Mr. Hoover:

There are quite a few things that come to ones mind these days, and one is, who will be chief after you retire? Do you have a trained man who is not a liberal minded fellow to step in?

Then too, is it a true fact that the founder of the NAACP died a full fledged communist? or is this propaganda?

Also, I wonder about this fellow James Baldwin who writes for "The Worker." An evangelist who spoke at our church kept quoting him. Are you allowed to tell us if a man is a known communist?

Thank you, and know one thing, you have been the one big hope for our future for a long time. It worries us to see time go by and retirement nearing for you.

Yours truly,

[redacted] b7C-5

62-108763

REC- 16

b7C October 24, 1963

Mr. J. Edgar Hoover, Chief
Federal Bureau of Investigation
Washington, D.C.

ALL INFORMATION CONTAINED
HEREIN IS UNCLASSIFIED
DATE 5-16-89 BY [illegible]

Dear Mr. Hoover:

There are quite a few things that come to ones mind these days, and one is, who will be chief after you retire? Do you have a trained man who is not a liberal minded fellow to step in?

Then too, is it a true fact that the founder of the NAACP died a full fledged communist? or is this propaganda?

Also, I wonder about this fellow James Baldwin who writes for "The Worker". An evangelist who spoke at our church kept quoting him. Are you allowed to tell us if a man is a known communist

Thank you, and know one thing; you have been the one big hope for our future for a long time. It worries us to see time go by and retirement nearing for you.

b7C Yours truly,

REC- 16 62-[illegible]

October 30, 1963

ALL INFORMATION CONTAINED
HEREIN IS UNCLASSIFIED
DATE 3-16-89 BY [illegible]

b7C-5 b7C-1

Dear

I have read your letter of October 24th.

While I would like to be of service, information contained in the files of the FBI is confidential and available for official use only pursuant to regulations of the Department of Justice.

You may wish to know, I have made no plans to retire. On the contrary, it is my desire to remain in my present capacity as long as I can be of service to our country.

Sincerely yours,

J. Edgar Hoover

MAILED 31
OCT 3 0 1963
COMM-FBI

John Edgar Hoover
Director

NOTE: Bufiles contain no information concerning Mr b7C-5
James Baldwin, author, is well-known to the Bureau in connection with his communist front and integrationist activities. He has in the past blamed Mr. Hoover for the racial strife in Alabama.

JCF:rls
(3)

Tolson
Belmont
Mohr
Casper
Callahan
Conrad
DeLoach
Evans
Gale
Rosen
Sullivan
Tavel
Trotter
Tele. Room
Holmes
Gandy

68 NOV 8 1963

MAIL ROOM ☐ TELETYPE UNIT ☐

19.

J. EDGAR HOOVER ASKS "IS BALDWIN ON OUR SECURITY INDEX?"

DECEMBER 1963

Hoover's mounting distrust and distaste for Baldwin boiled over at the close of 1963, when he asked Bureau underlings if the writer was "on our Security Index," a highly classified FBI database tracking American citizens judged to be grave threats to national security. The authority of the questioner—the director himself—guaranteed an affirmative answer. Baldwin was therefore rapidly elevated to the Security Index from the Reserve Index, a lesser FBI enemies list aimed at individuals "who, in a time of emergency, are in a position to influence others against the national interest." The first Security Index card on Baldwin was recommended on December 9, 1963. Like that of thousands of other suspects, this card threatened its subject with stripped rights and regulated mobility. It propelled street-level Bureau surveillance and regular updates of Baldwin's home address and physical description. It placed him on a register of undesirables "whose presence at liberty in this country in time of war or national emergency would be dangerous to the public peace and the safety of the United States Government." It exposed him to summary arrest, surrender of habeas corpus, and indefinite detention, if Hoover's will ever aligned with national crisis and presidential consent. As covert as it was legally dubious, the Security Index was long kept from public view: before its official elimination in 1971, Hoover ordered that it should never be "discussed with agencies or individuals outside the Bureau." By the late 1960s, however, many African American radicals—Baldwin included—rightly assumed they were among the targets of what Harlem congressman Vito Marcantonio christened "a system of terror by index cards."

FD-122 (Rev. 1-4-60)

Director, FBI (Bufile- 62-108763)

12/9/63

filed 12-17-63

SAC, NEW YORK (100-146553)

"Reserve Index card approved and prepared. Two copies attached. Cards should be filed in your Reserve Index."

JAMES BALDWIN
SM-C

[X] It is recommended that a Security Index Card be prepared on the above-captioned individual.

[ ] The Security Index Card on the captioned individual should be changed as follows (*specify change only*):

Name

James Baldwin

ALL INFORMATION CONTAINED HEREIN IS UNCLASSIFIED DATE 5-16-79 BY [illegible] Jap

Aliases

James Arthur Baldwin

[X] Native Born [ ] Naturalized [ ] Alien

[X] Communist [ ] Socialist Workers Party [ ] Independent Socialist League

[ ] Miscellaneous (*specify*)

[ ] Tab for Detcom | Race: Negro | Sex: [X] Male [ ] Female

Date of Birth: 8/2/24 | Place of Birth: New York, New York

Business Address (*show name of employing concern and address*)

~~UNKNOWN~~ *writer from residence*

Key Facility Data

Geographical Reference Number ______ Responsibility ______

Interested Agencies ______

100-146553-78

Residence Address

~~UNKNOWN~~ *81 Horatio St New York, New York*

SEARCHED ..... INDEXED .....
SERIALIZED ..... FILED .....
DEC 1 1963
... NEW YORK

b7C - 1

470 West End Avenue
New York, New York

REGISTERED MAIL

"Send S.I. [illegible] 1 photo"

FD-122 (Rev. 4-17-63)
OPTIONAL FORM NO. 10
MAY 1962 EDITION
GSA GEN. REG. NO. 27

5010-106

UNITED STATES GOVERNMENT

Memorandum

TO : Director, FBI (Bufile- 62-108763) DATE: 12/9/63

FROM : SAC, NEW YORK (100-146553)

SUBJECT: JAMES BALDWIN
SM-C

Card filed
Cards sent OO
12/10/63

MAKE RI-11 card.
-104

[X] It is recommended that a Security Index Card be prepared on the above-captioned individual.

[ ] The Security Index Card on the captioned individual should be changed as follows (*specify change only*):

Name
James Baldwin

ALL INFORMATION CONTAINED HEREIN IS UNCLASSIFIED DATE 5-16-89 BY

Aliases
James Arthur Baldwin

[X] Native Born [ ] Naturalized [ ] Alien

[X] Communist [ ] Socialist Workers Party [ ] Independent Socialist League

[ ] Miscellaneous (*specify*)

Tab for Detcom	Race	Sex
[ ] Tab for Detcom	Negro	[X] Male [ ] Female

Date of Birth	Place of Birth
8/2/24	New York, New York

Business Address (*show name of employing concern and address*)

~~UNKNOWN~~
writer, from residence

REC-22 62-108763 11

Key Facility Data

Geographical Reference Number ______ Responsibility

Interested Agencies ______

Residence Address
~~81 Horatio St.~~
~~UNKNOWN~~ ~~New York, New York~~

470 West End Avenue
New York, New York

REGISTERED MAIL

b7C-1

1052

OPTIONAL FORM NO. 10

UNITED STATES GOVERNMENT

Memorandum

Tolson
Belmont
Mohr
Casper
Callahan
Conrad
DeLoach
Evans
Gale
Rosen
Sullivan
Tavel
Trotter
Tele. Room
Holmes
Gandy

TO : Mr. W. C. Sullivan

DATE: December 10, 1963

FROM : Mr. [redacted]

1 - Mr. Belmont
1 - Mr. Rosen
1 - Mr. Sullivan
1 - Mr. [redacted]
1 - Mr. [redacted]
1 - Mr. [redacted]

SUBJECT: JAMES A. BALDWIN
SECURITY MATTER - C
RACIAL MATTERS

b7C-1

In connection with a summary of information in Bureau files on Baldwin the Director inquired "Is Baldwin on our Security Index?"

Baldwin's name is included in the Reserve Index (special group of individuals who will receive priority consideration with respect to investigation and/or other action following apprehension of Security Index subjects). Although Baldwin's name is not now in the Security Index, New York has this case under active investigation and, among other things, his Security Index status will be evaluated.

ACTION:

This is submitted in accordance with the Director's request. New York is being followed closely.

62-108763

ALL INFORMATION CONTAINED HEREIN IS UNCLASSIFIED DATE 5-17-89 BY

Expedite

Included in Security Index 12/19/63 IDH

IDH:cad
(7)

REC 33 62-108763-12

12 DEC 20 1963

66 DEC 26 1963

Let 12/18/63 WPJ:cad

1053

Memorandum to Mr. Rosen
Re: James L. Farmer, Et Al.

He has indicated publicly that he feels the Attorney General and the President have been ineffective in dealing with discrimination and in this connection has urged the removal of the Director. (157-6-34-78; 62-108763)

By memorandum dated 5/28/63 the Director indicated that the Attorney General had called and related a conversation he had had with James Baldwin, whom he considered a "nut." The Attorney General advised that the whole conversation started by Baldwin making two determinations: (1) Wouldn't think of fighting for the United States if the United States got into a war and (2) Thinking of getting guns and starting to shoot white people. The Attorney General indicated that Baldwin "is an important figure in the Student Nonviolent Coordinating Committee (SNCC)" and commented that the Negroes look up to this sort of leadership as the Negroes have no outstanding leaders with the exception of Martin Luther King. (100-439190-47)

ACTION:

This is for the Director's information.

It should be noted that all of the information set forth above concerning these individuals has been furnished to the Department over the past several months.

Is Baldwin on our Security Index?

20.

THE BIOGRAPHY OF JAMES ARTHUR BALDWIN, "SECURITY MATTER"

DECEMBER 1963

Baldwin's Security Index card was ushered in by a thirty-nine-page investigative report, suitable for sharing across the federal intelligence system, prepared by the New York field office at Washington's command. Following FBI conventions, the report took the form of an unembellished but paranoid life history of Baldwin seen from the perspective of Hooverite anticommunism. The initial summary captures Baldwin as a security threat "self-employed as a writer" and as a serial ally of radical groups, journals, and opinions. A fuller piecemeal description then sets out the facts of Baldwin's birth, citizenship, education, marital and military status, and credit rating (his application for a Diner's Club Card, the record showed, was rejected in 1961). Further on, three of his prior addresses in Paris are correctly recorded, and his current residence on West End Avenue in New York is verified by the quick but underhanded means of a pretext phone call. Indicative of Baldwin's many pre-echoes of the era of Black Lives Matter, a section on his short criminal record cites "a charge of disorderly conduct for refusal to move on the order of a policeman." The bulk of the report then establishes Baldwin's guilt by political association (his work on behalf of the Emergency Civil Liberties and the Fair Play for Cuba Committees beginning in 1960, etc.) and by freedom of speech (his 1963 statement to the *New York Times* that "Negroes have no cause to have faith in the

FBI," etc.). Unlike other, more indulgently literary portions of Baldwin's file, this synopsis strips his life of most creative highlights beyond his book titles. In their place, it offers a hostile but instructive portrait of the artist as a political dissenter, first and last.

FD-204 (Rev. 3-3-59)

UNITED STATES DEPARTMENT OF JUSTICE
FEDERAL BUREAU OF INVESTIGATION

SECRET

CONFIDENTIAL

Copy to: ALL INFORMATION CONTAINED HEREIN IS UNCLASSIFIED EXCEPT WHERE SHOWN OTHERWISE

Report of: [redacted] b7C-1 Office: New York, New York

Date: DEC 11 1963

Field Office File #: 100-146553 Bureau File #:

Title: JAMES ARTHUR BALDWIN

DECLASSIFIED BY AUC 94255SAH/8b
ON 2/17/99
CA97-5269

Classified by 6972 SQP1088
Declassify on: OADR 2-20-90
89 3016 JAE

Classified by DB2/BT3/08
Declassify on: OADR 5-18-89

Character: SECURITY MATTER - C

Synopsis: JAMES ARTHUR BALDWIN, Negro author, born on 8/2/24, in NYC, self-employed as a writer, resides in apartment 6A, 470 West End Avenue, NYC. Sources advised subject: sponsor of FPCC, April, 1960; currently subscribes to "Freedomways"; addressed public meeting of NLG, NYC, October, 1963; signed appeal for clemency for CARL BRADEN, identified as CP member August, 1961; received copy of "Workers World", August, 1961; observed in company of MALCOLM X, NOI Minister, NYC, July, 1963; addressed meeting in NYC under auspices of Liberation Committee for Africa, June, 1961; listed as sponsor of rally by NY Council to Abolish HUAC, NYC, April, 1961; addressed rally at Carnegie Hall, NYC, sponsored by Student Non-Violent Coordinating Committee, February, 1963; signed "Open Letter to President John F. Kennedy" urging U.S. cease intervention in Vietnam, July, 1963; ~~signed ad calling for abolition of House Committee on Un-American Activities, February, 1962~~. BALDWIN has made the following statements: "How many Negroes would fight to free Cuba when they can't be freed themselves?"; United States is confronted with "22,000,000 black people who can't be negotiated with any more"; and reportedly stated "Part of the problem in civil rights movement is J. EDGAR HOOVER", which statement reportedly was deleted from television program of U.S. Information Agency, Washington, D.C., 8/28/63. Description of BALDWIN set forth.

-P-

SECRET

CONFIDENTIAL

... automatic ...

This document contains neither recommendations nor conclusions of the FBI. It is the p... to your agency; it and its contents are not to be distributed outside your agency.

NY 100-146553

DETAILS:

Unless otherwise noted, allbackground information set forth hereunder was furnished by NY T-14 on December 10, 1963.

Information contained in the "Wilson Library Bulletin" set forth below, was obtained by SA [redacted] from the files of the New York Public Library, New York City on December 10, 1963.

Records of the Credit Bureau of Greater New York mentioned hereunder were reviewed by IC [redacted] [redacted] on December 10, 1963.

b7c-1

I. BACKGROUND

A. Birth Data

JAMES ARTHUR BALDWIN was born on August 2, 1924 in New York City.

The "Wilson Library Bulletin" dated February, 1959, page 392, indicates that JAMES ARTHUR BALDWIN was born on August 2, 1924 in New York City, the oldest of nine children of DAVID BALDWIN, a clergyman, and BERDIS EMMA (JONES) BALDWIN.

Records of the Bureau of Vital Statistics, Borough of Manhattan, New York City, reviewed by SA [redacted] on December 10, 1963, reflected no record of subject's birth.

B. Citizenship

Subject is a United States citizen by virtue of birth in the United States.

- 2 -

CONFIDENTIAL

NY 100-146553

C. Education

An article appearing in the June 3, 1963 issue of "The New York Times" reflected that the subject was graduated from DeWitt Clinton High School, Bronx, New York, in 1942.

The "Wilson Library Bulletin" reflects that subject was graduated in 1942 from DeWitt Clinton High School, New York City, where he served as a student judge and magazine editor.

D. Marital Status

An article in the June 3, 1963 issue of "The New York Times" indicates that subject has never been married.

E. Military Status

Subject registered with Selective Service, Local Board 11, 80 Lafayette Street, New York 13, New York, on September 17, 1948, and was assigned registration number 50-11-24-577. He was classified 1A on November 8, 1948, and on February 14, 1950, was classified 5A.

The subject was scheduled to take an Armed Forces examination in New York City on December 14, 1948. However, this examination was not taken due to subject's residence in Paris, France.

Subject is not known to have ever served in the Armed Forces of the United States.

F. Credit

Records of the Credit Bureau of Greater New York indicate that on February 25, 1958, a suit was

CONFIDENTIAL

CONFIDENTIAL

instituted against the subject by JOHN M. GARCIA to recover $1,000 which had been loaned to the subject, Docket Number 1M9348. No disposition of this suit was indicated.

On February 21, 1961, an application made by the subject for a Diner's Club Card was rejected by that organization. As of November 29, 1963, subject's credit rating was listed as satisfactory.

G. Employment

Records of the Credit Bureau of Greater New York indicate that as of November, 1963, BALDWIN's Business was listed as Dial Press, 461 Park Avenue South, New York City.

The subject has had the following former employments:

1945	"Saxton Fellowship"
1948	"Rosenwald Fellowship"
1948	Foreign Correspondent, Partisan Review, 1545 Broadway, New York City

On December 10, 1963, [redacted] 470 West End Avenue, advised that the subject is self-employed as an author. b7C-6

The "Wilson Library Bulletin" reflects that after graduating from high school, BALDWIN held a number of jobs helping to support his family.

However, his only interest was writing, and in 1945 a Eugene Saxton Fellowship enabled him to devote himself to literary work.

CONFIDENTIAL

His first publication was a book review in 1946 in "Nation" magazine, and following that he had articles appearing in such periodicals as "Partisan Review," "American Mercury," "Commentary," "Mademoiselle," "The Reporter," "Harper's" and "New Leader", and his play "The Amen Corner" has been produced at Howard University.

BALDWIN has written the following books "Another Country," "Go Tell It On The Mountain," "Notes Of A Native Son," "Giovanni's Room," and "Nobody Knows My Name."

H. Residence

By means of a pretext on December 9, 1963, it was ascertained that JAMES ARTHUR BALDWIN was then residing at 470 West End Avenue, New York City.

On December 10, 1963, [redacted] Security Supervisor, New York Telephone Company, New York City, advised that JAMES BALDWIN resides in Apartment 6A, at 470 West End Avenue, New York City, and has unlisted telephone number TR 7-7773. b7c-6

On December 10, 1963, [redacted] [redacted], 470 West End Avenue, New York City, advised that the subject has resided in Apartment 6A at that address for the past three months.

Records of the Credit Bureau of Greater New York indicate the following residences for the subject:

February, 1958	81 Horatio Street New York City
November, 1962	306 West 18th Street New York City

CONFIDENTIAL

CONFIDENTIAL

NY 100-146553

November, 1963 470 West End Avenue
New York City

The subject has had the following prior residences:

46 West 131st Street
Apartment 5F
New York City
(no date)

Hotel de Rome
7 Rue des Carmes
Paris, France
(November 18, 1948)

269 Rue St. Jacques
Paris, France
(December 13, 1948)

13 Rue St. Sal Pece
Paris, France
(August 24, 1950)

800 Oxford Road
Ann Arbor, Michigan
(May 1, 1952)

I. Criminal Record

Records of the Bureau of Criminal Identification, New York City Police Department, reviewed by SA [redacted] [redacted] on December 10, 1963, indicate that subject was arrested on September 3, 1954, on a charge of disorderly conduct for refusal to move on the order of a policeman. He was arraigned before Judge BALSAM and received a suspended sentence. b7c-1

CONFIDENTIAL

CONFIDENTIAL

II. AFFILIATION WITH THE COMMUNIST MOVEMENT

Emergency Civil Liberties Committee (ECLC)

The November 7, 1963 issue of the "National Guardian" contained an announcement on page 11, column 2, that JAMES BALDWIN would be one of the speakers at a "Bill of Rights Dinner" scheduled for December 13, 1963, at the Americana Hotel, New York City. The sponsor of this dinner was listed as the ECLC.

Characterizations of the ECLC and the "National Guardian" are contained in the Appendix of this report.

Fair Play For Cuba Committee (FPCC)

On May 20, 1961, NY T-1 made available information indicating that the name and address, JAMES BALDWIN, 81 Horatio Street, New York City, was in the possession of the FPCC, 799 Broadway, New York City.

On December 10, 1963, [redacted] b7c-1 [redacted] New York City Police Department, advised that on April 24, 1960, subject was listed as a sponsor of the FPCC, 799 Broadway, New York City.

A characterization of the FPCC is contained in the Appendix of this report.

Freedomways Associates, Inc.

On October 25, 1963, NY T-2 advised that [redacted] [redacted] stated she had received a letter from JAMES BALDWIN, b7c-2 Negro author, in which BALDWIN wrote that he wanted to renew his subscription to "Freedomways" for two years. (U)

CONFIDENTIAL

BALDWIN added that he will give subscriptions to "Freedomways" as Christmas presents. NY T-2 further advised that [redacted] stated that [redacted]

b7c-2

[redacted] the quarterly publication, "Freedomways", published by Freedomways Associates, Inc.

[redacted] JAMES JACKSON, who, according to the October 27, 1963 issue of "The Worker", is its Editor.

"The Worker" is an East Coast Communist newspaper.

A characterization of Freedomways Associates, Inc. is contained in the Appendix of this report.

National Lawyers Guild (NLG)

The October 3, 1963 and October 10, 1963 editions of the "National Guardian" on pages 8 and 4, respectively, contained an announcement that the New York City Chapter of the NLG would present an evening with JAMES BALDWIN, author of "The Fire Next Time", at 8:30 PM, on October 18, 1963, at Town Hall, New York City. Proceeds will go to the NLG's Committee to Assist Southern Lawyers.

On October 19, 1963, NY T-3 advised that the NLG held a public meeting at Town Hall, New York City, on the evening of October 18, 1963.

Principal speaker of the evening was JAMES BALDWIN, author, who gave a commentary on the laws concerning Negro rights. BALDWIN in general statements was critical of the Attorney General, President JOHN F. KENNEDY, and the Federal Bureau of Investigation (FBI) for alleged failure to live up to the civil rights promises of the United States Government.

CONFIDENTIAL

NY T-3 further stated that BALDWIN made the statement that the law was for the privileged and not for the poor, especially the colored people.

A characterization of the NLG is contained in the Appendix of this report.

New York Council to Abolish the House Un-American Activities Committee (NYCAHUAC)

The April 17, 1961 edition of the "National Guardian", on page 4, carried an announcement for a "rally to abolish the House Un-American Activities Committee" to be held at St. Nicholas Arena, New York City, on April 21, 1961, under the auspices of the NYCAHUAC. One of the listed sponsors of this rally was "JAMES BALDWIN, writer."

A characterization of the NYCAHUAC is contained in the Appendix of this report.

New York Committee to Secure Justice for MORTON SOBELL (NYCSJMS)

On May 6, 1963, NY T-4 advised that at the monthly meeting of the NYCSJMS, held on May 2, 1963, at 940 Broadway, New York City, HELEN SOBELL, wife of MORTON SOBELL, reported on program plans. She stated she was in close touch with JAMES BALDWIN, who was now in this country, and stated she was hopeful of having him on the program. (X)(U)

A characterization of the NYCSJMS is contained in the Appendix of this report.

CONFIDENTIAL

Southern Conference
Educational Fund, Incorporated
(SCEF)

On August 18, 1961, NY T-5 made available a copy of a news release-type communication from the Carl Braden Clemency Appeal Committee which was distributed by the SCEF.

This communication reflected that a delegation of Southern integration leaders would, on that date, take petitions signed by over 1800 leaders in the field of human rights, representing all 50 states of the United States, to President KENNEDY, asking him to free CARL BRADEN of Louisville, Kentucky. Among those listed as signers of the petitions from New York State was JAMES BALDWIN.

Concerning CARL BRADEN, it is noted that ALBERTA AHEARN, 2311 Payne Street, Louisville, Kentucky, a self-admitted former member of the Communist Party (CP) in Louisville, Kentucky, on December 11 and 13, 1954, in her testimony in Jefferson County, Kentucky Court House, in the prosecution of CARL BRADEN, testified that CARL BRADEN was known to her as a member of the CP in Louisville, Kentucky, from January, 1951, to December, 1954, which was during the period of her (AHEARN's) CP membership.

A characterization of the SCEF is contained in the Appendix of this report.

CONFIDENTIAL

NY 100-146553 

"Workers World"

On August 25, 1961, NY T-6 made available information that JAMES BALDWIN, 81 Horatio Street, New York, New York, received the "Workers World" on that date.

A characterization of the "Workers World" is contained in the Appendix of this report.

III. ASSOCIATES

On July 15, 1963, [redacted] b7C-7 [redacted] New York City Police Department, advised SA [redacted] that he b7C-1 had received the following information from [redacted] b7C-4,5

[redacted] advised that [redacted] is definitely anti-white and anti-American but was unable to furnish [redacted] with any specific information in support of this statement.

[redacted] stated that since [redacted] moved into the above apartment, in October, 1962, he has been visited by the well-known author, JAMES BALDWIN, on 5 or 6 occasions. On one occasion, about 6 weeks ago, [redacted] was visited by MALCOLM X, Minister of the Nation of Islam (NOI) in New York City.

CONFIDENTIAL

On July 16, 1963, [redacted] advised [redacted] that on 1:10 p.m., on that date, he observed [redacted] leave his apartment in the company of 5 persons, including JAMES BALDWIN and MALCOLM X. b7C-7 b7C-4,5

[redacted] further advised that [redacted]

On August 1, 1963, NY T-7 advised that the subject with attorneys, CLARENCE BENJAMIN JONES and DAVID LUBELL, was scheduled to fly to Birmingham, Alabama on August 5, 1963.

As of July 3, 1963, CLARENCE JONES was the General Counsel for the Gandhi Society for Human Rights, 15 East 40th Street, New York City.

On February 26, 1957, NY T-8 identified a photograph of CLARENCE JONES as the person whom he knew during late 1953 or early 1954, to be a member and in a position of leadership in the Labor Youth League (LYL).

On August 20, 1963, NY T-7 advised that CLARENCE JONES was at that time counsel to Reverend MARTIN LUTHER KING, JR.

The LYL has been designated pursuant to Executive Order 10450.

CONFIDENTIAL

In testimony before the House Committee on Un-American Activities at Boston, Massachusetts, on March 18, 19 and 20, 1958, ARMANDO PENHA, a former member of the CP, identified DAVID LUBELL as a Communist Organizer among the students at various institutions of higher education in the Boston area. PENHA also identified DAVID LUBELL as a Harvard student who was an Organizer for the CP at the same time. This information is pertinent to the period 1952.

IV. STATEMENTS ATTRIBUTED TO JAMES BALDWIN

In an interview appearing in the June 3, 1963 issue of "The New York Times," by reporter M.S. HANDLER, BALDWIN made the following statements:

"No man can claim to speak for the Negro people today. There is no one with whom the white power structure can negotiate a deal that will bind the Negro people. There is, therefore, no possibility of a bargain whatsoever."

"I was raised in the church but have abandoned Christianity as an organized religion. The church is the worst place to learn about Christianity. I have rejected it because the Christians have rejected Christianity. It is too pious, too hypocritical."

In his interview with HANDLER, BALDWIN also stated that he could not accept the black Muslim political ideology based on black supremacy, but thought that the Muslims were the only grass roots Negro movement in the United States.

The June 3, 1963 issue of "The New York Times" contained another article on the subject in which he stated:

"I left the country and abandoned everything in 1948, never intending to return. I couldn't bear it any longer. I knew that I would kill somebody or someone would kill me. I lived in Paris and elsewhere in Europe long enough to vomit up most of my hatred and to place America in perspective.

"It was in Paris that I realized what my problem was. I was ashamed of being a Negro. I finally realized that I would remain what I was to the end of my time and lost my shame. I awoke from my nightmare."

On May 29, 1963, NY T-9 advised that on May 28, 1963, JAMES BALDWIN addressed a rally sponsored by the Staten Island Chapter of the Congress of Racial Equality (CORE), which rally was held at Wagner College, Grimes Hill, Staten Island, New York.

At this rally, BALDWIN stated he was speaking as an individual Negro rather than as spokesman for the Negro. He gave a brief outline of his boyhood in the South. The theme of his talk was that integration in the South is the problem of the white man and not of the Negro. He said it was not a Southern problem but a national problem. BALDWIN said he was not interested in compromises for the Negro, stating that compromising was a way of evading responsibility.

CONFIDENTIAL

During a question and answer period which followed, BALDWIN, when asked about his recent meeting with Attorney General ROBERT KENNEDY, stated merely that he had spoken with the Attorney General and thought the Attorney General "was beginning to listen."

The June 21, 1963 issue of the "New York Post" carried an article reporting that the subject on June 20, 1963, had received the Alumnus of the Year Award from the Frederick Douglas Junior High School in Harlem, New York City, from which school he graduated in 1938. In addressing the graduating class on June 20, 1963, BALDWIN stated, "This is the first time in the history of the country that it is confronted with 22,000,000 black people who can't be negotiated with anymore."

On September 19, 1963, NY T-13 advised that on that date CLARENCE JONES, counsel of Reverend MARTIN LUTHER KING, JR. and the subject held a discussion concerning the subject's appearance on a television program by the United States Information Agency (USIA) in Washington, DC on August 28, 1963. JONES informed the subject that he had noted that the subject's remarks regarding the FBI and J. EDGAR HOOVER were not contained in the transcript of the program which had been furnished him by USIA. BALDWIN stated that he had witnesses to the statements he made on this program and recalled that the substance of his remarks regarding the FBI was "part of the problem of the civil rights movement is J. Edgar Hoover."

JONES stated that any legitimate critical opinion of the FBI is apparently "off limits or taboo," and further stated that he intends to inform the USIA that he knows of the deltion of BALDWIN's remarks and intends to bring this information to the attention of the public and the Attorney General.

NY T-13 further stated that BALDWIN and JONES discussed BALDWIN's public statement issued at a press conference in New York City on September 18, 1963.

According to the "New York Herald Tribune," September 18, 1963, BALDWIN is quoted as bitterly criticizing the KENNEDY Administration and the FBI for their lack of action," following the Birmingham bombing September 15, 1963. "The New York Times" of September 19, 1963, additionally quotes BALDWIN as saying, "I blame J. Edgar Hoover in part for events in Alabama. Negroes have no cause to have faith in the FBI."

NY T-13 further advised that JONES informed BALDWIN that he, JONES, had received a call from an attorney "who works in an office of the Justice Department" and who reportedly informed JONES that BALDWIN's statement had caused "quite a stir" and that, "You're going to be hearing from us."

The January 21, 1963 edition of "The Militant," a weekly newspaper of the Socialist Workers Party (SWP), on page 2, column 1, carried an article which indicated that BALDWIN was opposed to the "Kennedy Administration's persecution" of ROBERT WILLIAM WORTHY. BALDWIN's protest was a result of the Federal conviction of WORTHY for illegal entry into the United States, and it was voiced on January 11, 1963, over the Barry Gray radio program, in New York City.

NY 100-146553

The article quoted BALDWIN as saying, "Worthy is a journalist whom I respect. He happens to be a colored journalist, and that certainly has something to do with his indictment. But the main point is that no government on earth has a right to tell any writer what he can and what he cannot go to see. If it happened to Bill Worthy, it can happen to me."

Because of this, BALDWIN urged listeners to the radio program to support the picket line protest against the Anti-Defamation League's Democratic Legacy Award to President KENNEDY.

The SWP has been designated pursuant to Executive Order 10450.

Concerning WILLIAM WORTHY, JR., it is noted that he was convicted in the United States District Court, Southern District of Miami, Florida on August 8, 1962, for violation of Section 1185B, Title 8, United States Code, in that he entered the United States in October, 1961, from Cuba without a valid passport.

On September 17, 1962, WORTHY was sentenced to one year in the custody of the Attorney General, 3 months committed, 9 months probation. WORTHY has appealed the conviction to the Fifth Circuit Court of Appeals, New Orleans, Louisiana.

The September 30, 1963 edition of "The Militant," page 1, column 3, contained an article which indicated that the subject and others spoke at 2 meetings held in New York City in memory of the 6 Negro children killed in Birmingham, Alabama. The meetings were held on September 20, 1963, at Town Hall, New York

CONFIDENTIAL

and on September 22, 1963, at Foley Square, New York City, in front of the United States Court House. The former meeting was sponsored by the newly formed "Artists' and Writers' Committee for Justice," and the latter meeting was sponsored by the March on Washington Committee. In his speeches at these meetings, BALDWIN called for a break by the Negroes from the Republican and Democratic parties, and suggested the possibility of a 3rd party being formed to further the "Negro revolution."

The June 3, 1963, issue of "Newsweek" magazine carried an article captioned "Kennedy and Baldwin: the Gulf," which reports on an informal discussion between Attorney General ROBERT F. KENNEDY, BURKE MARSHALL, Civil Rights Chief of the Department of Justice, JAMES BALDWIN and several of BALDWIN's acquaintances, which meeting was held at the apartment of JOSEPH P. KENNEDY in New York City.

According to the article, a 2½ hour informal discussion took place, and on one occasion a young freedom rider waggled a finger in the face of Attorney General KENNEDY and informed him he would not take up arms against Cuba.

The article further relates that BALDWIN, when interviewed, in his apartment in New York City, stated "He (Attorney General KENNEDY) was surprised to hear there were Negroes who wouldn't fight for their country." BALDWIN continued, "How many Negroes would fight to free Cuba when they can't be freed themselves?"

At the above meeting, which was held on May 24, 1963, BALDWIN reportedly told the Attorney General that he would not think of fighting for the United States if the United States got into a war and that he was thinking of getting guns and starting to shoot white people.

CONFIDENTIAL

NY 100-146553

CONFIDENTIAL

"The New York Times" issue of May 13, 1963, contained an article which stated that JAMES BALDWIN who was in Los Angeles on May 12, 1963, for integration rallies, had cabled Attorney General ROBERT KENNEDY blaming J. EDGAR HOOVER, Director of the FBI, Senator JAMES EASTLAND, Democrat of Mississippi, and President KENNEDY for the turmoil in Birmingham, Alabama.

"The New York Times" issue of February 4, 1962, carried an article reflecting that a pledge to defy any United States ban of shipments of medicine and food to Cuba was made on February 3, 1962, by a group of 19 United States citizens.

In a letter to President KENNEDY, the group warned that it would "feel compelled" to send food and medical supplies to Cubans if Washington, "misguidedly" banned such exports.

Among the signers of this letter was JAMES BALDWIN.

The November 6, 1963, issue of the "Washington Daily News," a daily newspaper in Washington, D. C. carried an article concerning a civil rights conference held at Howard University, Washington, D. C., on November 5, 1963. Among those participating at this conference was JAMES BALDWIN concerning whom the article made the following statement "Mr. Baldwin dropped several veiled hints of future trouble. 'I wonder how long we can endure—stand and not fight back,' he said at one point. At another, he said he knew of 'Many...even members of my own family' who would 'think nothing of picking up arms tomorrow'." The article also states that BALDWIN advocates the use of the general strike as a means to achieve civil rights.

The "New York Herald Tribune" of September 17, 1963, contains an article dealing with plans of Negro civil rights leaders to hold mass meetings in New York to mourn the six Negro children killed in Birmingham, Alabama. The article indicates that BALDWIN bitterly criticized the Kennedy Administration and the Federal Bureau of Investigation for their alleged "lack of action" following the bombing of the church in

CONFIDENTIAL

Birmingham in which four Negro girls were killed. The article continued "He (Baldwin) said the mass meetings Sunday would serve 'as a warning, but not a threat, that Negroes in America, since the Birmingham atrocities, are dangerously on the edge of violence, violence that could erupt in Birmingham and spread across this Nation.'"

On June 20, 1963, the "Miami News," a local Miami, Florida, newspaper reported that a Negro writer who they described as "The angry young man of American literature," James Baldwin, warned that there are a lot of angry young people among his race and their tempers are wearing thin, and that the self-control which Negro integrationists use in their non-violence campaign for equality is reaching the breaking point. The article further reported Baldwin as stating that obstruction to the passage of President Kennedy's civil rights legislation in Congress could well be the spark to touch off widespread rioting.

The "Washington Post and Times Herald" of September 27, 1963, contained an Associated Press article date lined New York September 25th which states that Baldwin termed the appointment by President Kennedy of Kenneth C. Royall and Earl H. Blaik as peacemakers in Birmingham was "cynical." The article also quoted Baldwin as saying "We must make the establishment afraid of us."

NY 100-146553

V. MISCELLANEOUS

On June 26, 1961, NY T-10 advised that ELIJAH MUHAMMAD, National Leader of the Nation of Islam (NOI) spoke favorably of the subject and stated he admired him because there was no "Tom" in him (BALDWIN).

On July 15, 1961, NY T-10, furnished information that ELIJAH MUHAMMAD, mentioned above, wanted the subject to have dinner with him on July 16, 1961.

On June 7, 1961, NY T-11 advised that on June 2, 1961, BALDWIN spoke at a meeting at the Martinique Hotel, 32nd Street and Broadway, New York City, under the auspices of the Liberation Committee for Africa (LCA). This meeting was called "Nationalism, Colonialism and the United States One Minute to 12".

At this meeting, BALDWIN, who was identified as author of "Go Tell It On The Mountain", and who recently returned after nine years in Paris, France, stated that the world was confronted with a period of revolution and America had taken a position throughout the world against revolutions. BALDWIN stated that only through revolution will the problems of the United States be solved.

A characterization of the LCA is contained in the Appendix of this report.

The February 10, 1963 edition of "The Worker", page 12, column five, reflected that a message from the subject was read at a rally held in Carnegie Hall, New York City, on February 8, 1963. This rally was sponsored by the Student Non-Violent Coordinating Committee to

CONFIDENTIAL

honor those persons who were fighting for Negro rights in the South.

"The Worker" is an East Coast Communist newspaper.

Page two of the magazine section of "The New York Times", dated July 14, 1963, carries "An Open Letter to President John F. Kennedy" signed by 650 individuals and urging the United States to cease intervention in Viet nam. Among the signers of this letter was JAMES BALDWIN.

The August 22, 1963 issue of "The New York Times" on page 16, carried an article which reflected that in Paris, France, on August 21, 1963, JAMES BALDWIN, author, led a delegation of about 80 American writers, musicians, and artists, to the United States Embassy in order to present a scroll bearing nearly 300 signatures indicating the support of the signers of the Civil Rights March on Washington, D.C.

On August 19, 1963, NY T-7 advised that a chartered airplane, which would be flying the Hollywood celebrities to the March on Washington, Washington, D.C., was scheduled to arrive at National Airport, Washington, D.C. at 9:00 a.m. on August 28, 1963. According to the source, JAMES BALDWIN, author, and BURT LANCASTER, actor, were planning to come in from Paris and would attempt to join the above-mentioned California group in Washington, D.C.

On September 24, 1963, NY T-12 advised that the subject was one of the speakers at a demonstration

CONFIDENTIAL

held at Foley Square, New York City, in connection with a National Day of Mourning for the Children of Birmingham. There were approximately 10,000 people present, and they heard BALDWIN call for more action by the Federal Government in the field of civil rights and more protection for the Negro people.

On December 10, 1962, [redacted], New York City Police Department, advised that his records indicate BALDWIN was a member of the Americans for Right to Travel Committee (ARTC).

b7C-7

A characterization of the ARTC is contained in the Appendix of this report.

[redacted] further advised that the subject's name had appeared on an appeal published by the National Committee for a Sane Nuclear Policy, 17 East 45th Street, New York City, which appeal demanded a cessation of nuclear tests.

Confidential sources familiar with various phases of CP activity in the New York area were unable to furnish any additional information concerning the subject.

Confidential sources familiar with NOI activity in the New York area were unable to furnish any information concerning the subject.

VI. DESCRIPTION

The following is a physical description of the subject, as furnished by NY T-14 and records of Credit Bureau of Greater New York:

CONFIDENTIAL

Name	JAMES ARTHUR BALDWIN
Race	Negro
Sex	Male
Date of Birth	August 2, 1924
Place of Birth	New York, New York
Age	39
Height	Five feet, six inches
Weight	130
Eyes	Brown
Hair	Black
Complexion	Dark
Marital Status	Single
Occupation	Writer, journalist
Residence	Apartment 6A 470 West End Avenue
Mother	BERDIS BALDWIN

APPENDIX

AMERICANS RIGHT TO TRAVEL COMMITTEE

On July 13, 1962, a confidential source, advised that he had learned that DANIEL WATTS had organized the Americans Right to Travel Committee to protest the indictment of WILLIAM WORTHY for travel between Cuba and the United States without a passport.

> WILLIAM WORTHY was indicted on April 24, 1962, for violation of State Department regulations in that he travelled from Havana, Cuba, to Miami, Florida, without a valid passport. It is noted that his passport was revoked in 1956 when WORTHY made an unauthorized trip to China. On September 17, 1962, WORTHY was convicted in United States District Court, Southern District of Florida, Miami, Florida, for violation of this regulation and sentenced to one year, three months, committed, nine months probation. On the same date, he appealed the matter to the Fifth Circuit Court of Appeals, New Orleans, which appeal is still pending.

On January 4, 1963, the above source advised he had recently learned [redacted] that the Americans Right to Travel Committee was either out of existence or dormant. b7C-4 b7D-3

CONFIDENTIAL

NY-100-T4655

1. APPENDIX

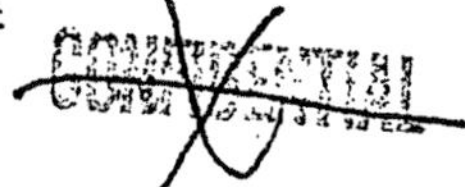

COMMITTEE TO SECURE JUSTICE FOR MORTON SOBELL

"Following the execution of atomic spies ETHEL and JULIUS ROSENBERG in June, 1953, the 'Communist campaign assumed a different emphasis. Its major effort centered upon MORTON SOBELL, 'the ROSENBERGS' codefendant. The National Committee to Secure Justice in the Rosenberg Case - a Communist front which had been conducting the campaign in the United States - was reconstituted as the National Rosenberg-Sobell Committee at a conference in Chicago in October, 1953, and 'then as the National Committee to Secure Justice for Morton Sobell in the Rosenberg Case'. . . ."

("Guide to Subversive Organizations and Publications" dated December 1, 1961, issued by the House Committee on Un-American Activities, page 116.)

In September, 1954, the name "National Committee to Secure Justice for Morton Sobell" appeared on literature issued by the Committee. In March, 1955, the current name, "Committee to Secure Justice for Morton Sobell," first appeared on literature issued by the Committee.

The Address Telephone Directory for the Borough of Manhattan, New York City, as published by the New York Telephone Company, on April 16, 1963, lists the "Committee to Secure Justice for Morton Sobell" (CSJMS) as being located at 940 Broadway, New York, New York.

NY-100-14655

1. APPENDIX

EMERGENCY CIVIL LIBERTIES COMMITTEE

The "Guide to Subversive Organizations and Publications," revised and published as of December 1, 1961, prepared and released by the Committee on Un-American Activities, United States House of Representatives, Washington, D.C., contains the following concerning the Emergency Civil Liberties Committee:

"Emergency Civil Liberties Committee

"1. 'The Emergency Civil Liberties Committee is an organization with headquarters in New York, whose avowed purpose is to abolish the House Committee on Un-American Activities and discredit the FBI. * * * The committee finds that the Emergency Civil Liberties Committee, established in 1951, although representing itself as a non-Communist group, actually operates as a front for the Communist Party. It has repeatedly assisted, by means of funds and legal aid, Communists involved in Smith Act violations and similar legal proceedings. One of its chief activities has been and still is the dissemination of voluminous Communist propaganda material.'

'FRANK WILKINSON was called as a witness when he appeared in Atlanta as a representative of the Emergency Civil Liberties Committee to propagandize against the Committee on Un-American Activities and to protest its hearings. In 1956 WILKINSON was identified as a Communist Party member by a former FBI undercover agent within the party. Summoned at that time to answer the allegation, his reply to all questions was, "I am answering no questions of this committee." This also became his stock reply to questions when he appeared during the Atlanta hearings. * * * WILKINSON has since been convicted of contempt of Congress and sentenced to one year in jail.'

NY-100-14655 3

2. APPENDIX

CONFIDENTIAL

EMERGENCY CIVIL LIBERTIES COMMITTEE (CONT'D)

'Disputing the non-Communist claim of the organization, the committee finds that a number of other individuals connected with the ECLC also have been identified under oath as Communists. * * *'
(Committee on Un-American Activities, Annual Report for 1958, House Report 187, March 9, 1959, pp. 34 and 35.)

'To defend the cases of Communist law-breakers, fronts have been devised making special appeals in behalf of civil liberties and reaching out far beyond the confines of the Communist Party itself. Among these organizations are the * * * Emergency Civil Liberties Committee. When the Communist Party itself is under fire these fronts offer a bulwark of protection.'
(Internal Security Subcommittee of the Senate Judiciary Committee, Handbook for Americans, S. Doc. 117, April 23, 1956, p. 91.)"

NY 100-14655 8

1. APPENDIX

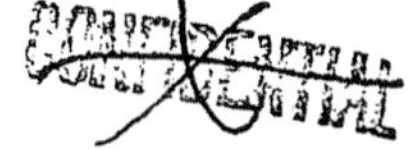

FAIR PLAY FOR CUBA COMMITTEE

The April 6, 1960, edition of "The New York Times" newspaper contained a full-page advertisement captioned "What Is Really Happening In Cuba," placed by the Fair Play for Cuba Committee (FPCC). This advertisement announced the formation of the FPCC in New York City and declared the FPCC intended to promulgate "the truth about revolutionary Cuba" to neutralize the distorted American press.

"The New York Times" edition of January 11, 1961, reported that at a hearing conducted before the United States Senate Internal Security Subcommittee on January 10, 1961, Dr. CHARLES A. SANTOS-BUCH identified himself and ROBERT TABER as organizers of the FPCC. He also testified he and TABER obtained funds from the Cuban Government which were applied toward the cost of the afore-mentioned advertisement.

On May 16, 1963, a source advised that during the first two years of the FPCC's existence there was a struggle between Communist Party (CP) and Socialist Workers Party (SWP) elements to exert their power within the FPCC and thereby influence FPCC policy. However, during the past year this source observed there has been a successful effort by FPCC leadership to minimize the role of these and other organizations in the FPCC so that today their influence is negligible.

On May 20, 1963, a second source advised that the National Headquarters of the FPCC is located in Room 329 at 799 Braodway, New York City. According to this source, the position of National Office Director was created in the Fall of 1962 and was filled by VINCENT "TED" LEE, who now formulates FPCC policy. This source observed LEE has followed a course of entertaining and accepting the cooperation of many other organizations including the CP and the SWP when he has felt it would be to his personal benefit as well as the FPCC's. However, LEE has indicated to this source he has no intention of permitting FPCC policy to be determined by any other organization. LEE feels the FPCC should advocate resumption of diplomatic relations between Cuba and the United States and support the right of Cubans to manage their revolution without interference from other nations, but not support the Cuban revolution per se.

The CP and the SWP have been designated pursuant to Executive Order 10450.

88

1. APPENDIX

FREEDOMWAYS ASSOCIATES, INC. CONFIDENTIAL

The records of the New York Secretary of State, Albany, New York, show that the certificate of incorporation of Freedomways Associates, Incorporated, was filed on March 2, 1961.

The Spring, 1963, issue of "Freedomways" is self-described as "A Quarterly Review of the Negro Freedom Movement" published by Freedomways Associates, Incorporated, 799 Broadway, New York City.

On May 24, 1961, a source advised that a report was given on "Freedomways" at a meeting of the National Board, Communist Party, USA (CPUSA), held on May 24, 1961. It was stated that the original plan called for the publication to be openly Marxist, but that it was later decided it would not be avowedly a Marxist publication. Editorials are in the hands of a mixed group of Marxists and non-Marxists. It was stated that the central purpose of "Freedomways" is to develop a theory and positive criticism of currents in the Negro movement, as well as to raise the level of understanding and discussion taking place in Negro life today and to project a socialist and pro-Soviet orientation.

On May 25, 1961, another source advised that "Freedomways" was set up for the CPUSA by James Jackson, a member of the National Committee of the CPUSA.

APPENDIX

1. LIBERATION COMMITTEE FOR AFRICA

DANIEL H. WATTS is Chairman of the Liberation Committee for Africa, an organization which has been described in newspaper articles as being nationwide with the aim of helping "African freedom fighters" and promoting awareness of a common heritage for Afro-Americans and Africans.

A source who has furnished reliable information in the past, advised in March, 1961, that WATTS was the guest speaker at a Philadelphia branch of the Socialist Workers Party (SWP) Public Forum held on March 4, 1961, in Philadelphia, Pennsylvania.

NY-100-14655

1. APPENDIX 

NATION OF ISLAM

In January, 1957, a source advised ELIJAH MUHAMMAD has described his organization on a nationwide basis as the "Nation of Islam" and "Muhammad's Temples of Islam".

On July 10, 1963, a second source advised ELIJAH MUHAMMAD is the national leader of the Nation of Islam (NOI); Muhammad's Temple of Islam No. 2, 5335 South Greenwood Avenue, Chicago, Illinois, is the national headquarters of the NOI; and in mid-1960, MUHAMMAD and other NOI officials, when referring to MUHAMMAD's organization on a nationwide basis, commenced using either "Mosque" or "Temple" when mentioning one of "Muhammad's Temples of Islam".

The NOI is an all-Negro organization which was originally organized in 1930 in Detroit, Michigan. MUHAMMAD claims to have been selected by Allah, the Supreme Being, to lead the so-called Negro race out of slavery in the wilderness of North America by establishing an independent black nation in the United States. Members following MUHAMMAD's teachings and his interpretation of the "Koran" believe there is no such thing as a Negro; that the so-called Negroes are slaves of the white race, referred to as "white devils", in the United States; and that the white race, because of its exploitation of the so-called Negroes, must and will be destroyed in the approaching "War of Armageddon".

In the past, officials and members of the NOI, including MUHAMMAD, have refused to register under the provisions of the Selective Service Acts and have declared that members owe no allegiance to the United States.

CONFIDENTIAL

2. APPENDIX

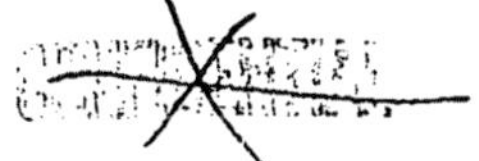

NATION OF ISLAM

On May 5, 1958, the first source advised MUHAMMAD had, upon advice of legal counsel, tempered his personal statements and instructions to his ministers concerning the principles of his organization in order to avoid possible prosecution by the United States Government; however, he did not indicate any fundamental changes in the teachings of his organization.

On July 10, 1963, a third source advised MUHAMMAD had early in July, 1958, decided to de-emphasize the religious aspects of the teachings of Islam and to stress the economic benefits to be derived by those Negroes who joined the NOI. This policy change, according to MUHAMMAD, would help him acquire additional followers and create more interest in his programs.

1.

APPENDIX

CONFIDENTIAL

"NATIONAL GUARDIAN"

The "Guide to Subversive Organizations and Publications," revised and published as of December 1, 1961, prepared and released by the Committee on Un-American Activities, United States House of Representatives, Washington, D.C., contains the following concerning the "National Guardian":

"National Guardian

"1. 'established by the American Labor Party in 1947 as a "progressive" weekly * * *. Although it denies having any affiliation with the Communist Party, it has manifested itself from the beginning as a virtual official propaganda arm of Soviet Russia.' (Committee on Un-American Activities, Report, Trial by Treason: The National Committee to Secure Justice for the ROSENBERGS and MORTON SOBELL, August 25, 1956, p. 12.)"

CONFIDENTIAL

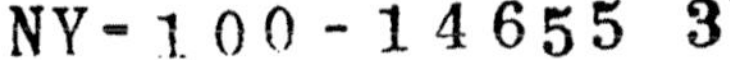

NY-100-14655 3

1. APPENDIX

CONFIDENTIAL

NATIONAL LAWYERS GUILD

The "Guide to Subversive Organizations and Publications," revised and published as of December 1, 1961, prepared and released by the Committee on Un-American Activities, United States House of Representatives, Washington, D.C., contains the following concerning the National Lawyers Guild:

"National Lawyers Guild

"1. Cited as a Communist front. (Special Committee on Un-American Activities, House Report 1311 on the CIO Political Action Committee, March 29, 1944, p. 149.)

"2. Cited as a Communist front which 'is the foremost legal bulwark of the Communist Party, its front organizations, and controlled unions' and which 'since its inception has never failed to rally to the legal defense of the Communist Party and individual members thereof, including known espionage agents.' (Committee on Un-American Activities, House Report 3123 on the National Lawyers Guild, September 21, 1950, originally related September 17, 1950.)

"3. 'To defend the cases of Communist lawbreakers, fronts have been devised making special appeals in behalf of civil liberties and reaching out far beyond the confines of the Communist Party itself. Among these organizations are the * * * National Lawyers Guild. When the Communist Party itself is under fire these offer a bulwark of protection.' (Internal Security Subcommittee of the Senate Judiciary Committee, Handbook for Americans, S. Doc. 117, April 23, 1956, p. 91.)"

CONFIDENTIAL

1. APPENDIX

NEW YORK COUNCIL TO ABOLISH THE HOUSE UN-AMERICAN ACTIVITIES COMMITTEE

On March 9, 1961, a source advised that the New York Council To Abolish the Un-American Activities Committee (NYCAUAC), 150 West 34th Street, New York City, New York, was formed at a meeting held in New York City on November 17, 1960. This organization was founded principally through the efforts of FRANK WILKINSON, Field Representative of the National Committee To Abolish the Un-American Activities Committee (NCAUAC).

A second source advised on September 17, 1952, that FRANK WILKINSON was a Communist Party member as of September, 1952.

A third source furnished on September 14, 1961, a copy of resolutions of the New York Council to Abolish the House Un-American Activities Committee (NYCAHUAC) which were adopted by the NYCAHUAC. One such resolution affirmed the intention to continue to work for the abolition of the House Committee on Un-American Activities (HCUA) and to continue its efforts to broaden the participation in this fight. Another resolution accepted as a modus vivendi the suggestion of the Field Representative of the "National Committee to Abolish the HCUA" (NCAHUAC) namely that local abolition committees may identify and co-ordinate their efforts as closely as they desire with NCAHUAC, still maintaining their autonomy for as flexible and independent a program as possible.

Various sources have advised during March, 1962, that Communist Party (CP) members in the New York City area have been solicited to support activities of the NYCAHUAC during attendance at CP club meetings.

On May 6, 1963, the first source advised that the NYCAHUAC continues to function from its office at 150 West 34th Street, New York City, New York.

APPENDIX

1.
SOUTHERN CONFERENCE EDUCATIONAL FUND, INC.

"The Southern Patriot," a monthly publication, shows that it is published by the Southern Conference Educational Fund, Inc., (SCEF).

"The Southern Patriot" was cited as an "organ" of the Southern Conference for Human Welfare (SCHW) by the Committee on Un-American Activities, House Report 592, on the SCHW, June 12, 1947.

The SCHW was cited as a communist front by the Committee on Un-American Activities, House Report 592, June 16, 1947.

An Amendment to the charter of the SCHW changed the name of that organization to the SCEF and listed its purpose as being to improve the educational and cultural standards of the Southern people in accordance with the highest American democratic institutions, traditions, and ideals. The amendment was dated April 26, 1946.

A source, who is familiar with some phases of Communist Party (CP) activity in the New Orleans area, advised on May 25, 1962, that during the time the SCHW was in existence, CP members were members of and worked actively in the SCHW. However, since the formation of the SCEF, rank and file CP members have not been encouraged to work in the SCEF. The source stated that the SCEF is a progressive, liberal organization, which he considers a CP front organization because it has gone along with the CP on certain issues, particularly on the racial question, and through the years certain CP members in the New Orleans area have been assigned to work in the organization to further CP principles.

NY 100-146553

2.

On May 25, 1962, the source advised that in the past he has considered JAMES DOMBROWSKI, the Executive Director of the SCEF, to be a communist, if not an actual CP member, because he followed communist principles.

The source also advised on May 25, 1962, that many people who are officials and members of the SCEF, while liberal in their views, are by no means communists.

Another source advised on March 2, 1961, that CLAUDE LIGHTFOOT, a CP functionary, stated at a meeting of the CP in Baltimore, Maryland, on February 25, 1961, that the CP is not connected with any progressive movement but indirectly they do have some influence in the SCEF.

1. APPENDIX

"WORKERS WORLD"

CONFIDENTIAL

On May 6, 1963, a confidential source advised that the "Workers World" is the official newspaper of the Workers World Party, published twice monthly, with editorial offices located at 46 West 21st Street, New York, New York.

CONFIDENTIAL

NY 100-14655 3

1. APPENDIX CONFIDENTIAL

WORKERS WORLD PARTY

On April 17, 1959, a confidential source advised that on February 12, 1959, a Socialist Workers Party (SWP) minority group, under the leadership of National Committee member, SAM BALLAN, split from the SWP.

The source stated that this minority group, referred to as the Marcyites, after many years of program and policy differences on varied issues concerning tactics and interpretation of political events, split from the SWP on the grounds that the Party was liquidating itself by departing from the Marxist precepts of LEON TROTSKY and retreating from the fight for the world socialist revolution. The final issue which ultimately forced the split was the minority's opposition to the SWP regroupment policy which involved cooperation with the Communist Party (CP) periphery - individuals characterized by the minority as petty - bourgeois.

The minority program, according to the source, advocates unconditional defense of the Soviet Union and has as its goal the building of a revolutionary party with a complete proletarian orientation for the purpose of overthrowing capitalism in the United States and throughout the world.

On May 12, 1960, the source advised that this minority group had chosen the name Workers World Party.

On May 6, 1963, a second confidential source stated that the headquarters of the Workers World Party were located at 46 West 21st Street, New York, New York.

The SWP and the CP have been designated pursuant to Executive Order 10450.

CONFIDENTIAL

21.

"A DANGEROUS INDIVIDUAL WHO COULD BE EXPECTED TO COMMIT ACTS INIMICAL TO THE NATIONAL DEFENSE"

DECEMBER 1963

Hoover's office welcomed with grasping arms the concise political biography of Baldwin prepared by the New York field office. As the FBI director saw it, this biography together with "the material in Bureau files" already held in Washington confirmed that the author was "a dangerous individual who could be expected to commit acts inimical to the national defense and public safety of the United States in time of an emergency." At the height of his fame and influence as an author and pundit, not a year after the publication of *The Fire Next Time*, Baldwin was branded a likely traitor and potential terrorist by his country's national police force. The more Baldwin spoke out against FBI failings, the more dangerous he was judged and the more starkly this tension was set: one of America's greatest living writers was also one of America's most wanted.

OPTIONAL FORM NO. 10
MAY 1962 EDITION
GSA GEN. REG. NO. 27

5010-106

UNITED STATES GOVERNMENT

Memorandum

TO : SAC, New York (100-146553)

DATE: December 18, 1963

FROM : Director, FBI (62-108763)

ALL INFORMATION CONTAINED HEREIN IS UNCLASSIFIED DATE 5-17-89 BY [illegible]

SUBJECT: JAMES ARTHUR BALDWIN
SECURITY MATTER - C

Rerep SA [redacted] dated 12/11/63 at New York and your FD-122a of same date.

A review of the material in Bureau files concerning captioned subject as well as the information contained in the summary report of SA [redacted] clearly depicts subject as a dangerous individual who could be expected to commit acts inimical to the national defense and public safety of the United States in time of an emergency. Consequently, his name is being included in the Security Index and Security Index cards will be forwarded to your office.

b7C-1

Transmitted herewith are copies of pages 18 and 19 and copies of new page 19a which should be included in SA [redacted] report. The material which has been added consists of statements made by Baldwin indicative of his dangerousness. It is possible that other statements made by him of a like nature have been published and you should thoroughly review the files of your office for any additional information of this nature.

The attention of the Washington Field Office is directed to Washington Field Office airtel dated 6/12/61 captioned "CORE, Racial Matters, Free Bus Racial Matters," Washington Field file 100-35588, and to Washington Field Office airtels dated 3/23/61 and 4/4/61 captioned "Witness for Peace, IS-C," and "Witness for Peace, Information Concerning-Security Matter," respectively, Washington Field file 100-38632. These files contain information concerning public appearances made by Baldwin in the Washington, D. C., area and statements attributed to him. Washington Field should review this material thoroughly for any information regarding inflammatory statements or statements made by Baldwin of a violent nature.

Enclosures - 9

2 - Washington Field (Enclosures-6)

100-146553-77

SEARCHED ____ INDEXED ____
SERIALIZED ____ FILED ____
DEC 1963
FBI - NEW YORK

Letter to New York
RE: JAMES ARTHUR BALDWIN
62-108763

Nrto

A review of Bureau files also indicates that New York Division is in possession of additional information concerning Baldwin which should be incorporated in a report. New York teletype dated November 29, 1963, captioned "CPUSA, Negro Question, Communist Influence in Racial Matters, IS - C," contained information indicating Baldwin was to fly to Washington, D. C., on November 29, 1963, to appear at a conference to be held at Howard University under the sponsorship of the Student Non-Violent Coordinating Committee. It should be ascertained whether Baldwin did, in fact, appear at this conference and whether any statements were made by him at the conference of an inflammatory nature. New York report dated November 16, 1961, captioned "Monroe Defense Committee, IS - Miscellaneous," New York file 100-146353, contains information regarding Baldwin's sponsorship of the Monroe Defense Committee which should be incorporated in a report. New York airtel dated January 29, 1963, captioned [redacted] IS - Cuba," New York file 10[redacted] contains information concerning Baldwin's participation in picketing in protest against the Anti-Defamation League's "Democratic Legacy Award" to President Kennedy. This information should also be included in a report.

b7C-3

22.

"HELLO, BABY, HOW ARE YOU?"— FBI SEXUAL LINGUISTICS

JANUARY 1964

The FBI's 1964 additions to its Baldwin file begin with a small batch of documents linking the writer to Hunter Pitts O'Dell. O'Dell, known as Jack to his friends, was a skilled executive assistant to Martin Luther King. His unapologetic involvement with the Communist Party, discovered by Hoover and protested by the Kennedy administration, forced his resignation from a Southern Christian Leadership Conference (SCLC) post in July 1963. In the January 1964 document reproduced here, Baldwin's slang and dinner plans are treated as just as relevant, and almost as worrisome, as O'Dell's politics. Reporting on the results of another phone tap, the New York field office "noted that in greeting O'Dell Baldwin stated 'Hello, baby, how are you' and in closing the conversation stated that 'It's good to hear from you, baby.' It also is noted that Baldwin mentioned that he was having dinner the following evening at [name redacted's] house." Both the "baby" and the dinner companion—a "degenerate" friend shared with Bayard Rustin—were flagged by the Bureau as signs of Baldwin's homosexuality. As we've seen, Baldwin's fondness for the hip endearment of "baby" in truth respected few sexual or racial barriers. (Practically quoting from the O'Dell transcripts, Baldwin's black bisexual character Rufus greets his too-platonic white friend Vivaldo this way in *Another Country:* "Hello, baby. How're you?") Like the many "brothers" and "sisters" of Cornel West, a later, similarly talkative black radical, Baldwin's "babies" were widely distributed and could be ironic as well as intimate. The imprecision of the linguistic gaydar on display in this document is par for the Bureau's course, further testimony to the corners cut and the reputations smeared when the FBI cemented queerness to "Communist Influence in Racial Matters."

CONFIDENTIAL

1/3/63

PLAIN TEXT

DECLASSIFIED BY [illegible] ON 3/9/99
CA97-5269

AIRTEL

ALL INFORMATION CONTAINED HEREIN IS UNCLASSIFIED EXCEPT WHERE SHOWN OTHERWISE

TO: DIRECTOR, FBI (100-38116)
(100-358916)

FROM: SAC, NEW YORK (100-151548)
(100-91330)

Classified by [illegible]
Declassify on: OADR 2-20-90

SUBJECT: CP, USA - NEGRO QUESTION
COMMUNIST INFLUENCE IN RACIAL MATTERS
IS - C
(OO:NY)

HUNTER PITTS O'DELL
IS - C
(OO:NY)

Classified by [illegible]
Declassify on: OADR 5-23-89

There are enclosed for the Bureau six copies of a letterhead memorandum containing information from [redacted] concerning a contact between HUNTER PITTS O'DELL and JAMES BALDWIN. It is noted that in greeting O'DELL, BALDWIN stated "Hello, baby, how are you" and in closing the conversation stated that "It's good to hear from you, baby". It also is noted that BALDWIN mentioned that he was having dinner the following evening at [redacted] (ph) house. This is being set forth because it is noted that in the obscene log sent to the Bureau relating to BAYARD RUSTIN, RUSTIN was in telephonic conversation with another degenerate named [redacted] LNU). There is no record in the NY indices for [redacted]

b2-1 b7C-4

Chief Clerk
Post

4 - Bureau (Encls.6) (RM)
(1 - 100-358916)
3 - Atlanta (100-6078) (RM)
(1 - 100-6078) (HUNTER PITTS O'DELL)
(1 - 100-5718) (SCLC)
1 - New York (100-146553) (JAMES BALDWIN) (#412)
1 - New York (#414)
1 - New York (#414)

100-146553-84

SEARCHED ... INDEXED ...
SERIALIZED ... FILED ...
NEW YORK

JFO:fjp
(11)

1 - Supervisor (#414)

CONFIDENTIAL

Classified by
Declassify on: OADR

b7C-1

CONFIDENTIAL

NY 100-151548
NY 100-91330

U(X)[NY 694-S*] The source used to characterize O'DELL is and the sources used to characterize Freedomways Associates, Inc. are [redacted] and NY 694-S*.](X)U b2-1

This letterhead memorandum is being classified "Secret" because it contains information from a highly sensitive source concerning [O'DELL's association with](X)U JAMES BALDWIN the well known Negro author.](X)

CONFIDENTIAL

23.

BALDWIN MEETS A DEADLINE

JANUARY 1964

Another discovery of the Bureau's wiretap of Jack O'Dell was the likely completion date of Baldwin's play *Blues for Mister Charlie*, his second work of drama and the first based on the lynching of young Emmett Till in Money, Mississippi. "A confidential source," more machine than human, let the FBI know that "O'Dell was in contact with James Baldwin" on January 2, 1964, and that both men had confessed to literary busyness: O'Dell with *Freedomways* magazine, the quarterly founded by W. E. B. Du Bois where he had begun working as a managing editor, and Baldwin with an unnamed play set for submission on January 3rd (the play's identity as *Blues for Mister Charlie* is clear from the timing and context). Agents in the New York field office were most concerned to document Baldwin's growing closeness with O'Dell, and thus his supposed closeness with Communism. Their hostile surveillance again produced a useful tidbit of literary history, the kind of nuts-and-bolts evidence drawn on in author timelines and biographies.

UNITED STATES DEPARTMENT OF JUSTICE

FEDERAL BUREAU OF INVESTIGATION

In Reply, Please Refer to
File No.

Bureau file
(100-3-116)
(100-358916)

New York, New York
January 3, 1964 CONFIDENTIAL

Communist Party, United States of America - Negro Question
Communist Influence in Racial Matters
Internal Security - C

Hunter Pitts O'Dell
Internal Security - C

A confidential source advised on January 2, 1964, that on that date O'Dell was in contact with James Baldwin. O'Dell stated that he has been very busy working on the All-Southern issue of "Freedomways" magazine and asked Baldwin about an unnamed play. Baldwin stated that he was turning in the play the next day, that it is opening in Washington, D.C., and that he wanted to get together with O'Dell. O'Dell commented that he wanted to see Baldwin and they agreed to meet at Baldwin's apartment the evening of January 3, 1964.

A second confidential source has advised that as of July, 1962, O'Dell was considered by the Communist Party (CP), United States of America as being a member of its National Committee.

James Baldwin is a well known Negro author.

A characterization of Freedomway Associates, Incorporated, publishers of the magazine "Freedomways", is set forth in the attached appendix page.

This document contains neither recommendations nor conclusions of the Federal Bureau of Investigation (FBI). It is the property of the FBI and is loaned to your agency; it and its contents are not to be distributed outside your agency.

Classified by
Declassify on: OADR

DECLASSIFIED BY AUC39677 SAH
ON 3/9/99
CA97-5269

CONFIDENTIAL

83

24.

BALDWIN SPEAKS—AFTER "ROBERT DILLON [THE] BEATNIK TYPE ENTERTAINER"

JANUARY 1964

Few of Baldwin's scheduled talks of the 1960s failed to attract the odd company of FBI agents or informers. But stranger company was sometimes provided by Baldwin's fellow speakers. In early 1964, the Bureau took notice of Baldwin's appearance at a December 1963 dinner of the Emergency Civil Liberties Committee (ECLC). At this fundraiser drawing over a thousand people to a New York hotel ballroom, Baldwin spoke on behalf of the leading radical alternative to the American Civil Liberties Union (ACLU). In distinction to the Cold War ACLU, the ECLC jumped to defend the free speech of Communists thought to advocate the overthrow of the US government. Two spies planted in the audience reported to the FBI about the night of speeches and donations. Both displayed imperfect understanding of Baldwin (the "author of [a] book") and the nature of the racism he protested ("[h]e spoke of the prejudice against Negroes in the civil rights movement"). One reason for their inaccuracy may have been the greater interest stirred by Bob Dylan, misidentified as "Bobby" or "Robert Dillon," and similarly mischaracterized as "a young beatnik type entertainer." Unlike Baldwin's closing address, the musician's typically shambling provocation was "rather one of free association."

Dylan's stoned-sounding confession that he saw "a lot of [himself]" in Lee Harvey Oswald, the man who murdered President John F. Kennedy a few weeks before, earned him boos at the scene and referral to an FBI case file on the Kennedy assassination.

SAC, CLEVELAND 1/3/64

SAC, NEW YORK (100-107419)

EMERGENCY CIVIL LIBERTIES COMMITTEE
IS-C
(OO:NY)

Identity of Source b7C-5 b7D-3 [redacted] (PS)who furnished reliable inf

Description of info ECLC Annual Bill of Rights Dinner

Date Received 12/16/63

Original where located b2-1 b7D-1 [redacted]

A copy of informant's report follows:

ALL INFORMATION CONTAINED
HEREIN IS UNCLASSIFIED
DATE 5/24/89 BY [illegible]

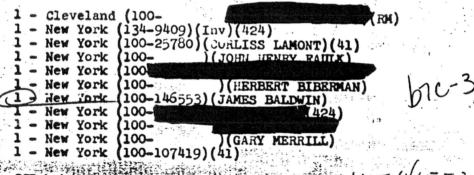

1 - Cleveland (100- [redacted] (RM)
1 - New York (134-9409)(Inv)(424)
1 - New York (100-25780)(CORLISS LAMONT)(41)
1 - New York (100-)(JOHN HENRY FAULK)
1 - New York (100 [redacted]
1 - New York (100-)(HERBERT BIBERMAN)
1 - New York (100-146553)(JAMES BALDWIN)
1 - New York (100- [redacted] (424)
1 - New York (100- [redacted]
1 - New York (100-)(GARY MERRILL)
1 - New York (100-107419)(41)

b7C-3

JJP:kmk
(11)

100-146553-85

SEARCHED ...... INDEXED
SERIALIZED ...... FILED
JAN 3 [illegible]

b7C-1

12/16/63

On 12/13/63 the Annual Bill of Rights Dinner sponsored by the Emergency Civil Liberties Committee was held in the Imperial Ballroom at the Americana Hotel, 52nd St. and 6th Ave., NYC.

CORLISS LAMONT was the master of ceremonies and he introduced JOHN HENRY FAULK as the 1st speaker.

FAULK's talk covered Civil Rights and he satirized the right wing conservative element and particularly Southerners. FAULK introduced the next speaker, Mrs. CYRUS EATON.

Mrs. EATON criticized the role American women are forced to play in that they are told what to do by the mass media of advertising. She called the American press "garbage". Mrs. EATON defended the right of the group of students to visit Cuba. She also stated that we have an idiotic foreign policy and that the CIA is a giant colossus with its foot in everyone's mouth. Mrs. EATON said the FBI is hypnotized by the Communist Party to the point that it does not see the vast network of crime in the United States right under its nose.

CORLISS LAMONT then presented the Thomas Paine award to ROBERT DILLON (ph) a young beatnik type entertainer. LAMONT said DILLON earned the award for his work and efforts on behalf of Civil Rights. DILLON is described as a white, male, 20-25 years, 5'9", 150 lbs., slender build, dark hair and medium complexion.

In his talk, DILLON said that the older people should move aside for the younger elements to push for civil rights. He said he agreed in part with LEE OSWALD and that he thought he understood him, although he would not have gone that far. DILLON was booed for his remarks concerning OSWALD and his talk was generally not well received. It appeared that LAMONT attempted to stop DILLON's remarks concerning OSWALD by tugging at his coat.

The fund raising was conducted by FNU BIBERMAN (ph) who asked for pledges and donations. No total figure on donation was announced but it is estimated that over $15,000.00 was donated.

The final talk was given by JAMES BALDWIN, the Negro author. He spoke of the prejudice against Negroes in the civil rights movements. He also said that J. EDGAR HOOVER had warned the Negroes against allowing Communists to get into the civil rights movement. BALDWIN said he could not see why they would want to get into the movement anyway. He also spoke of the non violent approach and said the Negroes were getting impatient using these tactics.

It was announced that 1200 people were in attendance at the dinner which started at 7 PM and ended about 11 PM.

Among those at the speakers table who were introduced were MOE FISHMAN of the Veterans of the Abraham Lincoln Brigade and BOB THOMPSON who was introduced as a World War II hero who was not receiving his disability from the government because of membership in the Communist Party.

An unknown female at the dinner was overheard to remark that GARY MERRILL the actor was in attendance at the dinner.

UNITED STATES GOVERNMENT

MEMORANDUM

TO : SAC, NEW YORK (100-107419) b7c-1 DATE: 1/6/64

FROM : SA [redacted] (41)

SUBJECT: EMERGENCY CIVIL LIBERTIES COMMITTEE
IS - C

b2-1
b7D-1

Identity of source: [redacted] who has furnished reliable info in the past (conceal)

Description of info: Info regarding Civil Rights Dinner held 12/13/63 at Hotel Americana NYC

Date received: 12/19/63

Received by: SA [redacted] b7C-1
(written)

Original location: NY [redacted] b2-1
b7D-1

b2-1 b7D-1 A copy of informant's written report follows:

1 - NY [redacted] (INV)(41)
1 - NY 100[redacted](22)
1 - NY 100-[redacted](412)
1 - NY 100- (JOHN HENRY FALK)(412) b7C-3
1 - NY 100-[redacted](412)
1 - NY 100- (JAMES BALDWIN)(412)
1 - NY 100[redacted]24)
1 - NY 100-[redacted](412)
1 - NY 105-38431 (ASSASSINATION OF PRES. JOHN F. KENNEDY)(22)
1 - NY 100-107419 (41)

100-146553-86

Searched Indexed
Serialized Filed
JAN 6 1964
FBI-New York
b7C-1

JPH:rvs
(10)

ALL INFORMATION CONTAINED
HEREIN IS UNCLASSIFIED
DATE 5/24/89 BY 2088 BJJ/ag

NY 100-107419

The following is an account of the Civil Liberty Committee meeting & dinner Dec. 13, 1963 at the Empire Room of Hotel Americana, N.Y.C. 8:30-12 (?)

This meeting consisted of a dinner with speakers seated at a table for (20) twenty people. The hall was filled to capasity. Admission was $15 per person.

Dr. & Mrs. AVIR KAGAN were seen amongst the audience and PEARL GER & TIBBY BROOKS were also said to have attended.

Speakers were as follows:

JOHN HENRY FALK (?) - appeared to be chairman or moderator for the evening.

Mrs. ANN EATON - spoke very ardently against U.S. newspapers. She repeadetly referred to them as "garbage". She said that there was nothing worse than a misinformed public - that newspapers lied.

JAMES BALDWIN - Introduced as author of book spoke about lack of equality for the negro in U.S. that he would sooner go to Cuba on his vacation with his family than Florida because in Cuba he at least was able to go to the best hdels and restaurants and that his child could go into any rest room in any gas station. (He was the last speaker.)

EDITH SEGAL - She recited herself composed poem called a "ballad for four girls and a President" whose most repeated stanza says: "How long shall free world freedom wait."

BOBBY DYLLON - Introduced as poet and writer and composer. He was informally dressed with sports slacks & jacket without a tie. Was presented the Tom Payne award. - His speech was rather one of free association. He started saying that he accepted the award in the name of the youths that went to Cuba. (One of which took a bow.) That everyone should go to Cuba to see for themselves. Then he said that it wasn't right that there so many older people (at this dinner), that he wanted to see young people. So many "bald heads" - He said his friends didn't wear fancy suits and ties that they just wore plain slacks and shirts like himself. He said: "I see a lot of myself in Oswald, - maybe wouldn't go that far." and repeated this several times in slightly different arrangements of words. The first time he said this, the audience who had cheered him profusely when he came in now "hissed and booed" at these statements. Various people in the audience yelled - "No - no" and "sing - sing" - He explained he didn't have a guitar with him and said that what he had just said (about OSWALD) he had a right to say because the Civil Rights Bill gave Freedom of Speech.

A monetary collection was started at $10,000 and then went down to smaller figures. No donation of four (4) digits or more was heard offered or accepted. There were about 5-9 three (3) digit donations and individuals envelopes from each table. No announcement as to the full amount was heard.

25.

PUBLIC SHAMING THROUGH PUBLIC SOURCES

JANUARY 1964

Baldwin's place on the Security Index was privileged information, not to be leaked outside the FBI. Everything that the Bureau discovered about him through its careful study of newspapers and magazines, by contrast, was fair game for an open war against the "novelist and writer" now "active in the Negro civil rights movement." In this memorandum, William C. Sullivan, the FBI intelligence official who doubled as Hoover's favorite ghostwriter, is supplied with a hot list of Baldwin quotations and associations drawn from public print sources. All of the information compiled paints Baldwin as a racial troublemaker and Communist sympathizer—barely distinguishable roles when seen by Hoover's FBI. All is intended for consideration by FBI Assistant Director Cartha DeLoach, chief of the Crime Records Division, the boiler room from which the Bureau directed its publicity and disinformation campaigns. The key player at the Bureau's ministry of propaganda would now know Baldwin as a rabble-rouser of "a mobilized Negro community."

OPTIONAL FORM NO. 10 5010-106
MAY 1962 EDITION
GSA GEN. REG. NO. 27

UNITED STATES GOVERNMENT

Memorandum

Tolson
Belmont
Mohr
Casper
Callahan
Conrad
DeLoach
Evans
Gale
Rosen
Sullivan
Tavel
Trotter
Tele. Room
Holmes
Gandy

TO : Mr. W. C. Sullivan

DATE: January 15, 1964

FROM : Mr. J. F. Bland

SUBJECT: JAMES ARTHUR BALDWIN
SECURITY MATTER - C

1 - Mr. Belmont
1 - Mr. Mohr
1 - Mr. Sullivan
1 - Mr. DeLoach
1 - Mr. Bland
1 - Mr. [redacted]
1 - Mr. [redacted]
1 - Mr. [redacted]

b7C-1

The attached contains information from public sources that could possibly be utilized by Assistant Director DeLoach.

Subject's name is included in the Security Index. He has recently played an increasingly active role in the Negro civil rights movement and as an advocate of a racial policy of a mobilized Negro community he has made many inflammatory statements. He was critical of the Kennedy Administration's handling of civil rights matters, termed the appointment by Kennedy of Kenneth C. Royall and Earl H. Blaik as peacemakers in Birmingham as "cynical" and stated that obstruction of civil rights legislation in Congress could well be the spark to touch off widespread rioting.

Baldwin has also been associated with several Communist Party front organizations. In April, 1960, he was a sponsor of the Fair Play for Cuba Committee and in October, 1961, was one of the sponsors of the Monroe Defense Committee. He addressed a public meeting of the New York City Chapter of the National Lawyers Guild in October, 1963. He was a sponsor of a rally to abolish the House Un-American Activities Committee held in April, 1961, under the auspices of the New York Council to Abolish the House Un-American Activities Committee. In December, 1963, he was a speaker at a dinner held in New York City under sponsorship of Emergency Civil Liberties Committee.

RECOMMENDATION:

It is recommended that this memorandum and the attached be furnished to Mr. DeLoach for his consideration.

Enc.

ALL INFORMATION CONTAINED
HEREIN IS UNCLASSIFIED
DATE 5-17-89 BY

62-108763

ENCLOSURE

WPJ:gad
(9)

62-108763-19

10 JAN 21 1964

53 JAN 23 1964

b7C-1

1 - Mr. B[illegible]
1 - Mr. Mohr
1 - Mr. Sullivan
1 - Mr. DeLoach
1 - Mr. [redacted]
1 - Mr. [redacted]
1 - Mr. [redacted]
1 - Mr. [redacted]

January 15, 1964 b7C-1

ALL INFORMATION CONTAINED
HEREIN IS UNCLASSIFIED
DATE 5-17-89 BY [illegible]

JAMES ARTHUR BALDWIN

James Arthur Baldwin, Negro novelist and writer, has recently become active in the Negro civil rights movement. He has made public utterances advocating a racial policy of a mobilized Negro community and has made many statements of an inflammatory nature. Baldwin was born August 2, 1924, in New York City and was educated in the New York City public schools. He lived in Paris for some time but presently maintains an apartment at 470 West End Avenue, New York City.

The June 3, 1963, issue of "Newsweek" magazine carried an article captioned "Kennedy and Baldwin; the Gulf," which reports on a meeting between Baldwin and Attorney General Robert Kennedy which was held on May 24, 1963, in New York City. The article relates that Baldwin, when interviewed, stated "He (Attorney General Kennedy) was surprised to hear there were Negroes who wouldn't fight to free Cuba when they can't be freed themselves."

"The New York Times" issue of February 4, 1962, carried an article indicating that a group of 19 American citizens, including Baldwin, had pledged on February 3, 1962, to defy any United States Government ban on shipments of medicines or food to Cuba.

On June 30, 1963, the "Miami News" reported that Baldwin warned that there are a lot of angry young people among his race and their tempers are wearing thin and that the self-control which Negro integrationists use in their non-violence campaign for equality is reaching the breaking point. Baldwin further was reported as stating that obstruction to President Kennedy's civil rights legislation in Congress could well be the spark to touch off widespread rioting.

The "Washington Post and Times Herald" of September 27, 1963, contained an Associated Press article under the date line New York September 25, which states that Baldwin termed the appointment by President Kennedy of Kenneth C. Royall and Earl H. Blaik as peacemakers in Birmingham as "cynical." The article also quoted Baldwin as saying "We must make the establishment afraid of us."

Tolson
Belmont
Mohr
Casper
Callahan
Conrad
DeLoach
Evans
Gale
Rosen
Sullivan
Tavel
Trotter
Tele. Room
Holmes
Gandy

62-108763

WPJ:cad
(11)

See Note Page 3

MAIL ROOM ☐ TELETYPE UNIT ☐

James Arthur Baldwin

On November 6, 1963, the "Washington Daily News" contained an article which stated that Baldwin, at a civil rights conference held at Howard University on November 5, 1963, made several veiled hints of future trouble. He is quoted as saying "I wonder how long we can endure--stand and not fight back." He also said he knew of "Many...even members of my own family who would think nothing of picking up arms tomorrow." The article also states that Baldwin advocates the use of the general strike as a means to achieve civil rights.

The April 6, 1960, issue of "The New York Times" contained an advertisement by the Fair Play for Cuba Committee in which Baldwin was named as one of the sponsors.

The October 2, 1961, issue of the "National Guardian" carried an advertisement listing Baldwin as a sponsor of the Monroe Defense Committee; according to the advertisement this Committee was formed to tell the story of the racial violence which occurred in Monroe, North Carolina, in August, 1961.

The January 10, 1963, issue of the "National Guardian" revealed that Baldwin was among the signers of a statement urging the Anti Defamation League to withdraw its award to President Kennedy unless the Department of Justice dropped its "harassment" of William Worthy, Negro journalist who traveled to Red China and Cuba in defiance of a State Department ban.

The April 17, 1961, edition of the "National Guardian" carried an announcement of a "Rally to Abolish the House Un-American Activities Committee" to be held April 21, 1961, under the auspices of the New York Council to Abolish the House Un-American Activities Committee. Baldwin was listed as one of the sponsors of this rally.

The October 3, 1963, and October 10, 1963, editions of the "National Guardian" contained an announcement that Baldwin would be a speaker at a public meeting of the New York City Chapter of the National Lawyers Guild to be held October 18, 1963.

The November 7, 1963, edition of the "National Guardian" contained an announcement that Baldwin was to be one of the speakers at a "Bill of Rights Dinner" to be held December 13, 1963, in New York City under the sponsorship of the Emergency Civil Liberties Committee.

James Arthur Baldwin

The New York Council to Abolish the House Un-American Activities Committee was founded principally through the efforts of the Field Representative of the National Committee to Abolish the House Un-American Activities Committee, an organization cited as a communist front group by the House Committee on Un-American Activities (HCUA).

The National Lawyers Guild and the Emergency Civil Liberties Committee have been cited as communist front groups by the HCUA.

The Fair Play for Cuba Committee is a militant pro-Castro organization whose announced intention is to promulgate the truth about revolutionary Cuba.

The Monroe Defense Committee claims to have been founded on a broad nonpartisan basis to aid four individuals jailed in Monroe, North Carolina, on "trumped up kidnaping charges." Its officers included an individual described in 1958 as a member of the Communist Party and another individual who, according to a source, is a member of the Workers World Party, a splinter group of the Socialist Workers Party.

The "National Guardian" has been cited by the HCUA as a virtual official propaganda arm of Soviet Russia.

NOTE: b7C-1

See memorandum [redacted] to W. C. Sullivan captioned "James Arthur Baldwin, Security Matter-C," cated 1/15/64, WPJ:cad.

26.

THE FBI COMBS BALDWIN'S PASSPORT

FEBRUARY 1964

Baldwin first moved from New York City to the French capital in 1948 and quickly enough published "Encounter on the Seine" (1950), "Equal in Paris" (1955), and other incisive, shape-shifting essays addressing what expatriation revealed about Frenchness, blackness, and his own black Americanness. Surprisingly, it took the FBI until 1964 to catch up to the lessons of his well-used passport. In these two communications to Hoover sent from the Washington field office, the Bureau tried to make up for lost time. FBI agents searched for Baldwin's passport records at the State Department on several occasions in 1963 and 1964, the documents reveal, and hit pay dirt in February of the latter year. The information gleaned from the author's renewal forms was underwhelming, yielding nothing about his "marital status" and no identifying photograph. Details on the legal team representing his literary properties were of greater potential use, as was evidence of the timing of a never-accepted invitation to visit Castro's Cuba. Later scourings of Baldwin's passport records provided the FBI with more exploitable riches: something Baldwin intuited when he proposed in his backlash-era memoir *No Name in the Street* (1972) that the same document "that proclaimed I was a free citizen of a free country" at European borders rendered him "a domestic nigger" when interpreted in the US. In the land of the free, his passport "underwent a sea change" and came to declare that "no foreign government would be offended if my corpse were to be found clogging up the sewers."

OPTIONAL FORM NO. 10
MAY 1962 EDITION
GSA GEN. REG. NO. 27
5010-106

UNITED STATES GOVERNMENT

Memorandum

TO : DIRECTOR, FBI (62-108763) DATE: 2/4/64

FROM : SAC, WFO (100-43011) (P)

SUBJECT: JAMES ARTHUR BALDWIN
SM - C
(OO:NY)

b7C-1

Rerep [redacted] at New York 12/11/63 with lead for WFO to check passport record of subject; Bulet 12/18/63.

b7C-8

On 1/2/64 [redacted] Agency Liaison Officer, Passport Office, U. S. Department of State, advised IC [redacted] no identifiable record was located concerning subject.

b7C-1

A recheck of passport office records was requested, pointing out subject known to have resided in Paris, France.

Passport record not located as of 1/29/64.
WFO following.

2 - Bureau
2 - New York (100-146553) (RM)
1 - WFO

LEW/acp
(5)

ALL INFORMATION CONTAINED
HEREIN IS UNCLASSIFIED
DATE 5-17-89 BY [illegible]

REC-139. 62-108763-21

8 FEB 5 1964

SUBV. CONTROL

OPTIONAL FORM NO. 10
MAY 1962 EDITION
GSA GEN. REG. NO. 27

5010-106

UNITED STATES G[illegible]ERNMENT

Memorandum

TO : DIRECTOR, FBI (62-108763)

DATE: 2/19/64

FROM : SAC, WFO (100-43011) (RUC)

SUBJECT: JAMES ARTHUR BALDWIN
SM- C
OO:NY

b7C-1

ALL INFORMATION CONTAINED
HEREIN IS UNCLASSIFIED
DATE 5/17/89 BY [illegible]

Rerep of [redacted] at New York 12/11/63 with lead for WFO to review passport record; Bulet 12/18/63 instructing WFO to review files concerning subject's appearances in Washington, D.C.

On 2/7/64, SA [redacted] reviewed available information concerning subject at Department of State Passport Office. This consisted of an application for renewal of passport 2365937 issued to JAMES ARTHUR BALDWIN 8/4/60.

Application for renewal dated 7/29/63 at New York, New York, contains following information furnished by subject:

Date and place of birth:	8/2/24, New York, New York
Permanent residence:	306 West 18, New York, New York
Mail address:	Lubell, Lubell and Jones, Attorneys 165 Broadway, New York, New York
Port of Departure:	New York, New York
Approximate departure date:	8/7/63
Mode of travel:	Air France
Intended stay abroad:	Four weeks
Proposed itinerary:	France
Purpose of trip	Pleasure
Person to be notified in case of death or accident:	DAVID BALDWIN, brother 9-13 West 110 Street, New York, New York
Number of trips abroad withing last twelve months:	Two

No information concerning marital status, description, or photograph of subject appears on renewal application.

REC 5 [illegible] 23

2- Bureau
2- New York (100-146553) (RM)
1- WFO

[illegible]W:pkg
(5)

6 FEB 20 1964

58 FEB 28 1964

1172

A handwritten notation on application indicates renewal was approved; therefore, passport 2635937 appears to have been renewed to be valid until 8/3/65.

Attached to renewal application was a letter to the Passport Office dated 7/19/63 from Lubell, Lubell and Jones, Attorneys at Law, 165 Broadway, New York, New York, which advised they are attorneys for BALDWIN in matters arising out of or relating to the creation, proprietorship, sale, license or other distribution of his literary properties.

This letter stated BALDWIN, on 6/25/63, received a cablegrammed invitation to visit Cuba in connection with the 10th anniversary of the "26th of July Movement", and, as a result of this invitation, the "New Yorker" magazine requested BALDWIN to undertake a specific writing assignment in connection with such a trip to Cuba.

The letter advises they have informed BALDWIN travel to Cuba without a specially validated passport is a violation of present laws.

The letter stated BALDWIN has a passport, and he has informed them he has had one for several years. The letter requested that BALDWIN be issued a special permit for travel to Cuba.

Also attached to the renewal application was a Passport Office memorandum dated 8/1/63 advising that CLARENCE B. JONES of the law firm of Lubell, Lubell and Jones had informed that BALDWIN was not going to Cuba at that time but was going to France, and if he decided to go to Cuba at a later date, he would reapply for validation of his passport for such travel.

b7C-8 [redacted] Agency Liaison Officer, Passport Office, advised numerous special searches have been made by the Passport Office, but they have been unable to locate the remainder of the Passport Office file on the subject.

Review of WFO files and pertinent issues of "The Evening Star" and the "Washington Post and Times Herald" newspapers disclosed BALDWIN was a speaker at a "Peace Rally" at Judiciary Square in Washington, D.C., on 4/1/61. No specific statements made by BALDWIN were recorded in above-mentioned newspapers or furnished by WFO informants.

STATEMENTS ATTRIBUTED TO BALDWIN

On 6/11/61, WF T-1, who has furnished reliable information in the past, advised that JAMES BALDWIN spoke at a mass rally for "Original Freedom Riders" on the evening of 6/11/61 at All Souls Unitarian Church, 16th and Harvard Streets, N.W., Washington, D.C., sponsored by the Washington Chapter, Congress of Racial Equality (CORE).

The informant stated BALDWIN told those present that the West had better re-evaluate its international policy in light of the potential strength of the new Afro-Asian countries. BALDWIN added that the white man had better realize the emerging strength of the Negro. He stated that he did not want to be in the shoes of the white man when the African nations become stronger.

b7C-1

b2-1 (Documentation-[redacted] to SA [redacted] 6/11/61. WFO [redacted])
b7D-1

The June 12, 1963, edition of "The Evening Star", a Washington, D.C., daily newspaper, carried an article captioned "Business Hit as Failing to Aid Freedom Riders" concerning a rally of the Congress of Racial Equality at the All Souls Unitarian Church in Washington, D.C., on the evening of 6/11/63, at which JAMES BALDWIN was a speaker. The article states: "JAMES BALDWIN, author of 'Negroes in our Society' and other books, said the Freedom Riders are trying to complete something long overdue--the American Revolution."

The June 12, 1963, edition of the "Washington Post and Times Herald", a daily newspaper published in Washington, D.C., carried an article captioned "Freedom Riders Acclaimed in Talks to Mixed Audience in D.C. Church" concerning the meeting at the All Souls Unitarian Church on the evening of 6/11/63. The article states: "The author JAMES BALDWIN declared at the mass rally for Original Freedom Riders, 'What we are here to accomplish is the American Revolution'....'The question that must be decided is: Am I a man or am I not? And if I am not, then white man, what are you.'"

The November 5, 1963, issue of "The Evening Star" newspaper carried an article captioned "Farmer Cites Problem of Staying Nonviolent" concerning a conference on "youth, nonviolence and social change" held at Howard University, Washington, D.C., at which JAMES FARMER, National Director of CORE, and BALDWIN were speakers. This article states:

"Author JAMES BALDWIN said he wondered how long civil rights advocates will endure various indignities before they begin to fight back." The article quoted BALDWIN as saying, "But in this terrible confrontation I see some opportunity which will liberate this country and change the world. The very gravity and danger of the situation can be turned into a tremendous opportunity. We will have to learn to live together here or not at all." The article continues, "BALDWIN scolded a Federal Government which can protect Viet-Nam and invade Cuba but does nothing to protect the Negro in the South." The article also states BALDWIN then suggested that mass strikes or acts of civil disobedience would force the Government to deal with Negroes as individuals.

"The Evening Star" newspaper edition of 11/6/63 carried an article captioned "Negro Authors Stress Truth and Survival" concerning a symposium on the "Negro Writer in American Society" held at Howard University on the evening of 11/5/63, at which BALDWIN remarked, "My problem is to tell the truth and survive society while doing it." The article states BALDWIN continued that the role of the writer is to excavate the real history of the country. BALDWIN described the American mind as one of "fantastic confusion". He said Americans want to believe things which are really not true. The article quoted BALDWIN as saying, "White Americans think this is a beautiful and wonderful country....and this is not true. The Negro is the only person who can unearth the truth about this country."

The "Washington Post and Times Herald" newspaper edition of 11/6/63 carried an article captioned "Negro Leaders Exort Followers Not to Stray From Nonviolent Path." This article states in part that JAMES L. FARMER, National Director of CORE, agreed with another analyst, JAMES BALDWIN, Negro author, who indicated the breaking point of Negroes in the civil rights struggle may be near. This article continues, "BALDWIN said Negroes may have to think of civil disobedience as a next tactic...." BALDWIN said, "I don't want to see Negroes adapt themselves to the American way of life....I don't think any Negro in this country, whether a drunk or what have you, has to prove anything to the white man."

The above newspaper articles were reviewed on 1/8/64 at the Library of Congress by SA [redacted]

b7C-1

27.

SIGNIFYING NOTHING

FEBRUARY 1964

Some pages of Baldwin's FBI file tell us nothing, or something very near it. This page, originally processed for FOIA release in 1989, is included to remind readers that dozens of documents in the file remain fully or partially classified fifty years after their composition. Examining the margins beyond the blocks of ink, we can only guess that the document addressed some link between Baldwin and Paul Robeson, the multitalented black radical actor and earlier victim of FBI passport pulling. In the twenty-first century, the hand-drawn, blacked-out look of FOIA-permitted censorship has given way to neat patches of electronic "white-out" applied to scanned documents. Despite this change in technique, FOIA law still allows for deletions from released materials in the name of privacy, law enforcement, and national security. Some of these deletions are understandable, some are harder to trust, and many (thanks to these same deletions) are difficult to judge.

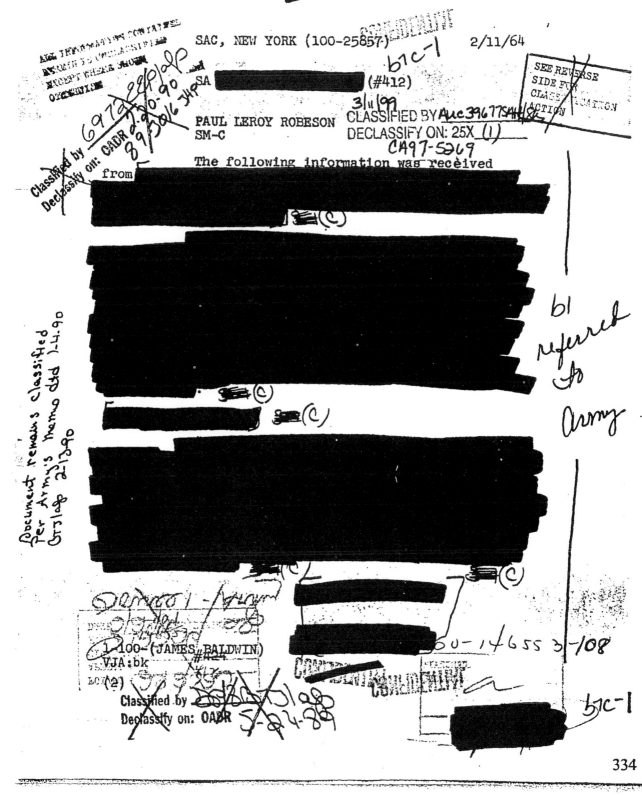

CONFIDENTIAL

ALL INFORMATION CONTAINED HEREIN IS UNCLASSIFIED EXCEPT WHERE SHOWN OTHERWISE

SAC, NEW YORK (100-25857) 2/11/64

SA [redacted] (#412)

PAUL LEROY ROBESON
SM-C

CLASSIFIED BY
DECLASSIFY ON: 25X (1)

The following information was received from [redacted]

1-100-(JAMES BALDWIN)
VJA:bk
(2)

SEE REVERSE SIDE FOR CLASSIFICATION ACTION

Classified by
Declassify on: OADR

28.

"AN ATTEMPT TO INTERVIEW HIM COULD PROVE HIGHLY EMBARRASSING"

MARCH 1964

This report from the spring of 1964 rehearses the reasons behind Baldwin's extended stay on the FBI Security Index. The "subject's outspoken stand on the civil rights issue, his current prominence as an author, and the inflammatory nature of his writings" all continued to prove him a likely danger in "time of emergency"—an exceptional time that in the sixties always seemed a breath away. What's new in the report is the explanation of why Baldwin had escaped an interview with FBI agents. "[H]is position as a prominent Negro author and his personal involvement in the current civil rights struggle," explained the New York office, "indicates that an attempt to interview him could prove highly embarrassing to the Bureau." Baldwin's habit of straight talk against the FBI occasionally saved him from FBI intimidation.

FD-263 (Rev. 5-1-59)

FEDERAL BUREAU OF INVESTIGATION

REPORTING OFFICE	OFFICE OF ORIGIN	DATE	INVESTIGATIVE PERIOD
NEW YORK	NEW YORK	3/26/64	12/18/63 - 3/19/64

TITLE OF CASE	REPORT MADE BY	TYPED BY
JAMES ARTHUR BALDWIN	[redacted]	11
	CHARACTER OF CASE: SM - C	

b7c-1

ALL INFORMATION CONTAINED HEREIN IS UNCLASSIFIED EXCEPT WHERE SHOWN OTHERWISE

REFERENCE:

Report of SA [redacted] dated 12/11/63, at NY.

- C -

DECLASSIFIED BY AUC 94255 SAH/8h ON 2/18/99
CA97-5269

ADMINISTRATIVE:

The sources used in the characterization of the Monroe Defense Committee in the order used are [redacted] and [redacted].

b2 b7D-1

Classified by 6972 SE 2/98
Declassify on: OADR 2-20-98

APPROVED — SPECIAL AGENT IN CHARGE

DO NOT WRITE IN SPACES BELOW

COPIES MADE:

4-Bureau (62-108763) (RM)
1-New York (100-146553)

100-146553-128

Searched
Serialized
Indexed

DISSEMINATION RECORD OF ATTACHED REPORT

CONFIDENTIAL

NOTATIONS

AGENCY				
REQUEST RECD.				
DATE FWD.				
HOW FWD.				
BY				

U.S. GOVERNMENT PRINTING OFFICE 16—76324-1

NY 100-146553

CONFIDENTIAL

INFORMANTS:

Identity of Source	File Number Where Located
NY T-1  (X) U	Instant report
NY T-2 NY 694-S* (X) U	Characterization of HUNTER PITTS O'DELL
NY T-3  (X) U	100-146353-111
NY T-4  (X) U	NY ▆▆▆ (X) U
NY T-5  (X) U	Characterization of Freedomways Forum Characterization of LILLIAN MARTINEZ
NY T-6 ▆▆▆ PSI	
NY T-7, Panel Source ▆▆▆ (X) U	U (X)
NY T-8 ▆▆▆ (X) U	(X) U

b2-1

b7D-1

b7C-5
b7C-3

- B -
COVER PAGE

CONFIDENTIAL

FD-305 (Rev. 9-19-62)

NY 100-146553

1. [x] Subject's name is included in the Security Index.
2. [x] The data appearing on the Security Index card are current.
3. [ ] Changes on the Security Index card are necessary and Form FD-122 has been submitted to the Bureau.
4. [x] A suitable photograph [x] is [ ] is not available.
5. [ ] Subject is employed in a key facility and __________ is charged with security responsibility. Interested agencies are __________.
6. [x] This report is classified ~~SECRET~~ because (state reason)

it contains information furnished by NY 694-S*, a highly sensitive source, regarding the association of HUNTER PITTS O'DELL with JAMES BALDWIN, well known Negro author. (U)

7. [x] Subject previously interviewed (dates) Never.
[x] Subject was not reinterviewed because (state reason)

of his position as a prominent Negro author and his personal involvement in the current civil rights struggle by the Negroes in the US indicates that an attempt to interview him could prove highly embarrassing to the Bureau.

8. [ ] This case no longer meets the Security Index criteria and a letter has been directed to the Bureau recommending cancellation of the Security Index card.
9. [x] This case has been re-evaluated in the light of the Security Index criteria and it continues to fall within such criteria because (state reason)

subject's outspoken stand in the civil rights issue, his current prominence as an author, and the inflammatory nature of his writings, show him to be a dangerous individual who could be expected to commit acts inimical to the national defense and public safety of the US in time of emergency.

10. [x] Subject's SI card [ ] is [x] is not tabbed Detcom.
[x] Subject's activities [ ] do [x] do not warrant Detcom tabbing.

~~CONFIDENTIAL~~

- C* -
COVER PAGE

29.

BALDWIN AS COINTELPRO AUDIENCE

APRIL 1964

Formed in 1938, the American Socialist Workers Party (SWP) fell under FBI suspicion as early as 1940, its Minneapolis headquarters then raided and stripped of its library by Bureau agents in 1943. Never pardoned for its early Trotskyism and opposition to American participation in World War II, the SWP was hit with a full-bore, largely illegal "COINTELPRO" or counterintelligence program in 1961. J. Edgar Hoover reasoned that the party deserved this extreme measure because of its recent support for Castro's Cuba and its long-term adherence to "the revolutionary principles of Marx, Lenin and Engels as interpreted by Leon Trotsky." Hoover's Bureau also feared and resented the SWP's backing of the Civil Rights Movement, the subject of this April 1964 memo concerning "a mimeographed anonymous letter prepared by the [FBI] Laboratory for use by the New York Office in a disruption tactic against the SWP." To make a strange story short, the letter forged by the Bureau aimed to separate the mostly white SWP from its mostly black allies around Monroe, North Carolina. In that area, a movement had grown to defend Robert Williams, the rebellious NAACP leader and author of *Negroes with Guns* (1962) falsely charged with kidnapping. Along with LeRoi Jones/Amiri Baraka, Baldwin was identified as a top target of this effort to resegregate an integrated radicalism. It's unclear if he was also sent a copy of "Georgie-Porgie, down in Monroe," a bit of FBI-composed verse designed to cause further disruption. In any event, the imaginative literature required in its COINTELPRO campaigns forced the Bureau to try on Baldwin's profession of authorship.

UNITED STATES GOVERNMENT

MEMORANDUM

TO: DIRECTOR, FBI (100-436291) DATE: 4/10/64

FROM: SAC, NEW YORK (100-146608)

SUBJECT: SOCIALIST WORKERS PARTY
INTERNAL SECURITY - SWP
DISRUPTION PROGRAM

ReBulet 4/3/64.

Relet enclosed copies of a mimeographed anonymous letter prepared by the Laboratory for use by the New York Office in a disruption tactic against the SWP. The New York Office had suggested this letter to bring discredit upon the Party in the Negro civil rights field, specifically through the activities of the SWP-controlled Committee To Aid The Monroe Defendants (CAMD). The letter implied that GEORGE WEISSMAN and BERTA GREEN of the SWP used the CAMD to their own advantage until they were finally repudiated by the defendants. It was written in a manner designed to direct suspicion as to its source upon the Workers World Party, a rival in the Monroe defense movement.

2 - Bureau (RM)
1 - New York (100-[redacted]
1 - New York (100-[redacted]
1 - New York (100-137309)(WWP)(413)
1 - New York (100-146359)(CAMD)(413)
1 - New York (100-[redacted]
1 - New York (100-[redacted]
1 - New York (97-169)("THE WORKER")
1 - New York (100-93572)("NATIONAL GUARDIAN")
1 - New York (100-146553)(JAMES BALDWIN)
1 - New York (100-[redacted]
1 - New York (100-[redacted]
1 - New York (100-[redacted]
1 - New York (100-147372)(PL)
1 - New York

b7C-3

GB:rmp
(16)

100-146553-136

ALL INFORMATION CONTAINED
HEREIN IS UNCLASSIFIED
DATE 5/24/19 BY [illegible]

SEARCHED ... INDEXED ...
SERIALIZED ... FILED ...
APR 1 ...
FBI — NEW YORK

Copies of the anonymous letter were mailed on 4/8/64, in commercially purchased envelopes addressed by a clerical employee of the New York Office. The letter was sent to the individuals listed below:

(1) DANIEL WATTS
Editor, "Liberator"
244 East 46th Street
New York, New York

(2) HAROLD CRUSE
203 West 14th Street
New York, New York

(3) Editor, "The Worker"
23 West 26th Street
New York, New York

(4) Editor, "National Guardian"
197 East Fourth Street
New York, New York

(5) JAMES BALDWIN
470 West End Avenue
New York, New York

(6) PETER KIHSS
c/o New York Times
229 West 43rd Street
New York, New York

(7) JAMES ROBERTSON
c/o "Spartacist"
Box 1377, G.P.O.
New York, New York

(8) TIM WOHLFORTH
160 West 95th Street
New York, New York

(9) LEROI JONES
27 Cooper Square
New York, New York

If any information re this mailing appears in New York files designated to receive a copy of instant letter, it should be directed to subject file, so the Bureau can be advised.

It is believed that a follow-up to this anonymous mailing may increase the effectiveness of the disruption operation. We can take advantage of the fact that GEORGE WEISSMAN reported to the Monroe police that while he was alone in the home of a Monroe Negro civil rights leader, two bandits came in and rifled a wall safe. A Xerox copy of a clipping from the Charlotte Observer of 2/27/64, outlining the story, is enclosed for information of the Bureau.

Since recipients of the first anonymous letter are familiar with the connection of the SWP's WEISSMAN with the Monroe defense, it will not be necessary to go into a detailed exposition if they are furnished copies of the clippong. Bureau authority is requested to send a Xerox copy of the Charlotte Observer article to the same individuals named above in instant letter. Bureau is also requested to authorize enclosing with the clipping, as a device to generate further suspicions, the following bit of verse:

Georgie-Porgie, down in Monroe,
Found himself alone with the dough,
Called the cops, and what did he say?
"Bad guys came and took it away".

If approved, Bureau is requested to have the Laboratory prepare the poen, as expeditiously as possible, using the same typewriter and paper as in the first letter. The poem should be on a mimeographed half-sheet, presumably an economy by the putative sender.

In addition to the addressees of the first anonymous letter, another will be added for the second letter, if approved by the Bureau. This is the editor of Progressive Labor, Box 808, G.P.O., Brooklyn 1, New York. This organization was also active in Monroe and as a rival of the SWP may be interested in the material to use in attacking the Party.

The Bureau is requested to advise the New York Office as soon as possible since interest in the Monroe case becomes less as time goes by.

30.

THE BUREAU STALKS BALDWIN ON BROADWAY

MAY 1964

In January 1964, FBI officials heard early that Baldwin was nearing completion of his play *Blues for Mister Charlie*. Four months later, they learned before nearly everyone outside the play's production team that its opening was threatened by financial crisis and racial tension, both of which could have been lifted from the play's uncompromising content. The Actors Studio, *Blues for Mister Charlie*'s downtown producer, had initially appealed to Baldwin because of its connections to his famous friends Marlon Brando, Tennessee Williams, and Geraldine Page. Actor Rip Torn, with whom Baldwin fell in love during rehearsals, had also been a "persuasive Studio advocate," as David Leeming notes. Even before the emergency discussed in these FBI documents, however, Baldwin's happiness with the studio was fraying: he doubted that its distinctive Method acting was indeed acting, and he fought tooth and nail to keep the play long and ticket prices low, the better to welcome and thoroughly educate a mixed audience. The last-minute fight over finances might have scuttled the Broadway opening if not for Jack O'Dell, who advised Baldwin to ignore the worst and "spend all his [remaining] time polishing scenes." The Actors Studio was merely one more fading Mr. Charlie feeling the blues: "O'Dell claimed that [this was] just another 'plantation' idea of 'white folks' where they will do as little as they can and let the 'nigger' do all the work." Hunting for

Communist plots and discovering only nuggets of literary history, FBI special agents spied on O'Dell and the playwright on Fifth Avenue, noting their entrance into a building and their boarding of an elevator up to a meeting "to decide the future of Baldwin's play."

CONFIDENTIAL

New York, New York
May 25, 1964

Bureau 100-358916
New York 100-91330

ALL INFORMATION CONTAINED HEREIN IS UNCLASSIFIED EXCEPT WHERE SHOWN OTHERWISE

DECLASSIFIED BY AUC94255SAH/[illegible] ON 2/18/99 CA97-5269

Hunter Pitts O'Dell

A confidential source advised on May 21, 1964, that on that date, Hunter Pitts O'Dell was in contact with an individual who was unknown to the source. They discussed the matter of keeping the play by James Baldwin ("Blues For Mister Charlie") going and O'Dell was told that Baldwin has given up royalty claims to the play and that there was going to be a meeting about the play on Friday, May 22, 1964. O'Dell stated that he would be there. (X)U

A second confidential source advised in July, 1962, that, as of that time, Hunter Pitts O'Dell was considered by the Communist Party, United States of America (CP, USA) as being a member of its National Committee.

The first confidential source advised on May 22, 1964, that, on that date, O'Dell and James Baldwin agreed to meet at the Actors Studio on the 17th floor of the Squibb Building at 3:50 PM. It was stated that Baldwin's lawyer would be there at 5:00 PM. (X)U

On May 22, 1964, Special Agents of the Federal Bureau of Investigation (FBI) observed Hunter Pitts O'Dell enter the lobby of the Squibb Building, 745 Fifth Avenue, New York City, and proceed to the elevator banks to the upper floors. Shortly thereafter, James Baldwin, the well-known Negro author, was observed entering this building and boarded an elevator to the upper floors.

It was noted that the directory of the Squibb Building lists office space for the Actors Studio, producer of Baldwin's play, on the 17th floor of this building.

CONFIDENTIAL

Classified by 6932EEP/08 Declassify on: OADR 2-26-99 JHP 84-3016

Group 1 Excluded from automatic downgrading and declassification

Classified by 8830 P/3/08 Declassify on: OADR 5-17-89

Searched Serialized Indexed

This document contains neither recommendations nor conclusions of the FBI. It is the property of the FBI and is loaned to your agency; it and its contents are not to be disseminated outside your agency.

100-146553-151

Hunter Pitts O'Dell

"The New York Times", Monday, May 25, 1964, in its theatre section, page 43, contains an advertisement stating that James Baldwin's "Blues For Mister Charlie" will be forced to close on May 30, 1964, "unless there is an immediate public response."

The first confidential source has furnished information, previously, indicating that O'Dell has been helping with promotion of the play "Blues For Mister Charlie" and also has been arranging theatre parties for the play.

5/25/64

AIRTEL

DECLASSIFIED BY AAC94255 SAH/
ON 2/18/99
CA97-5269

ALL INFORMATION CONTAINED
HEREIN IS UNCLASSIFIED
EXCEPT WHERE SHOWN
OTHERWISE

Classified by 6972/ECP/af
Declassify on: OADR
2-21-90
89-3014 JHP

TO: DIRECTOR, FBI (100-358916)

FROM: SAC NEW YORK (100-91330)

SUBJECT: HUNTER PITTS O'DELL
IS-C

(OO: NY)

CONFIDENTIAL
Classified by
Declassify on: OADR
5/1/89

There are enclosed 6 copies of a LHM showing that (U) HUNTER PITTS O'DELL has been closely associated with JAMES BALDWIN, the Negro author, in the presentation of BALDWIN's play "Blues For Mr. Charlie" which is currently appearing on Broadway in NYC. The source of this information is [redacted] (U) and the source used to characterize O'DELL is NY 694-S* (X)(U) b2-1

The Special Agents who observed O'DELL and BALDWIN entering the Squibb Building, 745 5th Avenue, on 5/22/64, were [redacted] and [redacted] Shortly before O'DELL and BALDWIN entered the building, BURGESS MERIDITH, the Director of "Blues For Mister Charlie", entered this building. It is believed that a meeting was held in the offices of the Actors Studio to decide the future of BALDWIN's play. (X)(U) b7C-1

The LHM is classified "Confidential" because it contains information from the above sources, the unauthorized disclosure of which could result in the loss of sources of great value and seriously impair the defense interests of the US.

The log reflecting the surveillance of O'DELL and BALDWIN is filed in NY file 100-91330-Sub A.

4-Bureau (Encls. 6)(RM)
(1-62-108763)(JAMES BALDWIN)
1-New York (100-146553)(JAMES BALDWIN)(45)
1-New York
JFO:rdu
(6)
1-Supervisor #42

100-146553-152

SEARCHED ___ INDEXED ___
SERIALIZED ___ FILED ___
MAY 26 1964
FBI — NEW YORK

b7C-1

31.

BALDWIN AND HIS "ALIASES"

JUNE 1964

Baldwin was "Jimmy" to most of his friends and to himself as well when he meditated on the various aspects of his personality. The numerous "strangers called Jimmy Baldwin," he observed of his own diversity, included an "older brother with all the egotism and rigidity that implies," a "self-serving little boy," and "a man" and "a woman, too. There are lots of people there." This secret FBI summary made the mistake of treating variations on Baldwin's name and identity as a set of potentially criminal pseudonyms. For the Bureau, "James Baldwin," "James Arthur Baldwin," "Jim Baldwin," and "Jimmy Baldwin" were "aliases" needing correlation and correction.

SECRET

SEE REVERSE SIDE FOR CLASSIFICATION ACTION

ALL INFORMATION CONTAINED HEREIN IS UNCLASSIFIED EXCEPT WHERE SHOWN OTHERWISE

CORRELATION SUMMARY

Main File No: 62-108763
See also: 145-2625

Date: June 2, 1964

Subject: James Arthur Baldwin

Date Searched: 1/6/64

All logical variations of subject's name and aliases were searched and identical references were found as:

James Arthur Baldwin
James Baldwin

Jim Baldwin
Jimmy Baldwin

This is a summary of information obtained from a review of all "see" references to the subject in Bureau files under the names and aliases listed above. All references under the above names containing data identical with the subject have been included except those listed at the end of this summary as not having been reviewed, or those determined to contain the same information as the main file.

This summary is designed to furnish a synopsis of the information set out in each reference. In many cases the original serial will contain the information in much more detail.

THIS SUMMARY HAS BEEN PREPARED FOR USE AT THE SEAT OF GOVERNMENT AND IS NOT SUITABLE FOR DISSEMINATION.

b7C

Analyst	Coordinator	Approved
[redacted]	[redacted]	[redacted]

RPD/elm

Classified by Multiple Sources BTJ/alp
Declassify on: OADR 5-17-89

ENCLOSURE

ENCLOSURE BEHIND FILE - SEARCH SLIPS ONLY

Pg 6, paras 3, 4 remains classified per CIA's memo dtd 3-6-90 6972 EEP lag 3-19-90 89-3016 JHP

Pg 2 para. 2, 3
Pg 12, para 1
remains classified per Army's memo dtd 1-4-90
BTJ/alp 2-13-90

SECRET

REC 62-108763-26

3/8/99
CLASSIFIED BY
DECLASSIFY ON: 25X (1)(6)
CA97-5269

17 JUN 3 1964

CONSOLIDATION

53 JUN 8 1964

32.

THE BLOOD COUNTERS AND BALDWIN COUNTERSURVEILLANCE, PART 1

JUNE AND JULY 1964

When did the Bureau lose sleep over the popularity of Baldwin's "recent books . . . ringing up best-selling figures," the "100,000 copies in hardcover" sold of *The Fire Next Time* and "the two million mark in soft covers" in sight for *Another Country*? It did so when a column in the *Washington Post* conveyed the news that Baldwin planned to publish another "book about the F.B.I. in the South." Hoover's sensitivity to literary competition and challenge, always acute, had been exquisite since 1950, when Max Lowenthal's study *The Federal Bureau of Investigation*, the first rigorously unauthorized history of the organization, somehow made its way to the printers without the Bureau's knowledge. "Mr. Hoover, if I had known this book was going to be published," swore Louis Nichols, then head of the Crime Records Division, "I'd have thrown my body between the presses and stopped it." Nichols's successors at Crime Records made certain that Baldwin's FBI book—shortly given the working title of *The Blood Counters*—would not take them unawares. The June memo to Cartha DeLoach identifies the book's expected publisher, the Dial Press, and indicates in an addendum that "should the book be published, naturally it will be reviewed." A July memo to the head of the New York field office requests a less passive form of vigilance: "Supervisor [name redacted] requested that if possible, through established sources at Dial Press, a copy of the proposed book concerning the FBI be discreetly obtained prior to publication." Where Baldwin was concerned, after-the-fact reviews were not enough. If the country's best-selling black author would devote his sharp tongue to the Bureau, the Bureau would be one of the first to know—and the first to try to respond in kind.

OPTIONAL FORM NO. 10
MAY 1962 EDITION
GSA GEN. REG. NO. 27

UNITED STATES GOVERNMENT

Memorandum

TO : Mr. DeLoach DATE: 6-22-64

FROM : M. A. Jones

SUBJECT: JAMES ARTHUR BALDWIN
INFORMATION CONCERNING

ALL INFORMATION CONTAINED
HEREIN IS UNCLASSIFIED
DATE 5-17-89 BY

Tolson
Belmont
Mohr
Casper
Callahan
Conrad
DeLoach
Evans
Gale
Rosen
Sullivan
Tavel
Trotter
Tele. Room
Holmes
Gandy

The book review section of "The Washington Post" for 6-21-64, contained an article concerning captioned individual. It stated he is contemplating at least four future books, among which will be one "about the F. B. I. in the South." These will be published by Dial Press.

The item goes on to point out that Baldwin's recent books have attracted an enormous response, ringing up best-selling figures all over the Nation. "The Fire Next Time," according to the article, sold 100,000 copies in hard-cover; its paperback version, just out, is likely to sell five to ten times that many. "Another Country" is nearing the two million mark in soft cover.

INFORMATION IN BUFILES:

James Arthur Baldwin is a Harlem-born Negro who resides in New York City, and who has become quite well known for his books regarding the relationship of Negroes and whites in our society.

He has been identified as a sponsor for the Fair Play for Cuba Committee and is one of its prominent members.

Baldwin is also listed as one of the sponsors of The Monroe Defense Committee, a group organized as the result of a race riot in Monroe, North Carolina, on 8-27-61. This Committee has received strong support from communist publications such as the "National Guardian."

REC- 57

The "New York Herald Tribune" of 6-17-61, in its "Letters to the Editor" section, contained a communication signed by Baldwin and William Styron which advocated abolishment of capital punishment. This letter said "If there were a shred of proof that the death penalty actually served to inhibit crime, that would be sufficient reason--even from the point of view of 'misguided do-gooders,' as J. Edgar Hoover calls its opponents--to maintain it." It goes on to state Mr. Hoover "is not a lawgiver, nor is there any reason to suppose him to be a particularly

1 - Mr. DeLoach
1 - Mr. Sullivan

JUL 16 1964

1246

HHA:cmk
(6)

(Continued, page 2)

M.A. Jones to DeLoach memo
Re: JAMES ARTHUR BALDWIN

profound student of human nature. He is a law-enforcement officer. It is appalling that in this capacity he not only oppposses the trend of history among civilized nations, but uses his enormous power and prestige to corroborate the blindest and basest instincts of the retaliatory mob."

On the subject of homosexuality, Baldwin states, "American males are the only people I've ever encountered in the world who are willing to go on the needle before they'll go to bed with each other. Because they're afraid of this, they don't know how to go to bed with women either. I've known people who literally died out of this panic. I don't know what homosexual means any more, and Americans don't either...If you fall in love with a boy, you fall in love with a boy. The fact that Americans consider it a disease says more about them than it says about homosexuality

In connection with a discussion of why he felt both Attorney General Robert Kennedy, the Justice Department and former President John F. Kennedy were ineffective in dealing with discrimination with the Negroes in the South, Baldwin said he was weary of being told desegregation is legal. He went on to say "...because first of all you have to get Eastland out of Congress and get rid of the power that he wields there. You've got to get rid of J. Edgar Hoover and the power that he wields. If one could get rid of just those two men, or modify their power, there would be a great deal more hope..."

RECOMMENDATION:

None. For information.

ADDENDUM, ECK:amr 6/22/64

In that this book "about the F. B. I. in the South" is one being contemplated by Baldwin, we will follow our sources, and should the book be published, naturally it will be reviewed and you will be advised.

A LITERARY CASEBOOK/BY DICK SCHA[illegible]

BEHIND THE LINES

Green for Mr. Jimmy

It reminds one, almost immediately, of an Ingemar Johansson fight camp. A few women scamper around; one of them is his sister. Males wander in and out; one of them is his brother. Telephones jangle constantly, offering deals, praises, pleas. In the middle of it all, the attention and the admiration swirling about him almost unnoticed but accepted, sits the champion, five feet and a few inches tall, maybe 135 pounds, wide-eyed, 39 years old—James Arthur Baldwin.

This is a seven-room apartment on New York's West End Avenue, in the 80s, and it is, at least temporarily, the training camp for Jimmy Baldwin. There are book shelves and modern paintings, posters and phonographs, telephones and sliding doors, and, permeating everything, there is the same weird, unreal, reverse race appeal that hung over a Johansson fight headquarters. Imagine! A white man who knows how to fight!

And then, in the best boxing tradition, there is the entourage, on scene and off scene. Writing is a lonely craft, and Jimmy Baldwin, with his art, is all alone—except for his lawyer, New York City Councilman Theodore Kupferman; his agent, Robert Lantz; his benefactor, Tom Michaelas; his photographer, Frank Dandridge; his song writer, Bobby Sharp; his publisher, Richard Baron; his disk jockey, Frankie (Downbeat) Brown; his minister-friend, the Rev. Sidney Lanier; and a supporting cast, changing every few months, of well-wishers, advisers and hangers-on.

And then there are Gloria Davis and Lucien Happersberger. They handle Jimmy Baldwin's money. That is, they handle most of Jimmy Baldwin's money. A suspicion persists, confirmed by some of his friends, that almost everybody handles some of Jimmy Baldwin's money, everybody but Jimmy Baldwin.

"I am impossible," says Baldwin, discussing his finances. "I am a positive menace." He gestures toward the room where Gloria Davis struggles to keep his finances straight. "I am locked out of that office," he says.

Money is one point where the personalities of James Baldwin and Ingemar Johansson part company. The strength of Johansson's great right hand was never greater than when he wrapped his fist around a dollar bill. But Baldwin and money are a mismatch; his generosity matches Johansson's thrift. At one stage in Baldwin's career, a literary agent, Bob Mills, set up parallel checking accounts in the same bank, one the agent's, one the author's. Mills, responding to phone calls from the bank, made a habit of switching funds from one account to the other, covering uncovered checks, later explaining the complexities of banking and currency to the author.

Baldwin's own standard of living has barely fluctuated over the years—he spends as much time as he can in Spartan seclusion writing on Fire Island—but he can't help giving money away to people who need it, acquaintances, friends and relatives ("We're not a family, we're a tribe," he says).

Mrs. Davis and Lucien Happersberger understand the problem.

"I ask them for cash from time to time," Baldwin says. "Sometimes they give it to me, and sometimes they don't."

Mrs. Davis is Baldwin's sister. "I can tell I'm solvent when she's smiling," he says.

Happersberger, a 31-year-old Swiss painter, has been Baldwin's friend—probably his closest friend—for some 14 years, since they met in a Left Bank cafe. "We have starved together in two cities," Baldwin says. "Paris and New York."

As recently as four years ago, even with three books in print, Baldwin's financial condition was shaky. He actually feared, he told friends, that he might have to go back to running an elevator, one of several dozen jobs that have kept him writing since he was 14 ("It's easier to name the jobs I haven't had").

The starving days are past for Jimmy Baldwin, and Mrs. Davis wears a permanent smile. Baldwin is box office now—perhaps not on Broadway, where a $10,000 gift from two of Nelson Rockefeller's daughters helped keep Baldwin's play, *Blues for Mr. Charlie,* going—but

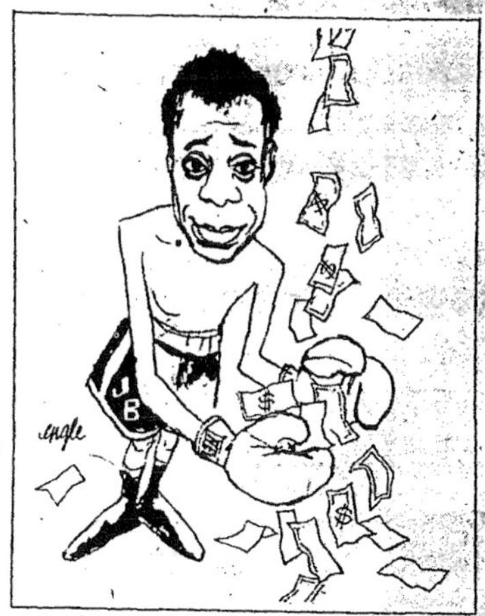

certainly in bookstores, where such recent Baldwin books as *The Fire Next Time, Another Country* and *Nobody Knows My Name* rang up best-selling figures. *The Fire Next Time* has sold 100,000 copies in hardcover; its paperback version, just out, is likely to sell five to ten times that many. All his books but *Blues* are now in paperback, and *Another Country* is nearing the 2-million mark in soft covers.

All this success, coupled with his knack for attracting well-meaning advisors, the departure last fall of Jim Silberman, Baldwin's editor at Dial

1 xerox 810RB.

ALL INFORMATION CONTAINED
HEREIN IS UNCLASSIFIED
DATE 5-17-89 BY [illegible]

62-108763-27

ENCLOSURE

Book Week
"The Washington Post"
6-21-64

Press, for ~~Random~~ House, and the merger of Dial into Dell Publishing Co., prompted talk in publishing circles that Jimmy was shopping around for a new publisher.

In fact, he was. Dial, though, was hardly anxious to let Baldwin go. Furthermore, it had him under a contract that provided for a $15,000 annual income after advances. But Baldwin's advisors told him, in effect, Jimmy, you're worth a million dollars. This notion was confirmed when a paperback house tried to woo him from Dial by offering Baldwin a million dollars—$50,000 a year for 20 years. The bid was never taken too seriously. "I knew it wasn't really a million dollars, with taxes and everything, you know," Baldwin says.

With new lawyers and new advisors intervening for him, Baldwin won a more liberal contract from Dial, signed in April just before the presses started turning out the book version of *Blues for Mister Charlie*. The negotiations, says Dial's Dick Baron, were cordial, and so Dial will publish at least four more Baldwin books, which might include a novel called *Talking at the Gates* (about a Southern plantation the day the news arrived that slavery had ended), a book about the F. B. I. in the South, a collection of short stories or a strictly autobiographical work. Before any of them, there will be one other book, previously committed to Atheneum —a two-man effort, Baldwin's words with Richard Avedon's pictures. The working title is, simply, *An Essay*, due next fall.

Baldwin, happy that the negotiations are over, is pleased with everybody. He doesn't sing any blues for the green. "You know," he says, logically, "the more money you make, the more you need."

OPTIONAL FORM NO. 10
5010-104

UNITED STATES GOVERNMENT

Memorandum

TO : SAC, NEW YORK DATE: 7/8/64

FROM : SUPERVISOR [redacted] #12

SUBJECT: JAMES BALDWIN
PROPOSED BOOK
FBI - SOUTH

b7C-1

[redacted] Bureau Supervisor, advised that information appeared in the "Washington Post," dateline of 6/21/64, setting out that JAMES BALDWIN had contracted with Dial Press for four books. One of the books was to be "The FBI - South." Allegedly this book was to depict the work of the FBI in the South during the recent civil rights incidents.

Supervisor [redacted] requested that if possible, through established sources at Dial Press, a copy of the proposed book concerning the FBI be discreetly obtained prior to publication. He said the office was to be most discreet in its contacts concerning this book.

ALL INFORMATION CONTAINED
HEREIN IS UNCLASSIFIED
DATE 5/25/18 BY

MMO'R:mrk
(1)

33.

THE BLOOD COUNTERS AND BALDWIN COUNTERSURVEILLANCE, PART 2

JULY 1964

In the summer of 1964, the same season in which voting rights activists descended on segregated Mississippi, FBI offices collected all the evidence they could of the whereabouts of Baldwin's book on the Bureau. Clippings from newspapers and magazines again accumulated in the author's FBI file, with portions once more rivaling the brag book of a proud relative or publicity agent. This envelope sent from New York to Crime Records in Washington, DC, included excerpts from the *Herald Tribune* and *Playbill*. The former teased the possibility that Baldwin's Bureau book would debut in *The New Yorker*, the premier home of American long-form journalism and the initial publisher of the better part of *The Fire Next Time*. The latter clipping spoke, in Baldwin's own words, of a lengthy piece "on the F.B.I. and how it treats Negroes. It will be called *The Blood Counters*, which is the Negroes' nickname for the F.B.I." The Bureau now had a name for the book it feared the most. And with Baldwin's explanation of the nickname behind the title, it had a window into African American attitudes to the calculating narrowness of FBI crime fighting.

ALL INFORMATION CONTAINED
HEREIN IS UNCLASSIFIED
DATE 5-17-89 BY [illegible]

b7c-1

ENCLOSURES - BUREAU (2)
ATTN.: CRIME RECORDS, SA

New York File 100-146553

Clipping from "New York Herald Tribune, 7/14/64, and copy of "Playbill".

62-[illegible]-28

FD-350 (Rev. 7-16-63)

(Mount Clipping in Space Below)

Books and Authors

James Baldwin is writing a book about the FBI and the South, which Dial Press will publish next Spring. Like "The Fire Next Time," the new work will be featured in the New Yorker before its appearance as a book. . . . . Columbia University Press is commemorating 70 years of publishing in a special exhibit at Butler Library this summer. Among the authors represented are four Presidents of the United States: Wilson, Taft, Truman and Eisenhower. . . . . The next book by Francoise Sagan, coming from Dutton in October, is a nonfiction work: a diary kept by the author during nine days in a special clinic undergoing disintoxication from the morphine she was given after her auto accident in 1957.

* * *

A Russian publishing firm, Detskaya Literatura, plans to publish an American juvenile about school integration in the South, "Mary Jane," by Dorothy Sterling. Mrs. Sterling's book, published here by Doubleday, was a winner of the Nancy Bloch Award for the children's book that best fosters intercultural understanding . . . . On Eugene Field's birthday, Sept. 3, Farrar, Straus and Company will publish a translation into French of his children's poem, "Wynken, Blynken and Nod," by Francis Steegmuller. In this version, the wooden-shoe sailors are named Papillot, Clignot and Dodo. Advance comments include 6½-year-old Lisa Millerand's: "The boys have beatle haircuts and night shirts. . . It is sort of like a dream" and 5-year-old Elizabeth Epler's: "It's in French. . . Let's give the book to Nicole."

* * *

Published tomorrow by Dutton will be Anthony Boucher's annual collection (the 19th) of "Best Detective Stories of the Year" (284 pages. $3.95). As usual, when the game's afoot, Mr. Boucher's questing talents and excellent taste are both in evidence, and the collection has its expected quotient of surprises, including the shortest murder story in history: Fredric Brown's 36-word "Mistake."

MAURICE DOLBIER

(Indicate page, name of newspaper, city and state.)

21 NY Herald Tribune

Date: 7/14/64
Edition: Late City
Author: Maurice Dolbier
Editor: James G. Bellows
Title: JAMES BALDWIN PROPOSED BOOK FBI - SOUTH
Character: INFO CONCERNING
or
Classification:
Submitting Office: NYO
☐ Being Investigated

Alvin Theatre

PLAYBILL

the magazine for theatregoers

ALL INFORMATION CONTAINED
HEREIN IS UNCLASSIFIED
DATE 5-17-89 BY

JAMES BALDWIN, *the brilliant burning tiger who is probably the monarch of the current literary jungle, has won international acclaim as both a major writer and as the angry conscience of a nation. This blunt, lonely, perceptive forty year old bachelor has created three novels, three books of essays and two plays. His latest work may be seen on Broadway in the Actors Studio's explosive production of* Blues for Mr. Charlie. *Alternately violent and vulnerable, Mr. Baldwin recently discussed his career and views on the American theatre in a two hour interview with Walter Wager, Editor of* PLAYBILL.

PLAYBILL: Let's start from the beginning—your birth.

BALDWIN: I was born in Harlem Hospital, and I've lived in New York all my years except for 1948 to 1957. I spent them in Paris. It saved my life.

PLAYBILL: When did you turn from the printed page to the stage?

BALDWIN: I wrote my first version of *The Amen Corner* in 1952 when I came home from France to sell my first novel — *Go Tell It On the Mountain*. I finished the play in 1954, and in 1955 *The Amen Corner* was produced at Howard University.

PLAYBILL: How was it received?

BALDWIN: Very good reviews, but I was told that Negro plays don't succeed in America. I put the script in my trunk, where it stayed until this year. Now I hear that it's a hit in Los Angeles.

PLAYBILL: What happened after *Amen Corner?*

BALDWIN: I decided that I might try to continue to work in theatre—if America had one—but I was not *about* to undergo the drab Shubert Alley scene.

PLAYBILL: Didn't you dramatize your second novel?

BALDWIN: Yes, John C. Wilson optioned *Giovanni's Room*. I wasn't too interested in the script until I saw the dramatization. I knew I couldn't do worse, so I wrote my own version—as a project for the Actors Studio.

PLAYBILL: That was before you were "apprenticed" to Elia Kazan?

BALDWIN: Yes, he'd read my writing and told me that he thought I should work in theatre. I was paid a nominal sum to carry his clip-board and take his notes in the production of *J.B.* and then *Sweet Bird of Youth*. It was very useful training.

PLAYBILL: What did you learn?

BALDWIN: The inner mechanics of how a play works—and other things. One of the most important was how essential it is to get along with the crew and stage-hands. If they don't like you, you've had it.

PLAYBILL: When and where did you write *Blues For Mr. Charlie?*

BALDWIN: I started in Istambul in April 1963, and then had to fly home for the March on Washington in May. I wrote the play in less than a year, working on it between civil rights meetings and appearances. I was afraid that if I didn't do it I wouldn't be a writer anymore. In the middle of it, Medgar (Evers) was shot and I knew I had to finish it.

PLAYBILL: Literally, *how* did you write it?

BALDWIN: On pads in planes, trains, gas stations—all sort of places. With a pen or pencil. Walter, this is a *hand-written* play. Then I typed it, editing in the process, and wrote it again—and typed it again. I've been rewriting and rewriting since the end of 1963. In the weeks before the opening, I did a lot more cutting and rewriting. I was buried in the tunnels under the ANTA Theatre so long that is seems as if I'd been born there.

PLAYBILL: Again literally, how did you *feel* when you were writing this play?

BALDWIN: Scared. I'm always scared when I'm writing. Both end of my digestive tract tense up. I hardly ate a regular meal in months.

PLAYBILL: Is it like that for other playwrights?

BALDWIN: I don't know. I'm not sure that the American theatre has many playwrights. As a result, the vacuum is filled by experts who can't read or write. The eminence of producers and directors in the U.S. theatre is the playwrights' fault.

PLAYBILL: Are the producers and directors solely responsible for the state of the American theatre?

BALDWIN: The people who make the decisions think that they know what a play—or a book—is, but they don't. They are genuinely *illiterate*. The only reason they are in theatre is because there is almost no genuine theatre in this country.

PLAYBILL: Do you have any personal philosophy as a playwright?

BALDWIN: I agree with Shakespeare: The Play's The Thing. It is the key, but it is the actors who bring it alive. A playwright and the performers should work in joy—with a common goal. You tell me — the audience—something I don't know.

PLAYBILL: Must the *something* be true or real?

BALDWIN: According to my definition, you write a play or you don't. If it's worth anything, it's real. There can't be an unreal play. Our theatre is not real, and when a people get this divorced from reality they can do *anything*. The state of our theatre is a sign of an unhealthy society.

PLAYBILL: Does our theatre reflect the truth about 1964 America?

BALDWIN: We see in the theatre what most people think Democracy is, but Democracy is not that simple. Unfortunately, the only virtues most Americans seem to respect are youth and ignorance. It is a crime to grow up, and "culture" is a dirty word. Remember that other country where "culture" was a dirty word? They exterminated 6,000,000 people.

PLAYBILL: Is the yawning flaw unreality or lack of proper proportion, Jimmy?

BALDWIN: Both. If we were living in a civilization with any sense of proportion, a non-writer such as Arthur Miller could never achieve any eminence. It's not Arthur Miller's fault that we think he's an artist. It's ours. He's watered-down Clifford Odets. His "love" is some panic-stricken attempt to hang onto his boyhood.

PLAYBILL: I cannot concur, although his latest play is plainly not his finest.

BALDWIN: *After the Fall* is the only play I ever walked out on. Anybody who could read it and not burn it obviously cannot be taken seriously as a theatre person. I'd say the same about anyone who could read *J.B.* and not realize that it was simply not a play.

PLAYBILL: To go back to *Blues For Mr. Charlie*, is it true that the Lincoln Center Repertory wanted to produce it?

BALDWIN: Yes, Kazan asked for it but I had an ethical commitment to the Actors Studio. I know that if I'd written this same play ten years ago *nobody* would have produced it—certainly not on Broadway. It is now born as a result of a meeting in time, a historical conspiracy or coincidence. The cast is also extraordinary. Take Diana Sands, a great actress. I wrote her part — every word — and she overwhelms me with her performance.

PLAYBILL: Will you write for the stage again?

BALDWIN: I will do more plays. I am now finishing a book with Richard Avedon on the way we now live in America. His pictures, my text—titled *An Essay*. Then I have a long article to do on the F.B.I. and how it treats Negroes. It will be called *The Blood Counters*, which is the Negroes' nickname for the F.B.I. After that, perhaps a play.

PLAYBILL: Thanks for an interesting and provocative interview.

BALDWIN: Do you know why it worked? Because you talked to me as a *writer*.

PLAYBILL: Doesn't everybody?

BALDWIN: No, Walter, not anymore. □

You call it icing. We call it Art.

And we built a gallery to prove it. You will see that all sorts of marvelous things can be Art, when you visit our exciting new Hallmark gallery. Now showing: The Art of the Wedding. Please stop in soon.

Hallmark Gallery 5th Avenue at 56th Street.

The setting tropical sun is just one of the delights of a Grace cruise.

Dream time away on a cruise to Haiti

And 5 other ports of call on a Grace Caribbean Cruise

GRACE

Grace Line's American-flag liners *Santa Rosa* and *Santa Paula* are the only ships specially designed for Caribbean cruising. You enjoy three vacations in one—resort living, foreign travel, the flavor of a private yacht. ■ You'll find more living space per passenger and an outdoor swimming pool that's the largest afloat. Every stateroom is outside with its own private bathroom and individually-controlled air conditioning. ■ 13-day Grace Line cruises sail every Friday from New York to Curacao, Aruba, Venezuela, Jamaica, Nassau or Haiti, and Ft. Lauderdale. See a Travel Agent. Grace Line, 3 Hanover Square or 628 Fifth Avenue (Rockefeller Center), New York. DI 4-6000.

34.

"ISN'T BALDWIN A WELL KNOWN PERVERT?"—HOOVER WEIGHS IN

JULY 1964

FBI headquarters urged the New York field office, also the FBI's consulate in the capital of the US book trade, to consult the grapevine about *The Blood Counters*. Tactful checks should be made "among its publication sources," the office was instructed, and agents should "remain alert to any possibility of securing galley proofs for the Bureau for review purposes." Possible exposure of Baldwin's book in *The New Yorker* made the hunt urgent: "over the years," wrote M. A. Jones of Crime Records, the magazine's careful urbanity had tolerated "irresponsible and unreliable . . . references concerning the Director and the FBI." The FBI's pilfering and pre-reading of Baldwin's book was not needed: as the introduction discussed, *The Blood Counters* was never completed, nor was it necessarily meant to be. But its rumored appearance was enough to send Hoover to the mattresses. "Isn't Baldwin a well known pervert?," the director asked in the lower right margin of this July 17th memo. Three days later, M. A. Jones answered both yes and no in a bravura critical performance also discussed in the introduction. "While it is not possible to state that [Baldwin] is a pervert," Jones concluded, "he has expressed a sympathetic viewpoint about homosexuality on several occasions, and a very definite hostility toward the revulsion of the American public regarding it." If Baldwin had intended the prospect of *The Blood Counters* to unhinge the very top of the Bureau, it succeeded flawlessly.

(Hoover, he pronounced in *The Devil Finds Work*, qualified as "history's most highly paid (and most utterly useless) *voyeur*.") Baldwin would not have guessed, however, that an FBI reader lower down could thoughtfully distinguish between sexual identity and sexual sympathy.

OPTIONAL FORM NO. 10
MAY 1962 EDITION
GSA GEN. REG. NO. 27

5010-106

UNITED STATES GOVERNMENT

Memorandum

Tolson
Belmont
Mohr
Casper
Callahan
Conrad
DeLoach
Evans
Gale
Rosen
Sullivan
Tavel
Trotter
Tele. Room
Holmes
Gandy

TO : Mr. DeLoach

DATE: 7-17-64

FROM : M. A. Jones

ALL INFORMATION CONTAINED
HEREIN IS UNCLASSIFIED
DATE 5-17-89 BY

SUBJECT: JAMES ARTHUR BALDWIN
INFORMATION CONCERNING

In my memorandum to you dated 6-22-64, I advised the book review section of "The Washington Post" for 6-21-64, announced captioned individual was contemplating at least four future books. Among these will be one about "the F. B. I. in the South." Our New York Office was advised and requested to make discreet checks among its publication sources in an attempt to verify this information. New York was also asked to remain alert to any possibility of securing galley proofs for the Bureau for review purposes.

The 7-14-64, edition of the "New York Herald Tribune" contained additional information concerning this matter. According to it, Baldwin's book will be published next spring; however, it will be featured in "The New Yorker" magazine prior to its publication in book form.

On 7-16-64, the New York Office telephonically advised that an interview with Baldwin appears in the current issue of "Playbill," the official program of the legitimate theater in that city. The article quotes Baldwin as telling the unidentified interviewer he will begin work soon on a long article about the manner in which Negroes are treated by the FBI. He referred to Bureau personnel as "The Blood Counters," which he claimed is the Negroes' nickname for them. New York is forwarding a copy of "Playbill" to the Bureau.

"The New Yorker" over the years has been irresponsible and unreliable with respect to references concerning the Director and the FBI. It has published articles of a satirical nature concerning FBI tours, "The FBI Story" (both the book and the movie) and crime statistics. Baldwin's book, "The Fire Next Time," appeared in the magazine before it was released in book form.

REC- 33 62-108763-29

The matter of Baldwin's contemplated book about the Bureau is being closely followed and you will be kept advised of pertinent developments.

JUL 27 1964

RECOMMENDATION:

1 ENCLOSURE

None. For information.

Isn't Baldwin a well known pervert.

1 - Mr. DeLoach
1 - Mr. Sullivan
HHA:cmk (7)

64 JUL 29 1964

COPY SENT TO MR. TOLSON

CRIME RE

OPTIONAL FORM NO. 10
MAY 1962 EDITION
GSA GEN. REG. NO. 27

5010-106

UNITED STATES GOVERNMENT

Memorandum

Tolson
Belmont
Mohr
Casper
Callahan
Conrad
DeLoach
Evans
Gale
Rosen
Sullivan
Tavel
Trotter
Tele. Room
Holmes
Gandy

TO : Mr. DeLoach

DATE: 7-20-64

FROM : M. A. Jones

SUBJECT: JAMES ARTHUR BALDWIN
INFORMATION CONCERNING

ALL INFORMATION CONTAINED HEREIN IS UNCLASSIFIED DATE 5-17-79 BY

b7C-1

My memorandum dated 7-17-64, which concerned the captioned individual's plans for a future book about the FBI, has been returned by the Director with this question: "Isn't Baldwin a well known pervert?" It is not a matter of official record that he is a pervert; however, the theme of homosexuality has figured prominently in two of his three published novels. Baldwin has stated that it is also "implicit" in his first novel, "Go Tell It on the Mountain." In the past, he has not disputed the description of "autobiographical" being attached to this first book.

The "New York Post" published a series of six articles about Baldwin in January, 1964. Written by Fern Marja Eckman, they were the result of a series of interviews by Mrs. Eckman with the novelist. She asked him why he used homosexuality in two of his novels and he corrected her by pointing out that all three novels contained this theme in one degree or another, using the term "implicit" in connection with the first book.

According to Mrs. Eckman, Baldwin explained the motivation for this recurrent theme in his fiction. He said there are two reasons for it, both of which are similar. He then launched into a diatribe about sex in America and actually never did state these so-called two reasons with any clarity. He says the situation he described in "Another Country" is true, only much worse than he depicted it. (Most of this novel dealt with the carnality of a group of whites and Negroes in Greenwich Village and Harlem. Included in it was one description of the homosexual deeds of a bisexual character in Paris.) Baldwin said he was exposed to all of this when he arrived in Greenwich Village as a Negro adolescent. He criticized American heterosexuality, saying it isn't sex at all but "pure desperation." He claims American homosexuality is primarily a waste which would cease to exist in effect if Americans were not so "frightened of it." He goes on to claim that Americans, Englishmen and Germans--the "Anglo-Saxons"--are the only people who talk about it. It should be noted, however, that he makes a point that it is these people, whom he calls the "Puritans" who speak of homosexuality in a "terrible way."

REC-33 62-108763-30

1 - Mr. DeLoach
1 - Mr. Sullivan

Continued on next page.

HHA:jol (7)

MORE

64 JUL 29 1964

CRIME

1258

M. A. Jones to DeLoach Memo
RE: JAMES ARTHUR BALDWIN

He then contrasts their approach with that of the Italians, stating, "In Italy, you know, men kiss each other and boys go to bed with each other. And no one is marked for life. No one imagines that--and they grow up, you know, and they have children and raise them. And no one ends up going to a psychiatrist or turning into a junkie because he's afraid of being touched."

He continues by saying that is the root of the "American" thing-- "it's not a fear of men going to bed with men. It's a fear of anybody touching anybody." Baldwin concluded this particular discussion with Mrs. Eckman by saying that Negroes were frequent targets of homosexual approaches on the part of whites because they were always looking for somebody to act out their fantasies on, and they seem to believe that Negroes know how to do "dirty things."

During this particular interview, Baldwin intimates that he has had experience in this type of activity, saying, "You wouldn't believe the holocaust that opens over your head...if you are 16 years old..." He ends by stating that they understand in Italy that people "were born to touch each other."

These remarks are similar to others Baldwin has gone on record with regarding homosexuality. While it is not possible to state that he is a pervert, he has expressed a sympathetic viewpoint about homosexuality on several occasions, and a very definite hostility toward the revulsion of the American public regarding it.

RECOMMENDATION:

None. For information.

35.

BALDWIN THE RIOT-STARTER

JULY AND AUGUST 1964

As if the Freedom Summer and *The Blood Counters* weren't enough, rioting in New York City in the summer of 1964 stoked the FBI's sense of a racial order turned upside down. A week of unrest in Harlem and Bedford-Stuyvesant was sparked by a painfully common incident: James Powell, a fifteen-year-old African American, was shot and killed by a white cop on July 16. Stores were looted and police precincts were attacked as perhaps four thousand black New Yorkers hit the streets to demand the shooter's arrest. This unsolicited postcard to the Bureau from a loyal—and morbidly racist—American offers a novel theory of the riot's causes. Trotskyites, some of them "married to U.S. citizens," were to blame. So were "Negroid Jews resembling Castro" and none other than James Baldwin, who had "interviewed Attorney General Kennedy" prior to his brother's assassination "and started it all." The FBI did not accept the credibility of the postcard at face value: its charges warranted "limited inquiries." But the Bureau's similarly race-baiting anticommunism still led it to wonder if the author was "in possession of any information of interest and/or value to the Bureau." Baldwin's quite different account of the riot, informed by his experience of earlier Harlem explosions in 1935 and 1943, was clipped from the *New York Post* in early August. "There is a very good reason for the Negroes to hate the police in Harlem," he explained, since law enforcement's "real role [there] is simply to corral and control the citizens." Baldwin had said much the same thing about Harlemites and their wardens in his moving autobiographical essay "Notes of a Native Son" (1955). This time around, however, collected and monitored by the FBI, he peered out from his file like a writer contemplating a final jailbreak.

S:

TROTZKYITES ARE BEHIND HARLEM RIOTS.

SOME ARE FOREIGN, IMMIGRANT TROTZKYITES MARRIED TO U.S. CITIZENS.

A NUMBER OF NEGROID JEWS RESEMBLING CASTRO ARE INVOLVED.

ALSO, JAS. BALDWIN, FEATURED BY "THE MILITANT" IS RESPONSIBLE. HE INTERVIEWED ATTORNEY GENERAL KENNEDY BEFORE THE ASSASSINATION AND STARTED IT ALL.

LOYAL CITIZEN

ANONYMOUS COMMUNICATIONS

62-108763-32

REC-98 ~~62-108763-30~~

6 JUL 31 1964

ALL INFORMATION CONTAINED
HEREIN IS UNCLASSIFIED
DATE 5/17/89 BY

CORRESPONDENCE

b7c-5

NEW YORK
PM
22 JUL
1964

U.S. POSTAGE 4c

THIS SIDE OF CARD IS FOR ADDRESS

U.S. POSTAGE

F.B.I. MAN IN CHARGE
OF HARLEM RIOTS INVESTIGATION
FEDERAL BUREAU OF INVESTIGATION
DEPARTMENT OF JUSTICE
WASHINGTON, D.C.

AIR MAIL

COMMUNICATIONS

SAC, Philadelphia 7/29/64

REC- 93

Director, FBI 62-108763-32

1 - Mr. [redacted]

b7C-1

JAMES BALDWIN
INFORMATION CONCERNING
(INTERNAL SECURITY)

There are enclosed two copies of a postal card addressed to the Bureau which was postmarked New York, New York, 7/22/64 and signed merely "Loyal Citizen."

It is noted that the postal card contains a return address in Philadelphia, Pennsylvania. The Philadelphia Office is accordingly instructed to make limited inquiries to attempt to determine the identity of the individual who directed this postal card to the Bureau. In the event he can be readily identified, he should be interviewed to determine if he is in possession of any information of interest and/or value to the Bureau.

This matter must be expeditiously handled and the results promptly submitted to the Bureau. It is not contemplated by the Bureau that the Philadelphia Office should expend considerable time and manpower in identifying the writer of this communication but inquiries should be made at the address given.

Enclosures - 2

ALL INFORMATION CONTAINED
HEREIN IS UNCLASSIFIED
DATE 5-18-89 BY SP8 [illegible]

Tolson
Belmont
Mohr
Casper
Callahan
Conrad
DeLoach
Evans
Gale
Rosen
Sullivan
Tavel
Trotter
Tele. Room
Holmes
Gandy

RDS:rbm
(4)

60 AUG 6 1964

MAIL ROOM ☑ TELETYPE UNIT ☐

James Baldwin on The Harlem Riots

James Baldwin sent this statement to The New York Post from Paris, where he is working on another novel.

I have lived through two race riots in Harlem, the riot of 1935 and the riot of 1943, and part of my family and many of my friends are living there now. I may, therefore, perhaps be pardoned a weary sharpness of exasperation when I observe the general reaction to the present disorder—which any citizen of Harlem could have foreseen, and which many of us, with no help whatever from the municipality or the government—and still less from the American citizenry—did our best to avert.

The riots always have the same stubborn cause—the conditions of life in the ghetto. These are conditions which almost no white American is willing to imagine, and from which he deliberately averts his eyes. On the other hand, the citizens of the ghetto are exposed to the white world, and under the most intolerable conditions, every working day. This means that, for Negroes the contrast between the black and white situations is perpetually and hideously vivid. White people, wishing to deny the contrast, have no idea whatever, therefore, of the resulting tension of fury and bitterness.

Lacking this, they are always reduced to a bewildered anger and guilt whenever the Negroes rise.

As for the fear which these up-risings evoke, it is not merely an objective fear, the fear, for example, of being physically attacked; it is a deeper fear, a sleeping fear which has been there all along, a fear of the Negroes' vengeance, or their will to vengeance, which then seizes on the objective disorder as a means of justifying injustice. This is why, in one of the most dangerous and lawless cities in the United States, the Negroes are immediately called upon to respect law and order. *Whose* law, one is compelled to ask, and *what* order?

The Police Angle

There is a very good reason for the Negroes to hate the police in Harlem. Leaving aside the general level of their competence, which is abysmal, and their terror, which is so great as to be indistinguishable from cowardice, and which is responsible for their brutality—for they *are* brutal: they know no other way of coping with the forces to which they are exposed—their real role in Harlem is simply to corral and control the citizens of the ghetto, and protect white business interests there. They certainly do not protect the lives or property of Negroes—I know people in my own family, who, having been robbed three times in as many months, simply ceased reporting these robberies (for which, of course, no culprit was ever found; it would appear that Negroes are arrested for robbing white people) and took steps to protect themselves.

Fear—on Both Sides

How can one be expected to respect the Law when it is overwhelmingly clear that the Law has no respect for you? And as for Order—are the citizens of Harlem seriously expected to become accomplices to that Order which locked them in the ghetto in the first place, and

Index
Test of
James Baldwin
on Harlem Riots
Ah 43

CLIPPING FROM THE

NY Post

EDITION

DATE

PAGE 3

FORWARDED BY NY DIVISION ✓

NOT FORWARDED BY NY DIVISION

ALL INFORMATION CONTAINED HEREIN IS UNCLASSIFIED DATE 5/25/89 BY

100-146553-19

which, according to almost all available evidence, intends to keep them and their children there forever? I know that these are very grave statements, but they petrain to very grave questions that we face—or, rather, alas, for the most part, do not face.

The police become the immediate focus, especially under specific tension, of the ghetto's discontent, and it is by no means insignificant that the people of the ghetto, and especially the youth, know that the police are afraid of them. In 1935, if I remember correctly, the specific tension involved the question of whether or not Negroes would ever be hired as clerks in the five and dimes and other stores on 125th St., where Negroes helplessly spent, and spend, so much of their money; presently, a policeman, or a plainclothes man, was accused of beating up a young Negro boy in one of these stores, and this was enough to set Harlem aflame.

(EDITOR'S NOTE: The 1935 riots actually were touched off by a rumor, not by an actual encounter between a policeman and a Negro boy.)

In 1943, the situation of the Negro soldier was a source of great anxiety and bitterness for everyone; presently a policeman was accused of shooting a Negro soldier in the back in the lobby of the Braddock Hotel.

These days, it is the situation of Negro youth—which is another way of saying the future of the race—which obsesses everyone; no Negro has forgotten, nor yet recovered from, the bombing of the Sunday school in Birmingham, and, once again, it is the fact that a policeman has been accused of killing a Negro youth—in self-defense!—which has precipitated chaos.

The Real Trouble

The policeman, in other words, immediately becomes the focus of the ghetto's preoccupations. He represents the power to which they owe their suffering and their danger; and, therefore, no policy could be more calculated to bring about disaster than the augmentation of the police force as soon as a more than ordinary tension is in the air. The augmentation of the police force simply guarantees a stiffening of resistance and an immediate increase of hostility.

And, finally, the ghetto, as best it can, and using the only means open to it, vents its despair. Nor will the problem be solved, or even seriously ameliorated, by assigning black policemen to Harlem. They, too, will be working for the white power structure, and will risk being even more hated than white policemen—to say nothing of the tensions that duty in Harlem must necesarily set up in a black policeman's breast and the ways which he will find, of coping with this tension.

For the trouble in Harlem is simply that it is a captive and mainly miserable population in the middle of one of the most important cities of a wealthy and pretentious nation. It is one thing to be captive or hungry in a captive and hungry nation. It is quite another thing to be captive and hungry in a nation which so vociferously and relentlessly boasts of itself as being affluent and free.

Mr. J. Edgar Hoover has been vastly more successful in discovering Communists and criminals than he has been in discovering those responsible for the bombings in the Deep South—so that I have no doubt that he and his so highly esteemed Bureau will, during their investigation in Harlem, flush out criminals by the score and Communists, possibly, by the dozen.

What the Negro Feels

I don't, to my knowledge, know any Communists in Harlem, but I know a great many criminals—maids stealing from kitchens, boys stealing from the garment center, janitors playing the numbers, junkies—but I suggest that he pay just a little attention to real estate boards and to landlords; to leave it only at that. It is grotesque and insulting, in any case, to suppose that race riots in Harlem are fomented by Communists.

They are, on the contrary, fomented by the American republic. Every Negro in America lives with the suspicion, which his daily life endlessly confirms, that his countrymen despise him—despise him so deeply and so helplessly, and from the very bottom of their hearts, that they will flee cities, as they do, and close libraries, parks, playgrounds, schools, and beaches, as indeed they do, rather than be contaminated by his presence.

One feels that they would pollute the very water one drinks and siphon off the air one breathes, if only they knew how. *The spirit of the South is the spirit of America*: this has been said to me more than once and, alas, alas, it is true. Or, as a black veteran of Mississippi work farms puts it: *"It's the same plantation, all over the United States."*

The Civil Rights Issue

And what better proof is needed than the grotesque wrangle over a Civil Rights Bill which should have been law a hundred years ago, and which yet remains, on many broken heads, and by way of many broken lives, to be tested, [illegible] *[illegible]*—one day, to be enforced?

What does the rise of Governor Wallace and still more the candidacy of Sen. Goldwater mean to a Negro, and what can it mean except that his countrymen are determined to [illegible] him? It is idle in the [illegible] expect that the black citizens of the United States will once more trust to the good will of white America. [illegible] scarcely possible, so runs [illegible] despairing reasoning, [illegible] ill-will of white America [illegible] him any more harm than [illegible] good-will has done already.

Some Questions

What is needed now [illegible] termined and clear-headed assault on those forces responsible for this despair and [illegible] common danger. Who, for example, runs the South, and for whose benefit? Who profits [illegible] Harlem, and by what means? To what forces and to what panic do we owe the extraordinary—extraordinary even in a country so enamoured of [illegible] mediocre—phenomenon of [illegible] water?

In my view, [illegible] questions, and questions [illegible] harder than these, to which we must address ourselves [illegible] hope ever to see peace or maturity or freedom in that country which arbitrarily calls itself America, but which actually occupies a small part of the American continent and (in spite of Texas) a much [illegible] part of the globe.

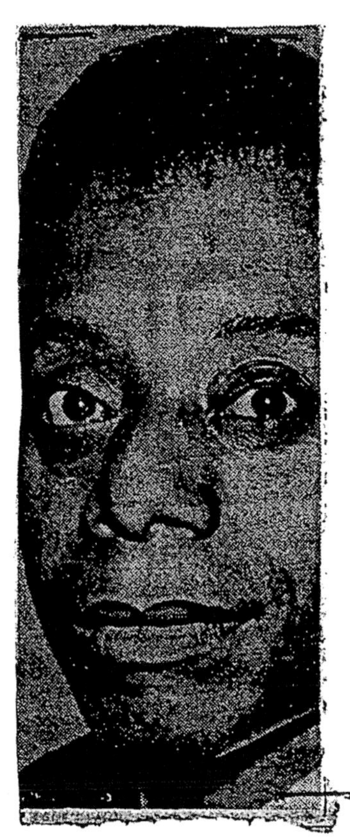

36.

THE BLOOD COUNTERS AND BALDWIN COUNTERSURVEILLANCE, PART 3

AUGUST 1964

In August 1964, the FBI finally became confident that it would get its man—or at least his galleys. M. A. Jones briefly and excitedly wrote Cartha DeLoach with the news that an informer in "the publishing field" expected "to secure the proofs" of *The Blood Counters* later that year and planned to "make them available immediately" afterward. Baldwin never delivered the manuscript of his "attack against the Bureau," of course, so its proofs remained secure against the FBI. There's little doubt that the Bureau could have hijacked completed versions if it tried hard enough, however. By the 1950s, the Bureau's connections in the New York book world made it difficult to criticize the FBI through a major publishing house. Claire Culleton's study of the FBI's file on Henry Holt, one of the oldest publishing firms in the United States, uncovers plentiful evidence of Hoover's "custodial relationship" with this pillar of the Cold War book industry. Holt employees sent Bureau agents all manner of intelligence on books-in-progress, from proposals to galley proofs (the latter being what the Bureau wanted of *The Blood Counters*). One Holt staffer confessed in a letter to Hoover that "I am beginning to feel like a member of the FBI myself." At Random House, another storied New York firm, the manuscript of Fred Cook's muckraking *The FBI Nobody Knows* was rejected after Hoover disapproved of a forwarded version; the book floated in limbo until Macmillan braved the Bureau's displeasure and eventually published copies in 1964. Baldwin's *The Blood Counters*, the rarely told story of the FBI known to African Americans, evaded a similarly complex fate by evading publication anywhere.

OPTIONAL FORM NO. 10
MAY 1962 EDITION
GSA GEN. REG. NO. 27

3010-106

UNITED STATE[illegible] [illegible]MENT

Memorandum

Tolson
Belmont
Mohr
Casper
Callahan
Conrad
DeLoach
Evans
Gale
Rosen
Sullivan
Tavel
Trotter
Tele. Room
Holmes
Gandy

TO : Mr. DeLoach

DATE: 8-5-64

FROM : M. A. Jones

SUBJECT: JAMES ARTHUR BALDWIN
INFORMATION CONCERNING

The New York Office has telephonically advised that one of its contacts in the publishing field has expressed the belief it may be possible to secure the galley of captioned individual's "The Blood Counters." As you are aware, this is the book that is to be based on the FBI and the South, and all current information regarding it indicates it will be an attack against the Bureau. New York's source expects to secure the proofs in November or December, 1964, and will make them available immediately.

This matter is being closely followed, and you will be kept advised of pertinent developments.

RECOMMENDATION:

None. For information.

ALL INFORMATION CONTAINED
HEREIN IS UNCLASSIFIED
DATE 5/18/89 BY [illegible]

1 - Mr. DeLoach
1 - Mr. Sullivan

62-108763-34

REC- 38

16 AUG 11 1964

HHA:cmk
(5)

EX-102

CRIME RESEARCH

70 AUG 17 1964

37.

TRASHING BALDWIN

SEPTEMBER 1964

The glamor of espionage: a reliable FBI source sifts through "trash which was collected from the China Daily News, 20 Elizabeth Street," New York City, and discovers an empty envelope that once contained a Baldwin letter (probably his bulk-mailed fundraising appeal for the Mississippi Freedom Project). Garbage can–raiding "trash covers," as they were termed in the trade, were regular features of FBI anti-subversive investigations. Rechristened as "dumpster dives" or "black forest" raids, they remain a standard tool of state and corporate spying. These days—witness the endless, world-changing investigations of Hillary Clinton's e-mail habits—the electronic files embedded in a discarded computer's memory are the highest-value targets. But the aim in Baldwin's paper-filled day was much the same: to hold one's nose, pick through a suspect's refuse, and come away with incriminating items, all in secrecy.

SAC (100-63825)

SEP 10 1964

SA JOHN M. DOGGETT (#312)

CHINA DAILY NEWS
IS - CH

ALL INFORMATION CONTAINED
HEREIN IS UNCLASSIFIED
DATE 5/25/18 BY

b2-1

On 9/2/64, [redacted] who has furnished reliable information in the past, made available trash which was collected from the China Daily News, 20 Elizabeth Street, NYC, to SA [redacted] b7C-1

Included in the trash were 3 envelopes addressed to the China Daily News bearing the following return addresses:

JAMES BALDWIN
100 Fifth Avenue
NYC

Progressive Labor
Box 808
GPO, Brooklyn 1, NY

Organization of Afro-American Unity
Hotel Theresa
125th Street and 7th Avenue
NYC

The above informant was unable to advise any information regarding the contents of the above correspondence.

100-146553-179

SERIALIZED ... FILED
FBI — NEW YORK

1 - 100-146553 (JAMES BALDWIN)
1 - 100-147372 (Progressive Labor)
1 - 100-153308 (Organization of Afro-American Unity)
- [redacted] (Investigative)

MD:mek
(5)

b2-1 b7D-1

38.

"BALDWIN WILL QUIT U.S. IF GOLDWATER WINS"

OCTOBER 1964

Arizona Senator Barry Goldwater, a leading opponent of the 1964 Civil Rights Act and the Republican Party's radically conservative conscience, lost his presidential contest with Democrat Lyndon B. Johnson in a landslide. As a result, Baldwin's vow to meet his election by emigrating permanently "to another country" went untested. Win or lose, the writer was ahead of the curve in sounding a liberal battle cry—"Give me a sane Democratic president, or give me exile"—mainstreamed in the wake of Donald Trump.

FD-350 (4-3-62)

Mr. Tolson
Mr. Belmont
Mr. Mohr
Mr. [illegible]
Mr. [illegible]
Mr. [illegible]
Mr. Conrad
Mr. Evans
Mr. [illegible]
Mr. [illegible]
Mr. [illegible]
Mr. Tavel
Mr. Trotter
Tele. Room
Miss Holmes
Miss Gandy

(Mount Clipping in Space Below)

Baldwin Will Quit U.S. If Goldwater Wins

BERLIN — James Baldwin has vowed he will emigrate to another country if Senator Barry Goldwater is elected President of the United States.

At the same time, he denounced the American Black Muslim movement and racial violence in the United States.

Baldwin discussed the American racial problem in an interview given in Paris to the West Berlin newspaper Spandauer Volksablatt.

The newspaper bannerlined the interview on the front page under the headline "Harlem Is A Ghetto."

Asked for his opinion of Goldwater's nomination as the Republican candidate for President the Negro writer, said, "That is a scandal for the United States. I do not believe in saying too much, but the San Francisco convention showed what the nation really thinks of us 20 million Negroes.

"It was a bitter lesson. If he becomes president I will emigrate. And I would not be the only one to do so."

Asked if he would support President Johnson's campaign for reelection, Baldwin replied, "As much as it is in my power to do so."

Baldwin condemned the Black Muslims as the Negro equivalent to the Ku Klux Klan.

"I have nothing in common with them," he said. It is criminal to want to solve the (racial) problem with force. Only mutual understanding can help here. No race is superior to another. To try and reverse the present relationship is to drive out the devil with Beelzebub."

Baldwin said Negroes regretted more than anyone the recent outburst of violence and looting in northern cities.

"Such demonstrations always and everywhere are used by dark elements for their criminal goals," he said. "And not only by Negroes. Look at what happened in Europe during the depression."

(Indicate page, name of newspaper, city and state.)

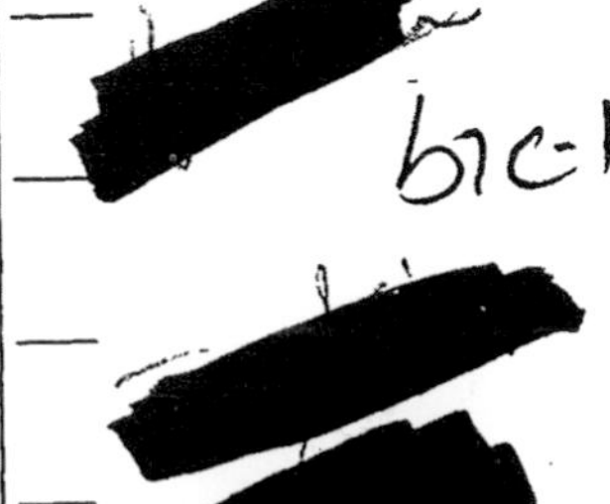

b7C-1

THE NEW CRUSADER
15 CHICAGO, ILLINOIS

Date: 9-26-64
Edition: WEEKLY
Author:
Editor: BALM L. LEAVELL
Title:

Character:
or
Classification:
Submitting Office: CHICAGO

ALL INFORMATION CONTAINED
HEREIN IS UNCLASSIFIED
DATE 5/18/89 BY [illegible]

62-108763-A
NOT RECORDED
OCT 22 1964

CT 26 1964

39.

CITIZEN LITERARY CRITICISM, PART 1: TEXAS ON *ANOTHER COUNTRY*

JANUARY 1965

Some of the ordinary citizens who regarded Hoover as a right-wing Dear Abby wrote the Bureau director with specifically literary questions. In this case, a correspondent from Texas inquires into the horror discovered at the end of a chain leading from a recommended books list in a Baptist quarterly, to Fort Worth stores selling paperbacks, to a seventy-six-cent copy of *Another Country*. Baldwin's novel, the correspondent reported, mixed loving depictions of degenerate behavior with the challenge of compound words and complex sentences. It "has every filthy word, compound word and phrasing that could be used to portray: Drug addition, Sex perversion at its vilest." The citizen-critic confessed inadequacy to the task of summary but instructed the Bureau where it could obtain a copy of its own: "Many Book stores and Drug stores here in Fort Worth . . . have it in stock." "Mr. Hoover," the critic pleaded, "is there any Federal law which would prohibit the publication or the sale of this degrading Book?" Hoover's answer must have disappointed: despite the Bureau's suspicion of *Another Country* since 1962, the critic's "communication [did] not present facts indicative of any violation of Federal law" under the FBI's jurisdiction. The critic wasn't mistaken, however, in assuming that Hoover would find Baldwin's phrasings and "perversions" disturbing: the four Hoover-authored pamphlets denouncing "obscene and pornographic literature" mailed out in return certified the director's personal disapproval of the novel. When looking to Hoover's FBI, such citizen-critics were right to see a fellow reader hopeful of better literary policing.

January 22, 1965

Hon. J Edgar Hoover
Federal Bureau of Investigation
Washington, D. C.

Dear Sir:

In a Baptist Young People's quarterly (B.Y .P.U.) published in Nashville, Tenn. by the Sunday School Board of the Southern Baptist Convention for the period of July, August, September, 1964, is a list of Books recommended for reading to the B.Y.P.U.

On page ~~six~~, six of this publication among the Books recommended is one titled "Another Country" by James Baldwin. This Book "Another Country" has every filthy w ord, compound word and phrasing that could be used to portray: Drug addition, Sex perversion at its vilest. Unless or/and until one has read this Book of degradation, any attempt the writer m makes to describe the contents will fall short of the degenerate nature of the B ook.

Many B ook stores and Drug stores here in Fort Worth, Texas have it in stock, with a price of 76¢ for paper bind.

Mr Hoover, is there any Federal law which would prohibit the publication or the s ale of this degrading Book?

Respt.

H

[redacted]

b7c-4 [redacted] Fort Worth, Texas

[redacted]

/cl

REC- 120 145-2625-4

JAN 29 1965

ack 1-28-65
DCL/~~ab~~ pp

CORRESPONDENCE

mml

January 28, 1965

REC-120 145-2625-4
EX-112

[redacted]

Fort Worth, Texas

b7c-4

Dear [redacted]

Your letter dated January 22nd has been received.

The concern prompting your writing me is very much appreciated; however, your communication does not present facts indicative of any violation of Federal law coming within the investigative jurisdiction of the FBI. I am referring a copy of your letter to postal authorities.

REC'D-READING ROOM FBI JAN 28 3 16 PM '65

Enclosed are publications which express my views on the widespread accessibility of obscene and pornographic literature.

Sincerely yours,

MAILED 10 JAN 28 1965 COMM-FBI

J. Edgar Hoover

Enclosures (4)
Combating Merchants of Filth: The Role of the FBI
Let's Wipe Out The Schoolyard Sex Racket!
The Fight Against Filth
1-60 LEB Intro

NOTE: Correspondent is not identifiable in Bufiles. Copy of incoming sent to PO Dept. by form.

DCL:pp (3)

Tolson
Belmont
Mohr
DeLoach
Casper
Callahan
Conrad
Felt
Gale
Rosen
Sullivan
Tavel
Trotter
Tele. Room
Holmes
Gandy

FEB 5 1965 MAIL ROOM ☐ TELETYPE UNIT ☐

40.

CITIZEN LITERARY CRITICISM, PART 2: MISSISSIPPI ON *BLUES FOR MISTER CHARLIE*

APRIL AND MAY 1965

A few months after filing the letter from Fort Worth, Hoover received a letter from Olive Branch, Mississippi, likewise triggered by the citation of Baldwin's books in a church publication. The denomination of the publication was Presbyterian, rather than Baptist, but the result was much the same. *Another Country* was again read with astonishment by a probably white, certainly Southern, conservatively Christian American, this time alongside the published version of *Blues for Mister Charlie*. Obscenity was again discovered in Baldwin's pages, and Hoover was again asked to sample it, then stop it. Hoover, with palpable regret, again answered that Baldwin's obscenity was "not within our investigative jurisdiction." Yet this time around, the citizen-critic mailed "one copy each" of *Blues* and *Another Country* to Hoover, both prepared for his examination: "Due to previous references some of the pages have been turned down or marked in ink. You might use that for quick check." The Mississippian's peculiar wish that Hoover would personally handle her copies in fact expressed a shared fantasy: more than one American reader understood the FBI director as an intimate, sympathetic audience for sexually tinged fears of James Baldwin.

Olive Branch, Miss.
Apr. 22, 1965

The Hon. J. Edgar Hoover
Chief of Federal Bureau of Investigation
Washington, D.C.

ALL INFORMATION CONTAINED
HEREIN IS UNCLASSIFIED
DATE 5-18-89 BY [illegible]

Sir:

I am sending to you one copy each of two books by the writer, James Baldwin. They are entitled "Blues for Mr. Charlie" and "Another Country." Also included are two copies of "Hi Way" dated November 1964 and February 1965.

The "Hi Way" Magazine is supplimentary material for the Senior High Young People's Sunday School Literature in the United Presbyterian Church U.S.A. As I understand it, this denomination is a member of The National Council of Churches.

I am a member of the United Presbyterian Denomination and so are all the members of my family. I was more than concerned

ENCLOSURE

when I read in these "Hi Way" magazines (I have a son in this Sunday School Class) and found these books by James Baldwin advertised, and which I was able to buy right from the book rack in the store.

When I bought these books and read them I was speechless. I was numb. I could not believe that any Christian Denomination would allow such writings to be advertised through their church materials. But it was true. It was there before me.

I don't know how far the FBI can go in church organization investigation but I see this as a matter of Obscene literature and poor church organization. My Faith in the Presbyterian Church has been thoroughly shaken, to say the least.

Mr. Hoover, will you please examine these books and advise me. Due to previous references some of the pages have been turned down or marked in ink. You might use that for quick check. Tell me, for the sake of Our God and Humanity, how and where these writings fit into Christianity. I find no connection whatsoever. One would not need to read the entire book to see the filth contained in its pages.

I do not know whether church materials can advertise such books as "Another Country" and "Blues for Mr. Charlie" and escape investigation or not, so that's why I need advice.

I will greatly appreciate any information you can give me about this matter. I feel that it is SERious.

I will help in any way I can if I know what to do. Some other church members feel as I do. We want this stuff out, if possible.

Thank you so very much for taking the time to read my letter. I will be very grateful for any advice and information

Respectfully,

b7C-5 [redacted]

Olive Branch, Miss.

TRUE COPY

Olive Branch, Miss.
Apr. 22, 1965

The Hon. J. Edgar Hoover
Chief of Federal Bureau of Investigation
Washington, D. C.

ALL INFORMATION CONTAINED
HEREIN IS UNCLASSIFIED
DATE 5-19-89 BY [illegible]

Sir:

I am sending to you one copy each of two books by the Writer, James Baldwin. They are entitled "Blues for Mr. Charlie" and "Another Country." Also included are two copies of "Hi Way" dated November 1964 and February 1965.

The "Hi Way" Magazine is supplimentary material for the Senior High Young People's Sunday School Literature in the United Presbyterian Church U. S. A. As I understand it, this denomination is a member of The National Council of Churches.

I am a Member of the United Presbyterian Denomination and so are all the Members of My family.

I was More than concerned when I read in these "Hi Way" Magazines (I have a son in this Sunday School class) and found these books by James Baldwin advertised, and which I was able to buy right from the book rack in the store.

When I bought these books and read them I was speechless. I was numb. I could not believe that any Christian Denomination would allow such writings to be advertised through their church Materials. But it was true. It was there before me.

REC 5

EX 110

62-108763-36

I don't know how far the FBI can go in church organization investigation but I see this as a matter of Obscene literature and poor church organization. My Faith in the Presbyterian church has been thoroughly shaken, to say the least.

b7c-5

21 MAY 24 1965

Olive Branch, Miss.

1-TC/4-29-65/ dll
ack/4-30-65
5-3
Kls/disfmlt faf 8 DTP

Mr. Hoover, will you please examine these books and advise me. Due to previous references some of the pages have been turned down or marked in ink. You might use that for quick check. Tell me, for the sake of Our God and Humanity, how and where these writings fit into Christianity. I find no connection whatsoever. One would not need to read the entire book to see the filth contained in its pages.

I do not know whether church materials can advertise such books as "Another Country" and "Blues for Mr. Charlie" and escape investigation or not, so that's why I need advice.

I will greatly appreciate any information you can give me about this matter. I feel that it is Serious!

I will help in any way I can if I know what to do. Some other church members feel as I do. We want this stuff out, if possible.

Thank you so very much for taking the time to read my letter. I will be very grateful for any advice and information.

Respectfully,
s/ [redacted]
Olive Branch, Miss.

b7c-5

REC 5 X 110

62-108763-30

May 3, 1965

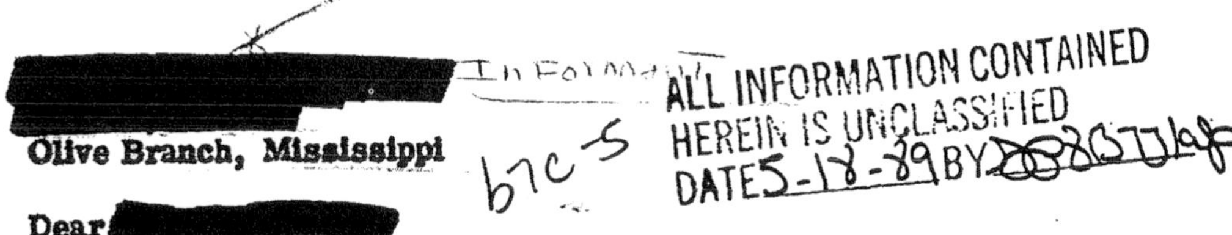
ALL INFORMATION CONTAINED
HEREIN IS UNCLASSIFIED
DATE 5-18-89 BY

Olive Branch, Mississippi

b7C-5

Dear

Your letter of April 22nd has been received, and the thought which prompted you to write me is appreciated.

With respect to your inquiries, the FBI, as strictly an investigative agency of the Federal Government, does not make evaluations of any kind. In addition, the advertising by any church of literature which may be construed as obscene is not within our investigative jurisdiction. I regret I cannot be of help in this instance but trust you will understand.

I am returning the booklets and magazines you sent.

Sincerely yours,

b7C-5

MAILED 7
MAY - 3 1965
COMM-FBI

Enclosures (4)

NOTE: We corresponded with on 11-10-64 at which time she was sent material on communism. The articles that she enclosed were the November, 1964, and February, 1965, issues of the magazine, "Hi Way," which is published monthly apparently by the Westminster Press and our files do not disclose any derogatory information concerning it. The other enclosures were two paperback books, "Blues for Mister Charlie" and "Another Country," written by James Baldwin and do contain feferences to pornography and obscenity. James Baldwin is well known to the Bureau.

DFC:asf (3)

Mr. Tolson
Mr. Belmont
Mr. Mohr
Mr. DeLoach
Mr. Casper
Mr. Callahan
Mr. Conrad
Mr. Felt
Mr. Gale
Mr. Rosen
Mr. Sullivan
Mr. Tavel
Mr. Trotter
Tele. Room
Miss Holmes
Miss Gandy

MAY 12 1965

41.

BUCKLEY ON "THE BALDWIN SYNDROME"

JUNE 1965

Judging from the sheer volume of writing clipped and filed, the FBI's favorite civilian critic of Baldwin was William F. Buckley Jr. In this June 1965 column on "The Baldwin Syndrome," circulated to at least five of Hoover's top lieutenants, Buckley turns from the poetic fervor of *The Fire Next Time* to Baldwin's "discouraging" words "on a television program in which I participated." Was it fair to say that "things couldn't be worse" for African Americans, as Baldwin apparently had claimed? Only if one had an excessive tolerance for hyperbole destructive "to the cause of a proper equality," thought Buckley. Setting Baldwin "and his coterie of America-haters" against properly moderate Civil Rights leaders, Buckley closed with the modest proposal that his debate opponent's "morose nihilism is a greater threat by far to prospects for the Negroes in America than anything that George Wallace," the arch-segregationist governor of Alabama, "ever said or did." Buckley's 1957 editorial "Why the South Must Prevail," a case for white supremacy over "Negro backwardness" in the region, was not his last dip into white Southern apologetics and the counsel of slow, sober, and patriotic black sympathy-seeking. Baldwin's updated Bolshevism, Buckley suggested, could not be allowed to intimidate the mild "socialist-humanitarians" at the NAACP, or a tragic repeat of the Russian Revolution would play out on American soil.

0-19 (Rev. 12-14-64)

Tolson
Belmont
Mohr
DeLoach
Casper
Callahan
Conrad
Felt
Gale
Rosen
Sullivan
Tavel
Trotter
Tele Room
Holmes
Gandy

The Baldwin Syndrome

By William F. Buckley Jr.

JAMES BALDWIN, the author and playwright whose reputation is in part owing to his fine writing, in part to the implacability of his theme (Hate the System), said a couple of discouraging things on a television program in which I participated. To wit:

That as regards the Negro, "things couldn't be worse." And that Negroes who throw their garbage out on the streets are doing so—legitimately, he suggests—as a form of protest against their plight.

When Mr. Baldwin says that the lot of the Negroes could not be worse, one necessarily reacts in either of two ways:

- He is correct — things couldn't be worse.
- Or he is engaging in hyperbole; in which case one must ask whether it is useful to the cause of a proper equality.

I conclude as regards the former that things could very easily be worse for Negroes than they are. Worse, for instance, if the overwhelming majority of the opinion leaders of this country cared not at all about the plight of the Negroes, which manifestly is not the case.

If the Negroes' lot is not improved by the kind of sympathy he receives and has received — sympathy registered in legislation, editorials, columns, books, sermons, catechisms, welfare payments — then what are we to do?

It is an interesting question, which is hardly answered by apocolyptic statements by such as Mr. Baldwin threatening us with The Fire Next Time — the next time we disagree with whatever poetical locution he comes up with concerning the delinquencies of the white people of this country.

On our program, Mr. Baldwin said that he was neither a socialist nor a Marxist. Let us take him at his word. But I wonder how, intellectually, he can reconcile his statements with his behavior?

In his writing he deplores the capitalist system, which he holds institutionally responsible for enslaving the Negro.

The crisis involving the American Negro has much to do with the fear that Negro leaders themselves have of their own most

The Washington Post and Times Herald
The Washington Daily News
The Evening Star
New York Herald Tribune
New York Journal-American
New York Daily News
New York Post
The New York Times
The Baltimore Sun
The Worker
The New Leader
The Wall Street Journal
The National Observer
People's World
Date

ALL INFORMATION CONTAINED
HEREIN IS UNCLASSIFIED
DATE 5-18-89 BY

62-108763-A

NOT RECORDED
46 JUN 28 1965

JUN 23 1965

56 JUN 29 1965

rabid representatives. There is a great deal to disagree with—for those concerned with the integrity of the Constitution—when dealing with the demands of such as Roy Wilkins of the NAACP, of Thurgood Marshall, of others who tend to seek out a fresh law to suture every offense against the Negro. But however much one disagrees with them, they are, in context, the voices of moderation: and we must ask them why they do not dissociate themselves from the swollen irrationalities of such as Mr. Baldwin.

The trouble is—and this is brilliantly recorded in the forthcoming book by Theodore White on The Making of a President, 1964 — that they dare not do so, for fear that they would thus suggest a lack of militancy in their own approach to the problem.

It was exactly so in the 20's, when many of the socialist-humanitarians who backed the Bolshevik Revolution found themselves indorsing the enormities of Lenin, and Totsky, and subsequently of Stalin — because they feared to alienate themselves from the leadership of the revolutionary protest.

The objective of those who seek equality for the Negro is equality for the Negro within the American system. If James Baldwin and his coterie of America-haters continue to give the impression that such others as Roy Wilkins go along with their indictments, then they may very well end up satisfying the American people that identification with the civil rights movements is an alternative to maintaining the American system.

How long, one wonders, before the Baldwins will be ghettoized in the corners of fanaticism where they belong? The moment is overdue for someone who speaks authentically for the Negroes to tell Mr. Baldwin that his morose nihilism is a greater threat by far to prospects for the Negroes in America than anything that George Wallace ever said or did.

42.

WHERE IN THE WORLD WAS JAMES BALDWIN?

MARCH, APRIL, AND OCTOBER 1966

In early 1966, the year he first spent long stretches in Istanbul and began drafting his fourth novel, *Tell Me How Long the Train's Been Gone*, Baldwin temporarily fell off the Bureau's map. "Nothing is known about [his] current location," noted the New York office, other than the facts that he had recently attended a tribute to Paul Robeson at the Americana Hotel and that he "appeared as if [he] may be a homosexual" while doing so. In October, the Bureau again picked up his trail, locating Baldwin as a "[s]elf-employed" author "presently in Turkey." When seen by the FBI, Baldwin could run and briefly hide, but would always carry identifying signs of sexual difference.

Cover Sheet for Informant Report or Material
FD-306 (3-21-58)

DATE: 4/26/66

Date received	Received from (name or symbol number)	Received by
3/29/66	b2-1 b7D-1 [redacted] (Reliable-Conceal)	SA [redacted] b7C-1

Method of delivery (check appropriate blocks)

☐ in person ☒ by telephone ☐ by mail ☐ orally ☐ recording device ☐ written by Informant

If orally furnished and reduced to writing by Agent:

Date

Dictated ______ to ______

Transcribed by SA

Authenticated by Informant 4/1/66

Date of Report 3/29/66

Date(s) of activity Current

Brief description of activity or material

Info re JAMES BALDWIN. b2-1 b7D-1

File where original is located if not attached

NY [redacted]

Remarks:

1 - [redacted] (INV)(43)
1 - 100- (PAUL ROBINSON)(43)
1 - 100-146553 (JAMES BALDWIN)(43)

LGB:rmp
(3) rmp

ALL INFORMATION CONTAINED
HEREIN IS UNCLASSIFIED
DATE 5-25-89 BY SP8 [illegible]

Block Stamp

100-146553-215

SEARCHED INDEXED
SERIALIZED FILED
APR 29 1966
FBI — NEW YORK

NY 100-146553

3/29/66

Nothing is known about the current location of JAMES BALDWIN, the Negro Aughor and Playwright. BALDWIN was met at an affair held for PAUL ROBINSON in 1965 at the Americana Hotel. It has been heard that BALDWIN may be a homosexual and he appeared as if he may be one.

FD-366 (5-6-64)

New York, New York
October 11,1966

BUfile 62-108763
NYfile 100-146553

SUBJECT: JAMES ARTHUR BALDWIN

REFERENCE: New York report dated 4/13/66.

Referenced communication contained subject's residence and/or employment address. A recent change has been determined and is being set forth below (change only specified):

Residence: 137 West 71st Street, New York, New York
(presently in TURKEY)

Employment: Self-employed Writer

ALL INFORMATION CONTAINED
HEREIN IS UNCLASSIFIED
DATE 5-18-89 BY

Disseminated to Secret Service on 10-11-66 C

2-Bureau(RM)
1-Secret Service (NY)(RM)
1-New York

JC/cmc
(4)

Searched
Serialized
Indexed
Filed

This document contains neither recommendations nor conclusions of the FBI. It is the property of the FBI and is loaned to your agency; it and its contents are not to be distributed outside your agency.

100-146553-217

43.

BALDWIN REPORTED TO THE SECRET SERVICE—THE AUTHOR AS ASSASSIN

APRIL 1966

When the FBI discovered Baldwin's residence in Turkey, it shared the news with the Secret Service, the branch of federal law enforcement charged with protecting US presidents since 1902. This document, likely filed in April 1966, reveals the reason why: Baldwin, already on the Bureau's Security Index, was now also listed among those individuals "covered by the agreement between the FBI and the Secret Service concerning Presidential protection." Put less bureaucratically, the author of several American classics was now considered a potential assassin of the American president. The Bureau knew that Baldwin had not "threatened bodily harm to any government official or employee," and had avoided "conduct or statements indicating a propensity for violence and antipathy toward good order and government"—the second of these criteria broad and flexible enough to cover most any social critic. Instead, his undefined "background" was found to be "potentially dangerous," or his ties to the "communist movement" were thought to be too strong, or he had "been under active investigation as a member of other group or organization"—SNCC perhaps?—"inimical to [the] U.S." Or maybe all three. Baldwin, who later admitted that he found it grueling to write between the assassinations of Medgar Evers, Malcolm X, Martin Luther King, and Robert Kennedy, was suspected of harboring the same kind of political violence that badly damaged his hopes in the late 1960s.

FD-376 (Rev. 11-12-65)

Director
United States Secret Service
Department of the Treasury
Washington, D. C. 20220

Bufile 62-108763
NYfile 100-146553

Re: James Arthur Baldwin

Dear Sir:

The information furnished herewith concerns an individual who is believed to be covered by the agreement between the FBI and Secret Service concerning Presidential protection, and to fall within the category or categories checked.

1. ☐ Has attempted or threatened bodily harm to any government official or employee, including foreign government officials residing in or planning an imminent visit to the U. S., because of his official status.

2. ☐ Has attempted or threatened to redress a grievance against any public official by other than legal means.

3. ☒ Because of background is potentially dangerous; or has been identified as member or participant in communist movement; or has been under active investigation as member of other group or organization inimical to U. S.

4. ☐ U. S. citizens or residents who defect from the U. S. to countries in the Soviet or Chinese Communist blocs and return.

5. ☐ Subversives, ultrarightists, racists and fascists who meet one or more of the following criteria:

   (a) ☐ Evidence of emotional instability (including unstable residence and employment record) or irrational or suicidal behavior:
   (b) ☐ Expressions of strong or violent anti-U. S. sentiment;
   (c) ☐ Prior acts (including arrests or convictions) or conduct or statements indicating a propensity for violence and antipathy toward good order and government.

6. ☐ Individuals involved in illegal bombing or illegal bomb-making.

Photograph ☐ has been furnished ☐ enclosed ☐ is not available
☐ may be available through ______

ALL INFORMATION CONTAINED
HEREIN IS UNCLASSIFIED
DATE 5-18-89 BY

Very truly yours,

J. Edgar Hoover

John Edgar Hoover
Director

Searched ____
Serialized ____
Indexed ____
Filed ____

2 - Bureau
1 - Special Agent in Charge (Enclosure(s) 1)
U. S. Secret Service
1 - New York , NYC

100-146553-204

Enclosure(s) 1)
EFU:g
fb

(Upon removal of classified enclosures, if any, this transmittal form becomes UNCLASSIFIED.)

44.

WHITE HOUSE VISITS AND NAME CHECKS

MAY 1966

A year before his clash with Bobby Kennedy on the subject of civil rights, Baldwin attended a dinner at John F. Kennedy's White House honoring American Nobel Prize winners. In April 1962, near the height of the Kennedys' new Camelot, the writer swallowed his compunctions, overcame the complication of a forgotten ID card, and strode into a grand ballroom containing Mary McCarthy, Carson McCullers, Katherine Anne Porter, and dozens of other friends and inspirations. In May 1966, Baldwin was invited to the White House once more, this time for a reception for African ambassadors, several of them the first representatives of newly liberated black nations. Baldwin declined the honor this second time around, but not before the FBI had flagged his name—now also known to the Secret Service—when asked to perform a standard security check on the evening's invited guests. The Bureau provided a special assistant to President Lyndon Johnson with a five-page rundown on the "prominent author and playwright," a kind of greatest hits of Baldwin radicalism ranging from his 1960 support for the Fair Play for Cuba Committee to a 1965 speech denouncing Western imperialism in Vietnam as well as South Africa. The FBI's fingerprint files—the nation's largest—contained no matches for Baldwin. Yet many paper items in the Bureau's collection raised Hooverite alarms, a state of suspicion now communicated directly to the Johnson White House.

May 13, 1966

BY LIAISON

Honorable Marvin Watson
Special Assistant to the President
The White House
Washington, D. C.

ALL INFORMATION CONTAINED
HEREIN IS UNCLASSIFIED
DATE 5/18/89 BY [illegible]

Dear Mr. Watson:

Reference is made to the name check requests from Mrs. Stegall relative to the White House affair on May 26, 1966.

The central files of the FBI contain no derogatory information identifiable with the following individuals:

Anthony Michael Astrachan	Lawrence E. Laybourne
William H. Beatty, Jr.	George N. Lindsay
Norman Blake	The Reverend Frederick A. McGuire, C.M.
Professor Henry L. Bretton	John F. McKiernan
Al Castagno	Irwin Miller
L. Robert Castorr	Doyle Mitchell
Ernest Dunbar	Professor Ruth Schachter Morgenthau
James A. Farrell, Jr.	Robert M. Norris
Frank E. Ferrari	Macaire Pidanou
Raymond C. Firestone	Hans Ries
Ralph Hatzel, Jr.	Mrs. Oscar Ruebhausen
Walter Hochschild	Kenneth Spang
Dr. Jerome Holland	Reverend Theodore L. Tucker
Professor William O. Jones	Dr. Marvin Wachman
Dr. Howard Jordan	F. Champion Ward
Mrs. Helen Kitchen	Gilbert M. Weinstein

ENCLOSURE

1 - Mr. DeLoach (sent direct) - Encs. (17)
1 - Mr. Gale - Encs. (17)
1 - Mr. Rosen - Encs. (17)

REC- 3 62-108763-39

MAY 16 1966

NOTE: Per request of Mrs. Mildred Stegall, White House Staff.

JMM:jol (8)

Tolson
DeLoach
Mohr
Wick
Casper
Callahan
Conrad
Felt
Gale
Rosen
Sullivan
Tavel
Trotter
Tele. Room
Holmes
Gandy

57 MAY 26 1966 MAIL ROOM TELETYPE UNIT

NOT RECORDED
145 MAY 17 1966

ORIGINAL FILED IN

Honorable Marvin Watson

The files of the Identification Division of the FBI were checked and no arrest data was located concerning the above individuals based upon the background information submitted in connection with these name check requests.

Attached are separate memoranda on the following individuals:

James Baldwin

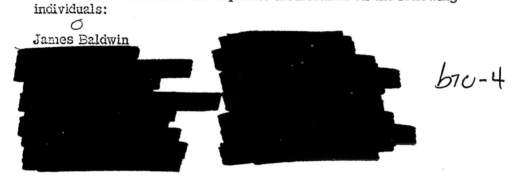

b7C-4

Sincerely yours,

Enclosures (19)

SECRET

DECLASSIFIED BY AUC 3962 ? SAH/8?
ON 9/27/99
CA97-5269

ALL INFORMATION CONTAINED HEREIN IS UNCLASSIFIED EXCEPT WHERE SHOWN OTHERWISE

May 13, 1966

JAMES BALDWIN — Summary

Captioned individual, prominent author and playwright, has been the subject of a security-type investigation conducted by the FBI which has revealed his association with individuals and organizations of a procommunist nature.

In July, 1965, he was the author of a form letter urging the recipients to renew their subscriptions to "Freedomways" magazine which is reportedly staffed by Communist Party (CP) members or sympathizers including Esther Jackson, its Managing Editor, who is the wife of James Jackson, a member of the National Committee of the CPUSA. (S)

In November, 1965, Baldwin made public appearances in Rome, Italy, at which he stated the United States has no right in Vietnam and that "Western interests" were responsible for events in South Africa and the Cuban "aggression." (S)

In December, 1963, Baldwin spoke before a dinner sponsored by the Emergency Civil Liberties Committee (ECLC), an organization cited by the House Committee on Un-American Activities (HCUA).

An advertisement entitled "What is Really Happening in Cuba" appeared in "The New York Times" of April 6, 1960. This advertisement, placed by The Fair Play for Cuba Committee, was sympathetic to the Castro regime and indicated that the American press had attempted to blacken Castro and his government by reporting untruthful information. The advertisement indicated The Fair Play for Cuba Committee, headquarters in New York, had been formed to furnish the true facts concerning the Cuban revolutionary government. James Baldwin appeared in the advertisement as one of the sponsors of The Fair Play for Cuba Committee.

Classified by / Declassify on: OADR

SECRET

NOTE: Per request of Mrs. Mildred Stegall, White House Staff.

JMM:mjl (8)

Tolson
DeLoach
Mohr
Wick
Casper
Callahan
Conrad
Felt
Gale
Rosen
Sullivan
Tavel
Trotter
Tele. Room
Holmes
Gandy

MAIL ROOM ☐ TELETYPE UNIT ☐

ENCLOSURE

62-108763-34

JAMES BALDWIN

The Washington, D. C., Chapter of the Congress of Racial Equality held a mass rally for the "Original Freedom Riders" in Washington on June 11, 1961. Among the speakers at this rally was James Baldwin. During his talk, Baldwin stated, in substance, that the West should re-evaluate its international policies in view of the potential strength of the new Afro-Asian countries. He stated that the white race had better realize the emerging strength of the Negro and that he would not care to be in the shoes of the white man when the African nations become stronger.

The "New York Herald Tribune" of June 17, 1961, in its "Letters to the Editor" section, carried a letter by James Baldwin and William Styron which advocated abolishment of capital punishment. This letter stated in part that "If there were a shred of proof that the death penalty actually served to inhibit crime, that would be sufficient reason--even from the point of view of 'misguided do-gooders,' as J. Edgar Hoover calls its opponents--to maintain it." It goes on to state that Mr. Hoover "is not a lawgiver, nor is there any reason to suppose him to be a particularly profound student of human nature. He is a law enforcement officer. It is appalling that in this capacity he not only opposes the trend of history among civilized nations, but uses his enormous power and prestige to corroborate the blindest and basest instincts of the retaliatory mob."

On June 2, 1961, the Liberation Committee for Africa (LCA) held a "first anniversary" celebration at the Martinique Hotel, New York City. James Baldwin, author, was listed as one of the principal speakers. During his address, Baldwin stated that he had spent the past nine years in Paris and advised that a period of revolution confronted the world and that America has taken a position throughout the world against revolutions. Baldwin asserted that only in revolution could the problems of the United States be solved.

It is understood that certain local chapters of the Socialist Workers Party have given support to the Liberation Committee for Africa. The March 24, 1961, issue of "Young Socialist Alliance Newsletter," which recognizes the Socialist

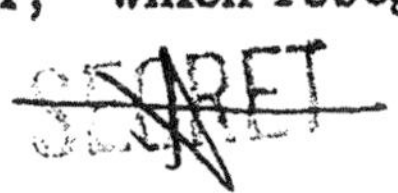

Workers Party as the only existing political party capable of providing the working class with political leadership, has given strong support to the LCA. The LCA claims to provide a public forum for African freedom fighters and to re-establish awareness of the common cultural heritage of Afro-Americans with their African brothers.

The name of James Baldwin appears as a sponsor on a news release communication in August, 1961, from the Carl Braden clemency appeal committee which was being distributed by the Southern Conference Educational Fund (SCEF). The SCEF is the successor organization to the Southern Conference for Human Welfare desceibed by the HCUA as a communist front organization. It is noted that on May 1, 1961, Carl Braden and Frank Wilkinson went to prison to begin a one-year sentence for contempt of the HCUA. The SCEF was endeavoring to obtain signatures in connection with a petition to President Kennedy for executive clemency for Braden and Wilkinson.

The April 17, 1961, issue of the "National Guardian" which the HCUA cites as a virtual official propaganda arm of Soviet Russia contained an advertisement announcing a rally to abolish the HCUA on Friday, April 21, 1961, in New York City. James Baldwin, writer, was listed as a sponsor supporting the rally.

The April 20, 1962, issue of "New America," an official publication of "Socialist Party--Social Democratic Federation," contains a clemency petition for convicted communist Junius Scales who was serving a six-year sentence in Lewisburg Penitentiary under the membership clause of the Smith Act. The petition was sent to President Kennedy on April 3, 1962, and allegedly contained the signatures of "550 prominent citizens" among whom was James Baldwin.

SECRET

JAMES BALDWIN

SECRET

Scales, who had a long history of membership and leadership in the CPUSA, was convicted in February, 1958, for violating the Smith Act. He was sentenced to six years in the Federal penitentiary, and after exhausting all appeals, he began serving his sentence on October 2, 1961.

On Christmas Eve, 1962, President Kennedy commuted Scales' sentence which he was serving in Lewisburg, Pennsylvania. During his trial and in connection with appeal motions subsequent to it, Scales endeavored to characterize himself as an ex-communist who had chosen to go to jail rather than name his former associates in the CP.

The cover of the May 17, 1963, issue of "Time" magazine is devoted to author James Baldwin. The cover story describes some of Baldwin's recent efforts in behalf of the American Negro's integration movements. He is described as "a nervous, slight, almost fragile figure, filled with frets and fears. He is effeminate in manner, drinks considerably, smokes cigarettes in chains and he often looses his audience with overblown arguments."

The May, 1963, issue of "Mademoiselle" contains an interview-type article with James Baldwin which was part of a series then currently being carried by the magazine under the caption "Disturber of the Peace."

As indicated by the title of the series, "Disturber of the Peace," James Baldwin gives a lot of gibes to both white and Negroes about the Negro situation in the United States. Baldwin answers many of the questions by introspection. In giving an answer to a question about his father and how he hated him and whether or not his father hated Baldwin in return, he stated "In a way, yes. He didn't like me. But he'd had a terrible time, too. And of course, I was not his son. I was a bastard. What he wanted for his children was what in fact I became...I changed all the diapers and I knew where the kids were, and I could take some of the pressures off my mother and in a way stand between him and her...."

SECRET

On the subject of homosexuality, Baldwin stated "American males are the only people I've ever encountered in the world who are willing to go on the needle before they'll go to bed with each other. Because they're afraid of this, they don't know how to go to bed with women either. I've known people who literally died out of this panic. I don't know what homosexual means any more, and Americans don't either...If you fall in love with a boy, you fall in love with a boy. The fact that Americans consider it a disease says more about them than it says about homosexuality." (157-6-34-78)

In connection with a discussion of why he feels Attorney General Robert Kennedy, the Justice Department and President Kennedy are ineffective in dealing with discrimination with the Negroes in the South, Baldwin makes the statement that he is weary of being told that desegregation is legal. He then states "...because first of all you have to get Eastland out of Congress and get rid of the power that he wields there. You've got to get rid of J. Edgar Hoover and the power that he wields. If one could get rid of just those two men, or modify their power, there would be a great deal more hope...."

The fingerprint files of the FBI Identification Division contain no arrest data identifiable with captioned individual based upon the background information submitted in connection with this name check request.

45.

SHARING WITH THE STATE DEPARTMENT—AND THE CIA

NOVEMBER AND DECEMBER 1966

In late 1966, when the Bureau confirmed that Baldwin was "engaged in travel abroad," it overcame institutional jealousy long enough to share this news with the Department of State and the CIA. State, responsible for American passports, was given an elementary sketch of Baldwin's identity: "a Negro male who is active in Civil Rights demonstrations and has authored several books." The CIA, responsible for foreign intelligence, was invited by an especially formal "John Edgar Hoover" to consult with the FBI's man in Rome, an agent who had been instructed to collect "any pertinent information" on Baldwin from non-American "security services." Such legal attaché agents, or "legats," in FBI dialect, had provided the Bureau with eyes and ears abroad since 1940. Posted in various foreign capitals even after the founding of the CIA in 1947, legats cooperated with local police and intelligence forces at the bidding of FBI headquarters in Washington. When Baldwin escaped the borders of the United States, then, he did not always escape the Bureau's attention; his expatriation was not full liberation from the FB eye. And when calling in the CIA, the Bureau's archenemy in the world of US intelligence, the FBI did not abandon its global posts and interests.

CONFIDENTIAL

1 - Liaison
1 - [redacted]
1 - [redacted]

ALL INFORMATION CONTAINED
HEREIN IS UNCLASSIFIED
EXCEPT WHERE SHOWN
OTHERWISE

(SC) 62-108763

SECRET

67C-1

Date: November 1, 1966

To: Director
Bureau of Intelligence and Research
Department of State

From: John Edgar Hoover, Director

Subject: JAMES ARTHUR BALDWIN
SECURITY MATTER - COMMUNIST

Information has been received to the effect that captioned individual has engaged in travel abroad. In this connection, there is enclosed for the information of each recipient of this letter one copy of a memorandum dated October 17, 1966, containing available information concerning Baldwin. Reports concerning captioned individual have previously been furnished to the recipients of this letter.

Enclosure

Classified by 6972 CEP/08
Declassify on: OADR
2-14-90
89-3016 JHP

1 - Mr. J. Walter Yeagley (Enclosure)
Assistant Attorney General

TJM:sjs (7)

NOTE:

Subject is a Negro male who is active in Civil Rights demonstrations and has authored several books. He is on the Security Index of the New York Office. [Central Intelligence Agency and] Legat, Rome, are being separately advised of subject's travel, and New York is being requested to ascertain additional details concerning his itinerary and the date of his expected return to this country.

(S)(U)

Classified by
Declassify on: OADR 5-18-90

REC-21 62-108763-41

NOTE CONTINUED PAGE TWO

Tolson
DeLoach
Mohr
Wick
Casper
Callahan
Conrad
Felt
Gale
Rosen
Sullivan
Tavel
Trotter
Tele. Room
Holmes
Gandy

BY COURIER SVC.
8 NOV 1966
COMM-FBI

FBI
NOV 1 1966

OCT 31 5 36 PM '66

CONFIDENTIAL

Upon removal of classified material, this letter becomes unclassified.

SECRET

62 NOV 8 1966

DECLASSIFIED BY 6972 CEP/08
5-19-90
Per CIA memo dtd 3-6-90
89-3016 JHP

MAIL ROOM ☐ TELETYPE UNIT ☐

CONFIDENTIAL

Director
Bureau of Intelligence and Research

SECRET

NOTE CONTINUED:

This letter is classified "Confidential" as it contains information from sources of continuing value. Unauthorized disclosure of information received from these sources may tend to reveal their identity and thus be detrimental to the defense interests of this country. The above-mentioned enclosure dated October 17, 1966, is enclosure to Serial 62-108763-40.

SECRET

CONFIDENTIAL

CONFIDENTIAL

SECRET

1 - Liaison
1 - [redacted]
1 - [redacted] b7C-1

ALL INFORMATION CONTAINED HEREIN IS UNCLASSIFIED EXCEPT WHERE SHOWN OTHERWISE

REC-138

(SC) 62-108763 - 40

4/27/99
CLASSIFIED BY [illegible]
DECLASSIFY ON: 25X (1)
CA97-5269

SEE REVERSE SIDE FOR CLASSIFICATION ACTION

Date: EX-110 November 2, 1966

To: Director
Central Intelligence Agency
Attention: Deputy Director, Plans

From: John Edgar Hoover, Director

Subject: JAMES ARTHUR BALDWIN
SECURITY MATTER - COMMUNIST

Information has been received to the effect that captioned individual is currently traveling abroad. In this connection, there is enclosed one copy of a memorandum dated October 17, 1966, containing available information concerning Baldwin. Pertinent reports regarding this individual have been previously furnished to your Agency.

This matter has been referred to the Legal Attache, Rome, for contact with appropriate security services to receive any pertinent information regarding this subject while he is in the area covered by that Legal Attache. (X) U

Referred to CIA

Enclosure (X) U

2 - Legat, Rome (Enclosure)
2 - New York (100-146553) (X) U

Classified by [illegible]
Declassify on: OADR

SEE NOTE TO LEGAT, ROME, AND SAC, NEW YORK, PAGE TWO.

1 - Foreign Liaison Unit (Route through for review)

TJM:sjs
(11)

SEE NOTE PAGE TWO

Tolson
DeLoach
Mohr
Wick
Casper
Callahan
Conrad
Felt
Gale
Rosen
Sullivan
Tavel
Trotter
Tele. Room
Holmes
Gandy

SECRET

56 NOV 8 1966

BY COURIER SVC.
92 NOV 3
COMM-FBI

MAIL ROOM ☐ TELETYPE UNIT ☐

CONFIDENTIAL

Upon removal of classified material, this letter becomes unclassified.

CONFIDENTIAL

[Director
Central Intelligence Agency] S (S)(4)

SECRET

NOTE TO LEGAT, ROME, AND SAC, NEW YORK:

U (X) Legat, Rome, alert your sources so as to receive pertinent information regarding the subject including advance information of travel to countries other than that mentioned in the enclosure. Notify CIA and appropriate Legats of such travel changes. Information contained in the enclosure may be furnished to your sources. For your ~~additional~~ information, James Arthur Baldwin is an author of several books and has been active in the Civil Rights movement. He is on the Security Index of the New York Office.

New York should continue its investigation to ascertain additional details concerning subject's itinerary and should be especially alert for information pertaining to the expected date of his return to this country. Submit pertinent results of your investigation in memorandum form suitable for dissemination to appropriate agencies and Legats.

NOTE:

Information has been received in October, 1966, that subject had then recently left the United States and is touring Turkey where he plans to write a book. Both the State Department and the Internal Security Division of the Department of Justice are being advised separately of subject's travel for information purposes.

The memorandum dated October 17, 1966, is an enclosure to Serial 62-108763-40. This letter is classified "Confidential" as it contains information from sources of continuing value. Unauthorized disclosure of information received from these sources may tend to reveal their identity and thus be detrimental to the defense interests of this country.

SECRET

~~CONFIDENTIAL~~

46.

FBI INTERNATIONALISM IN ACTION—BALDWIN TRACED AND TRANSLATED IN TURKEY

NOVEMBER AND DECEMBER 1966

Baldwin's complicated itinerary to and from Turkey in 1966—he aptly called himself a "transatlantic commuter" and, less believably, "a stranger everywhere"—was reconstructed more definitely that November. With the aid of passport numbers, ship manifests, and flight schedules, the FBI pinned his comings and goings down to the day, and accurately related that Baldwin stayed with Engin Cezzar while in Istanbul. Through the sociable Cezzar, a successful Turkish actor trained at the Yale Drama School, Baldwin "was literally and figuratively embraced" by the cream of Istanbul's intelligentsia. As his biographer David Leeming recounts, Baldwin found conversation and community among "theater people, journalists, writers, painters, and academics" who were like and excitingly unlike their American equivalents, particularly in their attitudes to race. One of Cezzar's acquaintances, the young Turkish critic Zeynap Oral, interviewed Baldwin for the *Yeni Gazette*, an Istanbul daily newspaper. Oral prompted Baldwin to reflect on the paradox of dreaming of Harlem in a "large green garden" overlooking the Bosphorus. The "noise and tumult of New York" ironically made writing about the city impossible while there, Baldwin offered, but permanent removal from his native country and its "black-white conflicts" was impossible as well. Among the interview's attentive readers was J. Edgar Hoover in Washington. Tipped off by an attaché agent in Rome, he arranged for a Turkish-to-English translation and distributed the results to various offices in copies on bond, standard, and "yellow" paper. For some good reasons, we don't remember Hoover's FBI as an eager literary translator. In the case of Oral's interview, however, it very likely produced the first English version of an illuminating Baldwin statement, its appearance a function of the Bureau's drive to shadow the author's transnationalism wherever it roamed.

UNITED STATES DEPARTMENT OF JUSTICE

FEDERAL BUREAU OF INVESTIGATION

In Reply, Please Refer to
File No.

WASHINGTON, D.C. 20535

ALL INFORMATION CONTAINED
HEREIN IS UNCLASSIFIED
EXCEPT WHERE SHOWN
OTHERWISE

November 25, 1966

JAMES ARTHUR BALDWIN

On November 10, 1966, a confidential source abroad made available the following information:

JAMES ARTHUR BALDWIN, born August 2, 1924, at New York, New York, and in possession of U. S. passport No. 440042, issued on August 2, 1965, at the U. S. Consulate, Berlin, Germany, arrived in Istanbul, Turkey, by ship on March 29, 1966. BALDWIN departed from Turkey on October 18, 1966, from the Istanbul airport on Air France flight No. 615, for an undisclosed destination. (S)(u)

During his stay in Turkey, BALDWIN resided with ENGIN CEZZAR, Ayaspasa Saray Arkasi 32/3, Istanbul, and was not known to be involved in any suspect activity. (S)(u)

Classified by 6912 Sep/ad
Declassify on: OADR 2-14-90

Classified by 3016 SEP/ad
Declassify on: OADR 5-18-88

GROUP 1
Excluded from automatic
downgrading and
declassification

PROPERTY OF THE FBI
This report is loaned to you by the FBI, and neither it nor its contents are to be distributed outside the agency to which loaned.

DECLASSIFIED BY AUC 39677 SAH/sh
ON 4/27/99
CA97-5269

100-146553-223

SEARCHED ___ INDEXED ___
SERIALIZED ___ FILED ___
DEC - 1966
FBI — NEW YORK

CONFIDENTIAL

b7C-1

Director, FBI (62-108763) SECRET November 25, 1966

Legat, Rome (100-1417) (RUC)

ALL INFORMATION CONTAINED HEREIN IS UNCLASSIFIED EXCEPT WHERE SHOWN OTHERWISE

JAMES ARTHUR BALDWIN
SM - C

ReBulet to the Director, Central Intelligence Agency, dated 11/2/66, enclosing New York LHM dated 10/17/66.

Enclosed for the Bureau is Form FD-350 with newspaper clipping from the 10/27/66, issue of the Turkish language newspaper, "YENI GAZETE," published daily in Istanbul, Turkey, which was made available by [redacted] on 11/10/66. Also enclosed is LHM containing information made available by [redacted] on that date and which information was classified confidential.

The Bureau may be desirous of translating the enclosed clipping and making a copy of the translation available to the New York office and Legat, Rome.

Encs. 9
5 - Bureau (1 - Liaison)
(2 - New York 100-146553)
1 - Rome (100-1417)
TAK:MEG
(6)

Classified by
Declassify on: OADR

SEARCHED INDEXED
SERIALIZED FILED
DEC 7 1966
FBI — NEW YORK

SECRET

7-41 (Rev. 5-7-63)
OPTIONAL FORM NO. 10
MAY 1962 EDITION
GSA GEN. REG. NO. 27
5010-106

UNITED STATES GOVERNMENT

Memorandum

TO : SAC, New York (100-146553)

DATE: December 6, 1966

FROM : Director, FBI (62-108763)

CONFIDENTIAL

DECLASSIFIED BY ALLC 39677 SAH/ON 4/27/99
CA97-5269

SUBJECT: JAMES ARTHUR BALDWIN
SM - C

REGISTERED MAIL

ALL INFORMATION CONTAINED HEREIN IS UNCLASSIFIED EXCEPT WHERE SHOWN OTHERWISE

Enclosed is certain foreign language material:

U (C) Article from "YENI GAZETE," Turkish newspaper, as described in a letter from Legat, Rome, dated 11/25/66, copy of which is attached.

This material should be processed as indicated below:

Full translation.

Following disposition should be made of enclosure and translation:

Both to the Bureau, attention FBI Annex. Please prepare one bond, three thins, and one yellow.

If the results of your review are not furnished the Seat of Government, in accordance with instructions set forth above, then the office initiating the request, to which translation is made available by you, has the responsibility of appropriately notifying the Bureau of any pertinent information contained therein.

Enc. - 2

Classified by 6922 EEP/alP
Declassify on: OADR 2-14-90
89-3016 JHP

Classified by SP3 ALJ/gg
Declassify on: OADR 5-18-99

100-146553-225

SEARCHED INDEXED
SERIALIZED FILED
DEC 7 1966
FBI — NEW YORK

CONFIDENTIAL

b7C-1

ALL INFORMATION CONTAINED HEREIN IS UNCLASSIFIED EXCEPT WHERE SHOWN OTHERWISE

CONFIDENTIAL

DECLASSIFIED BY [illegible] ON 4/27/93

Looking at New York from Istanbul

*

James Baldwin Finishes His Book In Hisar (X) U

*

In The Vefik Pasha Library the Negro Writer Pursues His People's Cause

In an old wooden building - circa 1800 - in an alley in Rumeli Hisar we found the noted American negro writer bent on his typewriter absorbed in his work so that he did not notice our entry. (X) U

The house, right in the middle of a large green garden, belongs to Vehik Pasha. From it one can see the entire strait of the Bosphorus which is why the writer had rented it. (X) U

The story of James Baldwin's decision to settle in Istanbul is quite old. Baldwin had met Engin Cezzar in New York and a friendship had developed. Sometime later Baldwin had come to Turkey to visit his friend. After that the visit was repeated every year. After five such visits Baldwin had settled in Istanbul in March of 1966. (X) U

Interrupting his work for a few minutes Baldwin told us of his intention of writing about his life iN New York. "Such a book cannot be written in the noise and tumult of New York", the writer said, adding that big city life bothers him. At the same time, without truly knowing a place, merely looking in from outside cannot work either. (X) U

The writer likes Istanbul for the following reasons. First of all he can be alone and relax much better. (Of course friends who love to visit him will make it difficult). (X) U

"If you decide to settle in Turkey permanently, would you chose Istanbul?", to this his answer was: (X) U

"Under the circumstances it cannot be a matter of preference. In the white-black conflicts in my country I must contribute my share by returning to America. To settle here permanently would be running away which I cannot do." (X) U

Classified by [illegible]
Declassify on: OADR

100-146553-226

CONFIDENTIAL

Classified by [illegible]
Declassify on: OADR

SEARCHED ____ INDEXED ____
SERIALIZED ____ FILED ____
DEC 20 1966
FBI — NEW YORK

CONFIDENTIAL

To help solve the white and black question in his country the writer gives interviews, holds conferences, writes articles and makes speeches. Before coming to Turkey Baldwin had been energetically active. He believes in hard work. "My professional and social life is very complex and jumbled up," said the noted writer.

What draws Baldwin to Istanbul and to Turkey is the people. He admires the warmth and liveliness of the Turkish people.

After finishing his book the author will return to America.

CONFIDENTIAL

47.

AN AIRLINE SOURCE AND A PRETEXT INTERVIEW

JANUARY 1967

Foreign legats and translations were not the only means through which the FBI followed Baldwin's globetrotting. Humbler domestic channels also offered information on his international travels. In January 1967, a confidential Bureau informer working at Air France in New York advised that Baldwin had flown on the airline from Istanbul to Paris. An FBI special agent then learned that Baldwin had failed to return to the US by phoning the author's New York literary agent, Robert Lantz, under an assumed identity. Such pretext interviews drew on the latent acting skills of G-men. Becoming the hippy enemy, the Bureau agent who called Lantz mimicked the voice of "a member of a peace organization soliciting a statement from James Baldwin."

DIRECTOR, FBI (62-108763) 1/18/67

SAC, NEW YORK (100-146553) (C)

JAMES ARTHUR BALDWIN
SM-C
(OO:NY)

ReBuFD-4, dated 12/6/66, with attached LHM, dated 11/25/66.

The confidential source employed in the enclosed LHM is [redacted] Air France, JFK International Airport, NY, NY, conceal at his request. b7C-6 b7D-2

Enclosed for the Bureau is an original and eight copies of LHM, and for Legat, Paris, one copy of same.

The pretext interview referred to was a telephone call made by SA [redacted] under the guise of a member of a peace organization soliciting a statement from JAMES BALDWIN. b7C-1

ALL INFORMATION CONTAINED
HEREIN IS UNCLASSIFIED
DATE 5-18-89 BY [illegible]

4 - Bureau (Encls. 9)
(1 - Legat, Paris)(Encl. 1)
(1 - Legat, Rome) (Encl. 1)
1 - New York

JJC:al
(5)

Searched
Serialized
Indexed
Filed

616

100-146553-233

New York, New York
January 18, 1967

Bufile 62-108763
NYfile 100-146553

James Anthur Baldwin

A confidential source advised on December 23, 1966, that Flight 615, Air France from Istanbul, Turkey, terminates at Paris, France. The source checked passenger manifests of all logical connecting flights from Paris, France, to New York, New York, for the period from October 18, 1966, to October 20, 1966, and advised that James Baldwin did not travel to New York, on any of these flights.

On December 29, 1966, a pretext interview with Robert Lantz, 111 West 51st Street, New York City, was conducted in an attempt to locate James Anthur Baldwin. Mr. Lantz who is Mr. Baldwin's agent advised that Mr. Baldwin had not returned to the United States. Mr. Lantz would not divulge his address.

THIS DOCUMENT CONTAINS NEITHER RECOMMENDATIONS NOR CONCLUSIONS OF THE FBI. IT IS THE PROPERTY OF THE FBI AND IS LOANED TO YOUR AGENCY; IT AND ITS CONTENTS ARE NOT TO BE DISTRIBUTED OUTSIDE YOUR AGENCY.

9 - Bureau
1 - Legat, Paris
1 - New York

ALL INFORMATION CONTAINED HEREIN IS UNCLASSIFIED DATE 5-18-89 BY [illegible]

JJC:al
(11)

Searched
Serialized
Indexed
Filed

100-146553-232

48.

BUREAUCRATIC DISCIPLINE AND THE "SUBJECT'S EVICTION FROM AN APARTMENT IN TURKEY FOR HOMOSEXUAL ACTIVITIES"

MARCH AND APRIL 1967

Baldwin's place on the Security Index meant that his case was reinvestigated regularly. In March 1967, the New York division attempted to fulfill this obligation with a short letter alone: Baldwin, after all, had "not been in the United States since the last report was submitted and his file fails to reflect any subversive activity since that time." Hoover's office in Washington was not pleased. Like an angry professor directing a corner-cutting student back to the syllabus, the FBI director called New York's attention "to the Manual of Instructions, Section 87D, page 74, wherein instructions are set forth as to when an annual report should be submitted." Only a full and "current report suitable for dissemination" would satisfy Hoover's assignment. Hoover took his paper-pushing deeply seriously—not only because he was a control freak, but also because his painstaking leadership had elevated the Bureau, something of a thieves' den in the teens and early twenties, to a clean-cut Progressive bureaucracy. In any case, contrary to New York's assessment, Washington trusted that there were "subversive activities" in Baldwin's Turkish life worth investigating. He was "preparing a book for publication," for one thing, and allowing himself to be interviewed "regarding racial problems in the U.S." The Office of Special Investigations (OSI), the police and intelligence division of the U.S. Air Force, had passed on a report that Baldwin had been evicted "from an apartment in Turkey for homosexual activities." Whether or not the report was accurate, Hoover assumed that Baldwin's ties to such activities were matters of national gravity.

DIRECTOR, FBI (62-108763) 3/31/67

CONFIDENTIAL

SAC, NEW YORK (100-146553) (C)

ALL INFORMATION CONTAINED HEREIN IS UNCLASSIFIED EXCEPT WHERE SHOWN OTHERWISE

JAMES ARTHUR BALDWIN
SM - C

Rerep of SA [redacted], dated 4/13/66, at New York.

b7C-1

Enclosed for the Bureau are 9 copies of a LHM.

The pretext employed by SA [redacted] was that of a publisher's representative.

This letter is being submitted in lieu of a report in view of the fact that the subject has not been in the United States since the last report was submitted and his file fails to reflect any subversive activity since that time.

The following informants of the NYO were unable to provide any additional information regarding the subject during February and March, 1967:

Classified by 6972 SP/0 8
Declassify on: OADR 2-14-90 89-3016 JHF

b2-1
b7D-1

Classified by [redacted] 5-18-89
Declassify on: OADR

In view of the fact that all logical stops have been placed that will be productive of information regarding the subject's return to the US, New York is considering this case closed.

DECLASSIFIED BY [illegible]
ON 4/27/99
CA97-5269

2-Bureau (Encls. 9) (RM)
1-New York

JC:pam
(3)

CONFIDENTIAL

CHIEF CLERK, CLOSE ON THIS
3/31/67

Searched
Indexed
Filed

628

100-146553-242

FD-305 (Rev. 3-17-64)

NY 100-146553

CONFIDENTIAL

1. [x] Subject's name is included in the Security Index.
2. [x] The data appearing on the Security Index card are current.
3. [ ] Changes on the Security Index card are necessary and Form FD-122 has been submitted to the Bureau.
4. [x] A suitable photograph [x] is [ ] is not available.
5. [ ] Subject is employed in a key facility and ________ is charged with security responsibility. Interested agencies are ________.
6. [ ] This report is classified ________ because (state reason)

7. [ ] Subject previously interviewed (dates) ________.
[x] Subject was not reinterviewed because (state reason)

he is not in the United States.

8. [ ] This case no longer meets the Security Index criteria and a letter has been directed to the Bureau recommending cancellation of the Security Index card.
9. [x] This case has been re-evaluated in the light of the Security Index criteria and it continues to fall within such criteria because (state reason)

of subject's outspoken stand on the civil rights issue, his current prominence as an author and the inflamatory nature of his writings, which show him to be a dangerous individual who would be expected to commit acts inimical to the national defense interests of the US in the time of a national emergency.

10. [x] Subject's SI card [ ] is [x] is not tabbed Detcom.
[ ] Subject's activities warrant Detcom tabbing because (state reasons)

CONFIDENTIAL

1 - Mr. Floyd
1 - Mr. McNiff

SAC, New York (100-146553) 4-11-67

CONFIDENTIAL

Director, FBI (62-108763) -46

EX 109 REC-59

DECLASSIFIED BY AUC39677SAH/TS ON 4/27/99 CA97-5269

JAMES ARTHUR BALDWIN
SECURITY MATTER - C

Reurlet 3-31-67.

Your attention is called to the Manual of Instructions, Section 87D, page 74, wherein instructions are set forth as to when an annual report should be submitted. Inasmuch as a review of subject's file at the Bureau indicates that your office is in possession of pertinent information concerning subject's foreign travel and activities while abroad, you should promptly submit a current report suitable for dissemination containing available information pertaining to the subject.

TJM:mh (5)

NOTE:

Referenced letter was submitted in lieu of an annual report. Since submission of the last annual report in this case on 4-13-66 subject has departed for Turkey where he is currently residing, reportedly preparing a book for publication (U) Bufile also contains results of an interview with the subject regarding racial problems in the U.S., which interview appeared in a Turkish newspaper and information has been received from OSI regarding subject's eviction from an apartment in Turkey for homosexual activities. (U)

Classified by 6972 EEP/af
Declassify on: OADR 2-14-90 89-3016 JHP

Classified by Multiple Sources
Declassify on: OADR 5-18-89

Tolson
DeLoach
Mohr
Wick
Casper
Callahan
Conrad
Felt
Gale
Rosen
Sullivan
Tavel
Trotter
Tele. Room
Holmes
Gandy

MAILED 4
APR 11 1967
COMM-FBI

OSI information was declassified per memo dtd 3-27-90. 6972 EEP/af 4-3-90 89-3016 JHP

CONFIDENTIAL

62 APR 18 1967

MAIL ROOM TELETYPE UNIT

49.

BACK IN THE USA— WITH A "LOOKOUT" WAITING

SEPTEMBER 1967

When Baldwin abandoned his Istanbul retreat in the fall of 1967, the Bureau wasn't caught napping. A Montreal inspector with the Immigration and Naturalization Service (INS) let the FBI know the day, time, and number of the author's flight to New York City and a protected source and/or chatty neighbor in Baldwin's building on West 71st Street informed New York agents that he "had returned to his residence, Apartment B." The INS inspector had been emboldened to call the Bureau at 11:45 at night by a "lookout" or "stop notice" placed on Baldwin some time before. Such "stops" were all-points instructions to advise the Bureau when a suspect passed through a US port of entry. Despite the term's literal meaning, they did not detain Baldwin for long once he reached the US. Even so, stops had the power to pinpoint their target's border crossings to the minute, sometimes before that minute had arrived. They provided a reason to interview suspects on arrival and to spread a common climate of suspicion across departmental lines. Most important, perhaps, was their unwritten service as federal travel advisories: if you had enjoyed lands beyond the ideological orbit of the United States, stops informally advised, you should continue to do so or return only with the utmost care. Beneath the just-the-facts surface, these September 1967 documents illustrate why Baldwin charged that his US passport, a ticket to liberty abroad, became a token of captivity at home.

OPTIONAL FORM NO. 10
MAY 1962 EDITION
GSA FPMR (41 CFR) 101-11.6
UNITED STATES GOVERNMENT

Memorandum

TO : SAC, NY (100-146553) DATE: 9/6/67

FROM : SA [redacted] - Supv. 16

b7c-1

SUBJECT: JAMES A. BALDWIN
SM-C

Inspector [redacted], INS, Montreal, Canada telephonically advised at 11:45 pm instant, that subject, who has an F-1 lookout placed on him with INS, is departing Montreal, Canada at 11:50 PM instant aboard Air Canada flight #572 to New York, N.Y. Subject has DOB of 8/2/24.

SA [redacted] Sec 43. advised of above at 11:55 pm.

ALL INFORMATION CONTAINED
HEREIN IS UNCLASSIFIED
DATE 5-25-80 BY [illegible]

b7c-1

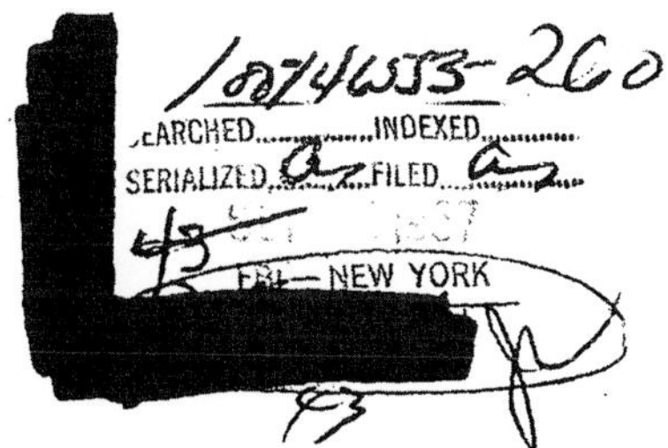
100-146553-260
SEARCHED....... INDEXED.......
SERIALIZED .... FILED ....
FBI — NEW YORK

Buy U.S. Savings Bonds Regularly on the Payroll Savings Plan

FD-122 (Rev. 4-21-66)

Director, FBI (Bufile- 62-108763) 9/13/67

SAC, New York (100-146553)

JAMES ARTHUR BALDWIN
SM-C
(OO:NY)

REMOVE FROM UNAVAILABLE SECTION

Re: ______

☐ It is recommended that a Security Index Card be prepared on the above-captioned individual.

☒ The Security Index Card on the captioned individual should be changed as follows *(specify change only)*:

Name

Aliases

NOTED
SI UNIT
DATE 9-13-67

☐ Native Born ☐ Naturalized ☐ Alien

☐ Communist ☐ Socialist Workers Party ☐ Miscellaneous *(specify)* ______

☐ Tab for Detcom	Date of birth	Place of birth	Race	Sex ☐ Male ☐ Female

Business Address *(show name of employing concern and address)*

Key Facility Data

Geographical Reference Number ______ Responsibility ______

Interested Agencies ______

ALL INFORMATION CONTAINED
HEREIN IS UNCLASSIFIED
DATE 5-19-89 BY [illegible]

Residence Address

Apartment B, 137 West 71st Street, New York, New York

REGISTERED MAIL
2-Bureau
1-New York
JO:gme
(3)

Searched ______
Serialized ______
Indexed ______
Filed ______

100-146553-262

New York, New York
September 13, 1967

Bufile 62-108763
NY file 100-146553

James Arthur Baldwin

b7C-8

Inspector [redacted] Immigration and Naturalization Service, United States Department of Justice, Montreal, Canada, advised on September 6, 1967, that James Baldwin departed Montreal, Canada, on Flight 572, Air Canada, at 11:50 p.m., on the same date. This flight terminated in New York on September 7, 1967.

On September 12, 1967, [redacted] b7C-6 137 West 71st Street, New York City, advised that James Baldwin had returned to his residence, Apartment B, in the same building.

ALL INFORMATION CONTAINED
HEREIN IS UNCLASSIFIED
DATE 2-19-81 BY [illegible]

This document contains neither recommendations nor conclusions of the FBI. It is the property of the FBI and is loaned to your agency; it and its contents are not to be distributed outside your agency.

Searched
Serialized
Indexed
Filed

100-146553-263

50.

OF LONDON, BALDWIN'S NEW YORK "WIFE," AND "FOREIGN AUTO SALES"

DECEMBER 1967

Never settled for long during the historical speed-up of the 1960s, Baldwin traveled to England at the end of 1967 to begin work on a film about the late Malcolm X. FBI officials on both sides of the Atlantic sprang into action to account for this latest excursion. Newspaper articles were gathered in the British capital ("The contrast between the Chelsea surroundings and the Black Muslim leader's life could hardly be more extreme," read a piece in the *London Evening News*). "[A]ppropriate stops" were placed with the INS at John F. Kennedy Airport, awaiting Baldwin's predicted return to New York City. And Baldwin's uptown Manhattan apartment was phoned by a Bureau agent "posing as a foreign auto sales representative" and thus confessing his shaky knowledge of Baldwin's skills and tastes. This agent did manage to hear an accurate account of Baldwin's purpose in London and a fully fictional tale about his marriage to his sister Paula. Paula Baldwin, who took the agent's call, may have been putting the agent on in the baiting style of *The Blood Counters*. Or the agent may have confused her relationship to her brother on his own. In either case, tax dollars would be spent to see if Paula Baldwin was indeed "the wife of the subject."

SAC, New York (100-146553) 12/19/67

Director, FBI (62-108763) 1 - Mr. S. S. Czarnecki

JAMES ARTHUR BALDWIN
SM - C

Enclosed herewith for New York is a Xerox copy of a newspaper article which was submitted by Legat, London, concerning subject.

In view of subject's presence in England, New York promptly submit letterhead memorandum concerning his travel.

Enclosed for the information of Legat, London, is New York letterhead memorandum dated October 17, 1966, concerning subject. For Legat, London's, additional information, Baldwin is an author of several books and has been active in the civil rights movement. He is on the Security Index of the New York Office.

Enclosure
1 - London (100-3409) (Enclosure)

1 - Foreign Liaison Unit
SSC:llr
(6)

NOTE:

Subject is on the Security Index of the NYO, is a Negro active in civil rights and has authored several books.

2 - ENCLOSURE

ST-115

REC-47 62-108763-56

18 DEC 19 1967

Tolson
DeLoach
Mohr
Bishop
Casper
Callahan
Conrad
Felt
Gale
Rosen
Sullivan
Tavel
Trotter
Tele. Room
Holmes
Gandy

MAILED 4
DEC 18 1967
COMM-FBI

ALL INFORMATION CONTAINED
HEREIN IS UNCLASSIFIED
DATE 5-19-89 BY

66 DEC 27 1967

MAIL ROOM ☑ TELETYPE UNIT ☐

Routing Slip
FD-4 (Rev. 6-14-66)

To:
☑ Director
Att.: SM - Section

☐ SAC
☐ ASAC
☐ Supv.
☐ Agent
☐ SE
☐ IC
☐ CC
☐ Steno
☐ Clerk

Date 12-4-67

FILE

Title JAMES BALDWIN
SM - MISC.

(LON FILE 100-3409)

RE:

☐ Rotor #:

b7C-1

ACTION DESIRED

☐ Acknowledge
☐ Assign ____ Reassign ____
☐ Bring file
☐ Call me
☐ Correct
☐ Deadline
☐ Deadline passed
☐ Delinquent
☐ Discontinue
☐ Expedite
☐ File
☐ For information
☐ Handle
☐ Initial & return
☐ Leads need attention
☐ Return with explanation or notation as to action taken.

☐ Open Case
☐ Prepare lead cards
☐ Prepare tickler
☐ Recharge serials
☐ Return assignment card
☐ Return file
☐ Return serials
☐ Search and return
☐ See me
☐ Send Serials
to
☐ Submit new charge out
☐ Submit report by
☐ Type

Re attached - Is he of current interest?

SAC Jim

____ See reverse side

Office London

ALL INFORMATION CONTAINED
HEREIN IS UNCLASSIFIED
DATE 5-19-89 BY

-56

ENCLOSURE

FD-350 (Rev. 7-16-63)

(Mount Clipping in Space Below)

The fire still burns in Mr. Baldwin

JAMES BALDWIN
"It would be a disaster"

In a quietly English, antique-filled town house where the back windows overlook a walled garden decorated by a Lake-land trompe l'oeil, James Baldwin is writing about Malcolm X.

The contrast between the Chelsea surroundings and the Black Muslim leader's life could hardly be more extreme. Mr. Baldwin seems not to notice it. He retires into himself and locks the door when he wants to write, ignoring outside stimuli.

He knew Malcolm X (who was assassinated in New York two years ago) well. "I was very fond of him and I think he was very fond of me.

"We always disagreed about dogma—the blue-eyed devils theory—but Malcolm had repudiated that himself before he died. It's a tremendous life—a man born in unimaginable conditions who managed to educate himself in prison.

The courage

"He had the courage to go even farther than that and repudiate eveything he had learned and start all over again."

The outcome of his stay in London will be a play about the Black Muslim which Elia Kazan is to direct on Broadway next year.

Mr. Baldwin author of "Go Tell It On The Mountain" and "The Fire Next Time," is a disarming man for so vehement a civil rights fighter. But at 43 the fire still burns fiercely just below the surface.

He still hopes we can avoid the United States tragedy in coming to terms with racial questions.

"One of the things I have observed around the world—and it's a bitter observation—is that many people wish to become more like the Americans. From my point of view that would be an unmitigated disaster.

"I can see why, it looks very attractive from afar. But I know what's in the package."

(Indicate page, name of newspaper, city and state.)
THE EVENING NEWS
LONDON, ENG.
PAGE 4

Date: 12-1-67
Edition:
Author:
Editor:
Title: JAMES BALDWIN

Character: SM-MISC.
or
Classification: 100
Submitting Office: LONDON

☐ Being Investigated

Let NY (enc)
1-London (enc)
12-19-67
SSC | llr

ALL INFORMATION CONTAINED
HEREIN IS UNCLASSIFIED
DATE 5-19-89 BY [illegible]

[illegible] - 56

ENCLOSURE

12/28/67

PLAINTEXT

AIRTEL

TO : DIRECTOR, FBI (62-108763)

FROM : SAC, NEW YORK (100-~~108763~~ 146553) (P)

SUBJECT: JAMES ARTHUR BALDWIN
SM-C
(OO:NY)

ReBulet to NY, 12/19/67.

Enclosed herewith are 11 copies of an LHM re captioned matter.

b7C-1 The pretext referred to in the LHM was conducted by SA [redacted] on 12/27/67, posing as a foreign auto sales representative.

NYO has appropriate stops placed with INS, JFK Airport, NY re subject's return to US.

Extra copies of LHM being furnished Bureau for dissemination to Legat, London.

FD 122 being submitted. ALL INFORMATION CONTAINED HEREIN IS UNCLASSIFIED DATE 5-19-89 BY [illegible]

LEAD:

NEW YORK

AT NEW YORK, NEW YORK. Will attempt to verify that PAULA BALDWIN is the wife of subject..

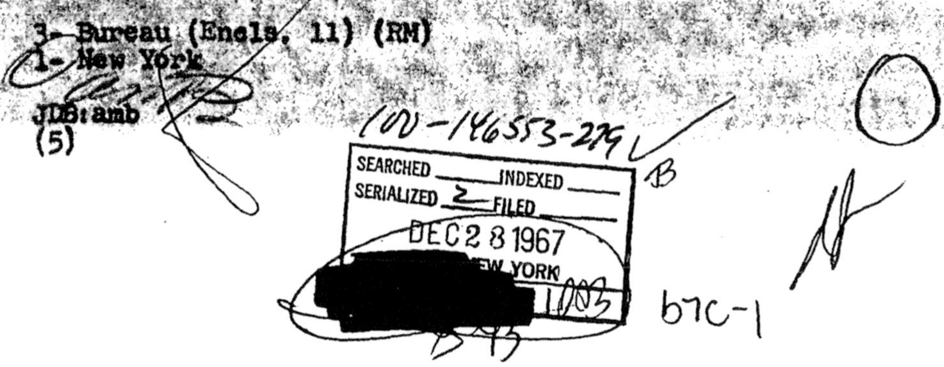

UNITED STATES DEPARTMENT OF JUSTICE

FEDERAL BUREAU OF INVESTIGATION

New York, New York
December 28, 1967

In Reply, Please Refer to
File No.

Bufile 62-108763
NY file 100-146553

James Arthur Baldwin

On December 27, 1967, by use of a suitable pretext, it was ascertained from Paula Baldwin, who identified herself as the wife of James Arthur Baldwin, Apartment B, 137 West 71st Street, New York, New York, that her husband is currently residing in London, England, the Chelsea section.

Mrs. Baldwin advised that she and her husband maintain a permanent residence of Apartment B, 137 West 71st Street, New York, New York; however, her husband is now in London while he completes work on his current book about Malcolm X, deceased leader of the Organization of Afro-American Unity (OAAU).

A characterization of the OAAU is attached hereto.

Mrs. Baldwin further advised that her husband departed for London a few days ago and she expects his return to New York City during the month of January, 1968, exact date unknown.

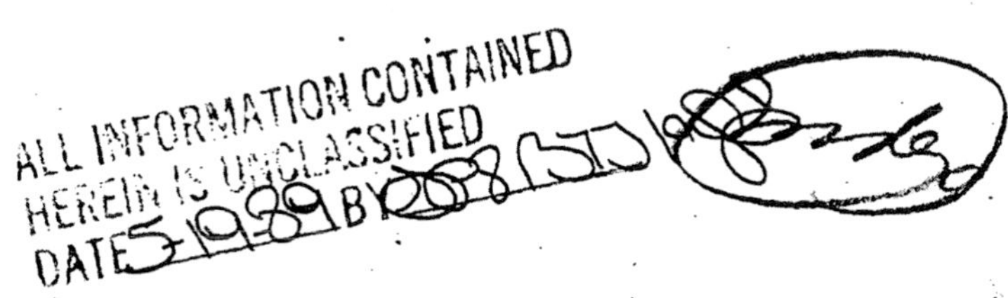

THIS DOCUMENT CONTAINS NEITHER
RECOMMEN[illegible] NOR CONCLUSIONS
OF THE [illegible] PROPERTY
OF [illegible] TO YOUR
AGE[illegible] ARE
NOT TO BE DISTRIBUTED OUTSIDE
YOUR AGENCY.

51.

BALDWIN AND OTHER "INDEPENDENT BLACK NATIONALIST EXTREMISTS"

JANUARY 1968

Baldwin's file was busy in the revolutionary year of 1968, a global "time of the barricades" in which student protests shook Rome, Paris, Warsaw, and New York City, assassinations took both Martin Luther King and Robert F. Kennedy in the space of two months, and the call for Black Power hurtled from curricular debates at Howard University to the winner's podium of the Summer Olympics in Mexico City. New York FBI agents greeted 1968 with a long report on the "Black Nationalist Movement" in the capital city of American radicalism, an analysis that reclassified Baldwin among "Independent Black Nationalist Extremists." Its toxic exaggeration aside, this new label underscored both Baldwin's ingrained habit of intellectual autonomy and his snowballing defense of a variety of militant groups, from the Black Panthers, to the post-nonviolent SNCC, to elements of the Nation of Islam, none of which captured or welcomed his exclusive allegiance. It also reflected the arrival in late 1967 of the Hoover Bureau's next-to-last COINTELPRO or counterintelligence program, this one targeting so-called "Black Nationalist-Hate Groups." (As we've seen, Baldwin's blessing of Robert Williams and the Monroe Movement in 1964 caught him in the web of an earlier COINTELPRO aimed at the Socialist Workers Party.) Hoover described his latest "counterintelligence endeavor" as a no-holds-barred crusade "to expose, disrupt, misdirect, discredit, or otherwise neutralize the activities of black nationalist, hate-type organizations and groupings, their leadership, spokesmen, membership, and supporters, and to counter their propensity for violence and civil disorder." Baldwin, an international explainer if not an elected leader of several of Hoover's most wanted black organizations, was retargeted in a dirty war to "prevent the rise of a 'messiah' who could unify, and electrify, the militant black nationalist movement." Strangely enough, at the same time that the FBI refocused on his political "extremism," would-be messiahs in the militant black nationalist movement began to attack his sexuality, an old Hoover saw, in public and in print. Advertising disgust for a "badly twisted and fragile weed, of too much use to the Establishment to be trusted by blacks"—Baldwin's own view of himself through the eyes of Black Panther leader Eldridge Cleaver—became something of a revolutionary rite of passage.

OPTIONAL FORM NO. 10
5010-104-01

UNITED STATES GOVERNMENT

Memorandum

TO: SAC, NEW YORK (100-161569)
Attn: SA [redacted]

DATE: 1/8/68

FROM: SA [redacted]

b7C-1

SUBJECT: BLACK NATIONALIST MOVEMENT
IS-BN

Re memo of SA [redacted], 12/29/67.

Referenced memo requested information concerning the identities of persons who could be included in the forthcoming report on the Black Nationalist Movement in the NY area.

The following information is hereby bewing submitted in connection with this matter:

<u>Independent Black Nationalist Extremists</u>

JAMES ARTHUR BALDWIN, Negro Author, NY file 100-146553.

[redacted] Harlem Unemployment Cenher, NY file 100-143564.

[redacted] Afro-Hispanic Community Alliance, West Side Unified Action Committee, NY file 157-1490.

b7C-4

1-100-161569 (#43) (SA [redacted] b7C-1
1-100-146553 (#43)
1-100-143564 (#43)
1-157-1490 (#43)
(4)
JDB/

ALL INFORMATION CONTAINED HEREIN IS UNCLASSIFIED DATE 5-25-08 BY [illegible]

100-146553-278

SEARCHED ___ INDEXED ___
SERIALIZED e FILED ___
JAN 8 1968
FBI — NEW YORK

b7C-1

att file
[illegible]

52.

THE BUREAU OF ACCURATE STATISTICS

FEBRUARY 1968

The FBI gets one right, the old-fashioned way: a special agent scrutinizing records at Manhattan's Bureau of Vital Statistics discovers no record "of marriage for James Arthur Baldwin to Paula Baldwin," now understood to be the author's sister—at least "for the period of August 18, 1967 to January 9, 1968," that is.

UNITED STATES DEPARTMENT OF JUSTICE

FEDERAL BUREAU OF INVESTIGATION
New York, New York

In Reply, Please Refer to
File No. Bufile 62-108763
NYfile 100-146553

February 12, 1968

James Arthur Baldwin

Reference is made to the previous memorandum on this matter dated December 28, 1967.

On January 10, 1968, a search of the records of the Bureau of Vital Statistics (Marriage Records) for the Borough of Manhattan, by Special Agent [redacted] b7C-1 failed to reveal any record of marriage for James Arthur Baldwin and Paula Baldwin for the period of August 18, 1967 to January 9, 1968. b7C-6

[redacted] On February 1, 1968, [redacted] 137 West 71st Street, New York, New York, advised that James Arthur Baldwin still resides in London, England. [redacted] further stated that Paula Baldwin, apartment B, 137 West 71st Street, New York, New York, is the sister of James Arthur Baldwin.

ALL INFORMATION CONTAINED
HEREIN IS UNCLASSIFIED
DATE 5-19-89 BY SP8CSJJ/afp

This document contains neither recommendations nor conclusions of the Federal Bureau of Investigation (FBI). It is the property of the FBI and is loaned to your agency; it and its contents are not to be distributed outside your agency.

100-146553-280

Searched
Serialized 3
Indexed
Filed 3

-1*-

53.

CLIPPERS AND INFORMERS ON *THE LIFE OF MALCOLM X*

MARCH 1968

Early in 1968, FBI newspaper clippers got busy documenting Baldwin's work on a movie about el-Hajj Malik el-Shabazz, the paramount hero of his black radical critics. "Baldwin Will Do Malcolm X," shouted the headline of an *Amsterdam News* item placed in Bureau custody, a brief announcement that the author had been signed by Columbia Pictures to write its big-budget translation of *The Autobiography of Malcolm X*. Marvin Worth, the film's producer, was friendly with an established FBI source—post-Ronald Reagan Hollywood still contained many—and this convenience allowed the Bureau to dig deeply into another not-yet-completed Baldwin manuscript. Paraphrased in a fill-in-the-blanks "Informant Report," the source's testimony conveyed that Baldwin was under contract "to write a treatment," not yet a screenplay, "to be used in a proposed film, 'The Life of Malcolm X.'" The author was headquartered in Palm Springs, but not even a pretext call to Worth Productions "seeking Baldwin's address . . . for a potential speaking engagement for the Peace and Freedom Party," could uncover exactly where. In the rented house the Bureau had yet to place, Baldwin launched his treatment with Aretha Franklin on the stereo, replaying the days when Bessie Smith records provided the soundtrack for his completion of *Go Tell It on the Mountain*. "He wanted to write the way that Aretha sounded," reports David Leeming, "to capture the combination of the 'heart-breaking' and the 'peaceful' that was in the Malcolm story and in

Aretha's music." Baldwin was listening to her music on the evening of April 4, 1968, when his brother David called to say that Martin Luther King had been shot and killed on a hotel balcony in Memphis. Baldwin cried out as he dropped the phone. He rallied to attend King's funeral in Atlanta and then returned to California determined to tell Malcolm X's story "my way or not at all." He could not resurrect Martin, but he believed he was "really creating Malcolm" once more.

FD-350 (Rev. 7-16-63)

(Mount Clipping in Space Below)

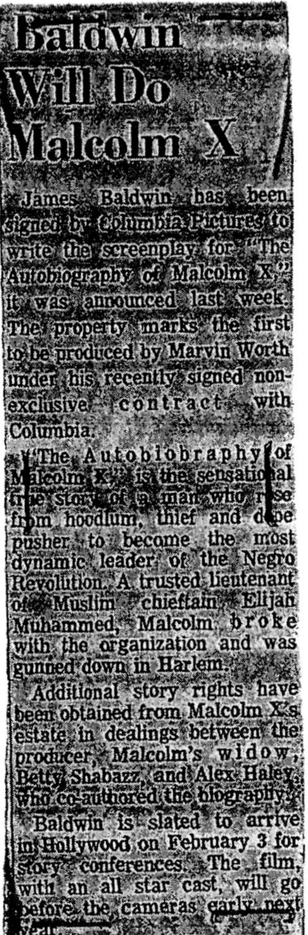

Baldwin Will Do Malcolm X

James Baldwin has been signed by Columbia Pictures to write the screenplay for "The Autobiography of Malcolm X," it was announced last week. The property marks the first to be produced by Marvin Worth under his recently signed non-exclusive contract with Columbia.

"The Autobiobraphy of Malcolm X" is the sensational true story of a man who rose from hoodlum, thief and dope pusher to become the most dynamic leader of the Negro Revolution. A trusted lieutenant of Muslim chieftain Elijah Muhammed, Malcolm broke with the organization and was gunned down in Harlem.

Additional story rights have been obtained from Malcolm X's estate in dealings between the producer, Malcolm's widow, Betty Shabazz, and Alex Haley, who co-authored the biography.

Baldwin is slated to arrive in Hollywood on February 3 for story conferences. The film, with an all star cast, will go before the cameras early next year.

(Indicate page, name of newspaper, city and state.)

19 Amsterdam News

Date: 3/2/68

Edition:

Author:

Editor:

Title:

Re: James Baldwin

Character:

or

Classification:

Submitting Office:

☐ Being Investigated

100-146553-289

INDEXED

SERIALIZED FILED

MAR 4 - 1968

ALL INFORMATION CONTAINED HEREIN IS UNCLASSIFIED DATE 5-25-89 BY

298325

#43

b7c-1

Cover Sheet for Informant Report or Material
FD-306 (3-21-58)

ESTABLISHED SOURCE
CONCEAL

b7C-5
b7D-2

Date received	Received from (name or symbol number)	Received by
3-21-68	[redacted]	SA [redacted] b7C-1

Method of delivery (check appropriate blocks)

☐ in person ☒ by telephone ☐ by mail ☐ orally ☐ recording device ☐ written by Informant

If orally furnished and reduced to writing by Agent:

Date

Dictated ______ to ______

Transcribed ______

Authenticated by Informant ______

Date of Report

Date(s) of activity

3-21-68

Brief description of activity or material

James Arthur Baldwin(100-71381)00: NY
SM-C

ALL INFORMATION CONTAINED
HEREIN IS UNCLASSIFIED
DATE 5-30-89 BY

File where original is located if not attached

Ref. NY Airtel 3-14-68 re Baldwin being in
Remarks: Hollywood and Palm Springs writing on the screen play "Malcolm X"

[redacted] said Baldwin under contract to Marvin Worth Productions,1438 N. Gower St., L. A. to write a treatment on the screen story to be used in a proposed film," The Life of Malcolm X ",to be produced by Marvin Worth Productions for Columbia Pictures Corp. release.Columbia Pictures has an option on the work being done by Baldwin,in their contract with Worth, where by if Columbia likes the treatment Baldwin will proceed with the full screen script. If not of course some other writer would be obtained.

b7C-5
b7D-2

No contact has been had with Baldwin by source,all negotiations have been done by Worth through Baldwins' Agent Robert Lantz,111 W. 57th St., NY,NY. No L.A. or Palm Springs or other local address has been obtained on Baldwin. Source understood Baldwin was currently in Palm Springs.

[redacted] asked for Baldwin's address in Palm Springs.Worth said Baldwin comes into the studio now and then and to send the mailings to Worth's office and Worth would see that Baldwin gets them.Worth works very closely with Baldwin. Source said he could not discreetly get the address from Worth with out making an issue of it and did not recommend trying it.He had no other source.

A pretecal to Worth Productions,3-21-68, seeking Baldwin's address in Palm Springs for a potential speaking engagement for the Peace and Freedom Party,ascertained from a female secretary that Baldwin was out of Palm Springs temporarily and declined to give the address or say where he was or would return.

Block Stamp

100-71381-2

SEARCHED ____ INDEXED ____
SERIALIZED ____ FILED ____
MAR 21 1968
FBI — LOS ANGELES

b7E-1

OPTIONAL FORM NO. 10
MAY 1962 EDITION
GSA GEN. REG. NO. 27

5010-108

UNITED STATES GOVERNMENT

Memorandum

TO : SAC, LOS ANGELES (100-71381)

DATE: 3/22/68

FROM : SA [redacted] b7C-1

SUBJECT: JAMES BALDWIN
SM - C

SOURCE	ACTIVITY	RECEIVED	AGENT	LOCATION
[redacted] PRI	Info re JAMES BALDWIN on 2/26/68	2/26/68	Writer	[redacted]

b2-1 b7D-1

Informant's report has been Xeroxed and is attached.

ACTION:

Informant was thoroughly interviewed concerning the above and could add nothing further.

All necessary action in connection with this memo has been taken by the writer.

ALL INFORMATION CONTAINED
HEREIN IS UNCLASSIFIED
DATE 5-25-89 BY SP8 DTJ/rbf

CC: 2 - NEW YORK (REGISTERED)
100- (BETTY SHABAZZ)
100- (JAMES BALDWIN) see att

b2-1 b7D-1

100- [redacted] -157- (BETTY SHABAZZ)
-157-DEAD [redacted] b7C-3
105-2604 (NOI)

GEA/lch
(8)

Read by

100-146553-303

SEARCHED INDEXED
SERIALIZED FILED
APR 5 1968
FBI — NEW YORK

b7C-1

2/26/68
Los Angeles, California

JAMES BALDWIN returned to Los Angeles, California, on the evening of February 26, 1968. He had accompanied BETTY SHABAZZ to New York City subsequent to the mass meeting in Los Angeles, California, on Sunday, February 18, 1968, to participate in a Malcolm X Memorial that was to be held inNew York City on February 20, 1968. After the New York meeting, SHABAZZ flew to Detroit, Michigan, to attend a Malcolm X Memorial Meeting being held in that city during the late afternoon hours or early evening hours of the same date.

BALDWIN flew to San Francisco from New York City, exact date unknown, and thereafter arrived in Los Angeles from San Francisco, California.

BALDWIN is scheduled to address a portion of the student body at Crenshaw High School at Los Angeles, California, on Tuesday afternoon February 27, 1968. He will be accompanied by Mr. EDMUND BRADLEY.

LAWSON JACKSON stated that BALDWIN plans to go into seclusion somewhere in Palm Springs, California, beginning February 28, 1968.

54.

"TWO SEPARATE FILMS ON THE LIFE OF THE SUBJECT"

MARCH 1968

Courtesy of the liberal *New York Times*, the FBI discovered that Hollywood in fact planned two biopics on Malcolm X. The first was the one under construction by Baldwin and Columbia. The second was in the hands of 20th Century Fox and Louis Lomax, the African American journalist and coproducer of *The Hate That Hate Produced*, a biting television documentary on the Nation of Islam that wound up doubling the movement's membership. Neither movie was ever completed as such, though Baldwin published an uncompromised version of his Malcolm script as the book *One Day, When I Was Lost* in 1972, and Spike Lee drew on his preliminary work in the film *Malcolm X*, successfully released twenty years later. (Respecting Baldwin's pledge that he "would rather be horsewhipped, or incarcerated in the forthright bedlam of Bellevue, than repeat the adventure" of film writing, Baldwin's heirs kept his name off Lee's credits.) Back in March 1968, the FBI did not anticipate the cancelling of either film and instructed its Los Angeles field office to "obtain advanced copies of these scripts in order that the interests of the Bureau may be protected." Preknowledge of Baldwin and Lomax's treatments would help the Bureau gauge incoming damage to the Nation of Islam, Malcolm's late enemy and likely killer (black radicals, for their part, often accused the FBI of conspiracy with his NOI assassins). As protective of its reputation as a teenager on Snapchat, the Bureau was also eager to know if it "will be mentioned or portrayed in either movie." As in the case of *The Blood Counters*, the FBI was the kind of Baldwin reader who just couldn't wait.

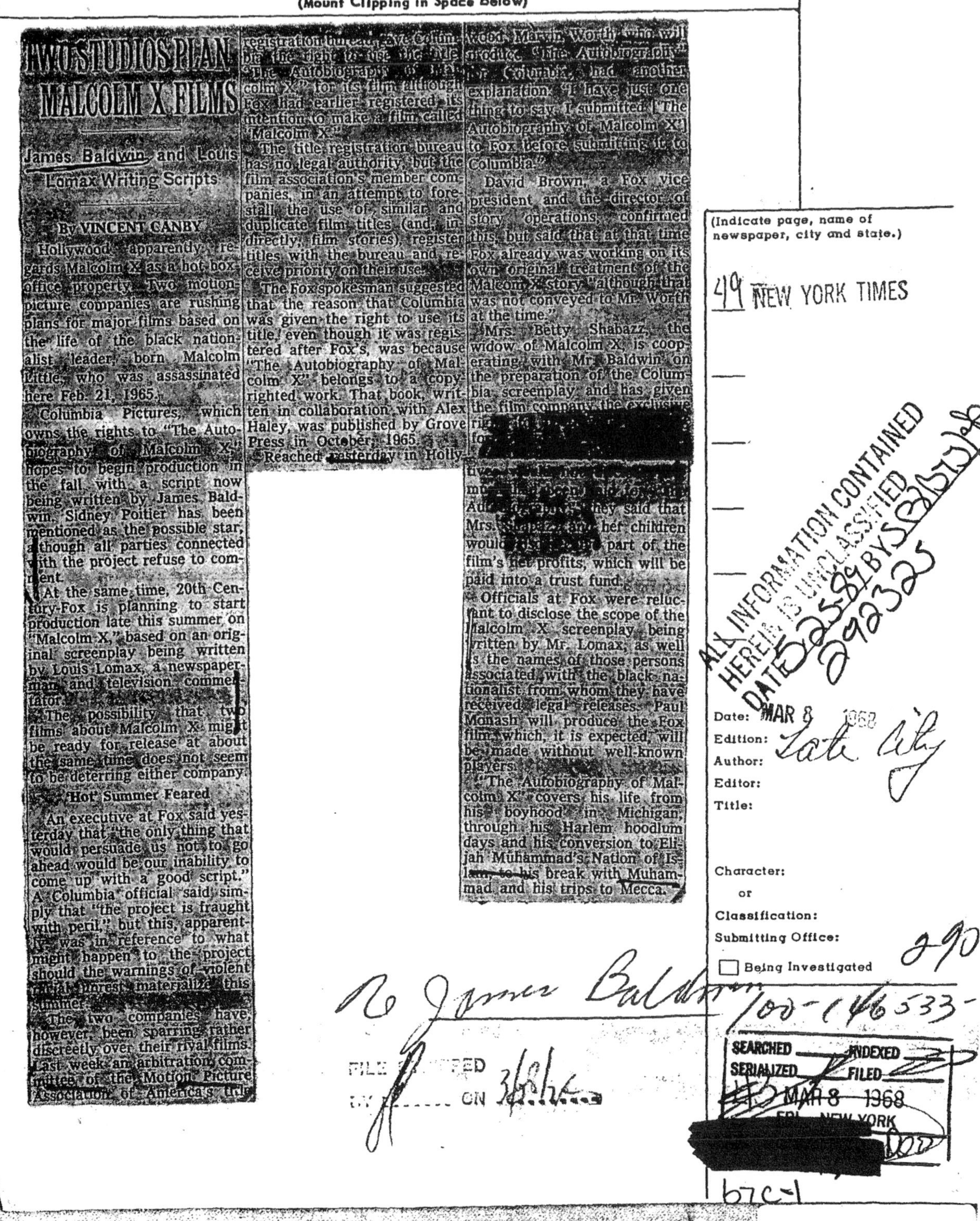

FD-350 (Rev. 7-16-63)

(Mount Clipping in Space Below)

TWO STUDIOS PLAN MALCOLM X FILMS

James Baldwin and Louis Lomax Writing Scripts

By VINCENT CANBY

Hollywood apparently regards Malcolm X as a hot box-office property. Two motion-picture companies are rushing plans for major films based on the life of the black nationalist leader, born Malcolm Little, who was assassinated here Feb. 21, 1965.

Columbia Pictures, which owns the rights to "The Autobiography of Malcolm X," hopes to begin production in the fall with a script now being written by James Baldwin. Sidney Poitier has been mentioned as the possible star, although all parties connected with the project refuse to comment.

At the same time, 20th Century-Fox is planning to start production late this summer on "Malcolm X," based on an original screenplay being written by Louis Lomax, a newspaperman and television commentator.

The possibility that two films about Malcolm X might be ready for release at about the same time does not seem to be deterring either company.

'Hot' Summer Feared

An executive at Fox said yesterday that "the only thing that would persuade us not to go ahead would be our inability to come up with a good script." A Columbia official said simply that "the project is fraught with peril," but this, apparently, was in reference to what might happen to the project should the warnings of violent racial unrest materialize this summer.

The two companies have, however, been sparring rather discreetly over their rival films. Last week an arbitration committee of the Motion Picture Association of America's title registration bureau gave Columbia the right to use the title "The Autobiography of Malcolm X" for its film although Fox had earlier registered its intention to make a film called "Malcolm X."

The title registration bureau has no legal authority, but the film association's member companies, in an attempt to forestall the use of similar and duplicate film titles (and, indirectly, film stories), register titles with the bureau and receive priority on their use.

The Fox spokesman suggested that the reason that Columbia was given the right to use its title, even though it was registered after Fox's, was because "The Autobiography of Malcolm X" belongs to a copyrighted work. That book, written in collaboration with Alex Haley, was published by Grove Press in October, 1965.

Reached yesterday in Hollywood, Marvin Worth, who will produce "The Autobiography" for Columbia, had another explanation: "I have just one thing to say. I submitted ['The Autobiography of Malcolm X'] to Fox before submitting it to Columbia."

David Brown, a Fox vice president and the director of story operations, confirmed this, but said that at that time Fox already was working on its own original treatment of the Malcolm X story "although that was not conveyed to Mr. Worth at the time."

Mrs. Betty Shabazz, the widow of Malcolm X, is cooperating with Mr. Baldwin on the preparation of the Columbia screenplay and has given the film company the exclusive rig[illegible] fo[illegible] ti[illegible] m[illegible] Au[illegible] they said that Mrs. [illegible] and her children would [illegible] part of the film's net profits, which will be paid into a trust fund.

Officials at Fox were reluctant to disclose the scope of the Malcolm X screenplay being written by Mr. Lomax, as well as the names of those persons associated with the black nationalist from whom they have received legal releases. Paul Monash will produce the Fox film which, it is expected, will be made without well-known players.

"The Autobiography of Malcolm X" covers his life from his boyhood in Michigan, through his Harlem hoodlum days and his conversion to Elijah Muhammad's Nation of Islam, to his break with Muhammad and his trips to Mecca.

(Indicate page, name of newspaper, city and state.)

49 NEW YORK TIMES

ALL INFORMATION CONTAINED HEREIN IS UNCLASSIFIED DATE 5-25-89 BY SP3 BTJ/pb 292325

Date: MAR 8 1968

Edition: Late City

Author:

Editor:

Title:

Character:

or

Classification:

Submitting Office:

☐ Being Investigated

Re James Baldwin

100-146533-

290

FILE [illegible]ED BY [illegible] ON 3/8/68

SEARCHED ___ INDEXED ___

SERIALIZED ___ FILED ___

MAR 8 1968

FBI — NEW YORK

b7C-1

ALL INFORMATION CONTAINED
HEREIN IS UNCLASSIFIED
DATE 5/26/89 BY

SAC, Los Angeles 3/27/68

Director, FBI (100-399321)

MALCOLM K. LITTLE
INTERNAL SECURITY - MUSLIM MOSQUE, INC.
(OO:NY)

Enclosed for Chicago, Los Angeles and Phoenix is a Xerox copy of an article which appeared in the March 9, 1968, edition of "The New York Times," page 23.

The above-mentioned article indicates that two film companies in Hollywood are currently preparing to start production on two separate films on the life of subject, now deceased, who is better known as Malcolm X. Columbia Pictures, which owns the movie rights to the book "The Autobiography of Malcolm X," will produce one of the movies to be released under that title. The script is being written by James Baldwin. The second movie is being produced by 20th Century-Fox and will be entitled "Malcolm X." The script for the latter is being written by Louis Lomax. All offices have previously been alerted under the "Nation of Islam, IS - NOI" caption to a possible movie on the life of Malcolm X since it is anticipated that such a film would be detrimental to the Nation of Islam and its leader, Elijah Muhammad.

Los Angeles is requested to discreetly contact sources at the above two studios to confirm the information in the article and to determine details relative to these two films. Los Angeles should be particularly alert for indications that the Bureau will be mentioned or portrayed in either movie. Los Angeles should obtain advanced copies of these scripts in order that the interest of the Bureau may be protected. Handle promptly and furnish the results in a form suitable for dissemination to the Bureau and all interested offices.

Enclosure
2 - New York (105-8999)
1 - Chicago (Enclosure)
1 - Phoenix (Enclosure)

Re James Baldwin

100-146553-38

105-8999

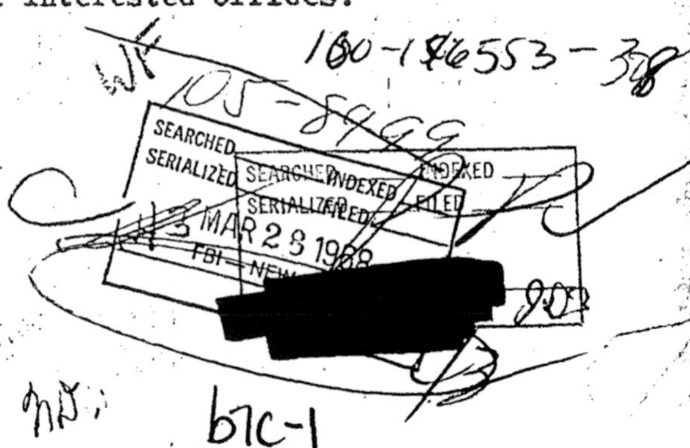

b7C-1

55.

THE PROBLEM WITH PARAPHRASE

APRIL 1968

Despite official instructions, it's difficult to paraphrase FBI file material when it's been censored so enthusiastically. What can be known beyond the blackouts on this document is this: a familiar confidential source told the Bureau something volatile enough to be classified "Secret—No Foreign Dissemination," and this something applied to Baldwin as well as to the Black Panther Party, the anti–Vietnam War Peace and Freedom Party, and the whole, vague "Racial Situation" in New York. Another ironically clear indication that the full story of the FBI's spying on Baldwin can't yet be told.

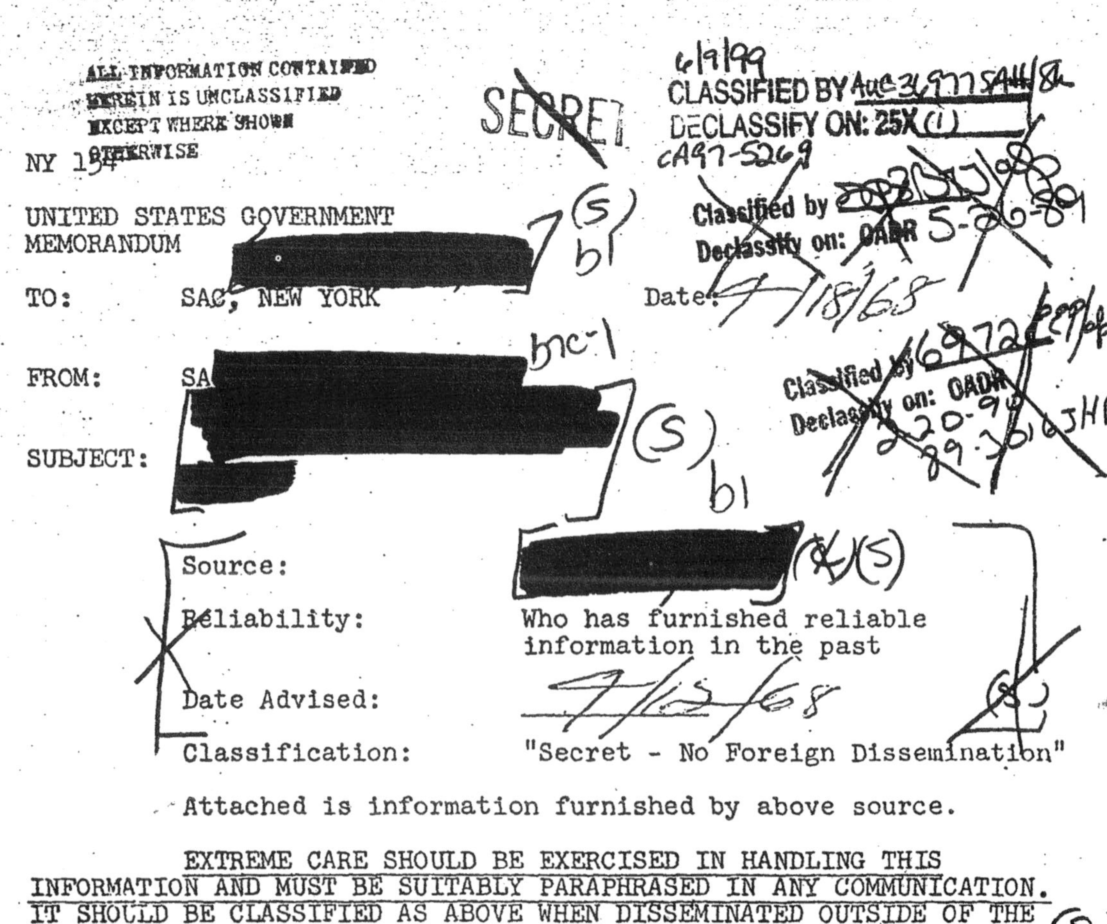

ALL INFORMATION CONTAINED HEREIN IS UNCLASSIFIED EXCEPT WHERE SHOWN OTHERWISE

SECRET

6/9/99 CLASSIFIED BY [illegible] DECLASSIFY ON: 25X(1) CA97-5269

NY 134

Classified by [illegible] Declassify on: OADR 5-26-89

UNITED STATES GOVERNMENT MEMORANDUM (S) b1

TO: SAC, NEW YORK

Date: 7/18/68

FROM: SA b7C-1

Classified by 6972 Declassify on: OADR 2-20-90 89-3616 JHF

SUBJECT: (S) b1

Source: (S)

Reliability: Who has furnished reliable information in the past

Date Advised: 7/12/68

Classification: "Secret - No Foreign Dissemination"

Attached is information furnished by above source.

EXTREME CARE SHOULD BE EXERCISED IN HANDLING THIS INFORMATION AND MUST BE SUITABLY PARAPHRASED IN ANY COMMUNICATION. IT SHOULD BE CLASSIFIED AS ABOVE WHEN DISSEMINATED OUTSIDE OF THE BUREAU. (S)

(S) b1

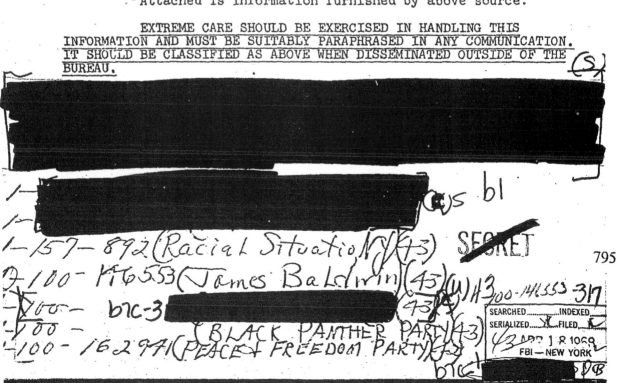

1 – 157-892 (Racial Situation NY) (43)

1 – 100-146553 (James Baldwin) (43)

1 – 100- b7C-3 (43)

1 – 100- (BLACK PANTHER PARTY) (43)

1 – 100-162971 (PEACE & FREEDOM PARTY) (43)

SECRET

795

100-146553-317

SEARCHED ___ INDEXED ___ SERIALIZED X FILED ___ APR 18 1968 FBI — NEW YORK

b7C-1

56.

BALDWIN THE BLACK PANTHER

MAY 1968

Like Stokely Carmichael, one of his most sympathetic contacts in SNCC, Baldwin found himself moving in the political and emotional direction of the Black Panther Party in 1967, attracted by its dramatic fearlessness and its Malcolm-stirred doctrine of black freedom by any means necessary. He first broke bread with Huey Newton, the Party's cofounder, in San Francisco that October, and he agreed to meet with Eldridge Cleaver despite the Panther minister's gay-bashing Oedipal attack in the essay "Notes on a Native Son," later collected in the bestselling *Soul on Ice*. Underlining the Panthers' shrewd cultivation of celebrity, it was Baldwin's old Greenwich Village pal Marlon Brando who introduced him to Bobby Seale, Newton's writing partner and the party's first chairman. By 1968, Baldwin was willing to host a fundraising birthday party for Newton and to address an Oakland meeting celebrating the first anniversary of the Panthers' armed invasion of the California state legislature. Recounted in this May 1968 report on the meeting filed by an undercover "Ghetto" informant, Baldwin's speech seems like relatively weak tea; while Seale called out "cracker, honky, racist, white pig cops," Baldwin promised "that his next book would be called 'The Fire This Time.'" Even this literary bow contained significant risks, however, as COINTELPRO tightened its noose around the party, Hoover's new nominee as "the greatest threat to the internal security of the country." Baldwin was reluctant to join the Panthers outright and surrender his liberties as an independent radical. But he was keen to lend his cultivated voice to the group because "the American state" was showing itself incapable of "self-confrontation, the power to change itself in the direction of honor and knowledge and freedom," the capacity the nonviolent Civil Rights Movement had banked on. Malcolm was right, Baldwin now suggested, in insisting that white America would never "atone."

Cover Sheet for Informant Report or Material
FD-306 (3-21-58)

b2-1 b7D-1

Date received	Received from (name or symbol number)	Received by
5-6-68	[redacted] (Ghetto)	SA [redacted] b7C-1

Method of delivery (check appropriate blocks)

[X] in person [ ] by telephone [ ] by mail [ ] orally [ ] recording device [XX] written by Informant

If orally furnished and reduced to writing by Agent:

Date

Dictated ______ to ______

Transcribed ______

Authenticated by Informant ______

Date of Report

Date(s) of activity

Brief description of activity or material

May 2, 1968 public meeting of Black Panther Party, 27th. and West Streets, Oakland, featuring JAMES BALDWIN as speaker

File where original is located if not attached

[redacted] b2-1 b7D-1

Remarks:

157-1204 (BPP)
100-53950 (BOBBY GEORGE SEALE)
157-636 (SOUL STUDENTS ADVISORY COMMITTEE)
100-54228 (MERRITT COLLEGE -)
157-0 (JAMES BALDWIN) — 157-245-239 (9/63)
100-[redacted]
100-[redacted]
157-[redacted]
157-[redacted]
157-0 [redacted] b7C-3

(10)

James Arthur Baldwin 157-1323 (5/68)

limited to 157's

ACTION RECOMMENDED: NO ACTION

ALL INFORMATION CONTAINED HEREIN IS UNCLASSIFIED DATE 5-30-89 BY [illegible]

Block Stamp

SEARCHED INDEXED
SERIALIZED FILED
MAY 24 1968
FBI — SAN FRANCISCO

157-1323-6

1752

A special report in reference to the BPPSD, Black Panther Party for Self Defense, Chairman BOBBY SEALE, Prime Minister STOKELY CARMICHAEL; ELDRIDGE CLEAVER, Minister of Information; HUEY P. NEWTON, Minister of Defense. May 2, 1968 - Approximately 125 people.

Subject a special meeting was held at Saint Augustine's Church, 27th and West Streets in Oakland, for the purpose to celebrate the first annual anniversary of the invasion of the State Legislature. BOBBY SEALE said we are going to control our neighborhoods if the cracker, honky, racist, white pig cops invade our society they will answer to the Black Panther Party. BOBBY SEALE made comments on the white power structure trying to destroy the leadership, but they will not succeed.

Comment: Incidentally off camera BOBBY SEALE said that this group calling itself John Brown Society wants to join the Black Panther Party. BOBBY said they will let them join and it will make a triangular coalition between the John Brown Party, Black Panther Party and the Peace and Freedom Party, but BOBBY SEALE said there will be one condition and that's if the Black Panthers can control everything.

JAMES BALDWIN, author of many books and his best selling novel "The Fire Next Time" and the first statement he

2

made was that his next book will be called "The Fire This Time." He said that he is working on a movie for MGM, the life story and autobiography of MALCOLM X. He said he would be back to the area. Incidentally, this meeting was [redacted] b7c-4 [redacted] and will be shown on TV at a later date, on Sunday show.

BOBBY SEALE spoke on his and HUEY NEWTON's starting of the SSAC at Merritt College. Soul Students Advisory Council, it is the only college with black representation, that does not call itslf the Black Activists Union although their ideology are about the same.

Present that were known:

BOBBY SEALE, Chairman, Black Panther Party
JAMES BALDWIN, World famous author
DAVID HILLIARD
MELVYN NEWTON
KATHLEEN CLEAVER (20th Century Joan of Arc), wife of ELDRIDGE CLEAVER
HARRIET WILLIAMS, Merritt College Militant
JOEL DURHAM, well known bandleader
JAMES CARTER, engineer

57.

TRUMAN CAPOTE, FBI SOURCE, AND JAMES BALDWIN, "NEGRO"

MAY AND JUNE 1968

Still struggling to locate Baldwin's exact address in Palm Springs, the Bureau's Los Angeles field office tapped a concealed source who in turn drew on a friendship with Truman Capote. Baldwin had known Capote, the flamboyant author of *Breakfast at Tiffany's* (1958) and *In Cold Blood* (1966), since his rookie year in Paris, 1948, when the two could be overheard in the Montana Bar talking writing and where it should be done, "back where we all come from," as Capote put it, or in another country. They remained friends for decades despite dividing political paths and Capote's far greater success in translating his prose for the screen (there may be aspects of Capote, in fact, in the sympathetic character of Eric in *Another Country*, a fair-haired Southerner with a fondness for truth-telling and darker men). It's unlikely, then, that the fellow gay author would have tattled to the FBI about Baldwin's address on "some 'Circle'" had he known he was doing so. It took an anonymous postal carrier, more literal-minded than Capote, to advise "that James Baldwin was a Negro" who was tackling his Malcolm X treatment at 822 Topaz Circle in Palm Springs. By the time of this confirmation of race and address, however, Baldwin had shifted scenes yet again, this time to Beverly Hills—closer to Capote's Hollywood but even further from Malcolm's Harlem.

OPTIONAL FORM NO. 10
MAY 1962 EDITION
GSA GEN. REG. NO. 27
5010-108

UNITED STATES GOVERNMENT

Memorandum

TO : DIRECTOR, FBI (62-108763) DATE: 5/23/68

FROM : SAC, LOS ANGELES (100-71381) (P)

SUBJECT: JAMES ARTHUR BALDWIN
SM - C

OO: New York

Re: New York airtel to Bureau, dated 3/14/68, and Los Angeles letter to Bureau dated 4/9/68.

b7C-6
b7D-2

On 4/1/68 [redacted] (conceal), [redacted] advised that he had asked TRUMAN CAPOTE, the well-known author, if JAMES BALDWIN was staying in Palm Springs. He was advised by CAPOTE that BALDWIN is staying in some friend's home in Palm Springs while he is re-writing some portions of his book, "MALCOLM X". CAPOTE could not recall the name of the street but said it was some "Circle" approximately one mile from downtown Palm Springs.

On 4/8/68, [redacted] b7C-8 Palm Springs (conceal), advised that JAMES BALDWIN is receiving mail at 822 Topaz Circle, Palm Springs. He did not know if this BALDWIN was identical with subject.

On 4/30/68 and 5/13/68, spot checks at 822 Topaz Circle, Palm Springs, failed to observe BALDWIN residing at that address.

LEAD

LOS ANGELES

AT PALM SPRINGS, CALIFORNIA: Will continue efforts to determine if BALDWIN temporarily residing in Palm Springs.

2 - Bureau (RM)
2 - New York (100-146553) (RM)
2 - Los Angeles
JWW:gcw
(6)

100-146553-37
SEARCHED ___ INDEXED ___
SERIALIZED ___ FILED ___
MAY 2 9 1968
[redacted] YORK

b7C-1

ALL INFORMATION CONTAINED
HEREIN IS UNCLASSIFIED
DATE 5/19/89 BY [illegible]

OPTIONAL FORM NO. 10
MAY 1962 EDITION
GSA GEN. REG. NO. 27
5010-108

UNITED STATES GOVERNMENT

Memorandum

TO : SAC, LOS ANGELES (100-71381) DATE: 6/19/68

FROM : SA [redacted] b7C-1

SUBJECT: JAMES ARTHUR BALDWIN
SM - C
OO: New York

b7C-8

[redacted] On 6/11/68, [redacted] (Conceal) [redacted] [redacted], Palm Springs, California, advised that on 4/30/68, JAMES BALDWIN, 822 Topaz Circle, Palm Springs, issued a change of address to 1230 La Colina, Beverly Hills, California. [redacted] checked with the postal carrier and he advised that JAMES BALDWIN was a Negro.

He advised that on 5/7/68, JAMES BALDWIN issued another change of address to have all mail forwarded to 1326 Benedict Canyon, Beverly Hills, California.

The Beverly Hills city directory revealed that E.F. LYNCH resides at 1230 La Colina and E. E. HATTER resides at 1326 Benedict Canyon. Both Beverly Hills.

ALL INFORMATION CONTAINED
HEREIN IS UNCLASSIFIED
DATE 5-30-79 BY [illegible]

100-71381-8
SEARCHED ...... INDEXED ......
SERIALIZED ...... FILED ......
JUN 19 1968
FBI — LOS ANGELES

b7C-1

JCT/jmb
(1)

58.

RETURNING ON A JET PLANE

JULY 1968

Typically rapid, sometimes compulsive, Baldwin's movements passed the speed limit in the long, hot summer of 1968, with the FBI not the only outfit wondering where he would be found next. In this July memorandum, the Bureau beat Columbia Pictures to the punch, locating Baldwin on a Pan American flight from Paris to New York. Thanks to the stop notice the FBI had sicced on the author, the New York field office learned the precise time and place of his arrival. It squeezed only a birthdate, "2/2/24," out of Baldwin in search of further "particulars," however, and even this was misleading. He was in fact born James Arthur Jones, the son of Emma Berdis Jones and a father he never met, in Harlem Hospital on August 2, 1924. (David Baldwin, the preacher Emma married in 1925, lent James his family name and little else without a struggle.) With impeccable timing, Baldwin took his first breath in the heart of Black Manhattan amid its first great cultural renaissance.

OPTIONAL FORM NO. 10
MAY 1962 EDITION
GSA FPMR (41 CFR) 101-11.6
UNITED STATES GOVERNMENT

Memorandum

TO : SAC, NEW YORK DATE: 7/11/68

FROM : [redacted] b7C-1

100-146553*

SUBJECT: JAMES ARTHUR BALDWIN.
INFO CONCERNING (F#1 Stop Notice).

[redacted] INS, Kennedy Airport, telephonically contacted the NY Office this date and advised that captioned individual, subject of an FBI F#1 Stop Notice, arrived Kennedy 2:00 p.m. instant date, 7/11/68, aboard Pan Am Flight #101 from Paris. Only particulars obtained concerning BALDWIN was his birthdate, 2/2/24 U.S.

b7C-8

[redacted] was thanked for his cooperation.

Destination: 137 W. 71st St.
NYC

ALL INFORMATION CONTAINED
HEREIN IS UNCLASSIFIED
DATE 5-26-89 BY [illegible]

#43

100-146553-336

SEARCHED....INDEXED....
SERIALIZED....FILED....
JUL 11, 1968
FBI — NEW YORK

b7C-1

5010-108

Buy U.S. Savings Bonds Regularly on the Payroll Savings Plan

59.

"HOSTESSES FOR THIS PARTY WORE LONG AFRICAN STYLE CLOTHES"—BALDWIN SPEAKS FOR SNCC

AUGUST 1968

Baldwin's new connection to the Black Panthers did not keep him from speaking on behalf of SNCC, an older political attachment. In 1967, H. Rap Brown had renamed the group the Student National Coordinating Committee, abandoning nonviolence in the conviction that political bloodshed "was as [A]merican as cherry pie." Indicted for inciting a riot, he resigned as SNCC chair in 1968 just as Kathleen Neal and Bobby Rush joined Stokely Carmichael in the Panthers. The departure of many of SNCC's most talented organizers did not help with fundraising, already damaged as well-off liberals, black and white, shied from its sharpening militancy. Into the breach stepped Baldwin, who joined jazz trumpeter Freddy Hill as the draw for a chic SNCC fundraiser in Los Angeles. The introduction to the FBI informer's report on the event dwells on the cultural revolution of Black Power, cocktails mingling with the "long African style clothes" of the hostesses in the largely black crowd (of the approximately "50 people" in attendance, "only 12 were white"). The report then recounts the highlight of Baldwin's speech, delivered near midnight, his pursuit of a middle way between self-defense in the tradition of Patrick Henry and costly "violence in the streets," an unwinnable "fight on white man's soil and white man's terms." It's in this same speech that Baldwin declared "that there probably was a CIA or FBI agent in the group" marking his words. The presence of government spies should be assumed everywhere, he suggested, and "one can never be sure who one is associating with." Courageously and a bit cryptically, he ended by warning "that those attending this party couldn't even be sure of him"—a call to suspect celebrity radicalism that may also have confessed the power of surveillance to infect its most wary targets.

OPTIONAL FORM NO. 10
MAY 1962 EDITION
GSA GEN. REG. NO. 27
5010-106

UNITED STATES GOVERNMENT

Memorandum

TO : SAC, LOS ANGELES (100-63822) DATE: 8/1/68

FROM : SA [redacted] b7C-1

ALL INFORMATION CONTAINED
HEREIN IS UNCLASSIFIED
DATE 5-26-89 BY [illegible]

SUBJECT: STUDENT NON-VIOLENT COORDINATING COMMITTEE
(SNCC)
IS - C

SOURCE	ACTIVITY	RECEIVED	AGENT	LOCATION
[redacted]	Fund rais. affair for SNCC, fea. J. BALDWIN, 6/27/68.	6/27/68	Writer	[redacted] (WR)

b2-1 b7D-1

Informant's report is quoted as follows:

"Canoga Park
June 27, 1968

"On the evening of May 29, 1968, the Los Angeles Friends of SNCC held a cocktail party at the home of [redacted] This affair was a fundraiser for L.A. SNCC. b7C-4

"The black women of SNCC who acted as hostesses for this party wore long African style clothes.

"There were several young boys acting as guards who wore black sweatshirts bearing the letters SYC (SNCC Youth Corps).

"There were approximately 50 people who attended this party. Of these, only 12 were white.

"There was a live band conducted by FREDDIE HILL.

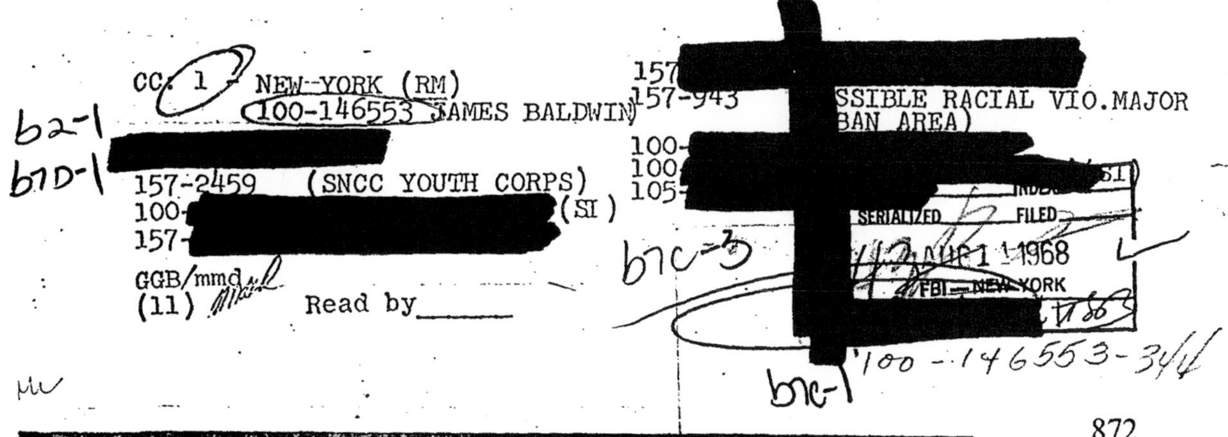

CC: 1 - NEW YORK (RM)
(100-146553 JAMES BALDWIN)
b2-1 b7D-1 [redacted]
157-2459 (SNCC YOUTH CORPS)
100-[redacted] (SI)
157-[redacted]

157-[redacted]
157-943 [redacted] SSIBLE RACIAL VIO. MAJOR [redacted] BAN AREA)
100-[redacted]
100-[redacted] (SI)
105-[redacted]

SERIALIZED FILED
AUG 1 1968
FBI — NEW YORK

b7C-3

GGB/mmd
(11)

Read by______

100-146553-344

b7C-1

"JAMES BALDWIN, the guest speaker, didn't arrive until after 11 p.m.

"A Mr. CROOK, who is a staff worker at the L.A. SNCC office, told of some of the projects SNCC was working on. They were:

"1. Liberation schools to 'unbrainwash' black people.

"2. Establishing survival centers where food and aid can be obtained during a revolt. He said that during past 'revolts' aid was not immediately available to those involved in the action. They had to wait till Negro ministers and sympathetic groups collected what was needed and brought it to the area. This slowed down the revolt. These survival centers will be stocked ahead of time and will be prepared to give instant aid whenever the uprising or revolt happens.

"3. Legal gun clubs are already underway. CROOK pointed out that if the police could teach housewifes and other white people how to shoot then the blacks had better be trained in the use of weapons to defend themselves.

"CROOK also brought out the fact the LASNCC has to raise $250,000 bail money for 5 LA SNCC workers who were arrested in New Orleans. CROOK said these workers had gone there to attend the trial of H. RAPP BROWN.

"JAMES BALDWIN was then introduced. BALDWIN said he would not encourage his black brothers to go out & commit violence in the streets. Neither would he encourage them to stand by and let one of the brothers be hurt or killed. He warned his brothers not to be goaded into a fight on white man's soil and white men's terms. He said this could result in a whole generation of black activists being wiped out.

"He said the people of the U.S. must approve of what JOHNSON's doing or he wouldn't be able to do it. He said he "wouldn't vote for anyone in the Republican or Democcratic party.

"He knocked belief in God and Christianity. He called Christians hypocrits. He accused them of going to church by day and sinning by night. He said they were bigots and murderers. He said that blacks and whites were on a colision course.

"He said it was alright for PATRICK HENRY to say 'Give me liberty or Give me death' but it not alright for black people to say this now."

"He pointed out that American history books make big heroes out of those who fought the British to be free and indipendent. However, the black people are looked upon as evil when they fight for their rights and freedom.

"He mentioned that there probably was a CIA or FBI agent in the group attending this party but he didn't care. He said one can never be sure who one is associating with. Then he said that those attending this party couldn't even be sure of him.

"There were some questions from the floor after he finished speaking. One was asked by a lady from the Peace and Freedom Party who wanted to know what white people could do. He said they could work in their own white communities, but he went on to say that he thinks it's too late that the Blacks & whites were on a colision course and he didn't think anything was really going to prevent it.

"CLARE REESE ALLEN then gave a pitch for money to help get the 5 SNCC workers out of jail. A basket was passed around to collect the money donated for this cause.

"The following were among those attending the meeting:

LA 100-63822

"BRUCE INGRAHM
COLEEN and DON POOLE of Long Beach, SNCC.
MARY SEIFERT, (also of Long Beach SNCC) and the Save Cabrillo Beach Committee
HELEN CUNNINGHAM
FERN CUNNINGHAM
CAROL COLUMBO
PAULINE SCHINDLER
LENNIE REDMAN (phonetic)
CINDY COHEN (with REDMAN)
SAIDIA
BOBBIE HODGES (female LA SNCC staff worker)
JAMES BALDWIN
FREDDIE HILL & his orchestra
Mrs. SYLVANUS JONES (at whose home this fundraiser was held.)
CLARE REESE ALLEN
BROTHER CROOK and
many other Negro men and women some with African names."

ACTION:

b7c-5b7D-2

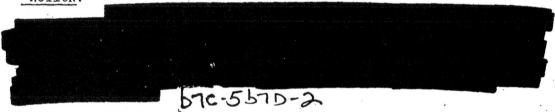

Since JAMES BALDWIN maintains his regular residence in the New York City area a copy of this channelizing memorandum is being furnished to that division (NY file 100-146553; LA file 100-71381).

All other necessary action in connection with this memo has been taken by the writer.

LA 100-63822

INDEX: SYLVANUS JONES
Mrs. SYLVANUS JONES
FREDDIE HILL
CLARE REESE ALLEN
COLEEN POOLE
DON POOLE
MARY SEIFERT
HELEN CUNNINGHAM
LENNIE REDMAN
CINDY COHEN

60.

FLYING THE COOP AND "PRESENTLY CHECKING HIS BAGGAGE THROUGH CUSTOMS"

FEBRUARY AND APRIL 1969

Baldwin's FBI file thins out beginning in 1969, and the Bureau wasn't the only observer that saw the writer in recoil in that year of Black Power, white rage, and President Richard Nixon's "law-and-order" restoration. In February, Baldwin published a short article in the *New York Times* on the unmanageable situation of the black American writer. Its title, "The Price May Be Too High," said it all, and its blunt conclusion—"White people don't want to hear what he knows, and the system can't afford it"—for now closed the case on the prospect of a mixed audience capable of healing and achieving the country. As the Bureau memo from February 14 suggests, Baldwin took meetings with Columbia Pictures executives in Los Angeles that same month. He finally quit their version of the Malcolm X project soon after, frustrated in part by their assignment of a white writer, Arnold Perl, to serve as co-wrangler. ("The question is not whether black and white artists can work together," Baldwin specified in "The Price May Be Too High," but "whether black and white *citizens* can work together." Baldwin put his single-authored, novelistic screen treatment of Malcolm's life to use three years later.) In April, the FBI caught him returning from a trip to Mexico via Mexicana Airlines—and caught him in the act, with an INS inspector phoning the Bureau as Baldwin was still "checking his baggage through customs." By the summer, Baldwin was off again to Istanbul. There, he threw himself into a fresh artistic role, directing a revival of John Herbert's 1967 drama *Fortune and Men's Eyes*, a study of prison slavery that spoke to him of entrapped gay desire and of jailed Black Panthers Huey Newton and Bobby Seale. Both the place and the play were the furthest thing from Hollywood he could conceive.

OPTIONAL FORM NO. 10
MAY 1962 EDITION
GSA FPMR (41 CFR) 101-11.6

UNITED STATES GOVERNMENT

Memorandum

TO : DIRECTOR, FBI (62-108763)

DATE: 2/14/69

FROM : SAC, LOS ANGELES (100-71381)

SUBJECT: JAMES ARTHUR BALDWIN
RM - MISCELLANEOUS
OO: New York

Re Los Angeles letter to Bureau, 1/13/69.

On 2/11/69, Columbia Picture's Corporation, 1438 North Gower Street, indicated that JAMES BALDWIN continues to list his address as 137 West 71st Street, New York City, New York, Apartment 1-B, and his Los Angeles, California address as 1601 Queens Road, Los Angeles.

BALDWIN is expected to be in Los Angeles on 2/14/69 and 2/15/69, in order to meet with movie officials.

LEAD

LOS ANGELES

AT LOS ANGELES, CALIFORNIA: Will continue to follow BALDWIN's activities while in Los Angeles area.

ALL INFORMATION CONTAINED
HEREIN IS UNCLASSIFIED
DATE 5-19-89 BY [illegible]

2 - Bureau (RM)
2 - New York (100-146553)
2 - Los Angeles

JWW/mdm
(6)

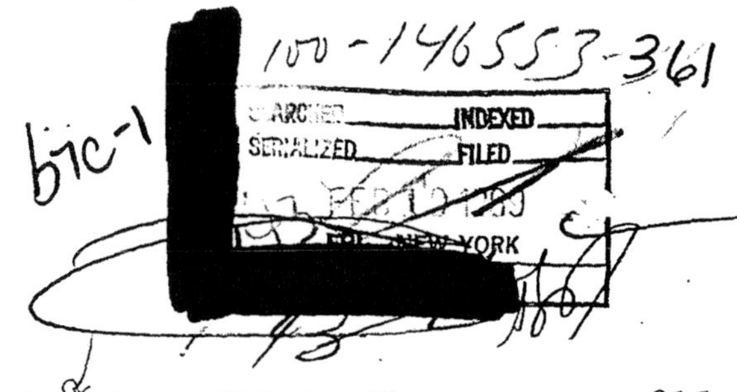
100-146553-361
b7C-1
SEARCHED INDEXED
SERIALIZED FILED
FBI - NEW YORK

Buy U.S. Savings Bonds Regularly on the Payroll Savings Plan

Complaint Form
FD-71 (Rev. 7-21-67)

NOTE: Hand print names legibly; handwriting satisfactory for remainder.

Indices: ☐ Negative ☐ See below

Subject's name and aliases	Character of case
JAMES ARTHUR BALDWIN	RM-Misc.
	Complainant INSPECTOR [redacted] b7C-8
	Complaint received ☐ Personal ☒ Telephonic Date 4-9-69 Time 12-04pm.
Address of subject	**Complainant's address and telephone number** Immigration and Naturalization Service 646-3965 or 646-3965

Subject's Description

Race	Sex	Height	Hair	Build	Birth date and Birthplace
	☐ Male				
Age	☐ Female	**Weight**	**Eyes**	**Complexion**	

Scars, marks or other data

Facts of complaint C advised he is an inspector for I.N.S. at International Airport. C said they have a "Fl interception" listed in their "Lookout Book" for the FBI on JAMES ARTHUR BALDWIN-the author. C said they are to immediately notify the FBI if he passes through the area.

C said he was calling to advise BALDWIN had just arrived, at approximately 11-50am this date, at International Airport. He had been aboard Mexicana Airlines flight 906, from Mexico. He is presently checking his baggage through customs. C said he would call to advise any additional information, such as an address, if he got it later.

ALL INFORMATION CONTAINED
HEREIN IS UNCLASSIFIED
DATE 5-30-89 BY [illegible]

100-71381-56

SEARCHED ____ INDEXED ____
SERIALIZED ____ FILED ____

ANGELES

b7C-1

Action Recommended See 100-71381*

(Agent)

61.

INDISCREET BOOK BUYING

JULY 1969

While new additions to the Baldwin file slowed, the Bureau Library in Washington continued buying his books. Into 1972, his titles were purchased directly by FBI agents, who sometimes patronized the new wave of black-owned bookstores sparked by the Black Power and Black Arts movements. The owner of Drum and Spear Books in DC, a supplier of titles to some of the first college courses in Black Studies, remembered Bureau shoppers—asked to be discreet, perhaps, but unconcerned to camouflage themselves. "They would come in and you always knew who they were," he reported, "they had those funny suits and the little ties and stuff and they were one of the few white people who would come in to the store." Whatever the nature of their interest in black literature, they "would spend lots of money" and were never barred from the door. Unsurprisingly, the New York field office rivaled DC's as a leading FBI book buyer. In July 1969, Hoover instructed it to pick up a copy of *Black Anti-Semitism and Jewish Racism*, an interfaith and interracial essay collection headed up by Baldwin's piece "Negroes are Anti-Semitic Because They're Anti-White." It's hard to picture FBI agents turning to this collection for "reference material" and not getting hung up on Baldwin's blunt and deliberately controversial opening: "When we were growing up in Harlem our demoralizing series of landlords were Jewish, and we hated them." But Baldwin's final two sentences, a return to his old argument with a whitewashed Christianity, in fact told the tale: "The crisis taking place in the world, and in the minds and hearts of black men everywhere, is not produced by the star of David, but by the old, rugged Roman cross on which Christendom's most celebrated Jew was murdered. And not by Jews."

1 - Mr. N. P. Callahan
1 - Mr. B. M. Suttler
1 - Mr. [redacted]

July 3, 1969

1 - Mr. [redacted]
1 - Miss [redacted]

SAC, New York (100-87235)
Attention: Liaison Section

Director, FBI (62-46855)

b7c-1

PURCHASE OF BOOKS
BOOK REVIEWS

You are authorized to obtain discreetly for the Bureau one copy each of the following books. Mark these books to the attention of the Research-Satellite Section, Domestic Intelligence Division.

1. "Black Anti-Semitism and Jewish Racism" with contributions by Julius Lester, James Baldwin, Rabbi Jay Kaufman, and others. Richard W. Baron Publishing Company, New York, October, 1969, $5.95

2. "America the Violent" by Ovid Demaris. Cowles Book Company, New York, October, 1969, $4.95

1 - Racial Intelligence Section (Route through for review)
1 - Mr. [redacted] 6221, IB

AMB:ckl
(10)

b7c-1

ALL INFORMATION CONTAINED
HEREIN IS UNCLASSIFIED
DATE 5-19-89 BY [illegible]

NOTE:

Books requested by SA [redacted] RIS, Domestic Intelligence Division, for review and use as reference material concerning black nationalism and racial matters; will be filed in Bureau Library, where not now available.

EX-111 REC-28

62-108763-74

XEROX
JUL 8 1969

UNRECORDED COPY FILED IN

19 JUL 3 1969

Tolson
DeLoach
Mohr
Bishop
Casper
Callahan
Contad
Felt
Gale
Rosen
Sullivan
Tavel
Trotter
Tele. Room
Holmes
Gandy

MAILED 8
JUL - 2 1969
COMM-FBI

55 JUL 18 1969

MAIL ROOM ☐ TELETYPE UNIT ☐

62.

BALDWIN IN OTHER FBI FILES

JULY 1969

What is a "Supplemental Correlation Summary," anyway? It's a type of FBI report that summarized references to a subject in Bureau files not specifically devoted to it. Picture a write-up of a pre-electronic Google search for Baldwin's name, performed painstakingly by hand and eye, that combed through many of the FBI's thousands of investigative files. Why did the Bureau subject Baldwin to so thorough a search in 1969? Because it had been five years since the last one, and following the FBI's declaration of war against "Black Nationalist-Hate Groups," there were plenty more "see" or cross references to the author to discover in the FBI archive. The results of the 1969 search into Baldwin and his "aliases" conveyed some familiar information taken from magazines and other public sources. The Bureau already had ample proof, for example, that Baldwin had appeared with Bob Dylan at political events. There was enough fresh material, however, some of it provided by confidential informers, to merit instructions that the summary was "not suitable for dissemination" outside "the Seat of Government," a self-important, Hoover-era term for FBI headquarters in Washington. Who knew that a Klansman had complained that a Louisiana state college "made the book 'Another World' by James Baldwin required reading"? And that the same Klansman who mistook *Another Country* for a bohemian soap opera objected to its depiction of "a Negro male making love to a white female"? After Baldwin's 1969 Supplemental Correlation Summary, FBI agents at headquarters could know all this by looking into the writer's file alone.

SECRET

SEE REVERSE SIDE FOR CLASSIFICATION ACTION

SUPPLEMENTAL CORRELATION SUMMARY
(See Correlation Summary dated 6/2/64 filed as 62-108763-26)

ALL INFORMATION CONTAINED HEREIN IS UNCLASSIFIED EXCEPT WHERE SHOWN OTHERWISE

Main File No: 62-108763 Date: 7-30-69
See also: 145-2625
Subject: James Arthur Baldwin Date Searched: 2/3/69

All logical variations of subject's name and aliases were searched and identical references were found as:

SUMMARY

James Arthur Baldwin
James Baldwin
James A. Baldwin
Jim Baldwin
Jimmy Baldwin

This is a summary of information obtained from a review of all "see" references to the subject in Bureau files under the names and aliases listed above. All references under the above names containing data identical with the subject have been included except any indicated at the end of this summary under the heading REFERENCES NOT INCLUDED IN THIS SUMMARY. References indicated in the block as SI contain the same information as the foregoing serial although the information may have been received from a different source.

THIS SUMMARY HAS BEEN PREPARED FOR USE AT THE SEAT OF GOVERNMENT AND IS NOT SUITABLE FOR DISSEMINATION. IT IS DESIGNED TO FURNISH A SYNOPSIS OF THE INFORMATION SET OUT IN EACH REFERENCE, AND IN MANY CASES THE ORIGINAL SERIAL WILL CONTAIN THE INFORMATION IN MORE DETAIL.

5/25/99 CLASSIFIED BY AUC 39677 EAH/8 DECLASSIFY ON: 25X(1) (6) CA97-5269

Analyst Coordinator Approved

VIW:sds

b7c-1

Classified by [illegible] Declassify on: OADR

62-108763-76

ENCLOSURE
Enclosure behind file-search slips only

Pg 15, para. 2 remains classified per CIA memo dtd 3-6-90 6972 EEP/ag 3-19-90 89-3016 JHP

54 AUG 14 1969

AUG 11 1969

SECRET

ABBREVIATIONS

SECRET

Add. info. ....Additional information appearing in this reference which pertains to James Arthur Baldwin can be found in the main file or elsewhere in this summary. This information may have been received from a different source.

CORE..............................Congress of Racial Equality

CP................................Communist Party

SNCC..............................Student Nonviolent Coordinating Committee

*****

b2-1 b7D-1 (X)U

[redacted] furnished a newsletter dated 1/12/63 of the Maryland Committee For Democratic Rights (100-435977). This newsletter entitled "Democratic Rights" urged people to protest against the McCarran Act. It stated "In the course of the past three years, thousands of individuals have registered against the McCarran Act. Recent addition to their ranks have been author James Baldwin and Rabbi Joachim Prinz, leader in the March on Washington. Will you join them?"

100-435977-33 p.10
(7)

b2-1 b7D-1 (X)U

[redacted] advised that on 5/9/63 James Baldwin, a Negro author and lecturer, addressed a group of approximately, 1,000 persons of Roosevelt Junior High School, San Diego, Calif. Baldwin spoke on "The Black Man in America" Baldwin said the Negro is imprisoned in America. He discussed Cuba and the strife in the South, stating that it would be hard for Negroes to find a valid reason for going to Cuba to free it and that Negroes in the South were striving to establish their own culture. [redacted], SWP member from San Diego, was present.

b7C-3

100-436031-15 p.7
(7)

SI 100-353475-51 p.3
(5)

SECRET

SECRET

b7C-5
b7D-2

former PSI (protect identity), advised that a rally was held on 5/20/63 at the Second Baptist Church, 24th and Griffith, Los Angeles, Calif. James Baldwin, National Head of CORE, was the guest of honor. from the Santa Monica Chapter of CORE was present.

b7C-3

100-368117-38 p17
(6)

b2-1 b7D-1 (S)(U)

and advised that a group of Negroes and Caucasians met at 5243 San Bernardo Terrace, headquarters of the San Diego Branch of the Socialist Workers Party (SWP) on 5/26/63. The meeting was called to hear a tape recording of a recent talk given in San Diego by James Baldwin a well known Negro author and lecturer. All Negro groups were invited to this meeting for a discussion which followed after the playing of the Baldwin tape. of the Black Muslims, members of the SWP and other groups participated in the discussion. (S)(U)

b7C-3

100-439704-4 p.13
(7)

b7C-10

Puerto Rico Department of State, Research Section, San Juan, Puerto Rico advised that James Baldwin, 470 West End Avenue, New York City, attended the Second Symposium of the Inter-American Committee, Incorporated, held in Puerto Rico 11/9-14/63, as a guest or delegate.

105-126017-6 encl.p.4
(10)

b2-1 b7D-1

furnished information concerning the bank accounts maintained by the "Emergency Civil Liberties Committee" (ECLC) (100-384660) at the Amalgamated Bank of New York, 11-15 Union Square, New York City, which indicated that on 12/13/63 the ECLC issued a check to James Baldwin (Bill of Rights Dinner) for the amount of $750.00.

Add, info.

100-384660-763 p.18,21,31,32,33
(6)

SECRET

SECRET

(S) (S) b1

(10,16)

b2 b7D-1

On 1/22/64 ████ PSI furnished a letter which contained "A Personal Appear from James Baldwin" that was written on the letterhead of the Committee to Aid Monroe Defendants. In his appeal, Baldwin discussed the "so-called kidnap case in Monroe, N.C., a case trumped up against those fighting racism there."

The serial indicated that ████ was listed as a sponsor of this letter.

b7C-3

100-380341-20
(6)

The 2/3/64 issue of the "Militant" contained an article entitled "Three Publications Discuss Indiana 'Subversion' Case." This article stated that prominent public figures in the fields of literature, the arts, journalism, religion, and the peace and civil rights movements had become sponsors of the Committee to Aid Bloomington Students (100-440538). Listed among the sponsors was James Baldwin, author and civil rights spokesman.

100-440538-A "The Militant"
(8) 2/3/64

b7C-5 b7D-2

████ (protect identity) furnished a circular type letter dated 2/14/64 which was issued by the Student Committee For Travel to Cuba (SCTC) (100-439769). This letter outlined a proposed trip to Cuba during July 1964 which was being organized by the SCTC. The letter indicated that the State Department had declared the passports of students going to Cuba invalid and filed criminal indictments against three individuals who went to Cuba last year, for conspiracy to violate travel regulations and sections of the McCarran-Walter Act. The letter further indicated that a statement of support for SCTC's criminally indicted members as well as the passport case had been issued and signed by many prominent professional people among whom was James Baldwin.

100-439769-894 p.10
(8)
SI 100-439769-821 p.7
(8)

SECRET

SECRET

The 4/10/64 edition of "Life" Magazine, a weekly published in New York City, contained a picture of Albert LaSater Maher [redacted] in the company of one Geno Forman and Bob Dylan on page 112. Maher and Forman were described as "bodyguards" for Dylan, a rising young folk singer. Dylan was described as an active participant in the civil rights movement and was pictured with novelist, James Baldwin.

b7C

105-122289-47 p.58
(10)

b2-1

On 4/19/64 [redacted] advised that [redacted] of McCody International New York City discussed the Angola Refugee Rescue Committee (ARRC) (105-133061) with Hunter Pitts O'dell and advised O'dell that "Carlos" (not further identified) wrote James Baldwin asking him to be co-chairman for the ARRC. [redacted] was desirous of having O'dell take this matter up with Baldwin and persuade him to be co-chairman. Baldwin's play entitled "Blues for Mr. Charlie" opened at the Anta Theater on 52nd Street, New York City, during the Spring and according to source was being promoted by O'dell. (X)U

b7C-4

This serial indicated that Hunter Pitts O'dell was a member of the National Committee of the CP, USA.

105-133061-6
(11)
SI 105-133061-3
(10)
SI 105-133061-1
(10)

A Bureau memo dated 5/8/64 captioned "Free Southern Theatre" (157-1661) indicated that the "Free Southern Theatre," a theatre project to reflect the struggle of the American Negro had begun at Jackson, Miss. The project was supported by SNCC and the Council of Federated Organizations. Author, James Baldwin, was one of the sponsors of this theatre group.

157-1661-2
(13)
SI 157-1661-1
(13)

SECRET

SECRET

A pretext telephone call by a SA on 5/12/64 to an unknown male at the Robertson Playhouse, 1024 South Robertson Boulevard, Los Angeles, Calif., revealed that Frank Alvin Silvera [redacted] was engaged as a theatrical producer for James Baldwin's Play, "The Amen Corner."

b7c-4

100-396292-16
(6)

The following references in the file captioned "Hunter Pitts O'dell" contain information pertaining to the relationship between James Baldwin, Negro author and O'dell a member of the National Committee, CPUSA, during the period from 11/29/63 - 6/10/64 in California, Washington, D.C., and New York. O'dell reportedly was to accompany Baldwin and his brother to a SNCC Conference at Howard University, Washington, D.C., on 11/29/63. Information indicated that O'dell and Baldwin were socially acquainted and that O'dell was in contact with Baldwin on several occasions. O'dell was to obtain a letter from Baldwin for Harlem CP organizer, Jesse Gray, authorizing the use of a mailing list whereby Gray could get money for legal defense and other needs such as printing and distribution of educational material. O'dell was one of the persons whom Baldwin was taking to California at his (Baldwin's) expense for the opening of one of his plays. Between April 20 - June 10, 1964, Baldwin met several times with O'dell to discuss the financing of his play, "Blues For Mr. Charlie." O'dell was doing publicity work for Baldwin in connection with his play. (X)U

REFERENCE	SEARCH SLIP PAGE NUMBER
100-358916-281 p.10	(5)
-285 p.19	(5)
-289 p.1,6,7,8,9	(6)

The following references in the file captioned "CP, USA - Negro Question, Communist Influence in Racial Matters" contain information pertaining to the activities of James Baldwin, from New York City in connection with civil rights during the period from 11/29/63 - 7/27/64, in Washington, D.C., New York and Canada. Baldwin was scheduled to speak on 11/29/63 at Washington, D.C., at a 3 day conference sponsored by SNCC. A CP member from Louisville, Ky., wanted Baldwin to write an introduction to a pamphlet which documented the role the HCUA played in stopping progress in the civil rights movement. Baldwin reportedly was a sponsor of the National Committee

(continued)

SECRET

(continued)

to abolish the HCUA, a new organization formed for the purpose of leading and directing the CP's abolition campaign against the HCUA. On 7/25/64 at a civil rights demonstration in New York City at which several CP leaders were in attendance and one CP leader appeared in a official capacity, it was urged that the writings of Baldwin be read. The speaker at this rally directed their comments toward police brutality and housing conditions regarding Negro people. Baldwin was to appear on a television show in Montreal, Canada along with other well known Negro entertainers and leaders of the civil rights movement. This program was to depict Negro problems relative to civil rights.

REFERENCE	SEARCH SLIP PAGE NUMBER
100-3-116-1127 p.2	(4)
-1191 p.2 encl.p.1,2	(4)
-1943 encl.p.1	(4)
-2077 p.28	(5)

bic-3

A mail cover on [redacted] at his residence, [redacted] Philadelphia, Pa., revealed that [redacted] during August, 1964 was in contact with James Baldwin, 100 5th Avenue, New York, N.Y.

An inspection of the building directory at 100 5th Avenue, showed no listing for James Baldwin, however, Room 803 at this address was occupied by SNCC and Baldwin had used this address on a form letter which solicited contributions for the Mississippi Summer Project. The New York telephone directory contained no listing at this address for Baldwin.

Add. info.

100-264519-129 p.3
(5)
SI 100-264519-121 p.3
(5)

b2-1 SECRET

[redacted] advised that on 8/11/63 Nat Schwerner, father of murdered civil rights worker Michael Schwerner, issued instructions to a representative of the SNCC office in New York City about preparing a large mailer containing a Baldwin letter and return envelope. The source was unable to furnish information concerning the contents or purpose of this letter.

On 8/11/64 a confidential mailbox of the New York Office furnished a copy of a mailing from SNCC, 6 Raymond Street, N.W., Atlanta, Ga., which consisted of a form letter bearing the signature of James Baldwin, a business reply envelope addressed to him at Suite 803, 100 5th Avenue, New York City, and a reprint of an article from "Newsweek" magazine dated 2/24/64. The form letter requested contributions for the Mississippi Summer Project be sent to Baldwin at SNCC, 100 5th Avenue, NYC.

100-442529-14 p.10,11
(8)
SI 94-50424-2
(4)

The Fall 1964 edition, page 20, of "Black America," published guarterly by the Revolutionary Action Movement (100-442684) Black Liberation Front of the USA, contained the excerpt "There are some wars ... that the American Negro will not support ...." by James Baldwin, author of "The Fire Next Time".

Publication enclosed
100-442684-9-9 encl.p.20
(8)

The following references in the file captioned "March from Selma to Montgomery, Alabama, 3/21-25/65," contained information pertaining to the activities of James Baldwin in connection with captioned march during the period 3/20-24/65 in New York City and Montgomery, Ala. Information indicated that Baldwin was to contact various literary people for the purpose of having them send telegrams to Martin Luther King in support of the above march. Baldwin along with other literary artists such as Shelly Winters and Leonard Bernstein were scheduled to arrive in Montgomery on 3/24/65. These individuals were part of a literary group who were to participate in Dr. Martin Luther King's march into Montgomery.

(continued)

SECRET

SECRET

(continued)

REFERENCE	SEARCH SLIP PAGE NUMBER
44-28544-47	(2)
-216	(2)
-275	(2)
-374 p.22	(3)

The 3/25/65 issue of "The Evening American" Pheonix, Arizona carried an article entitled "Trotskyite at ASU Predicts Violence." This article indicated that Ralph Levitt, self identified Trotskyite and former Indiana University student, spoke at a campus meeting at Arizona State University on 3/24/65. Levitt stated "We of the Young Socialist Alliance are revolutionary socialists." Levitt indicated that he was being sponsored by a national committee headed by prominent leftists including Negro author James Baldwin.

The above information appeared in the file captioned "Committee to Aid Bloomington Students."

100-440538-A "The Evening American," Phoenix, Ariz. 3/25/65

(8)

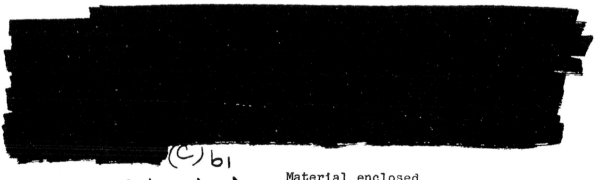

(C) b1

referred to Army

Material enclosed
100-434819-165 p.7
(7)

SECRET

b2-1

[redacted] advised that on 7/5/65 Elijah Muhammad** remarked to Richard Durham*** in connection with a discussion regarding the Nation of Islam (NOI) (25-330971) that James Baldwin and [redacted] (not identified) both wanted to do some writing and go 50-50 with him. According to Muhammad he told them he would have no part of it. b7c-4

25-330971-7387
(2)

**National leader of the NOI
***Editor of "Muhammad Speaks," the NOI newspaper

The September, 1965, issue of the "Liberator" (100-445048) magazine, 244 East 46th Street, New York, New York, listed James Baldwin as a member of its Advisory Board.

Add. info.

100-445048-1 p.7,11
(9)
SI 105-98055-A "The New York Times," 6/13/65
(10)

[redacted] (protect identity), advised that on 11/27/65, [redacted] met James Baldwin at the Hotel Boston, Rome, and shared a room with him. As of 11/29/65 Baldwin and [redacted] were still residing at the Hotel Boston. b7c-4 b7C-10 b7D-2

100-445043-6 p.2
(9)

b2-1 b7D-1

[redacted] (PROB) advised that on 2/1/66, [redacted] stated that the Northeast Louisiana State College at Monroe, Louisiana, made the book "Another World" by James Baldwin required reading. He advised the group that this book dealt with a Negro male making love to a white female. He suggested that Klansmen obtain copies of this book to determine whether it is suitable reading for college students. b7c-1

This serial indicated that [redacted] was an officer of the West Monroe Unit #2, United Klans of America Inc., Knights of the Ku Klux Klan, (157-370-33). b7c-1

157-370-33-320 p.97
(13)

b7c5b7D-2

[redacted] CS, (protect identity) advised that Issue No. 4 of "Logos" (100-445470) was distributed on Memphis State University Campus on 4/11/66.

A review of this issue revealed that it carried quotations from the Negro writer, James Baldwin, former Howard Professor; White House adviser Arthur Schlesinger, and William E. B. DuBois who joined the CP prior to his death. It also contained an editorial stating that "'Logos' recognized the present government of Red China, the Peoples Republic of China, as the official government of all Chinese people," and called for its immediate admission to the United Nations.

100-445470-8 p.9
(9)

The following references in the file captioned "Demonstrations Protesting United States Intervention In Vietnam" contain information pertaining to the activities of James Baldwin in connection with anti-war demonstrations during the period from 8/27/65-4/23/66 in Michigan and Italy. Baldwin spoke at a street rally in Detroit, Mich., sponsored by the Detroit Committee to End the War in Vietnam. His speech concerned the history of the Negro people and their travels. Baldwin also stated that he was against U.S. participation in the war in Vietnam. During late November 1965, he participated in a "Literary Tuesday" conference sponsored by the Italian Cultural Association in Rome, Italy, at which he stated "We do not have the right to remain in Vietnam and I don't know why we are there. We do not have to liberate anyone." Baldwin also participated in an all-night vigil sponsored by the Roman Committee to Promote Peace in Vietnam and an all-night Leftists vigil to protest U.S. action in Vietnam while in Rome. At the latter vigil on 11/29/65, he told the audience that "Western interests were responsible for the events in South Africa and the Cuban agression." A bombing attempt interrupted this all night vigil to protest U.S. action in Vietnam. Information indicated on 4/23/66 that a member of the Veterans and Reservists to End the War in Vietnam presented some books to St. Albans Naval Hospital, St. Albans, N.Y., for the casualties of the Vietnam war. Among those books was one by James Baldwin entitled "Going to Meet the Man." Background information concerning Baldwin from 4/24/60-1964 indicated that he was a sponsor for the New York Committee to Abolish the House Un-American Committee, the Fair Play for Cuba Committee, and the Committee to Aid the Monroe Defendants. He wrote a letter as an advertisement for "Freedomways" and participated in a Emergency Civil Liberties Committee function.

(continued)

SECRET

(continued)

REFERENCE	SEARCH SLIP PAGE NUMBER
105-138315-1536 encl.p.1	(11)
-2039 p.1,2	(11,16)
-3073 p.165	(11)
-3274 p.704-706,787,788	(11)
-4026 p.220,257	(11,16)

Washington Field Office letter dated 6/17/65 revealed that (S)

(S) b1

b7C-5 b7D-2

Confidential Source (protect identity), advised on 8/29/66 that claimed he had monitored some lectures at the Free University of New York during the Summer of 1966 and that two of the lecturers were the anti-white author, James Baldwin, a Negro, and Staughton Lynd, Yale University professor, who was an articulate spokesman for the "New left." b7C-3

100-447013-2 p.38
(9)

b2-1 b7D-1

(PSI) in interviews with SA's in San Juan, PR, during 11/12-18/66 stated that he was an acquaintance of Baldwin and not an associate. b7C-5 b7D-2

(12) b2-1- b7D-1

SECRET

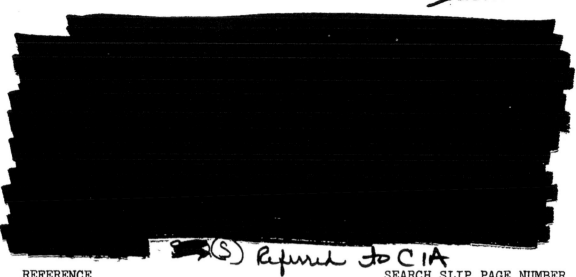

(S) Referred to CIA

REFERENCE SEARCH SLIP PAGE NUMBER

REFERENCE	SEARCH SLIP PAGE NUMBER
105-156243-121 p.2	(11)
-183 p.2 encl.p.6	(11)
-188 p.2	(11)
-190	(19)
105-156243-A "New York Herald Tribune-Washington Post," 4/11/67	(11)

b7C-4

The 8/1/67 issue of the "Berkeley Daily Gazette," a daily newspaper in Berkeley, contained an article by Ray Thompson entitled "Voice of the people - pro and con" with sub title "The open forum." In this article, Thompson wrote of the injustices imposed upon the Black people and quoted James Baldwin as having stated,"It is not necessary that they (white people) be wicked, but that they do nothing."

100-215110-54 p.4
(5)

SECRET

~~SECRET~~

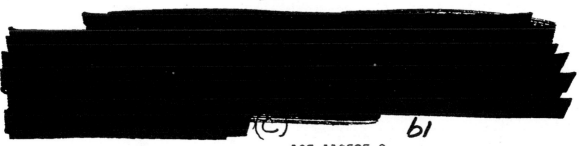

(C) b1

105-110525-9
(10)
SI 100-439190-9-34X10 p.64
(7)
SI 62-111181-1035 encl.p.30
(3)

b7C-7

On 9/6/67, [redacted], Cook County Sheriff's Office, Chicago, Ill., furnished a document concerning the American Council of Human Rights, Incorporated (ACHR) (157-8033). This document included a newsletter under the name of "The American Council Eagle, Post Office Box 42, Markhan, Ill." published by the ACHR. The newsletter also contained a quiz which listed the name of approximately 30 prominent Negroes including James Baldwin. Instructions set forth that a brief explanation of "who" the individuals were should be prepared and sent to ACHR, Post Office Box 42, Markham, Ill. The ACHR would mail $10.00 to each person with correct entry.

157-8033-1 encl.p.5
(13)

The 1/31/68 edition of "The New York Times" carried an article entitled "Writers and Editors to Protest War by Defying Tax." This article stated that James Baldwin was among the 448 writers and editors who announced in an advertisement in the 1/30/68 edition of the "New York Post," that they would not pay a proposed 10% surcharge of any other war designated tax increase. The article further stated that one-third of the signers would not pay the 23 per cent of the current income tax which was being used to finance the war in Vietnam.

The above information appeared in the file captioned "Writers and Editors War Tax Protest."

New York Times article enclosed
62-111830-4 encl.p.1
(3)
New York Post article enclosed
SI 62-111830-5 encl.p.2
(3)

~~SECRET~~

SECRET

The 5/6/68 issue of the "New York Times" contained a letter to the Editor of the "Times" which protested the killing of Bobby Hutton, Black Panther Party (BPP) (105-165706) official, and the wounding of another BPP member by the Oakland, Calif., Police. James Baldwin was one of the individuals who authored this letter dated 2/1/68 at New York.

105-165706-A "The New York Times"
(12) 5/6/68

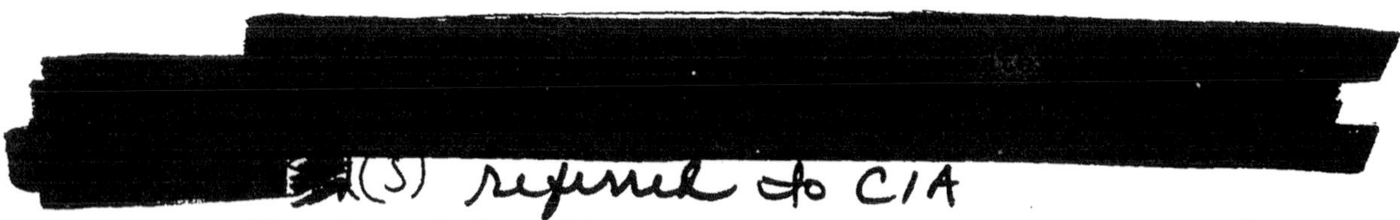

The above information appeared in the file captioned "Foreign Intelligence In the Black Nationalist Movement."

157-8141-111
(13)

The following references pertain to information received during the period from 1/24/65 - 2/14/68 regarding publications authored by James Baldwin. These books were described by various groups of the Klan as being obscene and communistic inspired. The Klans were critical of the Southern Baptist Association for the recommendation that they allegedly made in the "Southern Baptist Quartely" urging their young people to buy certain books by Baldwin. The following books by Baldwin were mentioned on their reading list: "Nobody Knows My Name," "The Fire Next Time," and "Another Country."

REFERENCE	SEARCH SLIP PAGE NUMBER
157-168-328	(13)
157-370-24-97 encl.p.11	(13)
157-9633-19 p.47,48	(14)

SECRET

The 3/3/68 issue of the "Washington Post Times Herald" contained an article "Baldwin Batting for Carmichael." The article indicated that it had previously been written by James Baldwin, the author of the "Fire Next Time," for the "Manchester Guardian." Baldwin was in Paris at the time he wrote the article. He stated that he first met Stokely Carmichael (100-446080) in the Deep South when Carmichael was just another nonviolent kid, marching and talking and getting his head whipped. Baldwin recalled an incident which took place in Selma, Ala., during a voter registration drive in which he saw two black boys beaten by the sheriff and his deputies. He was critical of the U.S. Government for lifting Carmichael's passport and for allowing the injustices against the black citizens.

100-446080-A The "Washington Post
(9) Times Herald" 3/3/68

The following references in the file captioned "Racial Matters" pertain to the activities of Negro author James Baldwin in connection with the racial situation during the period from 10/7/63 - 3/21/68 in Alabama, New York and California. On 10/7/63 Baldwin attempted to enter the Dallas County, Ala. Court House during a voter registration line-up. He was a founding member of the Association of Artists, an organization which grew out of the Birmingham bombings, when a group of artists got together to decide what they as artists would do. He was a panel member on a forum sponsored by the Association of Artists entitled "The Black Revolution and the White Backlash." Baldwin had agreed to attend a Students for a Democratic Society meeting entitled "Black Power and Its Challenges" at the University of California at Berkeley. On 2/21/68 Baldwin spoke at memorial services in NYC for Malcolm X, leader of the Muslim Mosque, Inc., who was assassinated. He labeled the U.S. as the "Fourth Reich" which was built on the principles of slavery and drudgery. He was scheduled to participate in a benefit performance on 3/12/68 at Town Hall, New York City, to raise funds for artists who were in legal difficulty because of demonstrations or censorship of work or similar circumstances.

REFERENCE	SEARCH SLIP PAGE NUMBER
157-6-34-805	(12)
-875 p.1,3,7	(12)
-2394 p.1,2,3,5,6	(12)
-2400	(12)
-2406 p,4,5	(12)

SECRET

(continued)

(continued)

REFERENCE	SEARCH SLIP PAGE NUMBER
157-6-47-936 p.2	(12)
157-6-61-410 (Photograph enclosed)	(2)

b7C-7

[redacted] Newark, New Jersey, Police Department, advised that on 3/22/68 at South Side High School, 80 Johnson Avenue, Newark, N.J., there would be an "Evening of Soul and African Culture." According to information received by his unit, Maulana Ron Karenga [redacted] leader of "US" organization, James Baldwin, novelist and playwright; and Leroi Jones, author, playwright, and poet, were the featured speakers. b7C-4

157-5877-26
(13)

[redacted] advised that at a meeting of the Black United Front (157-8471) held 4/30/68 in Washington, D.C., Gaston Neal (not further identified) announced that on 5/30-31/68 the grand opening of the Drum and Spear Bookshop located in the 2700 block of 14th Street, N.W., Washington, D.C. would be held. Neal advised that he hoped to have James Baldwin present if at all possible. He described the bookshop as a project of the New School for Afro-American Thought.

b2-1
b7D-1

157-8471-11 p.3
(13)

[redacted] furnished a printed notice announcing "Malcolm X Foundation Presents-Birthday Festival (Celebrating 43rd Birthday of Brother Malcolm X) Sunday, 5/19/68 at 8:00 P.M., Professional Arts Society of Los Angeles Theater, 8713 South Vermont, Los Angeles, Calif." James Baldwin was one of the speakers at this event sponsored by the Malcolm X Foundation (157-9335).

157-9335-1
(13)

SECRET

A SA monitored the Steve Allen Television Show, KTLA Channel 5, on 6/19/68 at 6:00 P.M., to 7:30 P.M. on which James Baldwin and Marlon Brando* were guests. The main topic concerned race relations between black and white. Baldwin alleged that there was a caste system among Negroes based on the degree of color of the skins. He also alleged that the white man's laws were designed to protect property and not Negroes as such. Brando commented on the extensive prejudice of the whites against the blacks in America. It was announced that one percent of the cost of the television broadcast would be contributed to the West Side Study Center, a Negro project in Pasadena, Calif.

The above information appeared in the file captioned "Cominfil of the Radio Television Industry."

100-340922-512 p.B,73,74
(5)

*Well known screen actor.

b7c-4

A New York letter dated 7/26/68 indicated that Daniel H. Watts [redacted] Editor-in-Chief of "Liberator" magazine, appeared on a local independent television station (WOR) program entitled "Black Power." On 6/27/68 Watts discredited James Baldwin and actor Ossie Davis as spokesmen for the black power movement in the U.S. The program was an uninformative disjointed discussion of black power.

105-96316-25
(10)

The 7/5/68 issue of the "Columbus Dispatch" contained an article captioned "CORE TO ANALYZE POLITICAL PARTIES," which indicated that during the 26th National Convention of CORE (100-225892) held in Columbus, Ohio, 7/3-7/68 a testimonial dinner was given in behalf of Floyd B. McKissick, national director of CORE. Among the Negro leaders who attended this testimonial dinner on 7/4/68 was Novelist, James Baldwin.

100-225892-10-55 p.40
(5)

SECRET

b7C-5
b7D-3

[redacted], racial liason source, Danville, Ill., made available the 4th publication of "The Black Vanguard" (157-9606), dated 7/15/68. "A letter to Americans," by James Baldwin appeared on page 6. This letter concerning the Civil Rights and Black Power Movements had originally been sent to the "London Times" and the "New York Times." Both declined to publish it. A photograph of Baldwin accompanied this letter.

Publication enclosed
157-9606-8 p.2, encl.p.6
(14)

b2-1 b7D-1

Approximately August 1968 [redacted] advised concerning the source of SNCC (100-439190) funds. SNCC had obtained financial assistance through the circulation of fund raising type letters over the signatures of such prominent Negroes as Harry Belafonte, the actor, and James Baldwin, the author, and through voluntary contributions from liberals, both Negro and white.

100-439190-34-106
(7)
SI 100-439190-34-103
(7)

b2-1 b7D-1

[redacted] advised during the period from July-September 1968 that James Arthur Baldwin continued to be active in the black nationalist extremist groups in the New York City area.

The above information appeared in the file captioned "Black Nationalist Movement."

157-8415-34-18 p.7
(16)

The 11/20/68 issue of the "New York Times," p.29, contained an ad captioned "On November 27, Eldridge Cleaver will be sent to prison. There is something you can do." This advertisement was sponsored by the "International Committee to Defend Eldridge Cleaver" (157-11302), 555 Hudson Street, New York, N.Y. It called for contributions to aid in the defense of Cleaver, Black Panther official, who faced imprisonment for breaking the terms of his parole. James Baldwin's name appeared among those individuals who endorsed the ad.

157-11302-A "New York Times" 11/20/68 p.29
(14)

SECRET

SECRET

The following reference on James Baldwin located in the Personnel Records Unit of Records Branch, Files and Communication Division, was reviewed and found to be identical with the subject of this summary; however, the information contained therein has not been included.

REFERENCE	SEARCH SLIP PAGE NUMBER
67-2-10241	(4)

*****

REFERENCES NOT INCLUDED IN THIS SUMMARY

The following references on James Baldwin located in files maintained in the Special File Room Records Section, Division 4, were not reviewed and it is not known whether they are identical with the subject of this summary:

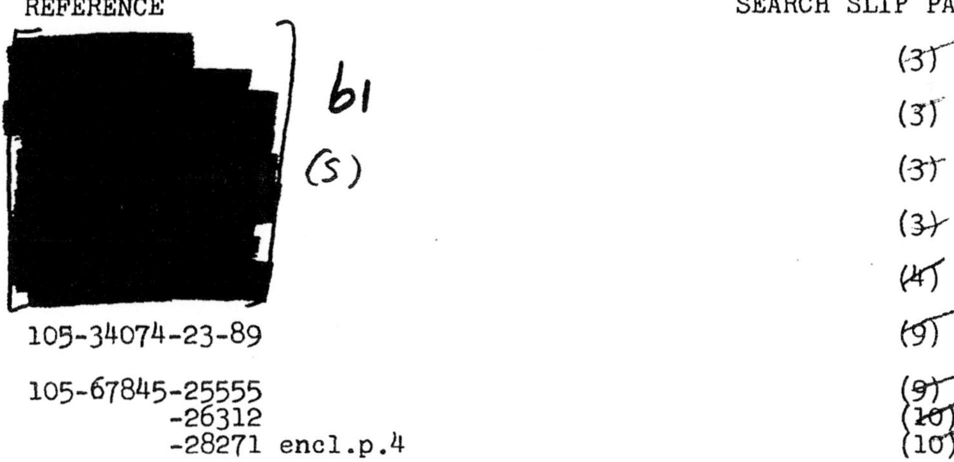

REFERENCE	SEARCH SLIP PAGE NUMBER
	(3)
	(3)
	(3)
	(3)
	(4)
105-34074-23-89	(9)
105-67845-25555	(9)
-26312	(10)
-28271 encl.p.4	(10)

SECRET

See the search slip filed behind file for other references on this subject which contain the same information (SI) that is set out in the main file. Although the information is the same it may have been received from different sources.

63.

"BALDWIN'S METHOD OF WORKING IS STRANGE"

DECEMBER 1969

With a little help from its friends in the CIA or the Office of Special Investigations (OSI), the FBI had discovered Baldwin's Turkish summer by the end of 1969. As it did two years earlier, it had an article from an Istanbul newspaper translated from Turkish to English and read something about Baldwin's writing life otherwise inaccessible in the US. "There is a Negro writer whose love for Turkey is as well-known as his fame on the world scale," the translated article began, waxing patriotic over Baldwin's compliment that he "cannot imagine a country in the world as beautiful as Turkey, a people as nice as the Turks, and another land where Negroes can live comfortably." Things turned less mutually flattering—and weirder—as Baldwin's "method of working" was described: "There are times when he writes continuously for 24 hours without food and drink. Under such circumstances, he does not even notice if you shout at him or hit him on the shoulder. Afterwards, he lies down and sleeps. Moreover, he is in a sound sleep for 48 hours. If you are able to awaken him, how fortunate you are." Embroidered as it is, this romanticized account of creative transport and stubbornness may be the single most memorable description of Baldwin at work to be found anywhere. And it was found first in English in Baldwin's FBI file.

UNITED STATES DEPARTMENT OF JUSTICE

FEDERAL BUREAU OF INVESTIGATION

In Reply, Please Refer to
File No.

New York, New York
December 23, 1969

b1

SECRET - NO FOREIGN DISSEMINATION

DECLASSIFIED BY 25638 SP4 JRM/GCL (C) memo 11/19/80 ON 2/12/81

5-13-89

James Arthur Baldwin
Racial Matter - Miscellaneous

NY T-1, ~~a United States~~ another Government agency ~~with investigative jurisdiction abroad~~ which conducts intelligence investigations, advised on July 31, 1969 that James Baldwin arrived at Istanbul, Turkey, from Athens, Greece via Air France on July 13, 1969.

The following article which appeared in the August 18, 1969 edition of "Milliyet" a daily newspaper published in Istanbul, Turkey was furnished by NY T-1 on October 22, 1969:

"Yasar Kemal, Engin Cezzar, And James Baldwin Have Formed A Partnership"

"There is a Negro writer whose love for Turkey is as well-known as his fame on the world scale. He did not hesitate to frankly state the following on the Paris television: 'I cannot imagine a country in the world as beautiful as Turkey, a people as nice as the Turks, and another land where Negroes can live comfortably.' The name of this writer, who celebrated his 45th birthday two weeks ago, is James Baldwin."

"Every summer for 5 - 6 years in succession, he has come to Istanbul, lived here, written a novel, and departed. His admiration for Istanbul is altogether different. Originally from the Harlem section of New York, he says, 'Look here; look there. It's as though one is drowning amongst the cement blocks without being able to see the sky and the sea. Its people have been turned into robots.

This document contains neither recommendations nor conclusions of the FBI. It is the property of the FBI and is loaned to your agency; it and its contents are not to be distributed outside your agency.

SECRET - NO FOREIGN

Excluded from automatic downgrading and declassification

932

100-146553-373

James Arthur Baldwin

"Whereas here, everyone is friendly and close to one another.' James Baldwin, who first came to Turkey in 1960, has many Turkish friends. Every year, he comes, writes a novel and departs."

"These are the titles of his novels:"

"Nobody Knows My Name; Go Tell It To The Mountain; Another Country; The Fire Next Time; and Giovanni's Room."

"These are his plays:"

"Amen Corner (now playing in Los Angeles) and Blues For Mr. Charlie."

"Before coming here, he stayed for 18 months in Hollywood and prepared a scenario which was taken from a biography which reflects the white - black problem. So much so that, because of this, he was a delegate at the famous meeting between the blacks and Kennedy; he explained all of the details of this problem to President Kennedy; and he wanted a remedy to be found for it."

"Baldwin's method of working is strange. There are times when he writes continously for 24 hours without food and drink. Under such circumstances, he does not even notice if you shout at him or hit him on the shoulder. Afterwards, he lies down and sleeps. Moreover, he is in a sound sleep for 48 hours. If you are able to awaken him, how fortunate you are."

"Baldwin is here again. This trip is for the purpose of establishing a new organization. He is establishing this company in order to get his books printed, translated, and sold, to get his plays produced, and to get his scenarios filmed. His partners are Yasar Kemal Gokceli, the originator

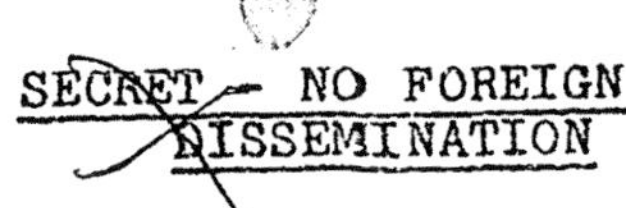
SECRET - NO FOREIGN DISSEMINATION

of Ince Memet and his friend Engin Cezzar who had introduced him to Turkey. The parties have reached an agreement in principle. They will be in operation soon."

b7C-b

On December 12, 1969, [redacted] 137 West 71st Street, New York City, advised that James Baldwin had returned from his trip to Turkey and resided in Apartment B at that address but that he is frequently out of New York on business.

SECRET - NO FOREIGN DISSEMINATION

64.

CITIZEN LITERARY CRITICISM, PART 3: CALIFORNIA ON *THE FIRE NEXT TIME*

APRIL 1970

It takes some doing to reach the end and the point of this letter to Hoover from a Southern California mom. The author shows boundless confidence in the director's interest in the stuff of anticommunist parenting in Orange County: summer sleep-away camp, the influence of star football and basketball players, and meetings of Young Life, the popular Christian youth ministry founded in 1941. Four paragraphs in, the author gets to the rub: some of the literature provided by Young Life sowed doubts about its political character. "In the July issue 1968 of Focus on Youth page 21, it gives a must list for suggested reading," she reports. "Somewhere in my studies of communism I have heard of the author James Baldwin and of course [Stokely] Carmichael and Malcolm X." A number of "FBI men supported Young Life," she had learned, but she preferred going straight to the top of the Bureau for the truth about *The Fire Next Time*. Hoover wrote back with nothing for her to chew on, a pro forma, two-sentence note explaining that "information in our files must be maintained as confidential pursuant to regulations of the Department of Justice." The extent of the Bureau's hidden action on the Californian's letter is remarkable all the same. Copies were sent to Clyde Tolson, Cartha DeLoach, William C. Sullivan, and several others in Hoover's domestic intelligence cabinet. The author was treated to a search for derogatory information in the FBI's enormous file collection. *Focus on Youth*, the Young Life magazine in question, was searched in the same dicey place. Hoover's 1964 award from the group was recalled and explained. And an account of this manifold inquiry wound up in Baldwin's personal file, among others. Never let it be said that Hoover's FBI was indifferent to the critical inquiries of undistinguished Americans.

Mr. Tolson
Mr. DeLoach
Mr. Walters
Mr. Mohr
Mr. Bishop
Mr. Casper
Mr. Callahan
Mr. Conrad
Mr. Felt
Mr. Gale
Mr. Rosen
Mr. Sullivan
Mr. Tavel
Mr. Soyars
Tele. Room
Miss Holmes
Miss Gandy

SANTA ANA, CALIFORNIA 92705

b7C-4

April 30, 1970

Dear Mr. Hoover,

My daughter has been attending Young Life on Wed. evenings for several months now. The parents were invited last night and it was held at Foothill High School. About 150 young people are present at these meetings and last night I saw the star football player and basketball player. All the kids seemed like good ones and I know a few of the parents who are backing this group.

b7C-1

The man in charge of this group is John Anderson. He says he is a minister. A film was shown of Malibu, their camp in Canada and they were encouraging the kids to go this summer.

Several times in the evening he mentioned having a personal relation with Jesus Christ but they mostly sang songs. Some were fun songs and some were out of a christian songbook. Apparently they are in a bad way financially. They claim it cost $10.00 a month per child.

EX-108 REC. 40 38 MAY 4 1970

What concerns me is the literature on the table. In the July issue 1968 of Focus on Youth page 21, it gives a must list for suggested reading. Somewhere in my studies of communism I have heard of the author James Baldwin and of course Carmichael and Malcolm X.

Can you please give me some information on this organization.

ENC. BEHIND FILE
ENCLOSURE

Sincerely,

b7C-4

REC-21 94-1-3266 - 166

b7C-1

EX-115

12 MAY 14 1970

CORRESPONDENCE

ack
5-8-70

1846

SANTA ANA, CALIFORNIA 92705

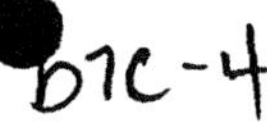

b7C-4

P. S. I spoke to Mr. Anderson after the meeting and showed him the article on page 21 of Focus on Youth and he said he was sorry I was suspicious. He said several FBI men supported Young Life and named one and suggested I write to him.

VOLUME 2 NUMBER 2 JULY

focus ON YOUTH

94-1-32662-166 (EBF)

I'm not a problem. I'm a man.

1848

that the greatest rewards come to peopl who are willing to jump into the middle of the battle – even if they get killed doing it.

There are a vast number of people, I'm convinced, who love Christ and who want to do something to show it. They are willing to recognize and expose the race problems within themselves. They are willing to study, to be taught, to get out on the battlefield. These are the misfits in our culture. These are the people who will not fit the system – any system. These are the ones who really want to pay the price. The rest of you step aside. If you want to hate, that's your problem. If you're hung up on your racism, go ahead and sing your hymns and build your picket fences. Sorry, we've got a job to do, and we don't have much time. □

Bill Milliken, originally from a Pittsburgh suburb, walked into New York City one day in 1960, and has stayed ever since. He is the Young Life Director on the Lower East Side, and a familiar figure to people of all colors and levels in that social "melting pot."

A MUST LIST for suggested reading

Report of the National Advisory Commission on Civil Disorders. *N. Y.: Bantam Books ($1.25).* Complete text and selected photos from the U. S. Riot Commission Report. The facts behind the racial crisis.

The Shadow That Scares Me, *Dick Gregory. N. Y.: Doubleday & Co., 1968 ($4.50).* With devastating wit and vivid illustration this comedian seriously exposes the wrong and upholds the right in America's social revolution.

The Nature of Prejudice, *Gordon Allport. N. Y.: Doubleday & Co., 1958 (Anchor Book, $1.95).* Probably the most comprehensive and penetrating study available on the origin and behavior of prejudice.

My People Is The Enemy, *William Stringfellow. N. Y.: Holt, Rinehart & Winston, 1964 ($3.95).* An intelligent appraisal of the Church's role in the racial crisis by a white Episcopal lawyer living in Harlem.

–BOB SENGSTACKE

Black Like Me, *John Howard Griffin. N. Y.: Houghton Mifflin Co., 1961 (Signet Edition, 60¢).* A white novelist crosses the color line to feel what it is like to be a "second-class" citizen in the South.

Autobiography of Malcolm X. *N. Y.: Grove Press, 1966 (Paperback, $1.25)* The absorbing personal story of the man who rose from hoodlum to become the most dynamic leader of the Black Awakening.

Worth Fighting For, *McCarthey and Reddick. N. Y.: Doubleday & Co., 1965 (Zenith Book, $1.45).** First of a series geared to junior high and high school level. Presents Negro history in a readable form from the Civil War to the Reconstruction.

Crisis in Black and White, *Charles E. Silberman. N. Y.: Random House, 1964 (A Vintage Giant, $1.95).* A powerful and unsparing analysis of the Negro problem in America. Cites concrete action as the key point of moral and ethical reality.

Before The Mayflower, *Lerone Bennett, Jr. Baltimore, Md.: Penguin Books, 1968 (A Pelican Book, $2.45).* A full history of the Negro from his origin in the great African empires till the present day.

Black Power, *Carmichael and Hamilton. N. Y.: Random House, 1967 (A Vintage Book, $1.95).* A revolutionary political framework and ideology by which Negroes can organize to produce needed social change.

White Man, Listen, *Richard Wright. N. Y.: Doubleday & Co., 1964 (Anchor Book, 95¢).* An historical analysis of how the white man gained his power, and the reactions of non-whites oppressed by that power.

The Fire Next Time, *James Baldwin. N. Y.: Dell, 1963 (50¢).* A compassionate, eloquent plea to end the racial nightmare which demands self-examination.

* Zenith Books is a series of stories of minority groups (American Negroes, Chinese, Mexicans, Puerto Ricans and Indians) and their part in the growth of the United States. They can be ordered hardbound or paperbound from Doubleday & Co., Inc., School and Library Division, Garden City, N. Y. 11530.

May 8, 1970

EX-115

REC-21 94-1-32662 166

Santa Ana, California 92705

Dear

I have received your communication of April 30th.

In reply to your inquiry, information in our files must be maintained as confidential pursuant to regulations of the Department of Justice.

Sincerely yours,

J. Edgar Hoover

b7c-4

MAILED 9
MAY 8 1970
COMM-FBI

NOTE: We have had limited correspondence with Last outgoing, March, 1966, at which time she wrote requesting information on an individual and was advised files confidential. There is nothing derogatory in Bufiles concerning her. She had enclosed a magazine entitled "Focus on Youth." This magazine, which is published by "Young Life," cannot be identified in Bufiles. She made reference to a suggested reading list on Page 21 which lists the work of Malcolm X, Stokley Carmichael and Dick Gregory who are well known to the Bureau. Although this group is not affiliated with the FBI in any manner, the Director was the recipient of an award by it in February, 1964, in connection with his work with the Nation's youth during the preceding 25 years. 720 W. Monument St. Colorado Springs, Colo.

Tolson
DeLoach
Walters
Mohr
Bishop
Casper
Callahan
Conrad
Felt
Gale
Rosen
Sullivan
Tavel
Soyars
Tele. Room
Holmes
Gandy

DMW:cfj (3)

60 MAY 26 1970 MAIL ROOM TELETYPE UNIT

b7c-1

65.

BALDWIN TESTIFIES FOR "SISTER ANGELA"—AND THE BUREAU RELAXES ITS VIGIL

JANUARY, MAY, JUNE, AND AUGUST 1971

Angela Davis, the African American philosophy professor turned Communist, radical feminist, and Black Panther, was the third woman ever named to the FBI's Ten Most Wanted List. Charged with homicide and lesser crimes after the bloody escape attempt of several black convicts in California in 1970, she fled the state and became a radical cause célèbre before her quick capture in New York. Baldwin, resettled far from the scene in Europe, wrote an open letter to Davis while she awaited trial. Addressed from "Brother James" to "My Sister," and discussed in this 1971 article clipped by the Bureau, Baldwin's update of "J'Accuse" praised Davis as the best of a rising black generation, one that had "assessed and absorbed their history" but had "freed themselves of it and will never be victims again." Despite the new liberation of black people twenty years younger, Davis's enemy remained his own: namely, "the bulk of our (nominal) countrymen," for whom all black people were "expendable. And Messrs. Nixon, [Spiro] Agnew, [John] Mitchell, and Hoover, to say nothing, of course, of the *Kings Row* basket case, the winning Ronnie Reagan, will not hesitate for an instant to carry out what they insist is the will of the people." Baldwin spoke in support of Davis in France, England, and Germany, with written offshoots of these talks reaching Italy and Switzerland. The Bureau, relying on its liaison in

Paris, watched Baldwin's words carefully, but judged that he was "currently far less militant than in the past and apparently is considerably removed from the mainstream of Black Power activities." One reason offered for Baldwin's withdrawal was his "poor health." This was a sane conclusion, given his real case of hepatitis and his hospitalization for exhaustion in Paris in late 1970, an experience of limits that inspired Baldwin to purchase his famous home in St. Paul-de-Vence in the south of France, the retreat built from an old farmhouse where he would pass away on December 1, 1987. For its part, the Bureau's suggestion that "considerable prosperity" was moderating Baldwin's politics missed his increasingly apocalyptic radicalism, freely expressed on the page if not in the street. It also forgot his willingness to spend in this radicalism's honor. For example, though he feared expulsion by the Gendarmerie, he wired money to Eldridge Cleaver's French hideout as the Black Panther leader fled an attempted murder charge in the US.

0-19 (Rev.

James Baldwin: 'for you, sister Angela'

SAN FRANCISCO—Black author James Baldwin, in an open letter to his "dear sister," Angela Davis, has pledged himself to "fight for your life as though it were our own —which it is."

Baldwin has lived the last few years in Europe. His letter was first published Dec. 26 in the British Manchester Guardian weekly. It has been published in full in a recent issue of the New York Review of Books. It is expected the letter will have a major impact on the black community.

In the letter, Baldwin sees Davis, Huey Newton, George and Jonathan Jackson as representing "a whole new generation of people" who are the hope of the struggle of both black and white against "a carnivorous economy." Yet Baldwin despairs of "white America" ever awakening from their racist delusions.

Baldwin struck one of several notes of despair in his letter as he said that "One might have hoped that, by this hour, the very sight of chains on black flesh, or the very sight of chains, would be so intolerable a sight for the American people, and so unbearable a memory, that they would themselves spontaneously rise up and strike off the manacles."

"But no," he says, "they appear to glory in their chains, now, more than ever, they appear to measure their safety in chains and corpses."

As an example of this Baldwin cites Newsweek magazine putting Davis on its cover, an attempt to "drown (her) in a sea of crocodile tears."

He acknowledged the tremendous change in young black people when he says, "a whole new generation of people have assessed and absorbed their history, and, in that tremendous action have freed themselves of it and will never be victims again."

To Davis he says, "You — for example — do not appear to be your father's daughter in the same way that I am my father's son. At bottom, my father's expectations and mine were the same, the expectations of his generations and mine were the same; and neither the immense difference in our ages nor the move from the South to the North could alter these expectations or make our lives more viable.

"The American triumph — in which the American tragedy has always been implicit — was to make black people despise themselves," Baldwin charges. The new black consciousness is countering this, he emphasizes.

"Only a handful of the millions of people in this vast place," Baldwin writes, "are aware that the fate intended for you, sister Angela, and for George Jackson, and for the numberless prisoners in our concentration camps — for that is what they are — is a fate which is about to engulf them too."

He warns that "white lives, for the forces which rule in this country, are no more sacred than black ones, as many and many a student is discovering, and as the white American corpses in Vitenam prove."

"We know that we, the blacks, and not only we the blacks, have been, and are the victims of a system whose only fuel is greed, whose only god is profit," he said.

"We know that the fruits of this system have been ignorance, despair and death," Baldwin said, "and we know that the system is doomed because the world can no longer afford it — if, indeed, it ever could have."

The revolution in black consciousness, "means the beginning of the end of America," Baldwin says. "Some of us, white and black, know how great a price has already been paid to bring into existence a new consciousness, a new people, an unprecedented nation. If we know, and do nothing, we are worse than the murderers hired in our name."

Baldwin emphasizes we must "render impassable with our bodies the corridor to the gas chamber." To Angela he says: "If they take you in the morning, they will be coming for us that night."

Tolson ____
Sullivan ____
Mohr ____
Bishop ____
Brennan, C.D. ____
Callahan ____
Casper ____
Conrad ____
Felt ____
Gale ____
Rosen ____
Tavel ____
Walters ____
Soyars ____
Tele. Room ____
Holmes ____
Gandy ____

ALL INFORMATION CONTAINED
HEREIN IS UNCLASSIFIED
DATE 5-22-89 BY

b7c-1

The Washington Post Times Herald ____
The Washington Daily News ____
The Evening Star (Washington) ____
The Sunday Star (Washington) ____
Daily News (New York) ____
Sunday News (New York) ____
New York Post ____
The New York Times ____
The Daily World ____
The New Leader ____
The Wall Street Journal ____
The National Observer ____
People's World PAGE 8

Date 1/9/71

62-108763 A

NOT RECORDED
170 FEB 22 1971

5 FEB 2

UNITED STATES DEPARTMENT OF JUSTICE

FEDERAL BUREAU OF INVESTIGATION

WASHINGTON, D.C. 20535

In Reply, Please Refer to File No.

May 26, 1971

ANGELA DAVIS

The May 24, 1971, edition of "L'Unita," the press organ of the Italian Communist Party (PCI) contained a photograph depicting various representatives of the "Committee of the Arts for the Freedom of ANGELA DAVIS" marching in Washington, D. C. The caption underneath the photograph states that the Committee has launched an appeal to artists throughout the world to intensify the international campaign in order to save the militant American communist ANGELA DAVIS. The caption continues that the Committee has launched an initiative in order to organize a showing and sale of paintings at the end of June, 1971, in Los Angeles, California, the birthplace of ANGELA DAVIS. The Committee has invited Italian artists to participate in this manifestation so that other artists can be mobilized in the struggle for a free society and at the same time raise funds desperately needed for the defense of ANGELA DAVIS. According to "L'Unita," the appeal was signed by writer JAMES BALDWIN; screen writer DALTON TRUMBO and actress JANE FONDA. The address of the Committee was shown as Post Office Box 8958, Los Angeles, California 90043.

ALL INFORMATION CONTAINED HEREIN IS UNCLASSIFIED DATE 5-21-79 BY SP-1 6sklcb

6972 EEP|alp 222.90 89-3016 JHP

PROPERTY OF THE FBI This report is loaned to you by the FBI, and neither it nor its contents are to be distributed outside the agency to which loaned.

- 1* -

JUN 22 1971

88-51548-805

ENCLOSURE

DIRECTOR, FBI (62-108763) 6-16-71

SECRET

LEGAT, PARIS (100-2660)(RUC) 100-146553-8

JAMES ARTHUR BALDWIN
RM - BN

Remylet 4-23-71 captioned "Black Panther Party (BPP), International Relations, mylet and LHM 3-24-71 captioned as above.

No information has been received from Paris sources which would indicate current involvement or activity by subject in connection with the BPP or other Black Power organizations in France. As noted in referenced letter dated 4-23-71, the "International Herald Tribune" issue of 4-20-71 reported BALDWIN had participated in a rally held in London on 4-18-71 on behalf of ANGELA DAVIS.

Paris sources have advised previously that BALDWIN is currently far less militant than in the past and apparently is considerably removed from the mainstream of Black Power activities. Sources indicated BALDWIN's poor health and considerable prosperity may have contributed to his withdrawal from these activities. (S) U

Sources are aware of our continuing interest in the activities of subject and will furnish any information developed upon receipt. All logical investigation at this time has been completed and captioned matter is being RUCed.

4 - Bureau
(1 - Foreign Liaison Desk)
(1 - New York, 100-146553)
1 - Paris
MGZ:jmw
(5)

100-146553-390

SEARCHED INDEXED
SERIALIZED FILED
JUN 25 1971
FBI—NEW YORK

RECEIVED WITH BUREAU ROUTING SLIP DATED

SECRET

990

UNITED STATES DEPARTMENT OF JUSTICE

FEDERAL BUREAU OF INVESTIGATION

89-3016 JHP
2/22/90

In Reply, Please Refer to File No.

August 9, 1971 697288

ALL INFORMATION CONTAINED HEREIN IS UNCLASSIFIED DATE 5-21-79 BY SP-1 GSK

ANGELA YVONNE DAVIS

The May 1, 1971 issue of the Swiss French-language communist newspaper contained an article which read as follows in translation:

"Free Angela Davis

"The life of Angela Davis is from now on in the hands of Ronald Reagan, racist and fascist governor of California, and of the tribunal which should judge her, but she will be among us if a unanimous and powerful protest is raised to disarm the executioner.

"Accused without evidence of being the instigator of an escape of black prisoners, she has been accused of worse: of being a young black woman, a philosopher, and above all, a communist.!

"Why are her accusers holding so to their prey? It is because in her are united in an exemplary manner the beginning struggles of the Americans with the principal problems of their society: youth and the students, the blacks, capitalism and Vietnam.

"But it is also because these problems are ours or that we solidarize with the struggles which they raise that we demand the immediate liberation of Angela Davis, member of the American Communist Party and of the Black Panther Party.

"'Free Youth,' supported by our newspaper, like other organizations in Geneva or in Switzerland, has conducted a campaign for her liberation and has sent a petition with more than 1600 signatures to the United States Embassy in Bern. They also sent a message of solidarity directly to Angela Davis. Vigilance should not be relaxed, and all sorts of actions should be pursued."

"This document contains neither recommendations nor conclusions of the FBI. It is the property of the FBI and is loaned to your agency; it and its contents are not to be distributed outside your agency."

88-51548-808

ENCLOSURE

SECRET

It is common knowledge in Switzerland that "Free Youth" is the youth organization of the Communist Party of Switzerland (CPS).

Information has been received from the American Embassy, Bern, that a printed sheet was circulated in Switzerland in May, 1971, which read as follows in translation from German:

"Help to free Angela Davis

"The story of Angela Davis is the story of political oppression: oppression as a woman, oppression as an Afro-American, oppression as a leftist. She was dismissed from the University of California on political grounds. Without regard to her unusual achievements as a student and professor, achievements which no one, not even her enemies, deny. Her participation in illegal activities has not been proven. Despite this, the American federal police, the FBI, placed Angela Davis on the list of the ten most wanted persons. Press and television gave this case the greatest publicity. President Nixon appeared before the American television cameras to personally thank Edgar Hoover, chief of the FBI, for capturing 'this dangerous woman'. Which means a sort of conviction-in-advance. With this he instigated hate and enmity against the Afro-American freedom movement as never before.

"Can Angela Davis still expect a just trial at all under such circumstances? She dedicated her life to the struggle against oppression and injustice, the struggle for the blacks and oppressed of the whole world.

"At present Angela Davis is confined in one of the most fearful prisons in the U. S. Her trial can last years. Regardless of whether she is innocent or guilty: her trial will be a trial of a society of violence and injustice. A society which is responsible for Angela's present situation. A society which is in the process of destroying its strongest accuser.

"Angela Davis is fighting for her life. Only the greatest protest throughout the world, a universal protest which will not let itself be stifled, can still save her life.

"Herbert Marcuse, Professor of Philosophy, University of California

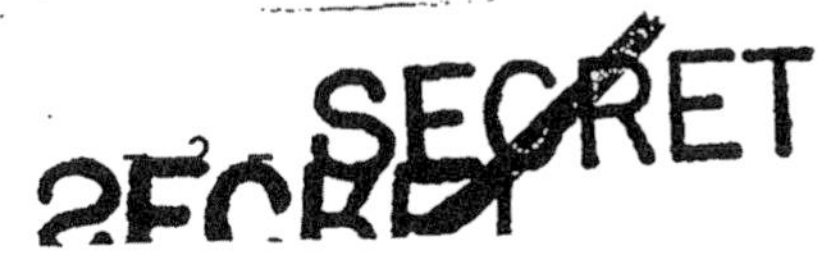

"James Baldwin, author USA
Shirley Mc Laine, film actress and representative of the Democratic Party

Jean Genet, author, France
Jane Fonda, film actress and freedom fighter

"Petition

"The undersigned persons protest against the injust arrest of Angela Davis and her delivery to the California authorities. We demand that the government of the United States use all its influence to prevent the threatening legal murder of Angela Davis, which would be only one in the endless chain of murders of Afro-Americans.

"Name: Address:

"Please send this stub signed with your name and address to Post Office Box 826, St. Gallen, as soon as possible. All stubs will then be sent by us to the American Embassy in Bern."

Approximately 430 of these slips, some with more than one signature, were received by the Embassy. In addition, a typed scroll on which the names of those signing the slips appeared, was also received at the embassy. This scroll was headed as follows:

"American Embassy, Jubilaeumstrasse 93
3000 Bern, Switzerland

Many people in the whole world are following with fear and increasing anxiety the destiny of Angela Davis, the fighter for civic rights. We wonder how the administration of the law of her country claims the right to charge Angela Davis with murder. The 'evidences' assembled by the Attorney General are, by the judgement of well known experts, more than doubtful. Nevertheless Angela Davis was put on the list of the most searched criminals, therefore the following people signed to protest against the unjustified arrest of Angela Davis and her extradition to the California Authorities.

66.

RAPPING ON *A RAP ON RACE*

APRIL AND SEPTEMBER 1971

Baldwin was now unable to ignore his declining health—a London doctor had even advised him to give up drinking, one of his deepest needs and pleasures, warning of a useless liver. His depression in response to his undeniable physical weakness made fresh writing sluggish. He could still talk brilliantly with the best of them, however, and he returned briefly to the United States to produce a book by speaking. *A Rap on Race*, one of the oddest contributions to his bibliography, memorialized a two-day conversation between Baldwin and Margaret Mead, the renowned cultural anthropologist whose *Coming of Age in Samoa* (1928) gave academic heft to the sexual revolution of the 1960s. (Some of Baldwin's bohemians in *Another Country*, black and white, were already exhausted by this revolution in the 1950s.) The white Mead agreed to the project because she hoped to go on record against racism; Baldwin hoped to extend the record at a time when the assassinations of Malcolm and Martin rendered him "the last witness." As stressed in the FBI's short review of *A Rap on Race*, Baldwin played the firebrand to Mead's scientist, defending limited doses of political violence and insisting that "our society is on the edge of absolute chaos." The two agreed to agree on the importance of being "as clearheaded as possible about all human beings" and on their exceptional exemption from common prejudice: "Mead indicated she could not possibly be a racist because of her impeccable upbringing. Baldwin related that he could not be an anti-Semite since one of his best friends is Jewish." The Bureau was unmoved by both speakers' protestations of innocence, racial and otherwise.

Mead "reportedly was a close associate of several individuals who were known members of communist front groups," while Baldwin "has been connected with several Communist Party front organizations." No part of *A Rap on Race*, added to the Bureau Library in 1971, was pro-capitalist enough to close either intellectual's FBI file.

b7C-1

1 - Miss [redacted]

SAC, New York (100-87235) 4/26/71

Attention: Liaison Section

Director, FBI (62-46855)

PURCHASE OF BOOKS
BOOK REVIEWS

You are authorized to obtain discreetly, and as soon as possible, one copy each of the following books for use of Bureau. Mark books to attention of Research Section, Domestic Intelligence Division.

Rec'd 6-10-71 AmB. 1. "A Rap on Race" by Margaret Mead and James Baldwin. Lippincott; May, 1971; $6.95

Rec'd 6-10-71 AmB 2. "Born Black: A Personal Report on the Decade of Black Revolt 1960-1970" by Gordon Parks. Lippincott; 5-20-71; $6.95

Rec'd 5-28-71 AmB 3. "Black Viewpoints" edited by Arthur C. Littleton and Mary W. Burger. NAL Mentor Original; 4-14-71; $1.50

Rec'd 5-25-71 AmB 4. "Beyond Racism: Building An Open Society" by Whitney M. Young, Jr. McGraw-Hill; 5-15-71; paperback, $2.95

MAILED 24
APR 26 1971
FBI

5. "Assault on Privacy: Computers, Data Banks, and Dossiers" by Arthur R. Miller. University of Michigan Press; March, 1971; $7.95 Rec'd 5-28-71 AmB.

1 - Racial Intelligence Section (Route through for review)
1 - Mr. [redacted] (6221 IB)

AMB:smh
(6)

b7C-1

REC-104 62-46855-924

19 APR 27 1971 b7C-1

NOTE:

First four books requested by SA [redacted] RIS, for review relating to work assignments on racial matters; book number five requested for review by Number One Man T. J. Smith, Research Section, Domestic Intelligence Division. Books will be filed in Bureau library.

Tolson
Sullivan
Mohr
Bishop
Brennan, C.D.
Callahan
Casper
Conrad
Dalbey
Felt
Gale
Rosen
Tavel
Walters
Soyars
Tele. Room
Holmes
Gandy

56 MAY 11 1971

MAIL ROOM ☐ TELETYPE UNIT ☐

AmB.

1 - Mr. W. C. Sullivan
1 - Mr. E. S. Miller

MR. E. S. MILLER

September 17, 1971

1 - Mr. G. C. Moore
1 - Mr. [redacted]
(Miss [redacted])
1 - Miss [redacted]
1 - Mr. [redacted]

b7C-1

MR. G. C. MOORE

BOOK REVIEW
"A RAP ON RACE," BY
MARGARET MEAD AND JAMES BALDWIN

This is a review of captioned book, published in 1971 by J. B. Lippincott Company. The book is being placed in the Bureau Library.

Synopsis:

"A Rap On Race" represents a tape-recorded dialogue between Margaret Mead, renowned anthropologist and author, and James Baldwin, well-known Negro author. Each expressed views concerning various issues such as their early childhood, slavery, Christianity, New Guinea, South Africa, Israel, Women's Lib, Huey Newton, the English language and the black bourgeoisie. Both Mead and Baldwin agreed they had to be clearheaded as possible about all human beings. Baldwin believes our society is on edge of absolute chaos.

ALL INFORMATION CONTAINED
HEREIN IS UNCLASSIFIED
DATE 5/22/18 BY [illegible]

Details:

Review of Bureau Files:

Margaret Mead, born 12/16/01 in Philadelphia, Pennsylvania, is Curator Emeritus of Ethnology at the American Museum of National History in New York City. She is a renowned anthropologist and author.

When Mead was being considered for employment as an anthropologist by the United States Public Health Service, an investigation during 1948 under the Loyalty of Government Employees Program revealed she had been affiliated with several communist front organizations. Later when she was an applicant with the World Health Organization, investigation under the Loyalty of Employees of the United Nations disclosed Mead reportedly was a close associate of several individuals who were known members of communist front groups.

ORIGINAL FILED IN 62-46855

1 - 62-46855 (Book Review File)
1 - 62-108763 (James Baldwin)
1 - 100-386818 (Margaret Mead)

62-108763-
NOT RECORDED
176 OCT 4 1971

LGB:ekw
(10)

58 OCT 8 - 1971

CONTINUED - OVER

Memorandum to Mr. E. S. Miller
RE: BOOK REVIEW, "A RAP ON RACE," BY MARGARET MEAD AND JAMES BALDWIN

When being considered for employment as a consultant with the Department of State in 1963, Mead indicated she had participated in various events which she later found to be communist controlled and that she had contact with individuals who were later publicly declared to be communists or members of communist front organizations.

James Arthur Baldwin, a well-known American Negro author, born 8/2/24 at New York City, has been connected with several Communist Party front organizations. He has lent his name to subversive causes and is an advocate of the black power movement in the United States. He has been critical of the Director. Baldwin is included on the Security Index.

Book Review:

This book represents a dialogue between Margaret Mead and James Baldwin, which was entirely tape-recorded in 1970. Each author relates views concerning issues such as their early childhood, slavery, Christianity, New Guinea, South Africa, Israel, Women's Lib, Huey Newton of the Black Panther Party, the English language and the black bourgeoisie. Baldwin is of opinion no one assumes any responsibility in our country and that our society is on the edge of absolute chaos. Both Mead and Baldwin agreed they had to be clearheaded as possible about all human beings. At times Mead and Baldwin showed anger as he was accused of mouthing anti-Semitic nonsense and Baldwin accused Mead of being one of his victimizers since she is white. Mead indicated she could not possibly be a racist because of her impeccable upbringing. Baldwin related that he could not be an anti-Semite since one of his best friends is Jewish.

Mention of the FBI:

On page 154 in discussing ethnic identification in the United States, Mead asked, "What about the Italians who are picketing the FBI as being unfair to Italians because they are persecuting the Mafia?" Baldwin had no comment. 1593

Mead undoubtedly is referring to picketing of our New York Office on a number of occasions within the past several years by an Italian-American group led by Joseph A. Colombo, Sr.

ACTION: For information

67.

FROM THE SECURITY TO THE ADMINISTRATIVE INDEX

APRIL 1972

Baldwin, a prominent name on the FBI's Security Index since 1963, was neatly shifted onto the new Administrative Index (ADEX) nine years later. The replacement of one secret directory of dissidents with another wasn't the Bureau's preferred path, but Congress repealed relevant aspects of the 1950 Internal Security Act in the spring of 1971, and Hoover's hand was forced. FBI managers knew that the old man's instinct would be to respect only the letter of the new law. Moreover, "the potential dangerousness of subversives was probably even greater now than before the repeal," or so thought Richard Cotter, the head of the Bureau's Intelligence Division. Attorney General John Mitchell, not yet snared in the Watergate scandal, was consulted with all this in mind. The FBI received his permission to flout the intent of Congress as efficiently as possible. "[T]he repeal of the aforementioned Act," Mitchell concluded, "does not alter or limit the FBI's authority and responsibility to record, file, and index information secured pursuant to its statutory and Presidential authority. An FBI Administrative Index compiled and maintained to assist the Bureau . . . is not prohibited." Compiled it was, and the only question about Baldwin's inclusion was whether he belonged in ADEX category III, meant for the "rank-and-file" of revolutionary groups, or category IV, reserved for "teachers, writers, lawyers, etc." who avoided active subversion but "were nonetheless influential in espousing their respective philosophies." Category IV won the day.

Baldwin, inactive over the past year "in black extremist activities," remained a thinker and espouser of real danger, "likely to furnish aid or other assistance to revolutionary elements because of his sympathy and/or ideology." Had he known about his grouping among the most treacherous intellectuals, Baldwin would have been proud as well as horrified.

OPTIONAL FORM NO. 10
MAY 1962 EDITION
GSA FPMR (41 CFR) 101-11.6

UNITED STATES GOVERNMENT

Memorandum

TO : SAC, NEW YORK b7C-1 DATE: 4/14/72

FROM : SUPERVISOR [redacted] (#43)

SUBJECT: JAMES ARTHUR BALDWIN- EM-

Bureau airtel to all offices dated 12/23/71, captioned "SECURITY INVESTIGATIONS OF INDIVIDUALS" instructed that all cases on subjects who were on the Security Index or Reserve Index be opended for the purpose of submitting an FD 122 concerning subject status on the New ADEX. This case is being opened now for that purpose.

To assure uniformity and ease of handling by the ADEX Unit, which will prepare all FD 122s, Agents should rough draft the information for the FD 122 on the special sheet which has been prepared for this purpose.

ALL INFORMATION CONTAINED HEREIN IS UNCLASSIFIED DATE 5-30-89 BY

100-146553-391

SEARCHED ___ INDEXED ___
SERIALIZED ___ FILED ___
4/14/1972
FBI—NEW YORK
[redacted]

b7C-1

RDS:sia

5010-108

Buy U.S. Savings Bonds Regularly on the Payroll Savings Plan

FD-122 (Rev. 11-22-71)
OPTIONAL FORM NO. 10
MAY 1962 EDITION
GSA GEN. REG. NO. 27
5010-106

UNITED STATES GOVERNMENT

Memorandum

TO : Director, FBI (Bufile- 62-108763) DATE: 4/18/72

FROM : SAC, NEW YORK (100-146553)

SUBJECT: JAMES ARTHUR BALDWIN
EM

OK for ADEX IV
ERS
GCI/TDR

Cards UTD
Cards Sent OC
6/7/72

Re:

Recommend: [XX] ADEX Card [ ] ADEX Card changed (specify change only) [ ] Subject removed (succinct summary attached)

Name

Aliases

[ ] Native Born
[ ] Naturalized
[ ] Alien

Card for IV

Tab
~~Category I~~
~~Category II~~
~~Category III~~
[X] Category IV

[ ] AWC [ ] COMMUNIST [ ] NL [ ] PLP [ ] PRN [ ] SNC [ ] SWP
[ ] BNT [ ] JFG [ ] NOI [ ] PPA [ ] SDS [ ] SPL [ ] WWP
[ ] BPP [ ] MIN [ ] Miscellaneous (Specify)

Date of Birth	Place of Birth	Race	Sex
			[ ] Male [ ] Female

Business Address, Name of Employing Concern and Address, Nature of Employment, and Union Affiliation, if any.

Residence Address

ALL INFORMATION CONTAINED
HEREIN IS UNCLASSIFIED
DATE 5/22/18 BY

REC-19

62-108763-84

Key Facility Data

ST-112

Geographical Reference Number Responsibility

(2)- Bureau (RM)
1- New York

LEB:bah
(3)

SEE ADDENDUM PAGE TWO

60 JUN 8 1972

APR 24 1972

RESEARCH SECTION
EXT. INF. SEC.

NY 100-146553

The following is a brief summary of the subversive activity of the subject and it is believed that it qualifies subject for Category III of the ADEX.

BALDWIN, well known American Negro Author, although formerly an advocate of Black Power Movements in the US, he has not been over the past year been engaged in black extremist activities.

The next report or LHM may be expected at the Bureau, 4/30/73; current report being submitted, 4/30/72.

ADDENDUM:

Baldwin, a well-known Negro author, has been connected with several Communist Party front groups. He has lent his name to subversive causes and is an advocate of the black power movement in the United States. It is believed the subject, due to his position as an author, is likely to frnish aid or other assistance to revolutionary elements because of his sympathy and/or ideology. Accordingly, he is being placed in Category IV of the ADEX rather than III as recommended by the New York Office.

68.

THE LAST BOOK PURCHASE—*NO NAME IN THE STREET*

JULY 1972

The final Baldwin book bought by the FBI—at least according his file—was his memoir *No Name in the Street* (1972), a non-chronological follow-up to the better-known autobiographical essays in *Notes of a Native Son* (1955) and *Nobody Knows My Name* (1961). The subject of Baldwin's new work of self-reflection was his life reconsidered in the short but eventful aftermath of the nonviolent Civil Rights Movement, a window in which egalitarian interracial education had given way to distortion of "the truth of the American black situation." "In this place, and more particularly, in this time," Baldwin reflected, time itself had seemed to change, and one could "say there are no longer any clear images," the very material needed for accurate and prophetic witness. Baldwin's sense of "kaleidoscopic, fragmented" vision did not extend to his view of the FBI, however, a clear and consistent danger in *No Name in the Street*. The "High Priest, J. Edgar Hoover," the book observed, once described Black Muslims exactly as he now demonized Black Panthers: time hadn't changed the racism at Bureau headquarters. The FBI's reaction to Baldwin's personal attack is unknown: the book review requested by the Extremist Intelligence Section has gone missing or was never undertaken. In any case, Baldwin only upped the ante in *The Devil Finds Work* (1976), a later autobiographical essay centered on his lifelong fascination with the movies. Hoover's death in 1972, more than fifty years after his start at the Bureau, seemed to tear down the floodgates of Baldwin's criticism, open since the early 1960s. In *The Devil Finds Work*, he complained that an early encounter with FBI agents who were chasing down military deserters was something "like being pissed on, or gang-raped." Whether you are guilty or innocent, he charged, "once you *have* come to the attention of the FBI, they keep a friendly file on you, and your family, and your friends." *The Devil Finds Work*, also the home of Baldwin's portrait of Hoover as "history's most highly paid (and most utterly useless) *voyeur*," is the closest thing we have to the missing *Blood Counters*, the book-length bomb promised the FBI way back in 1964.

b7c-1

1 - [redacted]

SAC, New York (100-87235) 7/14/72
Attention: Liaison Section

Acting Director, FBI (62-46855)

PURCHASE OF BOOKS
BOOK REVIEWS

You are authorized to obtain discreetly one copy each of the following books for use of Bureau. Mark books to attention Research Section, Domestic Intelligence Division.

1. "No Name in the Street" by James Baldwin. Dial Press; 1972; $5.95

2. "Black Religion and Black Radicalism" by Gayraud S. Wilmore. Doubleday; 8-18-72; $7.95

1 - Extremist Intelligence Section (route through for review) (Moore)

1 - Mr. [redacted] (6221 IB)

AMB:cjt/sra b7c-1
(6)

ALL INFORMATION CONTAINED HEREIN IS UNCLASSIFIED DATE 5/22/89 BY [illegible]

ORIGINAL FILED IN 62-46855-1062

NOTE:

Books requested by Inspector G. C. Moore, Extremist Intelligence Section, Domestic Intelligence Division, for review. Books will be filed in Bureau Library.

62-108763-
NOT RECORDED
185 JUL 18 1972

MAILED 9
JUL 13 1972
FBI

19 JUL 14 1972

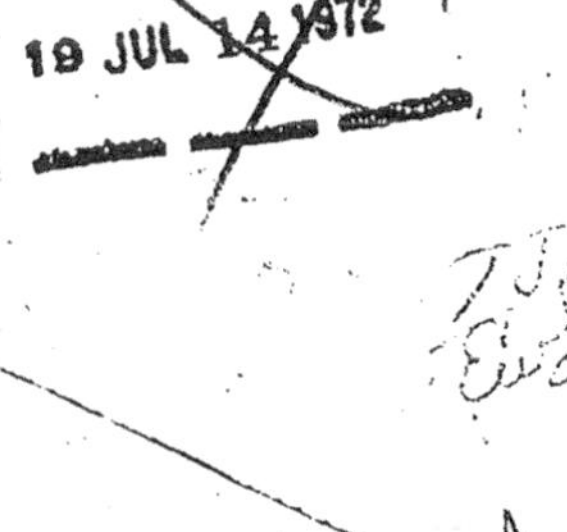

Felt
Bates
Bishop
Callahan
Campbell
Cleveland
Conrad
Dalbey
Jenkins
Marshall
Miller, E.S.
Ponder
Soyars
Walters
Tele. Room
Mr. Kinley
Mr. Armstrong
Ms. Herwig
Mrs. Neenan

62 JUL 21 1972 MAIL ROOM ☐ TELETYPE UNIT ☐

1600

OPTIONAL FORM NO. 10
MAY 1962 EDITION
GSA FPMR (41 CFR) 101-11.6

UNITED STATES GOVERNMENT

Memorandum

TO : ACTING DIRECTOR, FBI (62-46855)
ATTN: RESEARCH SECTION
DOMESTIC INTELLIGENCE DIVISION

DATE: 7/18/72

FROM : SAC, NEW YORK (100-87235)

SUBJECT: PURCHASE OF BOOKS
BOOK REVIEWS

ReBulets 5/12/72 and 7/14/72.

Enclosed herewith is one copy each of "Black America and World Revolution" by Claude M. Lightfoot. "No Name in the Street" by James Baldwin.

62-108763-

NOT RECORDED
183 JUL 27 1972

ORIGINAL FILED IN 62-46855-1063

ALL INFORMATION CONTAINED
HEREIN IS UNCLASSIFIED
DATE 5/22/18 BY

2 Encls. carded by and filed in Bureau Library. 7-20-72

JUL 20 1972

(2) - Bureau (62-46855)(Enc. 2)
1 - NY (100-87235)

RJL:chj
(3)

RESEARCH SECTION

(SEALED)
ENCLOSURE

60 JUL 28 1972

Buy U.S. Savings Bonds Regularly on the Payroll Savings Plan

5010-108

69.

THE LAST TRANSLATION—"*L'EXPRESS* CONTINUES WITH JAMES BALDWIN"

AUGUST 1972

The FBI's final translation of a Baldwin interview—again, at least according to his FBI file—came from *L'Express*, a news magazine still published weekly in Paris. "We ask only to be allowed to live," Baldwin was quoted on the first page of the French original. This and other early sections of the interview went untranslated by the FBI, whose selective English rendition began three pages in, ignoring earnest radical questions about the reality of Marx and Lenin for black Americans. What Bureau translators moved from French to English was somewhat more personal. Baldwin had been asked why he had returned to France after Martin Luther King's murder in 1968. "I hesitated for two years," he had replied, until "I felt that it was necessary to go away to begin again: as a writer, as a political militant, as a man. The death of Luther King was the end of a certain period of time in American politics in which I was closely involved. It was also the end of a certain hope." With its phone taps, informers, and aggressive reading in several languages, the FBI knew exactly how closely Baldwin had been involved. But what was the lost hope? "Hope in American morality," Baldwin specified, predicting the reaction of many of his most passionate twenty-first-century readers to the election of President Donald Trump. Among other lessons, Baldwin's passage through the early 1970s offers us instructions in processing what looks like another national catastrophe, the (temporary) ruin of both ethical and political optimism.

OPTIONAL FORM NO. 10
MAY 1962 EDITION
GSA GPMR (41 CFR) 101-11.6
UNITED STATES GOVERNMENT

Memorandum

TO : ACTING DIRECTOR, FBI (62-108763) DATE: 8/22/72

FROM : LEGAT, PARIS (100-2660)(RUC)

SUBJECT: JAMES ARTHUR BALDWIN
RM - BN

Enclosed is a copy of L'Express Magazine, a French weekly news magazine, dated 8/21-27/72, containing an interview with JAMES BALDWIN beginning on Page 68. In the event this is considered of sufficient interest the Bureau may wish to translate the article for information purposes.

3 - Bureau (Enc.- 1) ENCLOSURE
(1 - Foreign Liaison Desk)
1 - Paris
NWP/jmd
(4)

ALL INFORMATION CONTAINED
HEREIN IS UNCLASSIFIED
DATE 5/22/89 BY

REC-61 62-108763-87

AUG 31 1972

T-94236
MMC/

9/1/72

RESEARCH SECTION

EXT. SEC.

54 OCT 12 1972

JAMES BALDWIN.
« Nous demandons qu'on nous laisse vivre. Un point c'est tout. »

1952, c'est une chose que je n'arrivais pas à faire comprendre à mes amis à Harlem. Ma vie à Montmartre. La pauvreté, la faim, la saleté, l'angoisse de mon Montmartre à moi. Pour eux, Montmartre ne pouvait être qu'un fantastique paradis. Moi, j'avais vécu parmi les « misérables ». C'est-à-dire essentiellement les Algériens. Dans leur nostalgie de saveurs, d'odeurs, de soleil — et malgré leur présent sinistre — leur situation était beaucoup plus cohérente que la mienne. Ils n'étaient pas venus en France pour y rester. Un jour, ils rentreraient chez eux. Mais nous, les Noirs, en Amérique, nous n'avions nulle part où aller : nous étions chez nous.

L'Express : Et chez vous, on commençait à se détester ? Que voulez-vous dire ?

J. Baldwin : La première fois qu'on est traité de sale nègre, on est un enfant. Un tout jeune enfant de 5 ou 7 ans. On ne comprend pas ce que cela veut dire, mais on a le sentiment d'être méprisé. Et, ce qui est pire, c'est que l'on regarde autour de soi et que l'on s'aperçoit que sa mère, son père, ses frères, ses sœurs sont aussi de sales nègres. On se rend compte brusquement que l'on est condamné à vivre parmi des gens qui vous méprisent, vous, votre famille. Vous cherchez pourquoi. Et vous découvrez la raison : parce que vous n'êtes pas blanc. Dès qu'un enfant naît dans une famille noire, son père, sa mère savent qu'un jour il rentrera à la maison en demandant : « Maman, qu'est-ce qu'un nègre ? » Plus ou moins consciemment, les parents essaient de se préparer à ce jour où il leur faudra répondre. Et d'y préparer l'enfant.

L'Express : Vous vous souvenez de ce jour-là ?

J. Baldwin : Assez vaguement. C'était à l'école. Des professeurs blancs qui traitaient les enfants noirs de façon différente des autres élèves. Et puis cela a continué avec les policiers.

L'Express : C'était à Harlem ?

J. Baldwin : Oui, dans les années 20. C'était, à l'époque, un quartier blanc, mais très pauvre. Des immigrés italiens, finlandais. Harlem n'a commencé à changer, à devenir noir, qu'après la crise de 1929.

L'Express : Que faisaient vos parents?

J. Baldwin : Je suis l'aîné de neuf enfants. Mon père était ouvrier. Le matin, il mettait son chapeau melon, sa chemise blanche et son complet noir, et prenait sa gamelle pour aller travailler en usine. De véritables travaux forcés. Il était aussi prédicateur. Il gagnait 27 dollars par semaine ; pour nourrir ses neuf enfants. Il était inévitable qu'il

Suite page 70 ⟶

not classified!

62-108763-87

Suite de la page 69

Il y a, aux États-Unis, un risque de clash social qui n'avait jamais existé jusqu'ici

devint fou... Ma mère, bien sûr, avait assez à faire à la maison. C'est à elle — aux mères en général — qu'il incombe d'inculquer aux enfants une dignité intérieure. C'est ma mère qui m'a fait comprendre : « Bon, tu es nègre. Mais ça ne signifie rien. Ceux qui te traitent de nègre, laisse-les dire ou bats-toi contre eux. Mais tu vaux mieux qu'eux. Et, de toute façon, moi, je t'aime. »

Elle est parvenue à nous faire croire que la chose la plus importante au monde, c'était de nous aimer les uns les autres et d'aimer autrui. Malgré la pauvreté, malgré la violence, malgré cette espèce de mépris dont les Noirs se rendent responsables les uns les autres, nous sommes finalement sauvés par une sorte d'amour entre parents et enfants. Même si le père ne peut rien, même si la mère ne quitte pas sa cuisine, on ne se sent pas rejeté de chez nous. Cela nous donne une force, un style.

L'Express : Et l'on réagit comment ?

J. Baldwin : Au début, on essaie d'imiter les Blancs. On s'efforce d'aplatir ses cheveux. On se lave quatre fois par jour, on s'exprime avec correction, on évite les gestes, les éclats de voix. Et puis on s'aperçoit qu'il n'y a rien à faire. On reste un sale nègre. C'est dans cet effort pour cesser de se mépriser que cela se révèle. Alors, on commence à comprendre et l'on agit selon son instinct, comme on a envie d'être. Mais c'est un voyage assez pénible. Jusqu'au moment où l'on se met à douter de cet héritage, on ne sait pas combien on en est prisonnier.

L'Express : Si vous aviez 20 ans aujourd'hui, seriez-vous venu en France ?

J. Baldwin : Il est difficile de s'imaginer plus jeune qu'on ne l'est. Mais je pense que je ne serais pas venu en France. Depuis 1947, la France a beaucoup changé. Les Etats-Unis et le monde aussi. Et les Noirs. Une des différences essentielles entre la nouvelle génération et moi, c'est que le tableau de ce passé que j'ai esquissé n'est plus aussi marqué. Le mépris qu'un Noir pouvait avoir de lui-même est beaucoup moins fort aujourd'hui. Le monde blanc n'a plus le prestige, la puissance qu'il a connus. Le dogme de la suprématie blanche n'a plus, aujourd'hui, la même valeur, la même infaillibilité. A l'extérieur et à l'intérieur des Etats-Unis. Je pense qu'un garçon de 20 ans est plus libre dans sa lutte intérieure que je ne l'étais à son âge. Il n'a plus besoin de faire le même voyage. Peut-être songe-t-il à aller en Afrique ou en Amérique latine, mais sans doute pas en Europe, comme je l'ai fait, pour me retrouver. Les jeunes sont plus à l'aise que nous ne l'étions dans nos rapports mutuels. Il nous a fallu du temps pour nous accepter entre nous, nous aimer entre nous, nous libérer de cette espèce de cauchemar.

L'Express : Comment cela a-t-il été possible ?

J. Baldwin : Il y a plusieurs causes à ce changement. La première est sans doute économique. La misère des années 30 n'est pas, malgré tout, celle des années 50 ou de 1970. Par rapport aux autres Américains, les Noirs, dans leur ensemble, restent pauvres, défavorisés, mais ce n'est plus cette misère que j'ai connue et dont il semble que l'on ne puisse jamais sortir. Et puis, il y a eu la libération africaine, après la décolonisation. Tout cela a donné aux jeunes Noirs d'aujourd'hui une sorte d'ouverture qui n'existait pas dans ma génération : leurs luttes, leur façon de voir leur avenir, la vie, le monde, la possibilité d'entrevoir comment changer ce monde, c'est pour moi un grand espoir. Cela ne liquide pas la génération précédente, mais cela me donne, en quelque sorte, une nouvelle vie, comme des enfants peuvent le faire. C'est pour cela qu'on a des enfants.

L'Express : Ces jeunes Noirs, ils essaient de faire autre chose que ce que vous avez fait ?

J. Baldwin : Oui. Mais cette prise de conscience est sortie de quelque chose d'existant. Comme ma génération, comme moi-même je suis sorti de quelque chose. Mon esprit n'a pas uniquement été formé dans le cadre officiel américain. Il s'est forgé, aussi, dans la cuisine de ma mère, dans les rues de Harlem.

L'Express : Depuis votre enfance, votre adolescence, des pas ont été faits vers l'intégration. La jeunesse noire est pourtant, aujourd'hui, beaucoup plus radicale que vous ne l'étiez. Pourquoi ?

J. Baldwin : Parce qu'il ne s'agit nullement de pas, mais de simples gestes. Il est toujours difficile, pour la plupart des Noirs, de gagner convenablement leur vie, d'avoir un avenir concret, et même, s'ils sont sur les bancs de l'université, de se lier avec des Blancs. La société n'a pas changé, les syndicats n'ont pas changé. Et là où des villes sont devenues presque entièrement noires, on ne sait pas ce que l'on va en faire.

Le radicalisme des Noirs, il se superpose, aujourd'hui, à une panique générale des Blancs et à une sorte de doute, de dégoût de la jeunesse noire ou blanche — sous le coup de la guerre du Vietnam. Il y a, aux Etats-Unis, un risque de clash social qui n'avait jamais existé jusqu'ici.

L'Express : La prise de conscience politique est beaucoup plus aiguë, beaucoup plus précoce qu'il y a trente ans ?

J. Baldwin : C'est certain. Le problème est beaucoup plus visible, la situation est beaucoup plus claire aujourd'hui. J'étais, moi, déjà adulte, lorsque est venue cette prise de conscience. Aujourd'hui, par exemple, il n'est pas possible de vivre en Californie, sous l'œil bienveillant du gouverneur Ronald Reagan, sans comprendre quelque chose. Les flics de Californie, ce sont les hommes mêmes, que John Steinbeck a décrits dans « Les Raisins de la colère ». Ils vivaient dans la misère, ils ont traversé les plaines. Ils sont tous devenus flics en Californie. Le flic californien, c'est un personnage terrifiant. Mais il travaille, finalement, pour M. Reagan.

L'Express : Marx, Lénine, pour un Noir américain, c'est une réalité concrète ?

J. Baldwin : Ma vision n'est pas purement politique, parce que je parle en écrivain, c'est-à-dire que je conserve, bon gré, mal gré, une certaine distance. Et que, dans ma jeunesse, le problème ne se posait pas de cette manière. Le Parti communiste américain était, à l'époque, essentiellement composé de Blancs, qui n'étaient pas libérés de leur peur de Blancs parce qu'ils appartenaient au P.c. Les Noirs qui y militaient se trouvaient dans une situation bizarre, à la fois appelés camarades, mais traités en nègres. Lorsqu'il s'agissait de sortir avec des Noirs, d'aller danser avec eux, de jouer aux cartes avec eux, ils étaient plus rigides encore que les Blancs non communistes. Et, par-dessus le marché, ils prétendaient nous donner les clefs de notre libération.

Ils savaient, eux, ce qu'il nous fallait. Ce qui n'avait aucun rapport avec nos aspirations, nos possibilités. Pire que cela, dans l'affaire Scottsboro, par exemple, dans les années 30, le P.c. américain a utilisé ces garçons noirs, accusés d'avoir violé des Blanches, de simples ouvriers, qui n'y comprenaient rien, pour faire une démonstration politique et abstraite. Il n'a réussi qu'à en faire des martyrs. A quoi bon ? Les jeunes Noirs, aujourd'hui, quand ils ont une conscience politique, se

tournent plutôt vers la Chine ou l'Amérique latine. De la Russie, ils se méfient, comme ils se méfient de tout le monde blanc.

L'Express : La révolution est, pour vous, inévitable ?

J. Baldwin : Le mot révolution, il est facile de l'utiliser. Il est beaucoup plus difficile de préciser ce que l'on entend par révolution. Dans une situation aussi complexe que celle des Etats-Unis, c'est un mot qui ne veut pas dire grand-chose. Mais si vous voulez dire que, pour les Noirs, l'intégration dans les structures actuelles des Etats-Unis est impossible, alors oui. Car ces structures ont précisément été créées pour les exclure.

Tout a commencé après la guerre de Sécession, après l'abolition de l'esclavage. Le Nord et le Sud avaient, en fait, également besoin des Noirs pour réaliser des profits. Le Sud a libéré les esclaves, du point de vue légal, mais ces hommes libérés sont redevenus esclaves dans le Nord. Ils ont été jetés dans une condition pire encore : l'esclavage économique. L'abolition de l'esclavage a simplement permis à l'industriel de Nouvelle-Angleterre de faire tourner ses usines grâce à la main-d'œuvre noire du Mississippi.

Esclavage économique, esclavage intellectuel. Aujourd'hui encore, qu'apprend un enfant noir à l'école ? Les manuels le décrivent comme un être inférieur, un sous-Tarzan...

L'Express : Qui était d'ailleurs fils d'un lord anglais...

J. Baldwin : Oui, ironie... Bref, un sauvage qui a eu beaucoup de chance que des chrétiens aient le courage d'affronter la jungle pour le sauver et l'emmener en Amérique. Voilà l'Histoire enseignée aux enfants américains. On a essayé sans succès de changer ces manuels. Ce serait un scandale en Alabama, en Caroline, dans le pays tout entier.

L'Express : C'est une volonté délibérée ?

J. Baldwin : C'est le but même du système d'éducation. L'enfant noir continue d'être éduqué pour être esclave. Comment peut-il, à l'école, avoir une idée de sa propre identité, de sa propre valeur ? Lorsqu'il quitte l'école, à 17 ans, il est déjà, psychologiquement, conditionné. Et le travail qu'il trouve est généralement le plus minable. Le Garment Center, ce gigantesque centre de la confection à New York, c'est l'illustration même du travail des Noirs. Toutes les tâches les plus rebutantes sont réservées aux Noirs et aux Portoricains, sous la protection vigilante du plus raciste des syndicats.

L'esclavage se perpétue même dans la vie privée. Le Noir qui a le malheur de tomber amoureux d'une Blanche et de lui faire un enfant risque encore la prison à vie.

L'Express : Il n'y a pas d'issue possible ?

J. Baldwin : Je n'en vois pas. Il y a un mur qui, peut-être, se nomme l'Histoire. Des attitudes avec lesquelles on a vécu si longtemps qu'on ne sait pas comment faire pour s'en libérer. Un terrain si usé qu'on ne pourrait plus y construire. Un vocabulaire qui, de part et d'autre, n'a pas le même sens. Il n'y a même pas de termes, de langage communs. Qu'est-il possible de faire avec un M. Nixon, un M. Reagan, ou le leader du syndicat de la confection ? Les structures américaines sont condamnées à mort. Ce n'est qu'après leur chute qu'on pourra commencer à parler d'espoir.

L'Express : Vous croyez à la victoire possible de la minorité noire ?

J. Baldwin : Nous représentons un dixième environ de la population américaine. Sans parler de faire la révolution, c'est certainement suffisant pour détruire la société.

L'Express : De quelle façon ?

J. Baldwin : Il nous est facile, par exemple, de rendre les villes inhabitables. Ce sont les Noirs qui forment le gros des services urbains. Dans l'immeuble, nous sommes, nous, à la cave, et la cave commande la vie des étages. C'est très simple. Pour organiser ce type de résistance, il n'est pas nécessaire d'être très nombreux. Et la guerre du Vietnam est, à cet égard, très significative. Que le pays le plus puissant du monde n'arrive pas, en douze ans, à venir à bout d'un des pays les plus pauvres et sous-développés du globe, cela fait réfléchir beaucoup de Noirs.

L'Express : Il y a déjà des symptômes de cet ébranlement ?

J. Baldwin : Ce qui s'est passé, récemment, dans les prisons américaines, est très grave. Et très révélateur. Il y a des années que l'on connaît la situation de ces prisons. Mais l'Administration américaine n'a ni l'imagination ni les moyens nécessaires pour changer la situation. Et d'ailleurs, maintenant, il est trop tard. Mais jusqu'à quand réussiront-ils à garder leurs prisonniers ? Et tous ces prisonniers ont des rela-

Suite page 72

ABONNÉS DE L'EXPRESS

Pour toute correspondance relative à votre abonnement en cours, échu, en renouvellement ou nouveau :

Envoyez-nous l'étiquette collée sur votre dernière bande. Elle porte tous les renseignements nécessaires pour vous répondre utilement.

Adressez cette correspondance à L'EXPRESS
Service Abonnements
6, rue de Berri
75 PARIS VIII
(359-96-44) **Merci.**

VOTRE ENVIRONNEMENT ?

Grâce à notre "SERVICE-CONSEIL", nous vous aiderons à le créer, à l'améliorer, à le renouveler.

Nous résoudrons vos problèmes :

pratiques : revêtements, murs, sols, ameublement ;
esthétiques : harmonisation des matériaux, des volumes, des couleurs ;
de confort : insonorisation, climatisation, ventilation, etc.,

à votre domicile et dans vos locaux commerciaux et industriels.

256-16-60
heures de bureau

BALDWIN
Suite de la page 71

Le Noir paie, chaque jour, pour l'Histoire écrite dans la couleur de sa peau

›s avec l'extérieur. A Attica, les ›ncs qui ont été tués au cours de ›neute ont été enterrés avec tous les ›nneurs, comme des héros. Mais, ›dant une semaine, on n'a même › su combien il y avait eu de morts ›mi les Noirs.

›xpress : La violence, pour vous, nécessaire ou seulement inévitable ?

›Baldwin : On ne peut pas parler la violence comme si elle devait produire demain. Elle est déjà là, › est installée. Mais la violence où, ›tre qui ? Lorsque le président ›on déclarait : « Nous ne tolérerons › la violence », je me suis toujours ›nandé à qui il parlait. Qui ne doit › tolérer ? Lui ? Ou nous ? Car les ›ncipales victimes de la violence amé›ine, ce sont les Noirs. Je préfé›ais, certes, que l'on puisse éviter les ›ontements violents. Mais cela ne ›end pas des Noirs. Le choix n'est › entre leurs mains.

›xpress : Vous êtes rentré aux ›ts-Unis, en 1957, parce que vous ›tiez que quelque chose bougeait. ›inze ans plus tard, vous avez décidé vivre en France. Pourquoi ?

›Baldwin : J'ai décidé de revenir en ›nce, puis d'y rester, après l'assassinat Martin Luther King, en avril 1968. › hésité pendant deux ans. Et puis, › senti qu'il fallait que je m'éloigne ›ur pouvoir recommencer. Comme ›ivain, comme militant politique, ›nme homme. La mort de Luther ›ng, c'est la fin d'une certaine époque la politique américaine à laquelle › été mêlé de près. La fin, aussi, d'un ›tain espoir.

›xpress : La voie choisie par Martin ›ther King, c'était une issue possible ?

Baldwin : Je ne sais pas. Il est diffi›e, aujourd'hui, de le dire. Peut-être › moyens utilisés par Martin n'étaient-pas, à terme, les plus efficaces, mais ›taient, à l'époque, les plus puissants. › toute façon, je n'aurais pu sup›rter l'idée de rester en France, alors ›e l'on tentait, chez moi, de changer ›elque chose. Je suis rentré pour me ›ettre au travail, aux côtés de Martin de Malcolm X.

Express : C'est cet espoir qui s'est ›isé avec la mort de Luther King ?

Baldwin : Oui. Un espoir dans la ›oralité américaine.

'Express : Vous vous êtes rendu ›mpte, ce jour-là, que les Américains › voulaient pas jouer le jeu ?

Baldwin : C'était le jeu du men›nge. Et c'est beaucoup plus grave ›u'on ne le pense. Car ce sont les institutions mêmes qui sont en cause.

L'Express : Martin Luther King était pasteur, chrétien et protestant. Et ces institutions, elles sont précisément liées, en Amérique, à l'idéologie, à la religion chrétiennes. N'y a-t-il pas là une contradiction ?

J. Baldwin : C'est là toute l'ironie de l'histoire des Noirs américains. On nous a donné cette religion lorsqu'on nous a débarqués en Amérique. Nous l'avons prise, en assumant votre Jésus-Christ, mais nous l'avons transformée, sans même nous en rendre compte, en une espèce d'outil à notre usage. Les negro spirituals sont, pour la plupart, une sorte de code entre les esclaves. Une chanson comme « Steel away to Jesus » n'a rien à voir avec Jésus. Elle permettait un dialogue entre les esclaves. C'était une façon de dire : « La route est libre. Tu peux partir. » Tout le langage noir américain vient de là.

Pour Martin, l'Eglise, c'était notre seul forum, le seul endroit où nous étions ensemble, entre nous. Mais il pensait, peut-être avec une certaine naïveté, que cette Eglise, aux structures démocratiques, avait une valeur. Comme une lettre de crédit, dont le débiteur doit s'acquitter. Cela supposait que le peuple américain honore sa créance. Elle n'a pas été honorée.

C'était un pari sur l'honneur américain. Même ceux qui n'aimaient pas Martin, ou qui n'étaient pas d'accord avec lui, avaient du respect pour cet homme. Qu'il puisse, dans notre pays, avoir une telle fin, c'était si choquant, cela nous obligeait à ouvrir les yeux pour regarder autour de nous et découvrir une autre réalité. Malgré les pétitions, les collectes, les marches, les gens restaient en prison, J. Edgar Hoover restait chef du F.b.i., et Nixon s'installait à la Maison-Blanche. Il fallait donc trouver d'autres moyens de nous libérer. Lesquels ? J'ai commencé à comprendre qu'il ne m'appartenait pas d'en décider.

L'Express : Et vous êtes rentré en France ?

J. Baldwin : Oui, pour respirer. Et prendre, à nouveau, du recul. Essayer d'y voir clair. J'avais été très lié au mouvement des Panthères noires, et je craignais, désormais, d'être inutile pour eux, si, moi-même, je ne faisais pas d'abord un bilan. Ce qui se fera se fera par les jeunes dans un monde différent, déjà, du mien. Le seul moyen de les aider, c'est d'apporter son témoignage. De les écouter, de les respecter, avec l'espoir, parfois, de se faire entendre. Je suis, après tout, d'abord un écrivain. Si je ne trouve pas le temps de réfléchir, d'écrire, je ne serai plus d'aucune utilité, à personne. Je n'ai plus de raison d'être.

L'Express : Comment vous situez-vous par rapport à Angela Davis ?

J. Baldwin : Je ne la connais pas personnellement. Elle est beaucoup plus jeune que moi. Elle appartient à une autre génération. Celle que je ne peux qu'écouter et essayer d'aider, en étant là. Ce que je sais, c'est que son procès est absurde. Elle a l'unique tort d'être un mauvais exemple pour les autres esclaves. Angela Davis comme Paul Robeson sont, aux yeux des Blancs, de mauvais nègres.

L'Express : C'est-à-dire ?

J. Baldwin : Paul Robeson allait dans le monde, comme si ce monde lui appartenait. Le Blanc ne peut pas supporter d'être entouré de terres noires. Il faut vite faire un exemple. Angela Davis a répondu à Reagan qu'elle était communiste. Le problème n'est pas ce dont elle est accusée. Qu'importe la réponse lorsque l'on vous demande ce que l'on n'a pas le droit de vous demander. Ce qui est important, pour moi, c'est de sentir, chez elle, une véritable impulsion, une véritable liberté. Que je sois d'accord ou non avec ses idées n'a rien à voir. Parce que, ayant vingt ans de plus qu'elle, j'ai forcément une autre optique. De toute façon, elle est victime. Donc, elle est ma sœur.

L'Express : Pour vous, le dialogue, même, semble désormais impossible. Est-ce aussi la conclusion que vous avez tirée de votre entretien avec Margaret Mead (1) ?

J. Baldwin : Je ne pensais pas que nous pouvions trouver une voie commune. Elle a beaucoup de courage, de cœur et d'honnêteté intellectuelle. Mais, d'abord, il y a, entre nous, plus de vingt ans de différence. Ensuite, elle est ethnologue, c'est une autre recherche que la mienne. Moi, je n'ai jamais rien appris par mon esprit. J'ai tout appris par le cœur et les entrailles. Et, surtout, elle est blanche. Derrière ce que je dis, il y a Harlem, son église, la cuisine de ma mère, la musique, l'angoisse, tout le voyage du Noir américain. Ce voyage, il est impossible de le comprendre si on ne l'a pas fait.

Ce dialogue entre Margaret Mead et moi, c'était un peu comme si on avait demandé à Ray Charles et à Frank Sinatra de jouer ensemble. Cette

(1) « Le Racisme en question », éditions Calmann-Lévy.

Angela Davis.
« Elle est ma sœur. »

distance entre un homme noir qui vient de la rue et une ethnologue blanche qui n'a jamais crevé de faim, elle est énorme, infranchissable. Et si, avec la meilleure volonté du monde, nous ne sommes pas parvenus à nous mettre d'accord, c'est dire à quel point la situation peut être grave.

L'Express : Quel a été, disons, le point de rupture ?

J. Baldwin : Margaret Mead refuse d'assumer la culpabilité de ce que d'autres Blancs ont fait avant elle ; le crime commis par ceux de sa race contre la race noire, ce péché contre le Saint-Esprit pour lequel il n'y a pas de pardon. Elle ne l'a pas commis, elle ne s'en sent pas coupable. Elle ne se sentirait coupable que de ce qu'elle-même pourrait avoir fait. Le reste appartient à l'Histoire. Mais, moi, je dis, chacun doit accepter l'Histoire qui l'a *créé* tel qu'il est. Car quelque chose descend d'une génération à l'autre. Lorsque nous parlons d' « Histoire », c'est trop souvent une facilité, un moyen d'échapper à la responsabilité de ce qui s'est passé. L'assassinat de Martin Luther King, ce n'est pas un événement historique, cela peut arriver encore, demain, avec un autre. C'est le présent. C'était mon frère, mon ami. Il ne s'agit pas de choses faites avant nous, il s'agit de choses faites devant nous, devant nos yeux. Le Noir paie, chaque jour, pour l'Histoire écrite dans la couleur de sa peau.

L'Express : Le fossé, pourtant, n'est pas toujours infranchissable. L'Amérique du Sud, elle, a réussi son métissage.

J. Baldwin : Oui, mais il s'agissait d'une tout autre société. Le poids du puritanisme américain, il ne faut pas l'oublier. Car cette panique profonde qu'éprouvent les Blancs américains à l'égard des Noirs, elle n'est pas uniquement d'origine sociale. Elle a des racines sexuelles. Le mythe de la puissance sexuelle des Noirs, ce sont les Blancs qui l'ont créé, mais ils y croient profondément. Ce sont des phantasmes, bien sûr, mais des phantasmes blancs. Le Blanc est convaincu que si un Noir entre dans sa maison, ou passe dans la rue, il va enlever sa femme comme un paquet et qu'il sera incapable de la garder. C'est de la folie pure, mais c'est ainsi.

L'Express : Comment cela se manifeste-t-il ?

J. Baldwin : Même lorsqu'un Américain libéral essaie loyalement de lutter contre le poids de l'Histoire, il découvre à quel point il est enchaîné. Demandez-lui, brutalement, en face : « Que feriez-vous si votre fille voulait épouser un Noir ? » Il vous dira : « J'espère que ce sera un type bien, qui la rendra heureuse. Mais il faudra vraiment qu'elle réfléchisse. Car, non, vraiment, la société n'est pas préparée à cela. »

L'Express : Le racisme, pour vous, a une origine sexuelle ?

J. Baldwin : La sexualité lui donne, en tout cas, une force. Personnellement, j'ai vécu ce cauchemar. Et j'ai dû enterrer tant de choses en moi-même que c'est un problème qu'il m'est pénible d'aborder. A cause de l'ambiguïté totale des relations sexuelles entre Noirs et Blancs.

L'Express : Quelle ambiguïté ?

J. Baldwin : Prenons l'exemple d'une jeune fille blanche de bonne famille qui se brouille avec son père, et quitte la maison. Que peut-elle faire de pire pour se venger de lui, l'humilier ? Coucher avec un Noir. Mais, moi, le Noir, qui ignore tout de ce drame, je pense qu'elle a été attirée par moi, qu'elle m'aime. Et, peu à peu, en vivant avec elle, je me rends compte qu'elle est là pour d'autres raisons. Lorsqu'on est jeune, que l'on croit à l'amour, il est affreux de se rendre compte qu'on est un instrument. Que l'on fait jouer à votre corps un rôle social et anonyme. Que l'être qui fait l'amour avec vous vous méprise. Que, même s'il ne vous méprise pas, vous pensez qu'il vous méprise. Et vous vous méprisez. C'est la façon la plus horrible d'émasculer un homme.

L'Express : Cela vous est arrivé ?

J. Baldwin : Oui, cela m'est arrivé. Et, après cela, on ne peut plus avoir confiance en qui que ce soit. Pour moi, d'ailleurs, non seulement le racisme est lié au sexe, mais la révolution l'est aussi. Voyez ce qui se passe avec les mouvements de libération des femmes, ou les mouvements de libération des homosexuels. Cette lutte qui commence contre l'espèce de bannissement, presque théologique, dont sont victimes les femmes, les Noirs, les homosexuels, tous enveloppés du même opprobre, du même mépris. L'idée qu'il faut mortifier sa chair est pour moi, tout simplement, obscène.

L'Express : N'y a-t-il pas maintenant, chez les Noirs, le même ostracisme à l'égard de la communauté blanche ? Le même refus : « Ah non ! tu ne vas pas épouser un Blanc ! »

J. Baldwin : C'est vrai. Il y a eu une époque où la grande ambition des Noirs, c'était de « passer », de se fondre dans la communauté blanche. Un Noir respectable essayait d'épouser une Noire aussi « pâle » que possible. Un bon exemple, c'est le pasteur Adam Powell, qui avait un grand prestige auprès des Noirs, des femmes noires, parce qu'il était à peine teinté et qu'il avait les cheveux raides. Mais, depuis dix ans, les choses ont beaucoup changé. Ce n'est plus, aux yeux des jeunes Noirs, un avantage d'avoir la peau claire, c'est presque une tare. Les filles ont non seulement cessé de se défriser les cheveux, mais elles portent des perruques à l'africaine.

Cela a des côtés ridicules, mais c'est très significatif. Le Noir veut être noir, il veut vivre comme il lui plaît, et non plus selon les canons de la communauté blanche. Je me souviens de m'être trouvé à Chicago, comme journaliste, tous frais payés, donc, dans un de ces grands hôtels style Hilton, horriblement chers. Une nourriture aseptisée, sans goût, une clientèle d'automates, de morts ambulants. J'étais le seul Noir de l'établissement. Le soir, je n'avais qu'une idée : quitter ce mausolée et aller à South Side, le ghetto noir de la ville, où ce que l'on mangeait avait du goût et où les gens étaient vivants.

L'Express : Cette réaction ségrégationniste de la communauté blanche, elle est quand même beaucoup plus marquée au Sud qu'au Nord ?

J. Baldwin : Le Sud est terrifiant. Je

Suite page 74 →

Jean-Pierre Couderc

Le seul espoir de la société américaine c'est de se négrifier

→

ne l'ai d'ailleurs découvert qu'en 1957. Et j'ai eu peur. Dans le Sud, si j'ouvre la bouche, j'ai tort. J'ai tort, même quand je regarde les gens. J'ai tort par ma seule existence. Je ne suis pas seulement un étranger dans la ville, je suis un ennemi. Les gens, là-bas, sont si enchaînés par leurs préjugés, si misérables dans leur façon de vivre, qu'ils en deviennent pathétiques. Ce doit être horrible d'être enfermé dans une telle prison morale et mentale. Affreux pour les femmes, surtout. Le mythe de la supériorité sexuelle des Noirs atteint là-bas à une sorte de démence. Le côté sexuel du problème est essentiel. C'est la racine du racisme, c'est le danger. D'un côté, le Noir est présenté comme un surhomme qu'il est interdit aux femmes blanches d'approcher. De l'autre, le Blanc compense sa prétendue infériorité... avec des femmes noires. C'est à la fois terrifiant et ridicule. Quand j'entre dans un restaurant, les Blancs ont peur. Au point que si j'insistais pour me faire servir, là où je ne dois pas manger, il m'arriverait malheur. Le Sud, c'est ça. Une prison dont on n'a aucun espoir de sortir, parce que l'élément essentiel d'identité pour chaque race, c'est de ne pas appartenir à l'autre race.

L'Express : Vous avez pourtant écrit : « Si la catastrophe arrive un jour, la renaissance ne pourra venir que du Sud. » Que voulez-vous dire ?

J. Baldwin : Parce que les gens vivent dans un tel cauchemar, qu'inconsciemment ils chercheront à se libérer. Pour sortir de cet enfer, le Sudiste aura un prix énorme à payer. Mais peut-être finira-t-il, précisément, par se dire : tout plutôt que cet enfer. Tandis que le Nordiste, lui, ne vit pas entouré de Noirs. Le Noir n'est pas un élément quotidien, permanent de sa vie. Il le croise dans l'ascenseur, sur un trottoir. Ce n'est pas son... paysage. Le voyage sera pour lui beaucoup plus long.

Je me souviens d'être arrivé un jour à Birmingham, en Alabama, fort tard dans la nuit. Ce qui, pour un Noir, n'est pas recommandé. Pour comble, portant une machine à écrire à la main. Dans le Sud, un Noir avec une machine à écrire est un homme dangereux. C'est pire que s'il transportait une bombe. Et, dans le Sud, un Noir ne prend pas le premier taxi venu. Il faut qu'un porteur aille demander à un employé de téléphoner à une station qui se trouve à quarante minutes de la gare.

J'ai donc attendu, assis sur ma machine. Et j'avais peur, parce que tous les gens qui passaient me dévisageaient, hostiles, agressifs. Au bout de quarante minutes, j'ai appris que l'employé avait oublié de téléphoner. Avoir subi l'épreuve de l'attente sans incident, c'était un miracle. Recommencer, c'était fou. A ce moment-là, un chauffeur de taxi blanc a proposé de m'emmener. C'était contraire à la loi. Je me trouvais devant un dilemme. J'ai fini par partir avec lui, pas du tout rassuré. Et c'était un très brave type, qui a essayé de me parler. Mais il n'a pas pu. Parler à un Noir de New York, en Alabama, ce n'était pas possible. Moi non plus, je n'ai pas pu. D'un côté comme de l'autre, nous étions bloqués, à cause de cette ambiguïté, de cette suspicion dont nous ne pouvons pas sortir.

L'Express : Vous avez plusieurs fois employé le mot « peur ». Cette peur des Blancs, elle n'est pas uniquement d'origine sexuelle. De quoi ont-ils peur

J. Baldwin : Les Blancs savent combien de fois ils m'ont mutilé, combien de fois ils m'ont castré, combien de fois ils m'ont pendu, brûlé, combien de fois ils ont violé ma femme. Ils le savent très bien. Leur prétendue innocence leur coûte un énorme effort de volonté. C'est pour cela qu'ils ne vont jamais à Harlem. C'est pour cela que la femme peut trouver du travail, alors que l'homme ne le peut pas. Car c'est de l'homme noir qu'ils ont peur. Ils ont peur qu'un jour cet homme noir vienne leur faire la même chose.

L'Express : C'est plus que la défense de privilèges ?

J. Baldwin : Il y a cela, bien sûr. La crainte que l'oppresseur peut avoir de l'opprimé. Mais il s'agit d'une réaction plus personnelle, liée à la vie privée et inconsciemment compliquée par le fait de la couleur. On ne peut pas, paraît-il, ne pas avoir une réaction en face de la couleur. Lorsque les Européens sont arrivés en Amérique du Nord, pour sauvegarder leur pureté, leur intégrité, ils ont commencé par exterminer les Indiens. Parce qu'ils descendaient d'une civilisation blanche et chrétienne, c'était, pour eux, le seul moyen de préserver leur identité. Tolérer les Indiens, c'était renoncer à leur héritage, à leur civilisation. Ce génocide les a menés sur le chemin de la folie.

L'Express : Vous voulez dire que le racisme a été institutionnalisé ?

J. Baldwin : Absolument. Alors qu'il ne repose sur aucune base ethnique. La race blanche n'est pas plus pure qu'une autre. Il n'y a pas de race pure. Le racisme est déjà odieux lorsqu'il se manifeste à l'égard des Algériens, des Juifs, des Portugais ou des Irlandais. Mais, aux Etats-Unis, il est officialisé. Comme il l'était en Allemagne sous le IIIe Reich. C'est une situation fasciste. Et le drame est là. Nous ne demandons pas à être intégrés. Nous demandons qu'on nous laisse vivre. Un point c'est tout. Que tout le monde soit libre de vivre. Seulement, les structures sociales sont devenues si écrasantes qu'elles seront tôt ou tard insupportables et qu'il faudra les détruire.

L'Express : L'image des Etats-Unis a pourtant considérablement changé en dix ans. C'est une société en mouvement. N'y a-t-il pas là, pour vous, un espoir ? Comment vous situez-vous, par exemple, par rapport au mouvement hippie ?

J. Baldwin : Les hippies, c'est un peu le même phénomène que celui que j'évoquais tout à l'heure. Etre hippie pour un jeune Blanc de bonne famille, c'est prendre une sorte de revanche. C'est, comme coucher avec un Noir, un moyen d'humilier sa famille, de rejeter les conventions. C'est si vrai, que lorsqu'un garçon ou une fille devient hippie, pour la société, il devient un nègre. Nous, nous l'étions déjà !

L'Express : La société américaine, en quelque sorte, se négrifie ?

J. Baldwin : Le seul espoir de la société américaine, c'est de se négrifier. C'est l'objet même de notre lutte. Il faut accepter que l'Amérique ne soit plus un pays blanc. Elle ne l'a d'ailleurs jamais été. Ça a toujours été un rêve. Comment voulez-vous maintenir la fiction d'un pays blanc, où non seulement un habitant sur dix est un Noir, mais où les relations qu'il entretient avec le reste de la communauté sont aussi équivoques et aussi passionnelles ?

L'Express : Comment expliquez-vous cette mise à l'écart du Noir, comme être humain, et son acceptation générale, comme artiste ?

J. Baldwin : On accepte le Noir à condition qu'il reste à l'écart sur une scène. Ça, c'est notre rôle traditionnel. On faisait chanter et danser l'esclave et on lui jetait des pièces, parce qu'il chantait et dansait si bien, avec tant de charme. C'est exactement la même chose maintenant, il n'y a rien de changé. Je me souviens de Mahalia Jackson. Elle chantait, à Chicago, devant des milliers de gens qui pleuraient, qui hurlaient, qui l'adoraient.

Ces mêmes gens ont brisé ses vitres, ont essayé de mettre le feu chez elle, ont écrit des obscénités sur ses murs, parce qu'elle avait osé acheter une maison dans un quartier blanc. Cette grande artiste n'avait pas le droit de vivre parmi les Blancs.

L'Express : Cet « amuseur noir », il a quand même marqué, par des apports essentiels, la culture du XXe siècle. Ne serait-ce que le cubisme, la musique de jazz... La culture noire, l'influence que peut exercer la civilisation noire, ce n'est pas, pour vous, une voie possible ?

J. Baldwin : Je pense, en effet, que c'est de cette manière, par les apports culturels, que l'on peut arriver à changer profondément la société. Notre façon d'entendre, de regarder, notre façon de sentir, de penser, peut contribuer à ces changements, y contribue nécessairement. C'est pour cela que je trouve à notre époque le mot révolution un peu romantique. C'est, en réalité, le fonds caché de l'humanité qu'il faut exploiter, pour troubler, établir la communication.

Changer le monde de cette façon, c'est beaucoup plus long qu'on ne le pense. Et ma seule raison de vivre, c'est de témoigner en ce sens. Je désire ce que tout le monde désire, et qui viendra, sous différents aspects, sous différentes formes. Mais, dans le prix à payer, il y a le tarif universel, et, pour certains, il y a les suppléments. Naître, apprendre à marcher, grandir, vieillir, mourir, c'est difficile pour tout le monde. Personne n'a le droit d'ajouter à ces difficultés un supplément de prix, un fardeau insupportable : celui de la couleur de la peau. ■

Copyright © 1972 L'Express.
Tous droits réservés.

L'EXPRESS
25, rue de Berri
75 380 PARIS Cédex 08
Tél. : 256.45.00
Directrice de la publication : Françoise Giroud
Directeur de la publication délégué :
Bruno Monnier
Composition de Typo-Elysées
Imprimerie de Montsouris, Paris
Impr. Georges Lang (couleur)
Impr. D.M.C. Arts Graphiques (couleur)
Impr. Paul Dupont (couverture)
Printed in France
ABONNEMENTS :
8, rue de Berri, Paris-VIIIe
Tél. : 359.98.44
Un an : 125 F
Etranger : tarif par avion sur demande
Règlement par chèque bancaire ou postal (envoyer les trois volets, nous inscrirons le n° de C.C.P.).
■ Toute demande de changement d'adresse doit être faite quatre semaines au moins avant la date effective du changement (joindre la dernière bande d'expédition).

Les livres de James BALDWIN dont vous venez de lire l'entretien
LE RACISME EN QUESTION
CHASSÉS DE LA LUMIÈRE
... en les commandant directement à la
LIBRAIRIE DE L'EXPRESS

Remplissez et postez simplement le bon de commande ci-dessous avec votre règlement. Les livres de James BALDWIN vous parviendront par retour et **franco de port** (France Métropolitaine seulement).
Si le bon a déjà été découpé, ou si vous préférez garder votre Express intact, vous pouvez aussi écrire à la Librairie de L'Express, 25, rue de Berri, 75380 PARIS Cédex 08, en joignant votre règlement et sans oublier de mentionner le titre de l'ouvrage.

BON DE COMMANDE

à retourner à La Librairie de L'Express, 25, rue de Berri, 75380-PARIS Cédex 08
Veuillez m'envoyer par retour et franco de port LE RACISME EN QUESTION de James BALDWIN □ 24 F. CHASSÉS DE LA LUMIÈRE de James BALDWIN □ 28 F. Vous trouverez ci-joint mon règlement sous forme d'un chèque à l'ordre de la Librairie de L'Express.

NOM . . . .
PRÉNOM . . . .
ADRESSE . . . .
. . . .
. . . .
. . . .

SECRET **SUMMARY FROM FRENCH**

The article "L'Express Continues with James Baldwin" is taken from the August 21-27, 1972, issue of "L'Express." p68

Question: You believe in the possible victory of the black minority?

Answer: We represent around 10% of the American population. Without talking about starting a revolution, it is certainly enough to destroy society.

Question: In what way?

Answer: It is easy for us, for example, to make the cities uninhabitable. It is the Blacks who form the bulk of the urban services. In real estate, we are in the basement and the basement directs the life of the rest of the floors. It is very simple. In order to organize this type of resistance, it is not necessary to have a lot of people. And the war in Vietnam, in this regard, is very significant. That the most powerful country in the world, in twelve years, cannot manage to get the better of one of the poorest and most underdeveloped countries in the world, makes many Blacks wonder.

Classified by [illegible]
Declassify on: OADR 6-14-89

Question: In your opinion, is violence necessary or only inevitable?

Answer: You cannot speak of violence as if it could take place tomorrow. It is already there. But violence where, against whom? When President Nixon said: "We will not tolerate violence any longer," I still wonder to whom he was speaking. Who must no longer tolerate it? He? Or us? Because the main victims of American violence are the Blacks. I would certainly prefer to be able to avoid violent confrontations. But it does not depend on the Blacks. The choice is not in their hands.

DECLASSIFIED BY 6972 EEP/ap ON 2-16-90 89 3016 JHP

100-146553-397

SECRET

(U) RECEIVED WITH BUREAU ROUTING SLIP DATED:

SEARCHED INDEXED SERIALIZED FILED 1972 FBI — NEW YORK

Question: You returned to the U.S. in 1957 because you felt that something was stirring. Fifteen years later, you decided to live in France. Why?

SECRET

Answer: I decided to return to France and then to stay there after Martin Luther King's assassination in April of 1968. I hesitated for two years. And then, I felt that it was necessary to go away to begin again: as a writer, as a political militant, as a man. The death of Luther King was the end of a certain period of time in American politics in which I was closely involved. It was also the end of a certain hope.

Question: The way chosen by Martin Luther King, was it feasible?

Answer: I do not know. That is very difficult to say today. Perhaps the methods used by Martin were not the most effective but they were, at that time, the strongest. Anyhow, I could not stand the idea of remaining in France, because they were trying to change me. I returned to work at Martin's and Malcolm X's side.

Question: Was this the hope which was broken when Luther King died?

Answer: Yes. Hope in American morality.

Question: And you returned to France?

Answer: Yes, to breathe. And, to withdraw once again. To try and see clearly. I was very strongly connected with the Black Panther Movement and I was afraid, then, of being useless to them. What they do is done by youths in a world which is already different from mine. The only way to help them is to contribute my support. To listen to them, to respect them, hoping sometimes to be heard. I am, after all, first a writer. If I do not find the time to reflect, to write, I will not be of any use to anyone. I would not have any reason for being.

ALL INFORMATION IN THIS
PAGE IS CLASSIFIED
UNLESS INDICATED OTHERWISE

SECRET

Question: What do you think about Angela Davis?

Answer: I do not know her personally. She is much younger than I. She belongs to another generation. All I can do is listen and try to help while there. I know that her trial is absurd. The only fault she has is being a bad example for the other slaves. Angela Davis and Paul Robeson are, in the eyes of the Whites, bad "niggers."

SECRET

Question: What do you mean?

Answer: Paul Robeson went through the world as if the world belonged to him. Whites cannot stand to be surrounded by black people. It is necessary to quickly give an example. Angela Davis answered Ronald Reagan that she was a communist. The problem was not what she was accused of. What does the answer matter when you have no right to ask the question anyway? Whether I do or do not agree with her ideas means nothing. As I am 20 years older than she is, I necessarily have another viewpoint. Anyhow, she is a victim. Therefore she is my sister.

Translator's note: James Arthur Baldwin's interview with Margaret Mead is called "Racism in Question", a Calmann-Levy publication.

Question: You have written that "If catastrophe comes one day, the rebirth will only be able to come from the South." What do you mean?

Answer: Because the people live in such a nightmare, that unconsciously they will be looking to free themselves. In order to leave this hell, the Southerner will have an enormous price to pay. But perhaps he will finish by saying to himself: "Anything but this hell." While the Northerner does not live surrounded by Blacks, the Black is not a daily element, permanent in his life. He passes by him in the elevator, on the sidewalks. He is not a part of the view all the time. The journey will take much longer for him.

ALL INFORMATION ON THIS PAGE IS CLASSIFIED UNLESS INDICATED OTHERWISE

SECRET

SECRET

Question: Do you believe that the cultural contributions of the Black civilization can influence society?

Answer: Yes, I believe that it is in this way, through cultural contributions, that you can manage to profoundly change society Our way of listening, seeing, feeling, thinking can contribute to these changes. It is for this reason that I find the word "revolution," in this day and age, to be a bit romantic. It is, in reality, the hidden fountain of humanity that one must exploit, in order to disconcert, to establish communications.

To be born, to learn to walk, to grow up, to grow old, all this is difficult for everyone. No one has the right to add another problem, that of the color of one's skin.

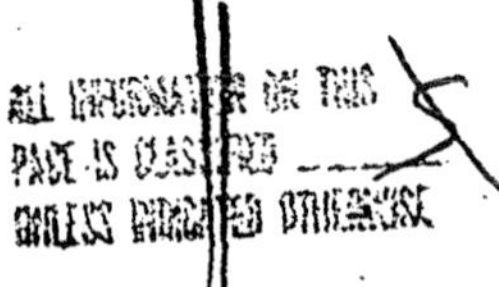
ALL INFORMATION ON THIS
PAGE IS CLASSIFIED
UNLESS INDICATED OTHERWISE

SECRET

70.

BALDWIN OFF THE ADMINISTRATIVE INDEX—THE FBI SAYS GOODBYE

MARCH 1974

James Baldwin's FBI file closed with his removal from the Administrative Index in 1974. The New York field office reviewed his dossier that spring and determined that the author no longer met the "criteria for inclusion" in this who's who of American radicals—his "propensity towards violence," for one thing, was hanging by a thread. The nearly two-thousand-page Bureau biography of Baldwin that took off with his speech before the Liberation Committee for Africa in 1961 thus landed with a whimper, a delisting rather an arrest, an escape, or a hard-to-imagine conversion to Hooverism. What were the reasons for the surprisingly quiet conclusion? On the FBI's side, several factors played a role: the appointment of the less dogmatic L. Patrick Gray in 1972, the first Bureau director not named J. Edgar Hoover since the Jazz Age; the legal extension of the Freedom of Information Act to cover many Bureau records in 1974; and the widening scandal of Watergate, from which the Bureau half-successfully sought to insulate itself by trimming some secret programs (Mark Felt, the number two man under Gray, turned out to be the legendary "Deep Throat" informer for the *Washington Post*). On Baldwin's side, meanwhile, the unseen closing of his FBI file complemented a year of rebuilding energy and taking stock, of fiftieth birthday tributes and a centennial "Artist as Prophet" medal presented by the Cathedral of St. John the Divine, the gigantic Episcopal church near Harlem that eventually hosted his funeral. Accepting this award in St. John's pulpit, Baldwin thundered against the ongoing betrayal of his birth country, cursing Richard Nixon and reminding his audience that the true artist was necessarily "disruptive of the peace." But peace made a comeback, in his lay sermon and in the best of the thirteen years remaining in his life. "It's time to think of the Messiah in a new way," his acceptance speech concluded, and "time to learn to love each other. The love of God," in the end, "means responsibility to each other."

OPTIONAL FORM NO. 10
MAY 1962 EDITION
GSA FPMR (41 CFR) 101-11.6

UNITED STATES GOVERNMENT

Memorandum

TO : SAC, NEW YORK (100-146553) DATE: FEB 21 1974

FROM : SUPERVISOR [redacted] 3A8 b7C-1

SUBJECT: JAMES ARTHUR BALDWIN
EM-

A review of subject's file fails to indicate that appropriate action has been taken with respect to the subject's Administrative Index (ADEX) status.

You are to determine subject's propensity towards violence and comment as to whether subject should remain or be deleted from the ADEX, in accordance with instructions contained in SAC Memorandum 21-72 (E), dated 9/12/72; you should submit Form -122 with appropriate recommendations for retention or deletion.

With regard to those subjects retained on the ADEX, the ADEX card should reflect that an FD-165 (Security Flash) and date was placed with the Identification Division (in cases where a fingerprint record exists) or that it was sent and date thereof when FD-165 returned with no record stamp.

Date FD -165 sent: ______________

Date FD-165 returned: ______________

ALL INFORMATION CONTAINED
HEREIN IS UNCLASSIFIED
DATE 5-30-89 BY [illegible]

100-146553-399

SEARCHED ___ INDEXED ___
SERIALIZED ___ FILED ___
FEB 21 1974
FBI—NEW YORK

[redacted] b7C-1

OPEN OR REOPEN CASE
ORIGIN ___ DATE 2/24/73
SUPV. ___ SECT. 3A8

JCS:sal

Bu 62-108763

Dissemination
Routing Slip
FD-417 (9-12-69)

(Copies to Offices Checked)

To: [X] Director, Att: INTD, [illegible] and D

[ ] SAC,

[ ] Albany
[ ] Albuquerque
[ ] Alexandria
[ ] Anchorage
[ ] Atlanta
[ ] Baltimore
[ ] Birmingham
[ ] Boston
[ ] Buffalo
[ ] Butte
[ ] Charlotte
[ ] Chicago
[ ] Cincinnati
[ ] Cleveland
[ ] Columbia
[ ] Dallas
[ ] Denver
[ ] Detroit
[ ] El Paso
[ ] Honolulu
[ ] Houston
[ ] Indianapolis
[ ] Jackson
[ ] Jacksonville
[ ] Kansas City
[ ] Knoxville
[ ] Las Vegas
[ ] Little Rock
[ ] Los Angeles
[ ] Louisville
[ ] Memphis
[ ] Miami
[ ] Milwaukee
[ ] Minneapolis
[ ] Mobile
[ ] Newark
[ ] New Haven
[ ] New Orleans
[ ] New York City
[ ] Norfolk
[ ] Oklahoma City
[ ] Omaha
[ ] Philadelphia
[ ] Phoenix
[ ] Pittsburgh
[ ] Portland
[ ] Richmond
[ ] Sacramento
[ ] St. Louis
[ ] Salt Lake City
[ ] San Antonio
[ ] San Diego
[ ] San Francisco
[ ] San Juan
[ ] Savannah
[ ] Seattle
[ ] Springfield
[ ] Tampa
[ ] Washington Field

Date March 25, 1974

RE: JAMES ARTHUR BALDWIN
EM

REMARKS:

FILE HAS BEEN REVIEWED AND SUBJECT DOES NOT MEET CRITERIA FOR INCLUSION ON ADEX AS SET FORTH IN BUREAU MEMORANDUM 21-72, DATED 9/12/72.

NOTED
ADEX UNIT
DATE 3/27/74

292325
ALL INFORMATION CONTAINED
HEREIN IS UNCLASSIFIED
DATE 5-30-89 BY [illegible]

1- BUREAU FILE #62-108763
(1) FILE #: 100-146553

~~SAC~~ ADIC JOHN F. MALONE

OFFICE New York

FILE STRIPPED
BY [illegible] 3/28/74

CHIEF CLERK
CLOSE ON THIS

100-146553 — 400

SEARCHED ___ INDEXED ___
SERIALIZED ___ FILED ___
MAR 25 1974
FBI — N.Y.
ADEX UNIT

SOURCES OF QUOTATIONS IN THE COMMENTARIES

Unless cited here, all quotations in the commentaries on documents in James Baldwin's FBI file can be found in those same documents.

Graphic Evidence: 1964: "[C]anon of Western thought: the self-determination of peoples," James Baldwin, *Conversations with James Baldwin*, edited by Fred L. Standley and Louis H. Pratt (Jackson: University Press of Mississippi, 1989), 60.

Graphic Evidence: 1966: "[A]n eyeballing disposition of his own," Maurice O. Wallace, *Constructing the Black Masculine: Identity and Ideality in African American Men's Literature and Culture, 1775–1995* (Durham: Duke University Press, 2002), 141.

Malcolm X and Elijah Muhammad Praise Brother Baldwin: July 1961: "[R]eally cowardly obtuseness of white liberals," James Baldwin, *The Fire Next Time*, in *Collected Essays*, edited by Toni Morrison (New York: Library of America, 1998), 320. "[I]t seemed to him . . . that I was not yet brainwashed," James Baldwin, *The Fire Next Time*, 324. "The glorification of one race," James Baldwin, *The Fire Next Time*, 334.

***Another Country* as Obscene Specimen: September and October 1962:** "[U]niversal blues," James Baldwin, quoted in David Leeming, *James Baldwin: A Biography* (New York: Arcade, 2015), 206.

"What Do Our Files Show on James Baldwin?": May 1963: "[S]till required to supplicate," James Baldwin, quoted in David Leeming, 224. "[A]n FBI file cabinet in his brain," Ed Pavlić, *Who Can Afford to*

Improvise?: James Baldwin and Black Music, the Lyric and the Listeners (New York: Fordham University Press, 2016), 126.

"Better Qualified to Lead a Homo-Sexual Movement than a Civil Rights Movement": September 1963: "[R]esponsible for Birmingham," James Baldwin, quoted in David Leeming, 228.

Baldwin Baits J. Edgar Hoover—and Bureaucratic Hell Breaks Loose: September 1963: "[C]ompletely ineffectual in resolving the continued mayhem . . . ," Martin Luther King Jr., quoted in William W. Keller, *The Liberals and J. Edgar Hoover: Rise and Fall of a Domestic Intelligence State* (Princeton: Princeton University Press, 1989), 104.

Photos of Baldwin in Selma: October 1963: "[D]estroyed by a plague called color," James Baldwin, "The American Dream and the American Negro," in *Collected Essays*, 716. "[A]ny right to throw us off *Federal* property," James Baldwin, "Open Letter to Mr. Carter," in *Collected Essays*, 768.

A Falling Out with "Sexual Proclivities": October 1963: "[I]nformal nighttime seminars . . . ," David Leeming, 275.

Ask J. Edgar Hoover—Is Baldwin "a Known Communist?": October 1963: "[P]ast midnight [to make] personal replies to citizens who write to him praising the FBI," Jack Alexander, "The Director—I" (*The New Yorker*, 25 September 1937: 20–25), 20.

J. Edgar Hoover Asks "Is Baldwin on Our Security Index?": December 1963: "[W]ho, in a time of emergency . . . ," quoted in Michael Newton, *The FBI Encyclopedia* (Jefferson, NCL: McFarland, 2003), 288. "[W]hose presence at liberty . . . ," J. Edgar Hoover quoted in William J. Maxwell, *F. B. Eyes: How J. Edgar Hoover's Ghostreaders Framed African American Literature* (Princeton: Princeton University Press, 2015), 92. "[D]iscussed with agencies or individuals . . . ," J. Edgar Hoover quoted in Michael Newton, 85. "[A] system of terror by index cards," Vito Marcantonio quoted in William J. Maxwell, 81.

"Hello, Baby, How Are You?"—FBI Sexual Linguistics: January 1964: "Hello, baby . . . ," James Baldwin, *Another Country*, in *Early Novels and Stories* (New York: Library of America), 377.

The FBI Combs Baldwin's Passport: February 1964: "[T]hat proclaimed . . . a domestic nigger . . ." and "underwent a sea change . . . ," James Baldwin, *No Name in the Street*, in *Collected Essays*, 378.

Sources of Quotations in the Commentaries

Baldwin as COINTELPRO Audience: April 1964: "[T]he revolutionary principles of Marx . . . ," J. Edgar Hoover, quoted in Michael Newton, 319.

The Bureau Stalks Baldwin on Broadway: May 1964: "[P]ersuasive Studio advocate," David Leeming, 231.

Baldwin and His "Aliases": June 1964: "[S]trangers called Jimmy Baldwin," James Baldwin, quoted in Douglas Field, *All Those Strangers: The Art and Lives of James Baldwin* (New York: Oxford University Press, 2015), 1.

***The Blood Counters* and Baldwin Countersurveillance, Part 1: June and July 1964:** "Mr. Hoover, if I had known . . . ," Louis Nichols, quoted in Curt Gentry, *J. Edgar Hoover: The Man and the Secrets* (New York: Norton, 1991), 386.

"Isn't Baldwin a Well Known Pervert?"—Hoover Weighs In: July 1964: "[H]istory's most highly paid . . . ," James Baldwin, *The Devil Finds Work*, in *Collected Essays*, 544.

***The Blood Counters* and Baldwin Countersurveillance, Part 3: August 1964:** "[C]ustodial relationship," Claire Culleton, "Extorting Henry Holt and Co.: J. Edgar Hoover and the Publishing Industry," in Culleton and Karen Leick, editors, *Modernism on File: Writers, Artists, and the FBI, 1920–1950* (New York: Palgrave, 2008), 237. "I am beginning to feel like a member of the FBI myself," quoted in Claire Culleton, "Extorting," 239.

Buckley on "The Baldwin Syndrome": June 1965: "Negro backwardness," William F. Buckley Jr., "Why the South Must Prevail," *National Review* (24 August 1957), 149.

FBI Internationalism in Action—Baldwin Traced and Translated in Turkey: November and December 1966: "[T]ransatlantic commuter" and "a stranger everywhere," James Baldwin, quoted in David Leeming, 197. "[W]as literally and figuratively embraced" and "theater people . . . ," David Leeming, 193–94.

Baldwin and Other "Independent Black Nationalist Extremists": January 1968: "[C]ounterintelligence endeavor . . . ," quoted in Michael Newton, 70. "[P]revent the rise of a 'messiah,'" quoted in Michael Newton, 71. "[B]adly twisted and fragile weed . . . ," James Baldwin, *No Name in the Street*, 459.

Clippers and Informers on *The Life of Malcolm X*: March 1968: "[H]e wanted to write the way that Aretha sounded . . . ," David Leeming,

297. "[M]y way or not at all," James Baldwin, quoted in David Leeming, 299. "[R]eally creating Malcolm," James Baldwin, quoted in David Leeming, 297.

"Two Separate Films on the Life of the Subject": March 1968: "[W]ould rather be horsewhipped . . . ," James Baldwin, *The Devil Finds Work*, 550.

Baldwin the Black Panther: May 1968: "[T]he greatest threat to the internal security of the country," J. Edgar Hoover, quoted in William J. Maxwell, 111. "[T]he American state" and "self-confrontation, the power to change itself . . . ," James Baldwin, *No Name in the Street*, 408. "[A]tone," James Baldwin, *No Name in the Street*, 409.

Truman Capote, FBI Source, and James Baldwin, "Negro": May and June 1968: "[B]ack where we all come from," Truman Capote, quoted in David Leeming, 60.

"Hostesses for This Party Wore Long African Style Clothes"—Baldwin Speaks for SNCC: August 1968: "[W]as as [A]merican as cherry pie," H. Rap Brown, *Die Nigger Die!* (Chicago: Lawrence Hill, 2002), 144.

Flying the Coop and "Presently Checking His Baggage through Customs": February and April 1969: "White people don't want to hear what he knows . . . ," James Baldwin, "The Price May Be Too High," *The Cross of Redemption: Uncollected Writings*, edited by Randall Kenan (New York: Vintage, 2010), 108. "The question is not whether black and white artists can work together . . . ," James Baldwin, "The Price May Be Too High," 105.

Indiscreet Book Buying: July 1969: "They would come in . . . " and "would spend lots of money," quoted in Colin A. Beckles, "Black Bookstores, Black Power, and the F.B.I.: The Case of Drum and Spear," *Western Journal of Black Studies* (20.2, 1996), 68. "When we were growing up in Harlem . . . ," James Baldwin, "Negroes Are Anti-Semitic Because They're Anti-White," in *Collected Essays*, 739. "The crisis taking place in the world . . . ," James Baldwin, "Negroes Are Anti-Semitic Because They're Anti-White," 748.

Baldwin Testifies for "Sister Angela"—and the Bureau Relaxes Its Vigil: January, May, June, and August 1971: "[A]ssessed and absorbed their history . . . ," James Baldwin, "An Open Letter to My Sister Angela Y. Davis," *The Cross of Redemption: Uncollected Writings*, 256. "[T]he bulk of our (nominal) countrymen . . . ," James Baldwin, "An Open Letter to My Sister Angela Y. Davis," 258.

Rapping on *A Rap on Race*: April and September 1971: "[T]he last witness," James Baldwin, quoted in David Leeming, 310.

From the Security to the Administrative Index: April 1972: "[T]he potential dangerousness of subversives . . . ," quoted in Michael Newton, 8. "[T]he repeal of the aforementioned Act . . . ," John Mitchell, quoted in Michael Newton, 9. "[R]ank-and-file," and "teachers, writers, lawyers, etc.," and "were nonetheless influential . . . ," quoted in Michael Newton, 9.

The Last Book Purchase—*No Name in the Street*: July 1972: "[T]he truth of the American black situation . . . ," James Baldwin, *No Name in the Street*, 462. "In this place . . . ," James Baldwin, *No Name in the Street*, 463. "[K]aleidoscopic, fragmented," James Baldwin, *No Name in the Street*, 464. "High Priest, J. Edgar Hoover," James Baldwin, *No Name in the Street*, 408. "[L]ike being pissed on, or gang-raped," and "once you *have* come to the attention of the FBI," James Baldwin, *The Devil Finds Work*, 547. "[H]istory's most highly paid . . . ," James Baldwin, *The Devil Finds Work*, 544.

Baldwin off the Administrative Index—The FBI Says Goodbye: March 1974: "[D]isruptive of the peace" and "[i]t's time to think of the Messiah . . . ," James Baldwin, quoted in David Leeming, 322.

INDEX

C

Index

G

H